MICHIGAN
STATE
COLLEGE

MICHIGAN STATE COLLEGE

JOHN HANNAH AND THE CREATION
OF A WORLD UNIVERSITY, 1926–1969

David A. Thomas

Michigan State University Press • *East Lansing*

Copyright © 2008 by Michigan State University

 This book was made possible by support from Michigan State University, the Office of the President, Michigan State University, and the Office of the Provost, Michigan State University.

⊗ The paper used in this publication meets the minimum requirements of ANSI/NISO Z39.48-1992 (R 1997) (Permanence of Paper).

Michigan State University Press
East Lansing, Michigan 48823-5245

Printed and bound in the United States of America.

14   13   12   11   10   09   08   1 2 3 4 5 6 7 8 9 10

ISBN 978-0-87013-772-3

LIBRARY OF CONGRESS CATALOGING-IN-PUBLICATION DATA
Thomas, David, 1944–
Michigan State College : John Hannah and the creation of a world university,
1926–1969 / David A. Thomas.
p. cm.
Includes bibliographical references and index.
ISBN 978-0-87013-772-3 (cloth : alk. paper)
1. Michigan State College—History. 2. Michigan State University—History—
20th century. 3. Hannah, John A., 1902–1991. I. Title.
LD3248.M5T46 2008
378.774'27—dc22
2008009825

Book and cover design by Sharp Des!gns, Lansing, Michigan

green press INITIATIVE   Michigan State University Press is a member of the Green Press Initiative and is committed to developing and encouraging ecologically responsible publishing practices. For more information about the Green Press Initiative and the use of recycled paper in book publishing, please visit *www.greenpressinitiative.org.*

Visit Michigan State University Press on the World Wide Web at www.msupress.msu.edu

Contents

Foreword

The study and understanding of history occupies a paradoxical and problematic place in contemporary American culture. On the one hand, it is widely believed that we face a general crisis of historical amnesia; on the other hand, there is a clearly enormous and growing public interest in history, manifest in museum attendance, historically oriented tourism, participation in festivals, and even the media driven excesses of nostalgia and commemoration of recent historical periods.

—Michael Frish, "Cracking the Nutshell: Making History-Making"

M ichigan State College: John Hannah and the Creation of a World University, 1926–1969, was conceived as the second of a three-volume series to commemorate the creation of what is now Michigan State University. Despite John Hannah's prominence in the title, the book very much describes the remarkable growth of America's pioneer land-grant college into a university that connected to all corners of the world. David Thomas set out to recapture the many stories within the larger narrative of the dramatic development of Michigan State University over an incredible thirty-year period.

Thomas came to this major undertaking well prepared to write a book that provides insights into this phase of the development of the university. A lifelong student of university and community history, Thomas literally grew up living on both sides of Grand River Avenue. The son of Gordon Thomas, a university faculty member as well as a mayor of East Lansing, David had the good fortune to become acquainted with President Hannah as a young man and to have an insider's perspective in the years to follow, during which time David became acquainted with many of the university's faculty and administrators, as well as civic leaders in the East Lansing and Lansing community.

Beyond his family experience, Thomas brought his training as a professional journalist to the task of preparing the lively history of these years. A former writer at the *Lansing State Journal*, Thomas drew heavily on newspaper accounts in tracing the early portion of this period. Thomas also coauthored a sesquicentennial history of the city of Lansing, *Lansing: Capital, Campus, and Cars*,[1] which provides a broad perspective on the connections between the growth of the university and the surrounding cities and communities.

What is most remarkable about this book is the flow of voices that converge to tell this impressive story of the development of a world university. Thomas effectively captures the multiple perspectives— those of the university leaders as well as those at many levels of the university and community.

As a folklorist, my initial reading of this manuscript provided great pleasure, as Thomas clearly made a major effort to collect the stories of everyday life of those who lived through this period. The accounts bring alive both moments of shared achievement and moments of contested visions for the university. By carefully listening to the stories recorded here, readers can more deeply assess the university's development as the contributions of thousands of men and women shaped it.

Richard Dorson, a professor in MSU's history department after World War II, was one of America's foremost folklore scholars. In the late 1950s, Dorson left East Lansing for Bloomington, Indiana, where he developed and directed Indiana University's world-renowned Folklore Institute. In *American Folklore and the Historian*, Dorson describes his vision of folk history as "the episodes of the past which the community remembers collectively. Folk history will be composed of a number of local traditions. These traditions may or may not be written in the formal histories, but their retention is chiefly by word of mouth, and so they will diverge from the printed accounts, if such exist."[2] This volume not only presents singular voices of lives lived during this period but also presents and explores the folk histories associated with the everyday life of an ever-changing university. By drawing on these interviews, Thomas draws the reader into the human experience of those who worked with and around President John Hannah—and who collectively were more powerful than Hannah himself.

As Thomas correctly notes, Hannah has taken on a larger-than-life quality over the past decades. Even today, nearly forty years after his retirement, it is not uncommon to hear stories of his years as president. Whether these tales relate how he stopped students for conversation while walking the campus, comment on his physical size and stature or his powerful theatrical voice, or note his presence in all phases of daily campus life, these accounts have all contributed to the rich folk history of this period.

The legacy of the Hannah years, so ably documented in this volume, has personal resonance in my life as the director of the Michigan State University Museum. The advancement of both President Hannah and the university can be seen by examining the history of this one campus unit. The college's first museum opened in 1857 in Old College Hall (now the site of Beaumont Tower). President Joseph R. Williams, in the founding address for the Agricultural College of the State of Michigan, called for the building of scientific collections to support scientific agriculture and an enlightened liberal education for farmers. The museum and its collections grew, and in 1881 a new Victorian Romanesque–designed Robert S. Linton Hall was built to house the "library-museum." In 1940, the museum moved to the ground floor of the Auditorium, a Public Works Administration supported project. While the museum served as a significant teaching and research center, only when Hannah became MSU's president did a much broader global vision for the museum emerge. Hannah sought to create a "general college museum"—a museum with collections and curatorial programs that extended to the social sciences, the humanities, and the arts—that focused not just on Michigan and the nation but on the world beyond.

President Hannah's constant quest for excellence for MSU was reflected in the museum's 1955 move into the old university library building on West Circle Drive. Hannah wanted the Michigan State University Museum to have a real professional home. He decided that MSU administrators needed to see some of the best museums in America, and while in New York City, he spent a morning touring the American Museum of Natural History, where he was fascinated by the dioramas and especially the murals. After lunch he sought out the museum's director and asked to meet the renowned staff muralist John Hope. By the end of the day, Hannah had invited Hope to come to East Lansing to paint murals and to serve as a staff artist for the Michigan State University Museum. Such accounts—a folk history of sorts—convey President Hannah's vision. The emerging Michigan State University was being shaped by a growing presence on the world stage, and its peers were the leading colleges and universities around the globe.

David Thomas's volume presents the ambitious quest for excellence that remained ever-present during these years of remarkable growth. The enterprising stories of the faculty, students, and leaders tell us much about where we have been and where we are headed. Today, Michigan State University proudly claims "boldness by design"—"by boldly daring to be who we are and who we were created to be. By doing it even more boldly and better than we are now. By boldly recasting our land-grant mission to meet twenty-first century challenges and opportunities."[3]

Michigan State College stands as a history in the best sense of how history functions in human terms. According to Roy Rosenzweig and David Thelen's *Presence of the Past,* "People who want to get as close as they can to experience as possible—to use the past on its own terms—recognize the need to reach toward people who have lived in other times and places."[4] In this book, Thomas has effectively presented the experiences of those who participated in and experienced the transformation of Michigan State College into Michigan State University. We all have much to learn by listening to these voices with care as we seek to better understand and use our collective university past.

C. Kurt Dewhurst, Ph.D.
Director, Michigan State University Museum
Professor of English
Senior Fellow for Outreach and Engagement

NOTES

1. Sallie M. Manassah, David A. Thomas, and James F. Wallington, *Lansing: Capital, Campus, and Cars* (East Lansing, Mich.: Contemporary Image Advertising, 1986).

2. Richard M. Dorson, *American Folklore and the Historian* (Chicago: University of Chicago Press, 1971), 150.

3. Lou Anna Kimsey Simon, "Boldness by Design," Sesquicentennial Convocation Address, 8 September 2005, available online at *http:// strategicpositioning.msu.edu/simon_s150_convocation_address.pdf.*

4. Roy Rosenzweig and David Thelen, *The Presence of the Past: Popular Uses of History in American Life* (New York: Columbia University Press, 1998), 12.

Preface

I T WAS THE EARLY 1960S, AND MY FATHER, GORDON THOMAS, WAS mayor of East Lansing and John Hannah was president of Michigan State University. Because my father was also a communications professor, Dr. Hannah was technically his boss. Consequently, they decided that the campus would not be an appropriate location for their meetings. The MSU president would definitely have the advantage over one of his employees. So our farmhouse on Hagadorn Road, built in 1849, several years before the creation of Michigan Agricultural College, hosted their occasional meetings. Late one Friday afternoon, President Hannah showed up at the house to talk about open housing in East Lansing. I followed my father and Dr. Hannah into the living room, hoping to overhear some entertaining conversation. After just two minutes of discussion, Dr. Hannah turned to me and said, "David, don't you have some homework to do?" I nodded and left the room. Looking back many years later, I wish I had said, "Dr. Hannah, someday I will be your biographer. Now is an opportunity to say something brilliant."

The following pages are not really a biography of John A. Hannah. They are an attempt to chronicle the Hannah years at MSU and to present the story of the incredible dynamics of what happened at the country's first land-grant college between John Hannah's appearance on campus in the early 1920s and his retirement as president in 1969. Madison Kuhn, MSU's premier historical chronicler, wrote in depth about Michigan State history from its beginnings to its centennial in 1955. Paul Dressel wrote a long history of the Hannah years, providing an incredible amount of detail about the academic structure. Still, those earlier works were mostly administrative histories, giving in-depth looks into the university's inner workings but relating limited information about the personalities who made MSU into the fine university it is today and their relationship to the global community. Many more specific works have also been produced, including Richard O. Niehoff's *John A. Hannah: Versatile Administrator and Distinguished Published Servant*; Victor Inzunza's *Years of Achievement: A Short History of the College of Education at Michigan State University*; and Fred W. Stabley's *The Spartans: A Story of Michigan State Football.*

The Hannah years were arguably the most significant in MSU history. When John Hannah took charge in 1941, Michigan State College was basically an agricultural school with an enrollment of around six thousand. When he left in 1969, it was a world-class university with a student population of more than thirty-nine thousand. In between, MSU joined the Big Ten Conference, won NCAA football championships, built some of the largest dormitories and classrooms in the world, and hired faculty members who earned international reputations for their expertise in a wide range of academic subjects and received frequent mention in magazines, newspapers, radio programs, and television shows.

This book gave me the opportunity to write about many of those achievements. I also was lucky to be able to approach this history in a way few authors could. In high school I was the debate partner of Dan Daugherty, the son of legendary football coach Duffy Daugherty; my first and only onstage kiss during a brief junior high school theatrical career was delicately provided by Jane Munn, daughter of celebrated football coach Biggie Munn. I ran track with John McQuitty, son of social science dean Louis McQuitty, and with Byron Treaster, son of longtime MSU public relations executive Lowell Treaster. My family had many dinners with Dr. Shao Chang Lee, the man who probably provided the impetus for MSU's ventures into the world of international relationships. I saw football star George Guerre score a touchdown against Marquette in 1949, stood along Grand River Avenue in East Lansing to watch the university's Centennial parade in 1955, and participated in campus civil rights marches during the 1960s.

But of course I did not write the book alone. Special thanks go to Dr. Robert Green, who provided valuable insight into the racial atmosphere at MSU during the 1960s; to Jim Cash, an MSU graduate and

Hollywood playwright who spent many hours giving me his insights into the MSU community; to my high school buddy Jim Votruba, a former MSU student, later assistant provost at the university, and now president of Northern Kentucky University, who so willingly provided me with his perspective on the Hannah years; to superalumnus Duane Vernon, whose uncontrolled enthusiasm for Michigan State helped me look for the positives even when the history looked bleak; and to my mother, longtime *East Lansing Towne Courier* fine arts editor Phyllis Thomas, who first taught me that there is much more to the East Lansing campus than just athletics.

Thanks are also owed to the people who helped me with the detailed production of the book, including Fred Honhart and his staff at Michigan State University Archives and Historical Collections; Val Berryman at the Michigan State University Museum; Diane Hutchins at WKAR; MSU Press Emeritus Director Fred Bohm; the staff at Michigan State University Press; Dan Leys of Mirage Technologies in Lansing, for letting me use his wonderful video histories related to Michigan State and East Lansing; historian Keith Widder, whose *Michigan Agricultural College: The Evolution of a Land-Grant Philosophy, 1855–1925,* gave birth to this three-volume sesquicentennial history of Michigan State University; C. Kurt Dewhurst, the director of the university museum, whose foreword to this volume helps put the Hannah years in perspective; and my wife, Gloria, who volunteered many hours of her time to scan old newspapers, interview retired MSU faculty, and read countless pages of my attempts to write about MSU history.

Early in my research of the Hannah years, I discovered a wealth of writings by contemporaries of President Hannah, most of them unpublished. Rather than reinvent the wheel, I appointed many of the authors of these histories, memos, and letters about Michigan State my unofficial coauthors and extensively used their material. Consequently, the book could not have been produced without the written memories of longtime *Lansing State Journal* sportswriter George Alderton, whose wonderful unpublished manuscript of his experiences during five decades of covering the Spartans is probably the most remarkable document ever produced about MSU sports. Also invaluable were the writings of university administrators William Combs and Floyd Reeves, Hannah administrative assistant James

Denison, university historian Madison Kuhn, university alumni association magazine editors Ron Karle and Bob Bao, dairy professor Malcolm Trout, and many others who played major roles at Michigan State during the Hannah years and had the historical foresight to write about their experiences.

Of course, this was all possible because of John A. Hannah. When I first began writing the book, several members of the MSU community expressed their hopes that the volume would not turn out to be a public relations piece for President Hannah. Maybe somewhat intimidated by their warnings, I made extensive efforts to look for the bad as well as the good. I did discover and wrote about some of the problems encountered or caused by the Hannah Administration. Nevertheless, in the end, I concluded that President Hannah made an enormous contribution to what MSU is today and that his legacy is worthy of a book dedicated to an immensely talented and compassionate human being. Thank you, Dr. Hannah.

The Names of
the Institution

During its history, Michigan State University has had six official names:

AGRICULTURAL COLLEGE OF THE STATE OF MICHIGAN
(1855–1861)

THE STATE AGRICULTURAL COLLEGE
(1861–1909)

MICHIGAN AGRICULTURAL COLLEGE
(1909–1925)

MICHIGAN STATE COLLEGE OF AGRICULTURE AND APPLIED SCIENCE
(1925–1955)

MICHIGAN STATE UNIVERSITY OF AGRICULTURE AND APPLIED SCIENCE
(1955–1964)

MICHIGAN STATE UNIVERSITY
(1964–)

I have aimed to use the chronologically appropriate name throughout the text.

Mr. Shaw and Mr. Hannah

R OBERT SIDEY SHAW WAS A NATURAL CHOICE TO BECOME THE new president of Michigan State College of Agriculture and Applied Science in 1928. He had already served three times as interim president—during the six-month gap between Frank Kedzie's and David Friday's presidencies; during the interval between Friday's and Kenyon Butterfield's presidencies; and while Butterfield was on leave in 1928. None were easy times. Kedzie left because many at the college believed new leadership was needed; Friday left after being accused of traveling with his female research assistant on college business; and Butterfield resigned after being charged with cronyism and poor financial management.

PRESIDENT BUTTERFIELD

In 1924, Kenyon Butterfield had seemed a good fit for the presidency of the small agricultural college in East Lansing. Born in 1868 in Lapeer, Michigan, he had received a bachelor of science degree from the State Agricultural College in 1891 and a master's degree from the University of Michigan in 1903. He had also served as secretary of the college, as superintendent of the Michigan Farmer's Institute, and as a field agent for the school. He was appointed to the presidency of Rhode Island College of Agriculture and Mechanical Arts in 1903 and assumed the top position at Massachusetts Agricultural College in 1910, receiving an LL.D. from that school the same year. Butterfield was considered a "rural sociologist," concerned about a wide range of agricultural issues, not just the technical side of planting and harvesting crops or raising healthy animals. His speaking and writing combined a little religion with some philosophical questions

Kenyon Butterfield graduated from Michigan Agricultural College in 1891 and served as the school's president from 1924 to 1928. Butterfield Hall, a dormitory in the Brody Residence Hall Complex, is named for him. Courtesy of MSU Archives and Historical Collections.

and a sprinkling of sociological jargon, unlike the more practical public musings of his former teacher at the State Agricultural College, William James Beal. Butterfield began a 1909 agriculture lecture at the Harvard Theological Seminary with the words, "When Jesus announced to the hearts overburdened with the cares of the daily toil that the birds of the heaven and the lilies of the field are the patterns for our industry, we can hardly believe that he intended to encourage thriftlessness or to abolish labor for bread. He was seeking to give proper proportion to human desires. What shall we eat? What shall we drink? Wherewithal shall we be clothed? are age-long queries. When men come to the full life of the spirit and when human justice is supreme, no doubt the ideal of Jesus will be realized and these questions will become incidental or at least subordinated to the quest for righteousness, and perhaps will be answered with less of sweat and toil than now."

It was not Butterfield's rhetorical gift that got him in trouble at Michigan Agricultural College but rather John D. Willard and John Phelan, friends and employees of Butterfield in Massachusetts whom he had urged to come to East Lansing and had given significant administrative responsibility. Both received bigger salaries than other senior administrators at the college, which caused resentment among many veteran faculty members. In addition, Butterfield was accused of mismanaging the college's budget, of conducting college business in secrecy, and of advocating continuing education programs for which the college lacked adequate funding. Butterfield quickly lost the support of the State Board of Agriculture, the college's governing board, and came under attack in Michigan's newspapers. In the early spring of 1928, the board seized control of the college budget while Butterfield was abroad on a visit to the Holy Land. In April 1928, the *State Journal* predicted that Butterfield would have no choice but to resign and claimed much of the credit for exposing the problems: "Investigation by the press, notably by *The State Journal*, was the most powerful factor in the solution of the tangled internal affairs of Michigan State College. [The board] made the resignation of President Kenyon Leech Butterfield almost imperative; politely eliminated President Butterfield's two 'vice presidents'; and effected salary economies of similar kind all along the line, throughout the faculty and administrative staff."

SHAW TAKES CHARGE

On 22 May the State Board of Agriculture unanimously accepted Butterfield's resignation and named Robert Shaw as Michigan State College's fourth president in thirteen years. "There are greater problems confronting the institution today than ever before in my twenty-six years of experience," Shaw declared upon accepting the position. "The presidency is a radical change for my plans for later life, but if I can be of any service to the institution, I am glad to do it."

A Canadian, Shaw had earned a bachelor's degree at Ontario Agricultural College (later Guelph University) in 1893 and had spent the next five years managing his father's farm in Woodburn, Ontario. He emigrated to the United States in 1898 to become an assistant professor of agriculture and animal husbandry at Montana State College, and four years later moved to the State Agricultural College, where he was appointed dean of agriculture in 1908. When he assumed the presidency, the college was running a deficit of about sixty-five thousand dollars; a year later, however, MSC boasted a reserve of around one hundred thousand dollars. The new president's talent for keeping costs under control was less important than his ability to cut weak programs and approve only new courses of study that seemed essential to the college's well-being.

Shaw also proved adept at raising funds by encouraging gifts to the college. In early 1938, MSC received five hundred thousand dollars from the Horace H. Rackham and Mary A. Rackham Fund, at the time the largest private grant the school had ever received. The money was earmarked for conducting research in agriculture with the aim of finding special industrial uses, other than food, for farm produce. During the 1937–38 school year, the college received a variety of other gifts, including six thousand dollars for entomology, four thousand dollars for sugar-beet research, nine hundred dollars for research in food preservation, and five hundred dollars for a fellowship in agricultural economics. Fred Jenison of Lansing donated flags for the band, the Detroit unit of the Women's Farm and Garden Society gave a stone sundial, and President Shaw provided more than two thousand trees to the college to "add more beauty to the campus."

After assuming the presidency, Shaw worked to transform the college's administrative structure, placing a bevy of new men and women in charge of key areas. After two stints as acting dean, Henry Bernard Dirks became dean of the engineering department in 1931. Dirks had come to East Lansing from Princeton University in 1919 and had served as East Lansing's mayor in 1928–29. During his first few years in office, Shaw also appointed Marie Dye as dean of home economics, Harold Smith Patton as head of economics, Everett Lewis Austin as acting dean of education, Elisabeth Conrad as dean of women, Joseph Cox as dean of agriculture, and Victor Gardner as head of the Extension Service. The *MSC Record* applauded Shaw's choices, proclaiming, "No one can say that President Shaw's appointments have not lived up to expectations and more. From home economics to athletics and from agriculture to a dean of women the individuals finally decided upon by the administration to fill the jobs have all been masters of their subjects not only in sound knowledge but in many cases have been able to lend inspirational guidance to their particular departments that is daily putting Michigan State more and more along the highway of continued success and prosperity."

Shaw also had to replace MSC institution Linda E. Landon, who in 1932 retired after forty years as head librarian. Shaw chose Jackson E. Towne, a Milwaukee native who held degrees from both Harvard University and the University of Illinois and who had previously served as head of the library at Peabody College in Tennessee. Towne remained at Michigan State until his retirement in 1959.

Towne was a meticulous administrator, often penning somewhat dull but detailed accounts of library activities. His history of the library written in the early 1960s offers extensive detail about his administration's committees, circulation procedures, ordering philosophies, and cataloging methods. He also provided valuable insight into Michigan State's faculty and student body. For example, he documented a 1936 survey of the reading habits of male MSC students that appeared in *Christian Education* magazine:

> Sixty-five and a half per cent read no books at all during the college year outside their assignments. Of this number, 67.5 per cent read some during vacations, which leaves from one-fifth to one-quarter of the men of the college never reading at all except when compelled to by class assignments. Those who do read spend about half of their time with novels, merely to "while away the

President Robert Shaw receives congratulations on his tenth anniversary as president of Michigan State College. *Courtesy of Michigan State University Archives and Historical Collections.*

time." Of the other books read the types mentioned particularly were biography, history, and world affairs. Seventy-eight [percent] of the men students read magazines. The magazine most read, interestingly enough, is *Collier's*, having almost twice the popularity of the next highest magazines in our count, the *American* and *Saturday Evening Post*. Then comes *Reader's Digest*, with about 10 percent reading it from time to time. About 4 percent read *Harper's* regularly or occasionally, 2 percent the *Atlantic Monthly*, with all sorts of other magazines, such as *Cosmopolitan*, *Christian Century*, *Review of Reviews*, having their one or two readers per hundred men students.

Towne apparently believed that students should be reading more, and early in his tenure he wrote a library handbook to be distributed to all entering freshmen. The back of the handbook offered students some suggestions:

1. Take time regularly each week to read books on some subjects entirely outside of your regular work.
2. Make the acquaintance of some of the standard magazines which you never read before.
3. Throughout your college course learn to use books as tools and as sources of information. Such knowledge will always be of value in countless ways.

4. Learn to know books as friends. Experience the pleasure of reading and the inspiration that can come from intimate contact with
the greatest minds of all ages.

By 1938, when Shaw completed his tenth year as president, the
MSC Record declared his tenure a resounding success. During the
preceding school year, Michigan State had enrolled a record 5,547
students from forty-one states and eight foreign countries. The school
had gained membership in the American Association of Universities
in 1931. Shaw's choices for dean of men and dean of women, Mitchell
and Conrad, had performed admirably in their positions, the *Record*
said, helping to create an atmosphere in which there had been "no
serious campus disciplinary problems" during the previous few
years. Shaw had also implemented a retirement system for faculty
members.

THE SCANDAL OF 1932

The biggest change during Shaw's early years may have been
precipitated by rumors of scandal at the highest levels of college
administration. In early 1932, East Lansing resident Sara R. Fagan,
an honors graduate of the University of Michigan, a member of Phi
Beta Kappa Society, and an observer and writer on government and
politics in Lansing for fourteen years, sent newspapers statewide a
series of stories criticizing Michigan State. Fagan urged the publications' editors to print the stories, to use her byline, and to pay her one
dollar for each story used. "They should prove valuable in building up
circulation for any newspaper," she suggested. "Their main purpose,
however, is to clean up a disgraceful, if not criminal, situation and
restore State College to the place it once held in the life of Michigan
and the world of education." At issue were alleged improprieties in
the music department, conflicts of interest related to board members
and college officials, possible illegal real estate deals, and illegal trans-
actions between a college official and an East Lansing bank where
college payroll funds were deposited.

Other observers were also concerned. The State Board of Agriculture asked special assistant attorney general Joseph Baldwin to

investigate on the board's behalf. In addition, five Ingham County residents requested that a grand jury be formed to investigate irregularities at the college. Several legislators also became interested. Baldwin found no wrongdoing and put out a 25 November 1932 press release in which he heaped praise on MSC. "It is the consensus of opinion that once the present difficulty is cleared up, the College stands on the eve of its greatest development. I have found a remarkable spirit of loyalty to the present administration, headed by President Robert S. Shaw." The faculty is largely "made up of trained, conscientious educators who are disturbed by the present situation only through a realization of the damage that can be done by careless charges and unfound gossip." Leland W. Carr, an Ingham County circuit court judge, served as a one-man grand jury and also found no evidence of "the commission of any criminal offense" by college officials.

Although the college had been exonerated, three MSC employees were terminated in late November 1932: agricultural school dean Joseph Cox, supervisor of publications James Hasselman, and college historian and former president Frank S. Kedzie. According to a statement issued by Shaw,

> Readjustments in the personnel of the staff of Michigan State College have become imperative for the reason that some individuals have aided in the constant circulation of rumors, criticisms and charges, both on and off campus, over a period of some months, which have been proven by the investigation of a grand jury and the office of the attorney general to be essentially without foundation or justification. These conditions have persisted despite repeated requests and warnings from the administration which has waited patiently even in the face of un-kept promises until now some corrective action must be taken. The continued repetition of these unfounded rumors, criticisms and charges against both members of the board and the faculty resulted in seriously affecting the morale of the staff, destroying harmonious relationships and engendering a spirit of distrust and unrest inimical to the best interests of the college. These conditions can no longer be tolerated.

Some Michigan newspapers suggested that the terminations were too harsh, but Shaw enjoyed widespread support on campus.

The student council passed a resolution expressing "confidence in the integrity and ability of the governing officers at this school," and numerous deans and professors met on 28 January 1933 and released an open letter to Shaw expressing their support of the administration. The statement concluded, "The record of this College is an open book. We pledge support to any action you may take to maintain the good name of the Institution and further the cause of education." The signers of the letter included numerous prominent college faculty members, including Ernst Bessey (mycology), Arthur Clark (chemistry), Jackson Towne (library), W. O. Hedrick (economics), Lloyd Emmons (mathematics), Ward Giltner (veterinary medicine), Marie Dye (nutrition), Rufus Pettit (entomology), Ernest Anthony (agriculture), and John Ryder (liberal arts).

Of the three dismissals, Kedzie's was the most notable. He had both taught at the college and had served as its president, earning the moniker the Grand Old Man of the college. Until his death on 5 January 1935 he remained a frequent visitor to campus. When he died, classes were canceled, and the chimes of Beaumont Tower tolled as his body was transported to Evergreen Cemetery in Jackson. "The news of Dr. Kedzie's death made me feel as I have often felt when a great tree on our College campus has been cut down," said college secretary John Hannah. "With it disappears something splendid and stalwart, something of long, steady, sound growth, something that flowered in foliage of beauty and helpfulness and filled out the landscape, making other trees near it seem stunted and insignificant. His passing will bring in a hundred alumni circles all over the country a sense of disturbing loss and a regret for a good man gone."

JOHN HANNAH APPEARS ON THE SCENE

While Shaw worked to stabilize the college's economic situation and to repair public relations damage caused by previous presidents, a young John Hannah began to make a name for himself in Michigan agricultural circles. Hannah had originally planned to become a lawyer but changed his mind and became an expert in chicken husbandry and a teacher to Michigan farmers. The choice made sense in light of his background. His ancestors had been blacksmiths, schoolteachers, and—perhaps most important for his future career—farmers and flower growers. His grandfather had emigrated from Britain and established a market gardening business and flower shop in Grand Rapids. "My father did not attend primary school," Hannah recalled many years later. "My grandmother felt that she could give him a better primary education at home than that provided by one-room country schools of the day. She was a scholarly person, able to read and translate rapidly from Latin and Greek, the academic language for scholars of her youth." Wilfred Steele Hannah apparently inherited his mother's intellectual curiosity. "My father had become very much interested in horticulture and was generally regarded as quite an authority on scientific agriculture," John Hannah wrote. "I remember the many large and impressive looking books in his library that dealt with botany and horticulture. He always referred to plants by their scientific names."

Mary Ellen Malone, John Hannah's mother, grew up on a farm in Grattan Township outside of Grand Rapids and attended Ferris Institute, where she became acquainted with future Michigan governor Woodbridge N. Ferris. She later taught grade school in Kent County. John Hannah was born on 9 October 1902, in Grand Rapids, and eventually had three younger siblings. The Hannahs raised flowers, vegetables, and chickens. John took over responsibility for the chicken flock when he was just five or six years old and became known for his Black Orpingtons, which he exhibited at local fairs. While in high school, he served as secretary of the West Michigan Poultry Association, and he later became secretary of the State Poultry Association. After graduating from Grand Rapids South High School and Grand Rapids Junior College, he went to the University of Michigan to study law.

"In the winter of 1921–22, E. C. Foreman, who had been on the Agricultural Extension staff at M.A.C. and was head of the Poultry Department, came to visit me in Ann Arbor," Hannah remembered. "He asked me what I was going to do when I finished law school, and I told him frankly I did not know. Before the conversation was over, he suggested that if I came to East Lansing and took a degree in agriculture, he would give me a job as an extension poultryman at an annual salary of $2,500. Two thousand five hundred dollars a year sounded to me like a tremendous amount of money." Hannah

John Hannah's first job after graduation was as a poultry specialist at Michigan Agricultural College. Courtesy of Michigan State University Archives and Historical Collections.

arrived in East Lansing in the fall of 1922 and, by transferring his credits from junior college and the University of Michigan, received a bachelor's degree just one year later.

As planned, he took the job as an extension specialist, a position in which he performed well. Former forestry department chair Paul Herbert remembered Hannah as "a poultry specialist and a bachelor. Once in awhile he ate breakfast with some of the other bachelor instructors in Hunt Food Shop [an East Lansing restaurant]. However, he did not mix much, partly I suppose because he was in the field so much. But he was well liked in the field. I remember once up near Newberry on a small cutover farm of brush and 100 Leghorns, the old farmer's wife waxed eloquent over John." Bacteriology professor Walter L. Mallmann wrote that he was "impressed with [Hannah's] desire to acquire knowledge as a student and to disseminate his knowledge to the poultry producers as an extension worker. He had

Longtime athletic trainer Jack Heppinstall was an early Hannah friend. Courtesy of Michigan State University Archives and Historical Collections.

the uncanny ability to appraise the knowledgeability of his audience and to accordingly set a pattern of presentation that was understood. He was well-liked and his teachings accepted." According to university historian Madison Kuhn, Hannah's success as an extension specialist came from his refusal to talk down to his farm audience. "He explained carefully until he could speak the language of science to men who understood. He impressed them with his quiet handsomeness, his modesty, his serious manner, and his quick understanding of the reasons that could prompt a listener's question. At his first culling demonstration in his home county, old friends hoped to trap him by slipping one little white hen into each new group of birds. After he rejected her repeatedly, they agreed to his competence."

Shortly after arriving in East Lansing, Hannah began his connection with the college's football team. According to longtime Michigan State athletic trainer Jack Heppinstall, Hannah "started coming to all the football games at Michigan State and to many practices, where he became acquainted with the coaches, the players, and others connected with the team." At a time when football players did not yet receive scholarships and had to provide for their own meals, Hannah "had an apartment on Grove Street which needed taking care of, so he always had some needy football player living with him to help with the cooking and dishes and cleaning, etc. By all accounts it was a very good place to eat." The team came to hold an important place in Hannah's heart, and *Lansing State Journal* sportswriter George Alderton recalled that "when State defeated Michigan in Ann Arbor for the first time in nineteen years—that was in 1934—I went around to the dressing room after the game and Dr. Hannah was there shaking hands with everyone, and I think I saw tears on his cheeks." Arthur F. Brandstatter, who later became head of Michigan State's criminal justice school, recalled that Hannah was "keenly interested in encouraging young people to enroll. . . . He occasionally accompanied Michigan State coaches on recruiting trips and assisted coaches in convincing high school athletes to cast their lot with Michigan State. I met him my senior year at Ecorse High School, and that meeting changed the entire course of my life. It ultimately gave me an opportunity to study at college and to know well one of the most dedicated and warm-hearted human beings I have ever met."

Alderton also remembered the future president's devotion to his work and to the school:

> I made a trip with him one time from Los Angeles to Lansing on a train and shared a state room with him. He was working all of the time during the ride, except when he slept, of course. He had a big briefcase that was packed. He pulled off his coat and started putting papers around on tables and chairs and beds, and walked back and forth studying first one and then another, and moving them from one pile to another. He was indeed a busy man at all times. . . . Another memory of Dr. Hannah: It was registration week on campus in one of those early years, and he was on the football sideline with me, as he was briefly many times, and he looked up at the clouded sky and said, "I just hope that we are not going to encounter rain for a few days." When I asked why, he replied, "'You know, there are a lot of young people here enrolling for classes, and if we have rainy days and nights, they go home in droves! Homesickness hits them hard." He wanted what was then Michigan State College to grow in numbers, students, faculty and buildings.

Marie Mercier, who later served as Hannah's secretary when he was secretary to the Board of Agriculture, similarly wrote in 1971 that she remembered Hannah in the late 1920s and early 1930s "as a very studious person—always reading books of an educational nature and never spending time on frivolous things."

In 1933, as president-elect of the International Baby Chick Association, Hannah played an instrumental part in the drafting of a fair trade code that protected honest hatcheries against unscrupulous competition. The code prohibited exaggerated advertising, set a minimum size for hatching eggs, established health standards, required that chicks be sold at or above the cost of production, and regulated hours and wages for workers. President Franklin D. Roosevelt signed the measure into law in late 1933. Hannah took a year's leave of absence from Michigan State to establish the Kansas City offices of the agency that would enforce the new code. "Hundreds of professors planned and advised in the New Deal," Kuhn observed, "but fewer occupied line executive positions. Hannah was an exception." Hannah and his staff became known as effective enforcers, and 95 percent of the attendees at Hannah's regional meetings voted to continue the code without amendment. But Hannah did not enjoy his stint working for the federal government. "I was sent to the Middle West to tell farmers how much to charge for their chickens and eggs," he told the *Detroit News* in 1966. "I decided it wasn't for me to tell farmers how they should run their business. So I left the NRA [National Recovery Administration], considered a Chicago packing firm's offer of an $18,000-a-year job, but decided my future was back at MSU."

Heppinstall remembered that Hannah "received a telegram from President Shaw offering him the Secretaryship of the College and the State Board. [Hannah] seemed very pleased when asked what he intended to do about the offer and said he was going to sleep on it that night, then think it over carefully, ask for time until we get home, and make some offers or concessions that he thought ought to be taken care of before he accepted the position. They must have been satisfactory to the Board for he got the position." According to Hannah's memoir, the new position came with a salary of $4,200 a year, much less than he received in his current position. However, Hannah "had already concluded that there were things more important to me than making money and I had about made up my mind that I would rather return to a university—particularly to Michigan State College—than do anything else. It seemed to me that when a person gets old and looks back over his life, what is

Lansing State Journal sportswriter George Alderton covered Michigan State athletics from the 1920s through 1962. He and journalist Dale Stafford are credited with giving the college its Spartan nickname. Courtesy of Michigan State University Archives and Historical Collections.

President Shaw meets with the State Board of Agriculture around 1940. Seated are (*left to right*) Melville B. McPherson, Forest Akers, James Jakway, Lavina Masselink, Shaw, Chair William H. Berkey, Clark L. Brody, Hannah, and Charles O. Wilkins. Courtesy of Michigan State University Archives and Historical Collections.

important in it is not prestige or the amount of money in the bank, but rather whether or not he feels his life has been useful. If he has been able to contribute, even in some small way, to making it possible for people to live lives that are more satisfying to them than they might otherwise have been, that, it seems to me, is probably the most meaningful of all life's satisfactions."

As the new secretary, Hannah worked with the state legislature to secure more appropriations, with the Works Progress Administration (WPA) to secure funding for additional buildings, and with the State Board of Agriculture to keep members informed of college needs. One of Hannah's most valuable contributions was convincing both Shaw and the board that the college needed additional land for future development. "We decided to move south, making the east boundary of the campus south of the Red Cedar River at Hagadorn Road; the west boundary of the campus was to be Harrison Road, south from Michigan Avenue," Hannah said. "We wanted to acquire everything between the east and west boundaries as rapidly as possible. We also decided to buy only through private negotiation, without the use of condemnation procedures. During the period when I was secretary and later when I was president, the university acquired a total of some 7,000 acres without ever condemning a single acre or a single lot. Sometimes it took a long time and much negotiation; sometimes we had to wait for people to die; sometimes we made it possible for the owners of the property to live in the houses after purchase, the land to be turned over to the university only after the current occupants had lived out their lives."

MSC began buying land, securing federal funds for buildings, and starting construction. Abbot Hall (1938), the Auditorium (1940), Campbell Hall (1939), Jenison Field House (1940), the Music Building (1939), and the Olin Health Center (1939) were all constructed in part with funds supplied by the Public Works Administration (PWA). In many cases, the "self-liquidating" approach, used extensively over the next few decades, paid for the college's share of construction. In the financing of the new hospital and health center, for example, MSC borrowed $137,500 to cover its share, and the PWA provided $112,500. The college paid back its loan by setting aside $16,000 in student fees each year for ten years. The WPA supplied funding for workers to build campus roads, sidewalks, lawns, and other projects. In 1940, Hannah reported, the college employed more than four hundred WPA workers to perform such tasks as seeding the lawns around Jenison Field House and the secret football practice field, building tennis courts near Mason and Abbot Halls, painting the interiors of classrooms and dormitories, and installing farm drains. WPA workers also helped install the museum on the ground floor of the new Auditorium. While the government funding was a boon to the college, it also required substantial amounts of paperwork. As Mercier remembered,

> If approval of a project was not forthcoming as soon as Mr. Han-
> nah thought it should be, he would send telegrams to Washington
> inquiring about its status, and some of the projects required three
> or four telegrams to pry them loose. I really believe they were sick
> and tired of being pestered, so one by one the projects that were
> requested were approved and Mr. Hannah's persistence paid off.
> During this time President Shaw did not approve of Mr. Hannah's
> aggressiveness with regard to all these PWA projects. He feared

that Michigan State could never fulfill its obligation . . . on each project. But he was overruled, and in the end I am sure he was very pleased when the buildings were completed. This did not bother Mr. Hannah in the least, for he knew he was doing what was right for Michigan State.

Another thing that Mr. Hannah accomplished shortly after he became secretary was the removal of several houses on West Circle Drive. In the early days these houses were used by the faculty and were still in use for one thing or another. One of the buildings was used as the Health Service. Women's dormitories stand on the sites of these houses today. This feat was not accomplished without a great deal of protest from older faculty members and from towns-people who thought the houses should remain as landmarks. Mr. Hannah knew this was necessary for expansion of the campus and he acted over these protests.

In its December 1938 issue, the *MSC Record* declared the college's building program a remarkable success. Reporter Ralph Norman explained that the total cost of the nine new structures and improvement of the college grounds was $6,012,770, with $1,429,470 supplied by the PWA and $1,429,470 supplied by the WPA. Most of the rest was funded by the college with bond issues, to be repaid with building income. Norman proudly pointed out that the new construction cost the state only $142,150. Nevertheless, Hannah wanted more, telling Norman, "Although the building program will relieve housing congestion and improve hospital facilities, the program does not permit construction of classroom and laboratory buildings. Construction is limited almost entirely to buildings which may be self-financed through building income or student fees. The need for state-financed buildings to provide for the rapidly growing student body at Michigan State College is nearly as great as ever."

One of the most ambitious of the new structures was the Music Building. Dedicated on 3 December 1939, the facility represented the fulfillment of the dreams of music department director Lewis Richards, who had arrived on campus in 1927. At the time, the program was housed in the old economics department building, a frame structure originally designed without any thought to acoustics. Richards saw endless possibilities for musical excellence, if only he

had a state-of-the-art facility, and devised a plan for an elaborate new curriculum and building. After seeing Richards's plan, world-famous pianist and Detroit Symphony Orchestra conductor Ossip Gabrilowitsch told Richards, "If the college will allow you to put into effect only half of what you have on these pages, you will have the most outstanding department of music in the country." The college approved the plan, mainly because it fell under the administration's definition of a self-liquidating building project. "The music building is paid for by those majoring in music," Hannah said. "The charge paid for the use of the music practice rooms is more than sufficient to take care of the interest and retire the bonds as they become due." When his new building was completed, Richards was elated.

Another major arts-related structure erected during this time was the band shell, a gift of the Class of 1937. Located behind the chemistry building, the shell was dedicated on 11 May 1938 and

Dedicated in 1939, the Music Building gave Michigan State a cutting-edge arts facility and enabled music department director Lewis Richards to put into practice his long-held dreams for the department's curriculum. Courtesy of MSU Archives and Historical Collections.

Michigan State's band shell, a gift of the Class of 1937, provided a venue for orchestral concerts, Shakespearean plays, and religious services.

Courtesy of Michigan State University Archives and Historical Collections.

subsequently "was used continuously," the *MSC Record* reported. "Besides attracting huge crowds to the band concert series, the open-air amphitheatre served as the locale for a new type of religious service, the Campus Inspirational Hour held every Sunday morning at 9 o'clock. Sponsored by the YMCA, the half-hour program consisted of music and poetry taken from the services of all religious faiths."

Other campus buildings constructed early in Shaw's administration included a new library, later to become a museum, on Circle Drive. Next door, on the site of old College Hall, the first building in the United States to be used for agricultural education, workers were completing 104-foot-tall Beaumont Tower. A gift of John and Alice Beaumont of Detroit, the structure featured a clock and a carillon that chimed every fifteen minutes. Across the Red Cedar River, Demonstration Hall was going up, eventually providing extensive facilities for military training as well as ice skating, equestrian, and athletic events; on Farm Lane, just south of the Red Cedar, new dairy barns, a state-of-the-art milk house, and a modern bull barn were nearing completion.

Lansing native Edwyn A. Bowd bore much of the responsibility for the architecture of these and other campus buildings constructed in the first half of the twentieth century. Bowd played key roles in the design and planning of Lansing's First Baptist Church (1891), City Hall (1894), and Pilgrim Congregational Church (1898), as well as several exhibits at the Louisiana Purchase Exposition and the St. Louis World's Fair held in 1904 and the refurbishment of the Ingham County Courthouse. In early 1902, he was appointed architect of Michigan Agricultural College. "He will design all buildings which may be required for the institution and supervise their erection," the *Lansing State Journal* reported. Over the next several decades, he and later his partner, Orlie Munson, would be responsible for such structures as the Intramural Recreative Sports–Circle, the library (now the museum), Olds Hall, Agriculture Hall, Marshall Hall, Human Ecology, the horticulture building, Natural Science, the Auditorium, Giltner Hall, Spartan Stadium, and Jenison Field House.

By 1939 Hannah was receiving almost as much attention both on and off campus as Shaw. Hannah perhaps became even better known after he married the president's daughter, Sarah Shaw, in 1938. Starting with the October 1939 issue of the *MSC Record*, Hannah penned a column describing current events at MSC, beginning his initial piece, "It is with considerable misgivings that I inflict upon you my first efforts as a columnist." Hannah used this forum to point out that Michigan State now had 6,663 students attending classes for college credit; two new dormitories, T. C. Abbot Hall for men and Louise H. Campbell Hall for women, each of which had cost more than a half million dollars, were now in use; and the old hospital (formerly President Snyder's house) had been converted to a cooperative residence for women.

In his July 1940 column, Hannah announced that the museum was moving from the third floor of the library to the ground floor of the new Auditorium; that a new building was being constructed to house the college's egg-laying contests; that Michigan muck farmers had petitioned the college for more muck-farming research and that five thousand dollars had been appropriated for that purpose; and

John Hannah married Sarah Shaw, daughter of MSC President Robert Shaw, in 1938. Courtesy of MSU Archives and Historical Collections.

that the old gymnasium, replaced by Jenison Field House, was being revamped for use as a women's gymnasium. Hannah also reported that the college's current enrollment stood at 9,201 students, an enormous increase from the 3,959 who had matriculated just six years earlier. The growing number of students and the additional buildings needed to house and teach them was putting tremendous pressure on the power plant and forcing extensive purchases of electricity. Consequently, the board approved the expansion of the plant, thereby allowing the university to manufacture its own power and save approximately thirty thousand dollars a year.

While Hannah was receiving increased attention, Shaw was contemplating retirement. He had arrived at the State Agricultural

Sarah Hannah views a portrait of her father, Michigan State President Robert Shaw. Courtesy of Michigan State University Archive and Historical Collections.

College in 1902 as a professor of practical agriculture. When he officially announced his retirement in 1941, Michigan State College had become the fifteenth-largest institution of higher education in the United States. He had presented degrees to 10,084 students—66 percent of all the graduates in MSC's eighty-six-year history. Numerous interviews conducted as Shaw neared retirement revealed that the president hated to wear dress suits; that he was a star baseball player in his youth; that he liked to dance but thought that students of the 1940s didn't know how to waltz; and that he liked to be called Mr. Shaw rather than President Shaw. "Since he shies away from displays of sentiment, and from that authoritative title of 'President' which he has borne so honorably, perhaps the best farewell from M.S.C. students would be, 'Goodbye, Mr. Shaw,'" student Peggy Trout wrote in the April 1941 *MSC Record*. "'Thanks for being sincere and straight with us, clear through.'"

Unlike some of his predecessors as the college's president, Shaw departed with the respect and admiration of virtually all segments of the college. "We as students were very close to him," A. L. Bibbins of the Class of 1915 wrote. "His patience and advice were of great value to us. His teaching and philosophy were supreme." Current students echoed these sentiments: "He is such a keen and natural person—so unaffected and genuine," said Jean Bills, *Wolverine* business manager. "President Shaw should be respected as a capable administrator, which is evidenced by the growth of the college," remarked senior class president Jim Otto. "He maintains a sincere attitude toward his work and is considerate of students and their activities." The chair of the Water Carnival, Harry Jackson, said, "The president certainly is a lot of fun and a good mixer, but take my advice, if you have a good looking date, he is likely to cut in." *Spartan* business manager Art Howland noted Shaw's numerous campus improvements: "I heard that he authorized damming up the Red Cedar in order to make canoeing possible and that he suggested the possibility of planting the sand hill behind Demonstration hall with the beautiful pines that are there today."

Shaw's retirement precipitated an impressive honorary dinner held on 6 June 1941. The event's honorary chairs included Michigan governor Murray D. Van Wagoner and Lansing industrialist Ransom E. Olds. Members of the sponsoring committee included Detroit industrialist Henry Ford, Lansing mayor Sam Street Hughes, *Detroit Free Press* publisher John S. Knight, *Detroit Times* publisher William E. Anderman, Detroit mayor Edward J. Jeffries Jr., Chrysler Corporation executive K. T. Keller, *Detroit News* president William E. Scripps, *Lansing State Journal* publisher Paul Martin, J. L. Hudson vice president Oscar Webber, and Michigan Bell Telephone president George M. Welsh.

John Hannah, President of Michigan State College

John Hannah was quickly selected as MSC's eleventh president. "Keeping in mind the fact that although the scope of the college activities has broadened greatly in its engineering, liberal arts, home economics, applied science, and veterinary divisions, and since Michigan State is primarily an agricultural college, it seemed best that its chief executive should come from the agricultural field, as does Mr. Hannah," W. H. Berkey, chair of the State Board of Agriculture, announced. "A graduate of the Agricultural division, he became an extension worker in the poultry department and internationally known for his work. He was engaged in special work in line for the U.S.

Department of Agriculture when he was asked to become secretary of the college, and gave up a more lucrative position to take over the work here, where his conduct of the business has made him a natural selection for the promotion to the office of president."

Media reports indicated that Ernest Anthony, MSC's dean of agriculture; Grover C. Dillman, president of the Michigan College of Mining and Technology; and Eugene Elliot, state superintendent of public instruction, had also been considered for the position. Hannah's selection had its detractors. Professor Walter L. Mallmann recalled that many faculty members with doctorates "believed the next president should have a doctorate, a good reputation as an educator and acceptance as a president by the great public and private universities of the United States. Hannah had a B.S. degree in poultry husbandry and no experience as an educator. Would he be accepted by other universities and would he be able to bring this growing school along the pathway leading to greatness as a teaching and research center based on the broad needs of a society created on research? . . . Although I had great respect for Hannah's ability I was disappointed—but not for long."

The new president did not disagree with Mallmann's assessment of his own résumé's shortcomings, writing in his memoirs,

> As a young man, I did not know that I was to spend most of my life in educational administration until I reached the point in my career where an earned doctorate would have made me no better and no worse at my job. I never apologized for it, but if I were to live my life over I should certainly try to earn a doctorate early in life. I called this to the attention of the State Board of Agriculture when they first raised the possibility that I might be offered the presidency of Michigan State, pointing out that in the eyes of some academics my lack of an earned Ph.D. degree would be viewed as a serious deficiency. The board brushed it aside. I was awarded honorary degrees by many respected universities—more than thirty of them, including several outside the United States. I was always grateful for this generous recognition but never regarded all of them put together as a substitute for an earned doctorate.

Ernest Anthony served as Michigan State's dean of agriculture from 1933 until his retirement in 1953. Courtesy of MSU Archives and Historical Collections.

John Hannah became president of Michigan State College in 1941. Courtesy of Michigan State University Archives and Historical Collections.

THE FOUR HORSEMEN OF MSC

During the years of John Hannah's rise to the presidency, MSC made great strides toward expanding beyond its agricultural beginnings and achieving numerous agricultural successes. When the *Lansing State Journal* summarized the previous year's significant campus events in its New Year's Day 1929 edition, horses were some of the biggest news: "Eleven horses from the college stables were entered in state fairs in Michigan and Ohio and also in the International Livestock Exchange in Chicago. The same horses were entered in all three exhibits. College Percherons won seven championships in the three exhibits, while Belgians were awarded six championships. . . .

Ralph S. Hudson graduated from the State Agricultural College in 1907 and subsequently spent forty-two years as head of the farm and horse department. Courtesy of Michigan State University Museum Collections.

The winnings this year serve to show that Michigan State College has the leading Percheron sires of the country." MSC's steers and cattle were also major winners; the sheep had less success "but nevertheless made a credible showing."

Ralph S. Hudson was born in Pentwater, Michigan, and grew up in Okemos. In 1907 he received a bachelor's degree from the State Agricultural College, and in 1917 he became superintendent of the farms. He served as head of the farm and horse department, during which time he and college blacksmith John MacAllan, college groomsman Jack Carter, and Harold Moxley, an extension specialist in animal husbandry, built a nationwide reputation for the school's horse show program. According to the *Draft Horse Journal*, "Notre

Groomsman Andrew Quirrie (*left*) and black-smith John MacAllan were part of the team that helped make MSC known for its excellent horse program. Courtesy of Michigan State University Museum Collections.

Dame's Four Horsemen played in the backfield. Michigan State's worked in the horse barn and out amongst the state's farmers and horse breeders."

Horses bred by these four men garnered equal fame. A Percheron mare, Maplegrove Leila, won three senior and grand championships at the Chicago International competition in the late 1920s. Coreen, another Percheron mare, was never shown but produced nineteen foals, many of which went on to win major competitions. A Belgian mare, Pervenche, was selected grand champion at Michigan State, Ohio, and Chicago International fairs; her offspring, Ginger, went on to win honors at the American Belgian Show in 1946. Rubis received a silver medal from the king of Belgium at the 1913 National Horse Show in Brussels. Rubis was especially well known for siring outstanding colts, and he bred mares up until two weeks before his death in 1935.

THE GREAT DEPRESSION

The Great Depression of the 1930s affected life at Michigan State much as the downturn affected life throughout the United States.

John Hannah posed with two of the college's championship horses. Courtesy of Michigan State University Archives and Historical Collections.

Students looking for work found themselves competing against more classmates for fewer jobs. New arrivals in East Lansing often had to work at odd jobs because steady jobs with better pay and hours had already been filled by returning students. The employment situation in East Lansing was better than in many other places: students found work as laborers on college farms, as typists for faculty members, and as waiters and dishwashers at the Student Union and local restaurants. The YMCA and YWCA established employment bureaus in the Peoples Church. Moreover, "Because of the strengthening of the curriculum in all divisions of the college, there appears to be very little likelihood that a student may carry a full college program and at the same time do enough work on the outside to support himself," Lloyd Emmons, a research professor of institutional management, reported. "There is, of course, an occasional student, sufficiently gifted to accomplish this, but those who try usually find the program too difficult and have to give up or readjust their affairs."

The New Deal brought some relief to the job situation by 1935, when a National Youth Administration program opened at the Union Building on the Michigan State campus. Headed by MSC Alumni Association secretary Glen Stewart, the program provided sixty-three hundred dollars per month in federal funds to employ students, who were chosen on the basis of need, character, and ability. The 405 students selected from among the 1,450 applicants in the fall of 1935 performed such duties as filing, clipping, mapmaking, and correcting papers. "I can't tell you how happy I am this year," one student wrote to the Youth Administration office. "I want to thank you for this opportunity to earn $15 a month. It pays half my board and room expense."

During the 1970s, Jack Green, a depression-era Michigan State student who later became a journalist and public relations executive, remembered his school days:

> I don't recall that life in college was a great deal different than it had been before or has been since except that none of us had any money; that put everybody on more or less equal footing. Tuition was thirty-five dollars a term. You could earn enough during the summertime for three terms. . . . There were very few apartments available for those students not living at home, and the few dormitories available (other than Wells Hall) were women's dormitories. Fraternity and sorority houses took care of a substantial number of the student body. The rest lived in rooming houses, in private homes, or in little one-room apartments over the business places downtown. . . . Many of them rented a single room with a drop bulb, a ramshackle bed, and a study table and chair, for two or three bucks a week. . . . People were able to preserve some semblance of entertainment with partying and dances, scraping together a little money here and there. This was during prohibition and there was no legal liquor. But there was a considerable amount of drinking going on. A lot of student drinking was based on pure grain alcohol which was swiped from the chemistry laboratory at the college. It was cut with water and made into "gin" by adding juniper flavor or into "whiskey" by coloring it with burnt sugar. It was terrible-tasting stuff.

The cold economic realities brought on by the Great Depression eventually caught up with the college's building program, and in 1934 no campus construction took place except for minor remodeling of existing structures. Shaw nevertheless remained hopeful, declaring, "The universal economic stress has brought about a change in the attitude of the student body. Students today are more purposeful, are thinking more correctly and acting more clearly than a year ago. From an administrative standpoint this means much need for disciplinary action has been entirely eliminated and the officials of the college are now enjoying the help and cooperation of the student body to an exceptional degree." Shaw went on to describe the college's situation and its efforts to help Michigan residents cope with the tough economic times: "For the second successive year operation on a greatly reduced budget has been necessary. . . . The extension organization, including administrative officers, specialists and county agents, has rendered a large and splendid service in aiding with the execution of relief readjustment measures of the federal government. Many members of the instructional staff have likewise been called upon to aid in solving difficult problems involved in the recovery program."

The Extension Service had originally been created to put college faculty in touch with farmers, and the Great Depression gave extension workers numerous opportunities to offer assistance. The Extension's home economics staff stressed self-sufficiency, teaching farm families how to become more proficient in canning meats and vegetables, helping them to make rugs with old materials and to create furniture covers out of dyed feed sacks, and assisting them in planning low-cost yet nutritious meals. Other extension specialists distributed improved celery seed developed by the botany department, helped introduce blueberry production to swampy wasteland, and taught poultry producers how to reduce the incidence of parasite infestations in chickens. Extension services extended beyond farmers as well: in the city of Midland, extension agents developed welfare gardens for the unemployed, resulting in ten acres of potatoes and forty-two individual gardens. On a larger scale, a cooperative effort between the Extension Service and the farm crops department helped to rejuvenate Michigan's ailing sugar-beet industry, adding seventy thousand acres of fields between 1929 and 1932.

STUDENT HEALTH

While the financial times may have been unhealthy, MSC students seem to have enjoyed excellent physical health. Dr. Richard Olin, former Michigan commissioner of health, was put in charge of medical care on campus in 1927. In a 1 January 1935 story in the *State Journal*, Olin pointed with pride to the more than 120,000 patients treated during his tenure; during that time only three deaths had occurred—a patient who succumbed as a result of an appendix that had ruptured before he entered the college hospital, a patient who had contracted scarlet fever and had originally been treated by an outside physician, and a person with a "previously infected liver." According to Olin, nine-tenths of the cases handled by the college health service were "irritations of the upper respiratory tract," and because the college focused on prevention, most illnesses were treated before they became serious.

MSC's hospital—one of the country's best equipped, according to Olin—was located at Faculty Row No. 1 (the Old President's Home), where Gilchrist Hall now stands. In 1939 the college began construction of a new medical facility, incorporating many of Olin's ideas into the structure. Olin died before the building was completed, and the building was named the Olin Memorial Health Care Center in honor of his contributions.

PUBLIC SAFETY

In 1939 the *State News* conducted a study of Michigan State's preparations in case of a fire and discovered that the campus had no fire alarms. Nevertheless, East Lansing fire chief Merle Croy remained unconcerned: "We think there is no great danger of fire for the simple reason that the heating system is centrally located and the electrical system is well checked," said Croy, whose department, along with Lansing's fire department, would respond to any fire emergency. He also cited the regular inspection of storage space, the presence of more than four hundred fire extinguishers around campus, and the employment of watchmen and janitors in the major buildings at night. In case of a fire, grounds department employees would turn off steam lines, turn up water pressure, and cut off electricity near the site of the fire. A study was also under way to determine if sprinkler systems should be installed in such danger spots as haylofts and chemistry laboratories. Hannah echoed Croy's reassuring words: "There is always the possibility of fire in the older buildings. However, the whole situation has been surveyed in the last three years by the underwriters. There's not much danger to the occupants although valuable material and documents might burn. The college is completely covered by insurance."

Traffic hazards, however, awaited those who ventured off campus onto Grand River Avenue, which featured such perils as students riding on the running boards of speeding cars, pedestrians who failed to look carefully before crossing the street, and drivers going up to sixty miles an hour in thirty-five-mile-an-hour zones. So many accidents occurred in the late 1930s that the East Lansing Police Department devised an elaborate study to figure out ways to assess traffic speeds. "We have two mirrors on tripods 220 feet apart," a police officer told the *State News*. "Both are set at angles to reflect passing cars. We time each car on the one-eighth mile stretch, starting the watch as the car's reflection flashes across the first mirror, and stopping as the car passes the second mirror. Charts transform the time in seconds into miles per hour." The study recommended stricter enforcement and stated a need for more speed-limit signs.

Strict enforcement of traffic laws was a priority for Harold Haun, a 1930 graduate of MSC who took over the duties of police chief in 1937, when the East Lansing and campus departments were merged. A former varsity football and basketball player at the college, Haun immediately announced that he would "clamp down" on all city and campus traffic rule violators. "After they know we're on the job," he said, "we won't have to be so strict. But right now all infractions of the law bring down a fine on the head of the offender."

Law enforcement officials also continually confronted rowdy students who celebrated too aggressively after athletic events. Prior to the mid-1920s, such celebrations often included a march to the Capitol. According to George Alderton,

It had become the custom at the college that whenever a football team or a baseball team won a signal victory, the students would walk to Lansing in a body picking up boards and other combustible material as they went, and heap it in front of the capitol, set it afire, and dance and sing and shout their happiness. The last one came in 1928, when State defeated the University of Michigan in baseball

. . . and the student body was ready to march, and downtown they went, a big horde, singing and laughing and cheering. . . . When they ignited [the bonfire], the Lansing police arrived on the scene and began asking questions and called the fire department to put out the fire, and, of course, the students were swarming around and it was a pretty difficult place for the policemen to find themselves in. A few of them were jostled. At the end, the crowd withdrew but were still laughing and shouting and cheering. They had pushed down a couple of the officers who tried to get to Skinny Skellinger, who was the ring leader of the invaders. Somewhere in the march he had picked up a fruit basket full of eggs, and when he saw the police were going to get him, he climbed a telephone pole with the basket in his hand and the policeman went after him. Skinny had an easy target. He was dropping eggs on the officer, who finally dislodged him and got him down, and got him to the police station. When we walked into the squad room, the cop stood there, spread out his arms and said, "Look at me, a damn omelet." They put Skinny in the cooler over night, and the crowd finally dispersed and went back to the campus. It was the last of an old tradition.

Despite the end of marches to the Capitol, students continued to conduct mass marches through the campus and city. In addition to police efforts to control the problem, private businesses sometimes attempted to intervene. East Lansing's State Theatre occasionally showed free films if students had behaved well after a football game. On 19 November 1934, for example, more than one thousand students attended a free showing of *Big Hearted Herbert*. "It was arranged for the students in appreciation of the fine spirit which was evidenced after the Michigan game," a theater spokesman explained. Other strategies used to discourage violence and destruction by students included pregame statements by Hannah, pleas from players and coaches, and the threat of arrest and prosecution.

WKAR

In 1934, Robert J. Coleman, a member of the music faculty, received the job of reorganizing the college radio station, WKAR, which had

Robert J. Coleman revitalized the mostly mori-bund college radio station, WKAR, in 1934, and oversaw its operations through 1958. Courtesy of WKAR Radio.

been founded in 1922. In May of that year, the station broadcast an address by college president David Friday; a year later, it covered a football game between MAC and the University of Chicago; and in 1925, it began a program of bedtime stories for children in rural homes. The station perhaps reached its early pinnacle in 1926, when a listener in Silverton, Oregon, wrote to tell station officials that he had picked up the signal. In 1934, however, "the entire staff of WKAR consisted of one person who was the program announcer and three operators, who in addition to handling the technical broadcasting equipment were responsible for the repair and maintenance of all keys and locks on the campus," Coleman wrote thirty-eight years later. "The program schedule consisted of a five-day farm program of 30 minutes drawn from the School of Agriculture and the School of Home Economics. . . . The studio was located on the fourth floor of the Home Economics building adjacent to the elevator motors, neces-sitating that the elevator be stopped during broadcasts. The faculty of the Home Economics Department resented this greatly. . . . There was no budget, no record library and no program resources except the live speaker from the agriculture and home economics department."

Coleman, who had several years of experience at Ohio State University's radio station and who had worked for the educational de-partment of the Victor Talking Machine Company, went to work. He reinstituted football coverage, which had been discontinued; moved

WKAR Radio's first real studios were built in
1924 and were located on the fourth floor of the
Home Economics building. Courtesy of WKAR Radio.

the station into the new Auditorium in 1939; greatly expanded the
staff and the hours of broadcasting; and, with Shaw's and Hannah's
support, created a separate radio department in 1940. During the
1930s, the station broadcast news stories taken directly from the
Detroit Free Press, with the paper's permission. On one occasion, a
WKAR announcer read a *Free Press* article about excess expenditures
by the Democratic legislature and then made a personal comment,
suggesting that more Republicans needed to get into office. "Our
first knowledge of this was when President Hannah called us over
and told us the office of Governor Frank Murphy [a Democrat] was
incensed and protested the partisanship of the station, mentioning
that the Legislature provided the budgets for the college," Coleman

Even in the 1930s, WKAR Radio was not a studio-only operation, as is shown in this photo of its 1939 mobile unit. Courtesy of WKAR Radio.

remembered. "Mr. Hannah told us to contact the proper people and to clarify the matter. We had a long conference with the Chairman of the Democratic Party in Michigan that afternoon and were able to convince him that this was a slip by a student announcer and did not reflect the policy of the station or the College." In most cases, however, Hannah was delighted by WKAR. After returning from a visit to Michigan's Thumb, he told Coleman, "Everywhere I go I find many people listening to WKAR; many of these have no other contact with the University except by radio. You have made many friends for the institution and have offended very few."

ATHLETICS IN THE 1930s

As early as 1930, Michigan State also gained public notice through football success, posting a 5-1-2 record, with its sole loss a 14-13 defeat by Georgetown. Led by head coach James H. Crowley and his two assistants, Miles "Mike" Casteel and Glen "Judge" Carberry, the team

Mike Casteel served as Michigan State's backfield coach under both Jim Crowley and Charlie Bachman. He also worked with the track team and was a polished after-dinner speaker and an excellent recruiter. Courtesy of Michigan State University Archives and Historical Collections.

Jim Crowley, Michigan State's football coach from 1929 to 1932 and one of the Four Horsemen of Notre Dame, led the team to great success. Courtesy of Michigan State University Archives and Historical Collections.

recorded its most successful season in fifteen years. Crowley, one of Notre Dame's famous Four Horsemen, had come to East Lansing in 1929, succeeding Lansing's Harry Kipke, who left for the top spot in Ann Arbor. Announced the December 1930 issue of the *MSC Record,* "Not only were the followers extremely pleased with the results of the games and the way the squad conducted itself at all times, but the fact that a new coaching combination had produced the desired results in two years. Coach Crowley commands the respect and admiration of everyone on the Campus. His personality, his ability to teach college men in a fashion that would meet the demands of the most critical and his standing with the faculty and business leaders of the community makes him a respected figure. Michigan State has fallen for Jimmy Crowley—and fallen in a big way."

During the next two seasons, Crowley's squads posted 5-3-1 and 7-1 records, and sportswriter George Alderton echoed the *Record*'s praise of the coach:

Jim called upon his players to play a high grade of the game against many major opponents and earned national attention. His teams never defeated Michigan, but in 1930 and 1931 they played the high-rated Wolverines to scoreless ties. Crowley asked his starting 11 players to play nearly every minute of every game. In one season there were only 13 players who earned their S's. . . . Three of his players at State went into professional football. Bobby Monnet and quarterback Roger Grove played with the Green Bay Packers for several years, and Arthur Buss was a standout tackle with the Chicago Bears for a long time. . . . Jim was a wit. He had a keen sense of humor that helped him with his witticisms. I enjoyed being around to hear them. . . . Jim, of course, had the nickname of "Sleepy Jim Crowley." I asked him one time if he slept well at night. His reply was that he slept pretty well at night but that he just pitched and tossed all day!

At Crowley's death in 1986, Tom O'Brien, a *State Journal* sportswriter during Crowley's time at the helm in East Lansing, remembered,

Fans loved to attend Crowley's practice sessions in East Lansing. He would yell at his squad, "I want you to play with zest and abandon."

. . . I'll never forget the 1930 game with the University of Michigan, a national powerhouse coached by Harry Kipke, a graduate of Lansing High School and an All-American at Ann Arbor. . . . Coach Crowley had lost his center, Harold Smead, a strapping giant and an All-Stater from Sturgis through a tragic motorcycle accident during the summer months. One leg had to be amputated. There was not an inkling of what was to occur minutes before kickoff time. Into the Michigan State dressing room came Smead in a wheelchair, an attendant moving it among the squad as the stunned players shook his hand. Emotions soared. The Spartans fought the highly favored Wolverines to a scoreless tie.

The 1932 Spartans defeated Fordham 19-13, impressing Fordham fans and officials so much that they hired Crowley at the season's end. "I am sorry that Crowley saw fit to ask us to release him from his contract," President Shaw stated. "We have enjoyed pleasant and successful relations with other institutions since he came to East Lansing. But, in view of the opportunity that was given him at Fordham, we could not stand in his way, especially since we all realize the career of a coach is, at best, rather brief. His departure does not mean that our attempt to produce good teams will be lessened. We shall, I firmly believe, find some coach who is fully capable of undertaking the responsibilities. I feel sure that an adequate and capable staff will be here to take charge of spring practice."

Although MSC amicably parted ways with the coach, an evaluation of the school's athletic programs by the North Central Association of Colleges and Secondary Schools soon discovered some problems with Crowley's team. "As the football coach James H. Crowley has been released from his contract which has a year more to run so that he may accept an offer at Fordham University, we need to say little regarding his activities or his salary," inspector B. L. Stradley reported in early 1933. "However, it is imperative that the conditions which existed while he was coach should not continue. . . . The opinion seems to be that the coach had been paid more and worked less than any man in the department. The assistant coaches have done most of the coaching and remained on the job and conferred with the students. It is estimated that thirty of the freshmen squad have never met the head coach and, therefore, we do not feel that he was being paid for

Charles W. Bachman became the Spartans' football coach in 1933 and compiled a 70-34-10 record during his thirteen years at the Michigan State helm. Courtesy of Michigan State University Archives and Historical Collections.

the educational or character building program which he contributed to the College, but rather for the ability to produce winning teams." Stradley advised that Crowley's successor "be sufficiently employed in the interests of the College that he may have little time available for outside activities. Competent faculty members resent the high salary paid to a football coach and particularly so when he is not giving his full time to the work of the College. Such a salary is an indication of the over emphasis on winning teams in intercollegiate athletics rather than any educational value the students receive from contact with a man who is absent from campus." According to the report, Crowley's annual salary had been $8,000; in contrast, athletic director Ralph Young made $5,250.

From among the more than sixty men who applied for the vacant MSC job, Young and other school officials chose another Notre Dame alumnus, Charles W. Bachman, head coach at the University of Florida. Bachman had a reputation for high-scoring teams—his 1928 squad had led the nation in scoring. To provide continuity for the players, MSC retained Casteel as one of Bachman's assistants. Wrote Alderton, Casteel "had been Ralph Young's star athlete in every sport that Kalamazoo College had when he was a student there, and Ralph wanted him in East Lansing. [Casteel was] a good after-dinner speaker, an excellent recruiter, and a trouble fixer."

With Casteel's help, Bachman surpassed Crowley's success, putting together six straight winning seasons and four consecutive wins over Michigan. The 1934 and 1937 squads went 8-1 during the regular season, and both guard Sydney Wagner and halfback John Pingel were named All-Americans. Other notable players during Bachman's early years included ends Ed Klewicki and Lou Zara; interior linemen Sam Ketchman, Harry Speelman, and Howard Zindel; and back Arthur Brandstatter. The 1934 season was especially exciting as the Spartans beat Michigan for the first time in nineteen years, 16-0, an occasion the *State Journal* described as "the greatest football day that the banks of the sleepy Red Cedar river, flowing through the Michigan State college campus, have seen in many a day":

State, in winning, left no room for a Michigan win. The Spartans were simply vastly superior in every department of the game and won a richly deserved victory. The score might easily have been

higher, for State had one or two opportunities to score while Michigan's men, pale and beaten, were apparently resigned to their fate.
But State out-thought, out-punted, out-passed and out-ran Michigan.
Michigan out-fumbled the Spartans, but it was only in this department that the statistics gave them the edge. Kurt Warmbein, the
blond galloper from St. Joseph, was the State spearhead in the
victory. He punted, passed, and ran the Wolverines dizzy. When
he took a place behind center, Michigan began guessing what he
would do and Coach Harry Kipke's young men guessed wrong,
many, many times.

Victories over Michigan and other prominent teams brought MSC
national attention, but the real public relations coup came at the end
of the 1937 regular season, when the Orange Bowl invited the Spartans to face off on New Year's Day against a tough Auburn team that
had posted a 5-3-1 regular season record. Playing in Miami's humid
eighty-degree weather, the Tigers defeated the Spartans 6-0, outplay-
ing Michigan State all the way, according to the *State Journal*.

Despite the loss in their first-ever bowl game, Bachman's teams
of the 1930s produced some of the most interesting, talented, and
successful men MSC had ever seen. Pingel subsequently played with
the Detroit Lions; served in World War II as a lieutenant colonel in
the infantry, earning a Bronze Star and Purple Heart; and became a
successful Detroit advertising executive. Klewicki, who was known
for having been whacked on the head by a steam shovel during a
summer highway construction job yet refusing to take the rest of
the day off, also played for the Lions, serving as the team's captain.
Brandstatter went on to become East Lansing's police chief and the
head of Michigan State's police administration school; in 1961, he
was named a *Sports Illustrated* Silver Anniversary All-American. And
Zara coached football at Wayne State.

In his memoirs, Alderton wrote fondly of several players from
this era. He remembered a 1934 game against Texas A&M in which
Klewicki had inadvertently blindsided an Aggie player: "I never saw
a player hit harder than that Texan was that day. He went in the air
like a rag doll when Ed hit him, and landed flat on the ground and
stayed there. They had to carry the guy to an ambulance and take
him to a hospital. That night Ed Klewicki was not eating dinner with

John Pingel was an All-American halfback during
the late 1930s who later played for the Detroit
Lions, earned a Purple Heart during World War
II, and became a Detroit advertising executive.
Courtesy of Michigan State University Museum Collections.

Howard Zindel starred in football at MSC during
the early 1930s and later served as a member
of the poultry husbandry faculty. Courtesy of MSU
Archives and Historical Collections.

the squad after the victory. He was at the hospital sitting at the boy's bedside until he regained consciousness about midnight. Ed was all man, a gentleman, and one heck of a football player."

Of halfback Eddie Pearce, Alderton wrote, "a good runner, a better blocker, and a happier guy I never knew." He described one occasion on which the Spartans were traveling on a ferryboat from British Columbia to Seattle:

A Chinese family had come aboard with us, pa, ma, and four or five kids, all dressed in native costumes. One of the little girls, three or four years old, was a darling child and Eddie spotted her. There was a piano in the room, and Eddie strolled over to the piano and started touching the keys with a single finger, and now and then looked over and smiled at this little girl. She started over toward him a couple of times but went back. The third time she went all the way, clambered up on the piano bench with Eddie, and it became a duet from that time on. I looked over at the parents and they were delighted. They were all smiling and so happy. Eddie said goodbye, reached over and kissed his little friend. Eddie was like that. It is too bad the whole world is not like that today. He graduated the next June and I didn't see him for a couple of years. One day he came out on the practice field dressed in his Air Force uniform, spic and span, puttees and all. We watched practice for a while, and he finally had to go. We shook hands. He said, "I have a strange feeling that I will never see this place again," and away he went, smiling, happy, straight-backed young soldier. A year or so later I saw his name in the newspaper again. His Thunderbolt fighter plane had rolled Eddie up in it, shot down over the desert in North Africa. I was walking over to the stadium for a game many, many years later and I was telling my companion about Eddie. As I finished, the man who had been walking in front of me in the crowd turned to me, smiled, reached out his hand, and said, "Thank you for the story about my father." You know, I think Eddie arranged our meeting.

The football team's success during this era led to the emergence of a new phenomenon, the athletic booster. Del Vandervoort, a member of the college's offensive line from 1914 to 1916 and again in 1919, after returning to campus from World War I, gained the unofficial title Spartan Fan No. 1 and rarely missed a Michigan State athletic event. He gave dinners for football coaches and players at his cabin, Rattlesnake Gulch, on the Grand River near Dimondale, and was one of the founders of East Lansing's Downtown Coaches Club.

And, as his early involvement with the football team continued, John Hannah became one of MSC's most loyal sports boosters. Wrote the school's longtime athletic trainer, Jack Heppinstall, "At one time [Hannah] attended better than 50 consecutive games. He knew all the players by their first names and what high school they were from. . . . At one of our games with Penn State at State College, we were assigned a general locker room for our dressing room. It was Homecoming day and the alumni were using a room next to the locker room and using our room as a runway to get there. The coaches could not talk to the players and the players could not get dressed. Dr. Hannah stood this traffic as long as he could, then locked the doors to keep them out. . . . On the away trips, Dr. Hannah was the first man of the party to take off his coat and help the tired and bruised players get their dirty, sweaty suits off and get them packed into the suit sacks."

In 1935, MSC named its football stadium in honor of former head coach John Farrell Macklin. The choice of Macklin did not please all members of the Michigan State community: Horace V. Geib, who had captained MAC's 1912 track team and was now a regional director for the U.S. Soil Conservation Service, questioned the decision in a letter to President Shaw, arguing that Macklin "was not at all in line with the traditions set up for good old M.A.C." Geib argued that another former coach, Chester A. Brewer, would have been a better choice, standing "for everything that was clean and fair and honest. I have seen him send the men off the athletic field because they swore. He never 'bawled out' an athlete. On the other hand he was always kind to them, spoke encouraging words, and in this way made the men love him and they all fought for him. Coach Macklin was exactly the opposite. He was a blusterer. He swore at the men on the field, instead of encouraging them. . . . If you will ask any of the men who were on the cross-country squad and the track team of 1912, I feel sure that every one of them will offer the same opinion."

Shaw's surprisingly candid response showed the influence that athletic boosters had come to wield:

When avid Spartan fan Del Vandervoort died in 1939, Spartan fans flew their flags at half-mast. Courtesy of MSU Archives and Historical Collections.

Michigan State honored former football coach John Farrell Macklin by naming the stadium after him in 1935. Macklin compiled a 29-5 record from 1911 through 1915, including two wins over the University of Michigan and a perfect 7-0 1913 season. *Courtesy of Michigan State University Archives and Historical Collections.*

I have read your letter with much interest, and must tell you frankly that I agree with almost all that you have said. The matter of the naming of our athletic field was virtually decided by large numbers of alumni who have for a number of years had a special interest in the success of athletics at the College. I am not positive but I think that [the members of the board] expect to guarantee financial support which I think has been coming to them for some years past. In view of the fact that suddenly there appeared to be such an overwhelming sentiment on the part of the alumni group referred to, the Board felt it would not be wise for them to interfere or present any counter proposals. . . . The stadium and field should really have been named after the Governor [Alexander J. Groesbeck] who was instrumental in getting the money for their construction, but in view of the fact that he has been almost continuously active in politics it would have been a delicate matter to present. Under the conditions, I myself would have liked to see the field named "Spartan field," since that name seems to have attached itself so firmly to the school. Chester Brewer is the only other coach whose name I would have cared to see used, but the field at the University of Missouri has already been named after him.

Macklin indeed had numerous supporters. The stadium's formal dedication on 9 November was followed by a banquet at Lansing's Olds Hotel that was attended by many of Macklin's former players and included the presentation of numerous gifts, among them a football autographed by the current football team and coaches. The previous day, more than twenty-five hundred Macklin supporters had gathered in the gymnasium to honor the former coach.

CAMPUS LIFE

Sororities and fraternities constituted another important part of campus life during the Shaw and Hannah years. The groups engaged in a variety of competitions, including tugs-of-war across the Red Cedar River and chess games in the Union, with winners taking great pride in their victories. The Greek organizations also competed academically, and in 1930 the women of Sigma Kappa celebrated the fact that they had achieved the best academic average on campus, edging out the previous year's winner, Alpha Chi Omega.

Another, more aggressive, competition had long existed in the traditional rivalry between the freshman and sophomore classes. Each year since the turn of the century, the two classes had engaged in what was known as the frosh-soph brawl. In 1940, classes were let out at 4 P.M. on 31 October for the competition. In keeping with tradition, all freshmen wore their "pots," or beanies, and had their graduating class year scratched on their foreheads with mercurochrome. Specific events included sophomores defending their class flag, which had been placed on the top of a greased pole in front of Demonstration Hall; a fight over twenty bags filled with leaves; the push-ball rush, in which each class tried to push a large ball over the opponent's goal line; and the tug-of-war, conducted over the Red Cedar River. Most years, the afternoon went fairly peaceably, with both sides claiming victory. In 1941, however, the friendly competition turned violent. Sixteen injuries were reported, two automobiles were dumped in the river, and a mysterious canister of tear gas was released. "So vicious was the struggling between the two groups after the regularly scheduled events were completed that the entire detail of four campus police assigned to the 'brawl' was kept busy transporting the injured to the college hospital," the *State News* reported.

For most students, however, the daily routine of campus life was considerably less dramatic. Longtime East Lansing resident Paul DeRose enrolled at Michigan State before leaving for military service in 1943. He ate his evening meal at a home where the Marriott Inn is now located. "It was a cheap dinner," he would later say. "I remember the Hungarian goulash. You'd put lots of ketchup on it." He got a job with the college athletic department, lighting the fires in the locker room for visiting teams. MSC was still a small college, and DeRose would occasionally run into John Hannah walking around the campus. "He always had time to talk to students. He never seemed to be in a hurry. He was an impressive figure. He had a presence and a remarkable voice."

DeRose and many other students frequently took breaks from their studies and part-time jobs to attend dances. Such events took place at the Dells Ballroom on Lake Lansing; at Deer Head Bar, just north of East Lansing; and on campus. In January 1935, for example,

Paul DeRose (*left*) began studying at MSC in the late 1930s. He married a fellow Spartan, Anne Kontas, and their three children, (*left to right*) Dan, Lynne, and Marc, all received degrees from Michigan State. Courtesy of the DeRose family.

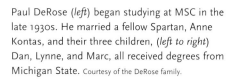

engineering students sold all three hundred tickets for the third annual Engineer's Ball, which was held at Lansing's Masonic Temple and featured Paul Specht and his orchestra, a "prominent musical aggregation from the east."

Dances were also held at the Union, which was the center of campus social life for many students. During the 1940s, Bill Krieg, a former Reo Motor Car Company employee, served as the Union's houseman, with duties including serving as official keeper of the keys, making sure the bulletin boards were kept up to date, maintaining comfortable building temperatures, and seeing to the needs of the thousands of people who visited each year. According to *State News* reporter Neva Ackerman, Krieg knew approximately two-thirds of each graduating class and viewed the students as "a mighty fine bunch of kids. . . . They all have been swell to me." He defended the "lounge lizards" and "grill hounds," students who spent large amounts of time at the Union, but also warned them against becoming too comfortable. The Union, said Krieg, "is a bill board advertising the college, and the campus is judged by what the many tourists see there."

Another campus fixture from the 1930s was Hungarian immigrant Sammy Esky. According to a 1941 article in the *State News,* "About 8 P.M. every day but Saturday, Sammy packs his two big baskets and his dry ice container over his shoulder and sets out for his first evening visit around East Lansing. Unannounced, he comes into the fraternity house, sets his packs down by the main stairs and begins to shout out in broken English all he has to sell. Around his short figure—he hardly measures five feet tall—gather the men of the house, dressed in typical 11 P.M. style, if dressed at all, to get a last minute snack." Sammy's most popular items included ice cream, apples, and candy bars. "Sammy says he likes his job and says he will really have a story to tell if he reveals all he has picked up in eight years of contact with college men. And that, by the way, is just what he plans to do someday." He was especially proud of his five children and liked to tell anyone who would listen that one of his kids, who was a senior in high school, would be enrolling at MSC in 1941.

Theatrical productions were a longtime fixture on the East Lansing campus. In a 1940 article for the *State News,* reporter Charlotte Whitten noted that "State's first Shakespearean venture began way back on June 16, 1916, when Prof. E. S. King directed *Twelfth Night.* One of the most fascinating productions of the early years was *Mid-Summer Night's Dream* given around Beaumont Tower in three settings, the audience moving from scene to scene. Chimes from Beaumont heightened one part of the play, and as the 'Queen' ascended the tower, lights illuminated the windows." After its construction, the band shell provided a site for summer productions, hosting *The Merchant of Venice* in 1938, *The Taming of the Shrew* in 1939, and *Henry VIII* in 1940.

During the late 1930s and early 1940s, William Fawcett Thompson dominated campus theatrical performances. Affectionately known as "Doc," the popular Thompson had worldwide professional theatrical experience. When the Great Depression caused acting jobs to become scarce, Thompson earned a doctorate at the University of Nebraska, arriving in East Lansing in 1936. In late November 1939, Thompson presented Thornton Wilder's *Our Town* in the Union ballroom. The *State News* ran numerous stories about the production, highlighting a wide range of its facets, including Thompson's belief that the play said much about the importance of living, as well as the simplicity of the stage design. Thompson left MSC in 1942 and moved to Hollywood to resume his acting career. In addition to minor roles in more than eighty movies, he found parts in several early television

Completed in 1940, the Auditorium provided
extensive facilities for the performing arts and a
new home for the MSC Museum. Courtesy of MSU
Archives and Historical Collections.

programs, including the *Gene Autry Show*, *Perry Mason*, *Bonanza*, and
Gunsmoke.

Thompson stayed on campus long enough to direct some of the
first plays in the new Auditorium, among them *What a Life*, a three-
act comedy by Clifford Goldsmith that appeared in early 1942. The
Auditorium gave Thompson and other faculty in MSC's entertainment community increased opportunities to develop students' skills
and allowed larger audiences to see the international talents brought
to campus as part of the Lecture-Concert Series. First Lady Eleanor
Roosevelt had spoken to a crowd of more than six thousand—the
largest ever to fill the Auditorium, according to Dean Stanley
Crowe—at the building's 1940 dedication.

One of the Auditorium's first tenants was the museum, which vacated its old home on the third floor of the library. Space had always been a problem, curator Joseph Stack explained to the *State News*, sometimes forcing the museum to refuse donations. The new location provided more room for both storage and exhibitions, and Stack quickly accepted the gift of a collection of firearms and other artifacts that demonstrated the development of modern weapons. Donated by Henry Haigh, a member of the Class of 1874 and honorary life president of the Michigan State Alumni Association, its oldest object was a sixteenth-century English crossbow valued at two thousand dollars. One of the items was a Confederate officer's dress sword captured by Captain George W. Haigh in 1863. The collection also included a French dueling pistol, a large German antitank rifle, and curved Turkish and Persian swords. Two-thirds of the guns were said to be in good firing condition. The museum also accepted Lansing resident Gladys Olds Anderson's donation of a collection of woven Native American baskets that had been preserved with a covering of cocoa butter.

Among the museum's roughly six thousand other items were collections of birds famous in English literature, a well-preserved Bolivian mummy donated by the U.S. ambassador to Bolivia, and many examples of South American wildlife. Because the museum curator had traditionally been a member of the zoology department, the facility was dominated by its collections of zoological materials. In the future, Stack hoped, the museum would "be developed into a general college museum rather than a collection of zoological specimens." The move to the new, more accessible facility brought the museum many new constituents—students, faculty, and theatergoers—who might not otherwise have been regular patrons.

Assistant football coach Bernard Traynor made one major off-field contribution to Michigan State's musical traditions. Concerned that MSC had few school songs, he created a festival, modeled after the ancient Greek festival of Carnea, which introduced new songs and dances to the citizenry. The Spartan version was held on 6 June 1927, and although new songs, including one written by Traynor, were sung, their "doubtful quality" (in the words of a student newspaper reporter) prevented a winner being selected. "After the 1928 season, Bernard Traynor left the college to begin studies on a law degree,"

John Hannah's friend Eleanor Roosevelt dedicated MSC's new Auditorium on 12 March 1940.
Courtesy of Michigan State Archives and Historical Collections.

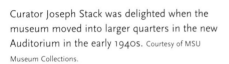
Curator Joseph Stack was delighted when the museum moved into larger quarters in the new Auditorium in the early 1940s. Courtesy of MSU Museum Collections.

the *Michigan State University Magazine* later reported. "One evening, many years later, he tuned to a weekly radio program featuring college campuses. His living room was filled with the music of his song, sung by the college Glee Club. It was the first time he had heard it since 1927. In 1947, the Student Council sponsored a campus poll which guaranteed lasting fame to 'Shadows.' Faculty-student votes favored it over the then-current alma mater, 'Close Beside the Winding Cedar,' which was sung to the tune of Cornell's official song. Today thousands of students sing 'Shadows' and millions of sports fans hear it. Whimsically enough, it is the only song Bernard Traynor ever wrote."

In 1938, the college inaugurated its student speakers bureau under the direction of speech instructor Paul Bagwell. During its first year of operation, thirty-eight students traveled 5,358 miles and spoke to audiences totaling more than twenty-four thousand people—rotary clubs, agricultural groups, church and community organizations, and other such institutions, which paid no fee for the speakers but had to cover their travel costs. With her thirty-nine appearances, junior dramatics major Jean Binkley was one of the busiest speakers, entertaining audiences with readings on such topics as "Lumber Lore of Michigan," "Hitler the Opportunist," and "Interesting Personalities in the Business World." Speakers received coaching from faculty members, rehearsed their speeches over the summer, and critiqued each other's performances. Bagwell tried to accompany individual members on their first two or three public performances. "The speaker's bureau was a great way for the citizens of Michigan to find out what wonderful students we had at Michigan State," Bagwell said. "It made the college look good and was consistent with our philosophy of reaching out to all segments of Michigan life."

HONORING MICHIGAN STATE'S PAST

The 1930s were a nostalgic time on the Michigan State campus. In addition to the naming of the stadium after former football coach John Farrell Macklin, the decade saw a variety of similar events. In 1931, students, staff, and faculty celebrated Scottish-born Thomas Gunson's forty years of service as supervisor of the campus grounds and greenhouses. "Uncle Tommy" had also served as mayor of East Lansing, and in 1907 he had presented a spade to Theodore Roosevelt so the president could plant an elm tree on the campus grounds in honor of the school's semi-centennial. "Thomas, you have done a good job for forty years," former horticulture professor Harry J. Eustace wrote in the *MSC Record*. "No amount of money would be enough to compensate for your forty years in the greenhouse on the Campus. It is the sincere wish of all your friends that a large part of the second forty may continue with all the joy and pleasure of the first." Gunson died nine years later, prompting another wave of tributes to his service. Glen O. Stewart wrote in the MSC alumni publication that Gunson had "witnessed the erection of practically every building on the campus, except for the old residences on Faculty row and several of the science buildings. His memory was replete with college lore. He was chief of the fire department when old Wells Hall burned in 1905; his hands planted or helped to plant more trees and shrubs on our beautiful campus than any other person; he knew more about early college history than any other person I ever visited; he was for years the most popular person requested by alumni clubs all over the country; he was popular for his humor and his jokes; to the alumni he was long considered a campus institution."

Scottish-born gardener Thomas Gunson was responsible for much of the beautiful landscaping on the college campus and served as mayor of East Lansing. Courtesy of Thomas Collection.

In 1932, more than one hundred students and friends of longtime botany professor William James Beal, who had died in 1916, gathered in the Pinetum, a forest of pine trees that Beal had planted in 1896 near the corner of Grand River Avenue and Hagadorn Road, to unveil a bronze memorial tablet donated in Beal's honor by the foresters of the Class of 1911.

Another frequent honoree, Lansing native and 1889 State graduate Ray Stannard Baker, symbolized the learned Spartan. Baker, who was William James Beal's son-in-law and a noted author who won the 1940 Pulitzer Prize for his biography of Woodrow Wilson, returned from his home in Amherst, Massachusetts, to East Lansing for his fiftieth class reunion in 1939. Baker later described his alma mater as one of the nation's leading educational institutions and reminisced that when he was a student, the State Agricultural College "had its own greatness, not so much in buildings, or variety of curriculum, but in the possession as members of its faculty of several great teachers. I am thinking especially of Dr. Beal, Dr. Kedzie and Professor Albert J. Cook, and a little later Professor Liberty Hyde Bailey and Dr. Howard Edwards. I left East Lansing to live next door to a number of colleges; and I can give it as my ripe opinion that few institutions of like size ever had a larger proportion of first-class teachers. I shall never cease to be thankful that it was my fortune to sit under them."

1930s MSC Notables

The 1936 edition of *Who's Who in America* included seven Michigan State administrators and faculty members: President Shaw; graduate school dean Ernst Bessey; Arthur Farwell, Frederick Patton, and Lewis Richards of the music department; health service director R. M. Olin; and librarian Jackson Towne. The campus itself also received honors: the Michigan Horticultural Society rated East Lansing the second most beautiful campus in the country, behind only Cornell University. Announcing the award, the *MSC Record* quoted Ralph Waldo Emerson: "If eyes were made for seeing, then beauty is its own excuse for being."

Some students during the Shaw years went on to become world-renowned professionals. Detroit-born Harry Callahan attended MSC for three semesters in 1935 and 1936, initially majoring in chemical engineering but later switching to business. Bored by college life, he left to work as a bookkeeper at Chrysler and then in the darkroom at General Motors. He subsequently became a prominent photographer, working extensively in Detroit, Chicago, and New York City and forming friendships with such photographers as Ansel Adams, Alfred Stieglitz, and Aaron Siskind. Alfred Hershey earned a bachelor's degree from Michigan State in 1930 and a doctorate four years later, and he went on to become a noted scientist and director of the Genetics Research Unit of the Carnegie Institute at Cold Spring Harbor, New York. In 1969, Hershey became the first Michigan State alumnus to win a Nobel Prize, receiving the award with two other American scientists for his work on the genetic structure of viruses. Hershey credited much of his success to two MSC scientists, Professors I. Forest Huddleson and Walter Mallmann.

RACE ON THE BANKS OF THE RED CEDAR

East Lansing was home to very few nonwhites in the early twentieth century, and Michigan State did not always distinguish itself with its treatment of minorities. In the summer of 1940, a black man, Franklin Duffy of Toledo, Ohio, applied for admission to the college and requested a room in one of the campus residence halls. Duffy was apparently admitted to the school but was denied housing, and Fred Mitchell, dean of men, explained in a 25 July letter, "We have a space in Wells Hall reserved for Negro men students, but this space has all been assigned." If Duffy filed an application to live in the section reserved for black students, wrote Mitchell, the college would "accept said application with the understanding that Mr. Duffy would have an option on the first vacancy occurring in said area." A subsequent letter from the director of men's housing, G. R. Heath, informed Duffy "that the area in the residence hall for colored students is still completely filled up. If you come to Michigan State College, it will be necessary for you to live in Lansing."

Duffy apparently was not satisfied with the college's response and brought the matter to the attention of state senator Charles C. Diggs of Detroit. On 4 September, Diggs wrote to the State Board of Agriculture requesting an explanation. Two days later, Hannah penned a two-page response to Diggs that offered a rare glimpse into the life of black students at Michigan State in the early 1940s.

I am sure that you are sufficiently well acquainted with Michigan State College to know that it is a very democratic institution where every effort is made to eliminate racial and religious prejudices and to provide educational opportunities on a democratic basis for all qualified students coming from the state of Michigan without reference to race, creed or color, and as many as can be accommodated with the facilities we have. I think if you will visit with the students of this college that are members of your race, you will find that they are very happy here. Several of them have told me at various times that they believe colored students are more fairly treated here than at any other College or University with which they are acquainted.

You will be interested to know that Walter Arrington is captain of our track team and a full-fledged member of the Varsity Club, which is a high honor. Harry Butler, who graduated in June, was a member of the cross country team, graduated in Veterinary Medicine, has now a fine position in the South and worked for the College in various capacities during all five of his five years in College, maintaining himself entirely by his earnings during that period. A young lady by the name of Cloteele Rosemond won our oratorical contest here last year and was sent at the expense of the College to the district and national contests, winning both of them. She is a very talented young woman. Hugh Davis, a colored boy from Lansing, has been working for the College all summer although he will not be enrolled as a student until the opening of this coming fall term. Hugh graduated from Lansing Central High School in February and was unable to find work elsewhere, came to see me and we have provided a job for him the last several months so that he can earn enough money to go on to college. Almost every colored boy or girl in College finds it necessary to earn part or all of their expenses and because of their difficulty in finding employment elsewhere every effort has been made to help them find employment and most of them work for the college in some capacity. I have personally made very substantial loans to colored students who were up against it so they might continue in school

and mention particularly Mr. William Smith of Hamtramck who
graduated in Engineering and Mr. James McCrary of Flint. I tell
you all of this only for the purpose of indicating to you my desire
to be helpful to the colored boys and girls that are making a struggle
to improve themselves by getting college training. I appreciate
the many obstacles they face. I know President Shaw and all the
members of the State Board of Agriculture have the same attitude
as I have toward colored students and feel with me that they should
be given every encouragement possible.

However, Hannah continued, "Upon inquiry at the Housing Director's Office, I find that a place has already been made available in
Wells Hall for Mr. Franklin V. Duffy of Toledo, Ohio, in whom you
are interested." These arrangements did not satisfy Duffy, and on 16
September he wrote to Hannah, "You will remember that I asked for
a room in Mason or Abbot Hall. However, in order to close the matter,
a single room in Wells Hall would be satisfactory provided that it is
not in the section of the dormitory, which in Dean F. T. Mitchell's
language would be that 'area set aside for Negro students.'" In the
face of Duffy's challenge, the college backed down, and Hannah wrote
to Duffy that "we are arranging for your housing in a single room in
the east end of Wells Hall entirely separate from the ward in which
colored students reside."

While Duffy apparently was satisfied with this resolution, other
observers remained angry about the college's racial policies. The
Detroit World Echo, a black newspaper, published a 14 September
article accusing Mitchell of discrimination and pointing out that he
had come to Michigan State "directly from the South." The Detroit
chapter of the National Association for the Advancement of Colored
People also criticized MSC, suggesting that the college's policy of
maintaining segregated housing in Wells Hall violated Michigan's
antidiscrimination laws. Student directories show that Duffy enrolled
at Michigan State and eventually resided in Mason Hall.

Less than a year after the Duffy incident, Hannah assumed Michigan State's presidency, and according to a 1957 article by *Lansing
State Journal* reporter William Burke, one of Hannah's first acts after
taking office "was to integrate white and Negro students in dormitory
rooms." Black students had previously been accommodated in what

The Natural Science building was built in 1948 and was touted as "one of the nation's largest buildings devoted to study and research in the natural sciences." Photo courtesy of Michigan State University Archives and Historical Collections.

Hannah described as "undesirable basement rooms in the dormitories or found housing off campus. The first Negro coeds on the campus were not even permitted to live in the women's dormitories . . . but were boarded in the house of the dean of women. Hannah's integration order brought gasps of dismay from some of his top members of his staff and faculty, but their predictions of strife and doom were soon forgotten as white and Negro students melted into one student body. Soon afterward, Pres. Hannah directed that racial designation be stricken from all student records at the university. 'It would be impossible for us to make a racial analysis of our student population today,' he said, 'or to distinguish a white from a Negro from any university record.'"

Records from the 1930s and 1940s show a conspicuous lack of attention to the matter of discrimination. Speeches by Hannah and other university officials preserved in the MSU Archives and Historical Collections contain almost no mention of minorities. Most stories in the *State Journal*, the *State News*, and campus publications such as the *Wolverine* concerned white males and females. Madison Kuhn's and Paul Dressel's books about Michigan State virtually ignore the subject of minorities. When asked directly about discrimination, Hannah would usually respond by reasserting the college's position on equal opportunity: everyone was treated the same.

Thus, Hannah's minority-related actions from this time can be discerned not through new policy or administrative decisions but through specific incidents recalled by university employees. For example, building manager Emory Foster's account of Hannah's presidency, written after his 1969 retirement, included his recollection of an incident involving the president of Landon Hall, a black woman:

> She accused the administration of segregating by house a group of black students in that hall. Mr. Hannah immediately charged me with the responsibility of finding why such a thing would occur. Investigation showed [that the segregation was] self-segregation on the part of these students. Incidentally, this same student at the same meeting in which she raised the question of segregation, asked that Mr. Hannah provide a place where black students could meet in private. Mr. Hannah's reply was if the institution were to build any facilities it would have to be for all students but that he could see nothing wrong with the formation of a black organization which might book rooms in the Union Building or elsewhere as freely as they wished. While this might seem as a reactionary position today without black studies and black cultural facilities set up in residence halls, at that time it was considered quite liberal thinking.

Maury Crane, retired director of MSU's Vincent Voice Library, recalled how Hannah integrated the Union's barbershop: "A black student came to Hannah and said he couldn't get a haircut at the barbershop. Hannah asked why not. The student said the barber was very polite but said, 'We don't cut black people's hair,' and he said, 'We don't know how to do it.' John Hannah said, 'Come with me,'" walked into the Union barbershop, and said, 'We'd like haircuts.' He sat in a chair and the student sat in a chair, and the barber said, 'I never cut a black person's hair.' Hannah said, 'It's time to learn.' The student got a haircut."

Lansing native Jennie Washington, a black woman who received a bachelor's degree from MSC in 1944, recalled that during her time on campus, "I didn't feel any discrimination by the white students, but even if there was, there weren't enough of us to raise any Cain." According to Washington, "There were virtually no blacks on campus in those days. Almost all the black males were in the armed forces." Washington lived at home, taking the bus back and forth to classes each day, and had a positive experience at Michigan State: professors and students treated her "just like anyone else." Washington dated white men and played bridge at the Union. On one occasion, she organized a display for Negro history week that was featured in the college library. In the classroom, she felt comfortable challenging the white professors if she thought their points of view were off base. Tellingly, however, she saw black employees cleaning dormitories, and her experiences across Grand River Avenue in East Lansing's business district were much less pleasant than those on the campus itself: "I didn't feel welcome there," she said.

2

The College Goes to War

V EGETABLE GARDENS WERE POPULAR IN THE 1970S, AND MANY mid-Michigan residents rented small plots of land from area farmers and grew produce to eat. Clusters of these rented plots could be found on the fringes of East Lansing and Michigan State University. Mathematics professor J. Sutherland Frame found the renewed interest in agriculture interesting. "It reminds me of World War II," he said. "Many places around both the city and campus had been converted to victory gardens to help relieve food shortages caused by the war. Lots of people pitched in to help raise food. It seemed everyone around here was patriotic in those days."

"UNCLE JOHN" AND THE COMING OF WORLD WAR II

John Hannah was one of East Lansing's most patriotic residents. After he became president in 1941, Hannah addressed the first freshman class of his presidency. Many students and faculty members later referred to him as "Uncle John," and on this warm September day he sounded very much like a kind but strict uncle. "You have reached maturity and the status of men and women," he told his audience of more than two thousand. "Michigan State College regards you as young men and young women able to do your own thinking—confident that each of you will exercise good judgment and discretion in determining the path and trend of your life for the years that you are here. We hope Michigan State College will be able to stimulate your curiosities, your desire for knowledge and wisdom, and your desire to become useful citizens so that your lives may bring satisfaction to yourselves and credit to the Nation."

While Hannah talked about his educational philosophy and his desire to have the freshman class succeed, he kept drifting back to the topic of war in Europe. He listed four beliefs that separated the United States from totalitarian states: dignity of the individual, respect for truth, government by law, and a good God. "These four simple beliefs are not shared by Adolf Hitler and his associates," he said. "To me they are what make life worth living, and their perpetuation is worth any amount of trial and sacrifice." Later in the speech, he talked about the changing world. "We are involved in a great war. To date it has been economic warfare and preparation for military defense. Some of us may become involved in military service through choice or compulsion. If called upon we have a fundamental obligation to do our part without shirking or evasion." While urging students to fulfill their military requirements, he cautioned them about leaving school to take high-paying industrial jobs to support the war. "If you succumb to this urge, you will find yourself one of a great army fitted only for industrial employment. There will come a time when there will be not enough jobs to go around, and the returning soldiers will be given preference. You may be able to return to college, but there will be a great surge of others doing likewise. The greatest contribution you can make to this nation, to your family, and to yourself is to complete your college work now as far as you can."

On 18 December 1941, eleven days after the attack on Pearl Harbor, the State Board of Agriculture approved a five-point plan "to utilize the facilities of Michigan State College most effectively in the nation's war and defense programs." The plan, formulated by Hannah, expanded summer school so that students could speed up their educational programs; established a two-year course designed for men who anticipated military service before they could finish their degrees; and created extracurricular courses that would prepare students to participate in community civilian defense, apply first aid in case of emergencies, fight fires, and serve as air wardens. In addition, he set up an office that provided information related to all branches of the armed forces and mandated that MSC cooperate with all government war agencies.

Hannah had suggested that students stay in college and complete their college work, and many did. More than 6,000 MSC students, however, entered military service between late 1941 and the end of the war; 285 are known to have died in the conflict. One hundred sixty-six faculty and staff received leaves of absence for military service; three were killed. In addition, many alumni lost their lives. Among the first MSC heroes was Carl F. Siglin of Tawas City and later Detroit, a graduate of the Class of 1938. Major Siglin participated in Operation Torch, the first Allied invasion of North Africa (Algeria and Morocco) in November 1942. Early newspaper stories told of an unidentified field major whom his comrades described as "the bravest man in the American army." The Associated Press later picked up the story: "The major, a tank-unit commander, won high tribute from the sergeant for defying heavy enemy fire to bring back a wounded soldier in a night battle of November 25. It was impossible to send a tank for the wounded soldier, because of the heavy danger of running over him in the darkness. Subsequently the major—now known to be Carl Siglin—was fatally wounded while directing a light tank in an attack on a German position. Sergeant Michael Swarte, of Philadelphia, removed him from the line of fire, but the major was too badly hurt to recover."

Seymour G. Knight was another MSC World War II hero. He withdrew from school in 1941 to join the Army Air Corps. The Detroit native and former Spartan football player first gained notoriety for piloting British Prime Minister Winston Churchill from Cairo to Moscow in August 1942 for a conference with Joseph Stalin. Captain Knight also flew thirty-four bombing missions in the Mediterranean and received the Distinguished Flying Cross and the Air Medal with Oak Leaf Cluster for meritorious service. He was killed in 1943, at the age of twenty-five, when two army planes collided in midair over Wright Field in Dayton, Ohio.

Sometimes the heroes came in very small packages. Captain James A. Gibb Jr., a graduate of Lansing Eastern High School and a member of MSC's Class of 1938, was only five feet, four inches tall. His small physical stature did not seem to deter him, however, as he was one of the first airmen to reach Pearl Harbor after the 7 December 1941 attack, racked up 407 flying hours, and received the Distinguished Flying Cross and the Silver Star.

While a few who fought in the war received public adulation for their service, most fought courageously and anonymously; many

Roger Keast won five varsity letters in the early 1930s in basketball, football, and track. An army captain during World War II, he was killed in action on 1 December 1942, in New Guinea.
Courtesy of Michigan State University Archives and Historical Collections.

died and were forgotten by all but family members and friends. The yearly reports of the State Board of Agriculture, however, religiously acknowledged the MSC service personnel who were war casualties. First Lieutenant Donald A. Rowden, a 1940 MSC graduate, died on 11 June 1943 in a Japanese prison camp. Captain Harry LeRoy Walters, a member of the Class of 1942, was killed in action on 23 October 1943, near Cloiseul Island in the Solomons. Reed Garrit Shanks, a radioman third class and a member of the Class of 1945, died on 3 January 1944 when the USS *Turner* exploded and sank off Sandy Hook, New Jersey. Second Lieutenant Robert Hamilton Henney, a 1942 graduate, was killed in action in Italy on 29 January 1944.

One MSC graduate never saw action on the battlefield but still played a significant role in ending the war. Lansing Central High School alumnus Harper Welton graduated from MSC in metallurgical engineering in 1942 and took a job with Westinghouse Manufacturing in Pennsylvania. He soon joined several other Westinghouse engineers in Los Alamos, New Mexico, assigned to a special project—developing the atomic bomb. A week before the Japanese surrendered, he wrote a letter to his parents that he shared with the *Lansing State Journal*. "It really gives a person a good feeling to be associated with such a successful project," he wrote.

SERVICE TO THE WAR EFFORT

MSC became one of 334 institutions selected by the U.S. War Department in late 1942 to train men and women for the armed forces. "The training programs assigned us by the War Department changed the campus from a quiet atmosphere to almost that of an armed camp, with boys in uniform marching everywhere in squads, singing cadence and occasionally turning 'eyes right' for some pretty coed," administrator and college archivist William Combs later recalled. "These programs brought more than ten thousand men to campus for varying lengths of time. Their curriculum generally included military subjects in the morning and a strong liberal arts curriculum in the afternoon. I'm not sure how the War Department was so enlightened, but the reasoning went that you couldn't govern a conquered country effectively without knowing something about it." At times,

military students made up more than 50 percent of the college's total enrollment, and virtually the entire campus played a role in training soldiers. The liberal arts division, for example, taught the men foreign languages, including Japanese, Russian, Portuguese, and Arabic. Military personnel learned about using radios from members of the physics department. Mapmaking, aerial photography, and geopolitics also made soldiers better prepared for the challenges they would face. Workshops were held to retrain former teachers so that schools could be kept open despite a teacher shortage.

Extensive war-related research also took place on the MSC campus. Horticultural specialists searched for ways to preserve food in hot combat zones. Plant pathologists experimented with methods to speed up the production of the raw materials that produced penicillin. Botanists studied the Russian rubber-producing dandelion in hopes that it could be utilized to manufacture badly needed materiel and worked on "quick" turfs for airport runways near combat zones.

Michigan State College was one of 334 institutions selected in late 1942 to train men and women for the armed forces. Courtesy of Michigan State University Archives and Historical Collections.

It seemed that almost every male on campus
was in a military uniform in the early 1940s.
Courtesy of Michigan State University Archives and Historical
Collections.

The MSC Extension Service directed the federal government's
Emergency Farm Labor Program in Michigan, helping farmers with
labor-shortage problems. The Extension Service also compiled a list
of sawmills that could produce lumber needed by wartime industries
and assisted farmers in increasing their crop production. Even MSC's
ROTC cadets became involved in helping farmers. When there were
not enough farm laborers to harvest the 1942 fall crop of sugar beets,
twenty-five hundred cadets were ordered into the fields. While the
students who did the actual harvesting may not have learned much
about warfare, the members of the field artillery unit gained experience they might someday use on the battlefield, coordinating logistics
and transporting truckloads of cadet workers to the fields.

Speech professor Don Buell played a major role in advancing the performing arts in the Hannah Administration. Courtesy of Michigan State University Archives and Historical Collections.

Because of government concerns about meeting production needs for both soldiers and the general population, MSC's agricultural division began expanding its fields to grow food for the college dormitories, allowing its usual suppliers to furnish food to military facilities. Agriculture dean Ernest Anthony reported harvesting more than two hundred acres of vegetables—peas, string beans, tomatoes, corn, beets, and carrots—during the 1942–43 school year. Even Hannah contributed. The 1944 *Wolverine* featured a photo of the MSC president with his sleeves rolled up and a bushel basket in his hand. "John Hannah enjoys his large farm just south of Pinetum," the caption read. "After his day on campus he often spends as much time as possible tending his extensive garden. Most of the produce goes to various campus kitchens, while Mr. Hannah gets the thrill of working the good earth with his hands." The home economics department also addressed the problem of food rationing by demonstrating how carp, previously considered an inedible fish, could provide an inexpensive substitute for rationed meats. "Stuffed and baked" was one of the ways the department recommended the fish be prepared. Zoology professor Peter Tack estimated that two million pounds of carp could be harvested annually from Saginaw Bay, Lake Erie, and rivers in Michigan's southern counties.

Even entertainment became an MSC product. Students and faculty with musical, comedic, and acting talents toured the state's hospitals and other facilities where wounded veterans were being treated or servicemen were being trained, giving performances designed to "lift the servicemen's spirits." On 12 July 1944, an MSC group led by speech professor Don Buell entertained the men at Fort Custer in Battle Creek with piano music, singing, and comedy. One of the star attractions was an all-women's accordion band featuring Lansing students Phyllis Blanchard, Phyllis Ostrom, and Dorothy Brook. Ostrom also led the troops in audience-participation singing, and the MSC entertainers received a standing ovation.

MSC's Media Go to War

The college radio station, WKAR, moved away from programming that might be considered merely entertainment, and devoted more airtime to providing information that supported the war effort. When war was officially declared, station officials wrote to both the Michigan governor's office and the Michigan Defense Council offering WKAR's services. The offers were accepted. The Victory Garden Committee, the War Bond Committee, and the Michigan Nutrition in Defense Committee sponsored regular programs, as did other MSC groups. The station featured government-created dramas such as *You Can't Do Business with Hitler* and *Meet Your Navy*. Locally, *MSC at War* reported wartime campus activities. And, in association with the *National Farm and Home Hour*, WKAR broadcast speeches by President Franklin D. Roosevelt, Winston Churchill, and Madame Chiang Kai-shek. The chair of MSC's radio broadcasting department, Robert Coleman, called on the college faculty to help explain war issues to Michigan citizens. E. C. Prophet presented *Geography in the News*; Hans Leonhart offered *Pre-War Germany*; R. P. Adams hosted *The Road to Peace*; J. W. Price presented *Post-War Issues*; and members of the English department took turns with their *Literature and the People's War* program. While war news dominated the airwaves, there were exceptions. WKAR continued to broadcast most football games and home baseball games. *Chats about College* was directed at recruiting Michigan's high school seniors. Classical music, a WKAR tradition, was played when the war news was light. And the station provided live broadcasts of MSC administrators' informational addresses directed at students.

The *Michigan State News* also informed faculty, students, and service personnel about what was happening on campus. Assistant editor Peg Middlemiss, a junior from Detroit, authored a 1944 column titled *Weekly Letter to the Men in the Service* and began each piece "Dearest Johnny." The columns summarized campus events, and Middlemiss encouraged readers to clip the column and send it to servicemen, especially those with MSC connections. She often ignored the war, probably assuming that soldiers needed a break from military duties. One 1944 column informed readers that:

> The canoe business is thriving as is usual when spring fever hits the campus. I like to go canoeing, of course, but I find it's a little different when you have to paddle yourself. The scenery is interesting, but so is the activity in some of the canoes.
>
> Our stately seniors got quite skittish this weekend and frisked about like mere freshmen when they had an informal game night. Monologues and magic tricks were only part of the three ring circus they put on.
>
> Coach Karl Schlademan is sending four track men to the Michigan AAU meet in Ypsilanti today. The meet is sponsored by the Detroit Police Department, although it seems strange that it should encourage quick getaways.
>
> The sorority sing came off last night with the Sigma Kappas taking top honors despite competition from Beaumont tower and a scrapiron special wheezing by. The Alpha Gams, last year's winners, took second place, followed by Chi Omega.
>
> Six hundred and forty-one students will bow out of Michigan State's picture this afternoon following commencement exercises in College auditorium. With proud mamas and papas beaming benevolently, they gathered their years' accumulation of books, rubbish and ponies and set out for a vastly different life.

Geography professor E. C. Prophet helped listeners better understand the war with his WKAR radio show, *Geography in the News*. Courtesy of WKAR Radio.

Math professor J. Sutherland Frame was one of several faculty members who wrote a column for the *Michigan State News* explaining their academic fields' contributions to the war effort. Courtesy of Michigan State University Archives and Historical Collections.

Lloyd Emmons served in several important positions at the college. One of his most difficult jobs was serving as liberal arts dean during the war years, when he continually had to shift teaching assignments because so many faculty members were on military leave. Courtesy of Michigan State University Archives and Historical Collections.

But the war nevertheless often dominated the paper's reporting. *Along Faculty Row* was a periodic column written by professors, who usually addressed their particular fields' contributions to the war. Music professor Roy Underwood, for example, told of a letter a serviceman and former MSC student—but not, he pointed out, a music major—had written to the department: "Nowhere will a man find anything so sublime, so pure, so clean, so expressive, so revealing, so beautiful as music. Sometimes it is my only salvation when loneliness approaches." Math professor J. Sutherland Frame used his column to point out technology's contributions to what he hoped would be an eventual Allied victory. "Without in any way detracting from the heroic contributions of the men who do the footwork, it must be realized that this war is more than ever a scientists' war, and that applied mathematics is one of the sciences which is called upon to solve many of the problems which arise in mechanized warfare."

Two large maps in the Union lobby, one of Europe and one of the world, also informed faculty, staff, and students about the latest war news. The bulletin board was sponsored by the International Relations Club, and members, obtaining their information from the latest issue of the *New York Times*, would track troop movements with pins. Students who could afford to buy newspapers and magazines were encouraged to leave them in the Union lobby so that other students could find out what was happening around the world. College secretary Karl McDonel said that similar efforts to distribute information had occurred during World War I but that students had expressed little interest. By contrast, the current war attracted far more attention.

THE WAR'S IMPACT ON THE CLASSROOM

While many departments saw significantly increased workloads, others shrank. "The work of the Economics Department has been curtailed owing to the fact that this subject matter is taken largely by business administration, hotel administration, and engineering students and these enrollments are almost completely depleted by the war," liberal arts dean Lloyd Emmons reported in 1944. "It is interesting to note, however, that the greatest demand for staff members for employment in governmental bureaus has fallen upon this department and has resulted in a long list of leaves for governmental service." Other liberal arts departments, however, saw no such decline in enrollment. "While it was freely predicted by almost everyone that the coming of the war would see a virtual elimination of liberal, non-technical training in colleges, quite the reverse has happened," Emmons wrote. "Enrollments in such departments as Art, Music, English, Speech, Education, Foreign Languages, Psychology and History have been reduced much less than enrollments in more technical departments—even without taking into consideration the soldier enrollments. Then too, much to the surprise of most persons, the soldier programs that are prescribed by the Army and the Navy are turning out to be predominantly Liberal Arts subjects, and thus the staffs of the departments of the Liberal Arts Division have borne a major portion of the burden of teaching contingents that have been sent here for further training."

Complicating the problem of unpredictable student enrollment were the numbers of faculty members who were leaving campus to assume key military-related jobs throughout the world, which played havoc with teaching assignments. Emmons reported that for the 1942–43 school year, thirty-seven members of his staff were on leave because of the war. Joseph Evans of the music department was an army private, Donald Hayworth of the speech department was heading the National Victory Speakers Bureau, art professor J. A. Person was a lieutenant colonel in the army, and Orion Ulrey of the economics department was an arbitrator for the regional War Labor Board. Others took temporary leaves to assist private companies involved in wartime production. Assistant math professor Everett Welmers helped the Bell Aircraft Division of Buffalo, New York; assistant professor of chemical engineering Robert Sweet accepted a temporary position with Chrysler Corporation; geology instructor John Young assisted the Sun Oil Company; and assistant professor of chemical engineering Albert Gower joined Connecticut Hard Rubber Company. These men and many others who took leaves eventually returned to campus and had distinguished academic careers.

But teaching both regular students and servicemen produced heavy workloads for faculty remaining on campus. "Consequently, additional help had to be sought outside the regular staff and in many

Joseph Evans of the music department served in the U.S. Army during World War II. Courtesy of Michigan State University Archives and Historical Collections.

Speech professor Donald Hayworth headed the National Victory Speakers Bureau during World War II. Courtesy of Michigan State University Archives and Historical Collections.

Band director Leonard Falcone was one of the many college faculty members and students who joined the armed forces during World War II. Courtesy of Michigan State University Archives and Historical Collections.

Fendley Collins was known for his success as the Spartans' wrestling coach. He also played a large role on campus during World War II, serving as an instructor in the Army Specialized Training Program. Courtesy of Michigan State University Archives and Historical Collections.

cases all instructors had to carry unusually heavy loads," Emmons reported. "[Adding] to the confusion generated by those conditions, groups of soldiers came and went at unexpected times, so that it was difficult to tell on one day what the teaching load would be on the next." Band director Leonard Falcone and the members of the music department learned how the war could both upset personal lives and play havoc with academic planning. Falcone joined the army in 1942 and was assigned to an Air Force band at Maxwell Field in Alabama. He was later transferred to Stuttgart, Arkansas, to organize and lead the 388th Air Force Band. Believing he could be more effective for the country as an educator, he secured his release and returned to MSC in the summer of 1943. But he was called back into service in September and assigned briefly to a munitions factory in Ann Arbor. By October, Falcone had again returned to campus, where he stayed until his retirement in 1967.

The absence of key faculty members was not the only problem facing those responsible for staffing college classrooms. For most of the period between 1942 and 1945, the campus hosted between six thousand and ten thousand servicemen, all of whom required specific training. One of the most taxed departments was men's physical education, since all army students were required to take physical education courses. One of the busiest teachers was wrestling coach Fendley Collins. The *MSC Record* reported that "as an instructor in the Army Specialized Training program, [Collins] is initiating the soldiers into the mysteries of personal combat for keeps, and his trainees have learned that if all weapons are lost, and a soldier is left with nothing but his bare hands, those hands can be dangerous weapons." The *Record* pointed out that an understanding of anatomy was essential because the soldier must be able to identify the vulnerable areas of the body. And the paper explained not too delicately that the soldier must learn the points where the blood vessels are close to the surface, where a quick slash would cut an artery, and how to break bones in the easiest, quickest manner. "Hand-to-hand combat combines techniques from many other sports and develops techniques of its own," Collins said. "It combines some of the physical combat techniques of wrestling, boxing, football, fencing and jujitsu. Add to those a few American police tricks used in searching, leading and controlling a prisoner, and you get an idea of the training the American soldier is receiving in the army."

Athletic trainer Jack Heppinstall also used his many years of experience in sports to aid the military effort. His suggestions for soldiers experiencing blisters because of long marches included applying a tannic-acid solution to the feet every day. It apparently worked: former MSC students who went into the service wrote to Heppinstall to express their appreciation. Fellow health and physical education professor King McCristal also physically challenged his male students. In a course specifically designed to prepare them for the rigors of military service, McCristal started the men out with basic calisthenics and then had them climb an eighteen-foot rope in twelve seconds, belly-crawl through a thirty-foot tunnel with a sand pack on their back in twenty-two seconds, jump thirteen feet from the balcony of Jenison Field House, and cross the Red Cedar River on a horizontal rope while carrying a sand pack. Twentieth Century

Physical challenges were a common sight on campus in the early 1940s as the physical education faculty prepared thousands of young men for overseas duty in the military. Courtesy of Michigan State University Archives and Historical Collections.

Physical education professor King McCristal conditioned his students for the rigors of military life. Courtesy of Michigan State University Archives and Historical Collections.

Fox was so impressed that it spent five hours filming the activities for a newsreel short. On 20 November 1942, more than one thousand students participated in a physical fitness demonstration in Jenison Field House that included boxing, wrestling, swimming, judo, and tumbling. Organizers hoped to highlight the level of physical readiness of students who left MSC for the armed forces.

Virtually every wartime department looked very different from just a few years earlier. The graduate school, for example, saw enrollment drop from 1,500 students during the 1940–41 school year to 836 in 1942–43. In the same years, the division of applied science experienced an approximate 50 percent drop in enrollment and had difficulty finding laborers to maintain the Beal Botanical Gardens. All twenty-three graduates of the police administration course entered military service after finishing a three-week in-service training session with the Detroit Police Department and serving as temporary campus police officers.

Opportunities for Women

The war years opened up many new opportunities for women. For the first time in the college's history, the regular student population consisted of more women than men. Coeds, as women students were called, had traditionally been concentrated in such academic programs as home economics and elementary education, but with many male students in the armed services, openings developed in what had previously been considered male fields. Agriculture was one of the more popular new areas, and women began receiving training in tractor operation and repair, feeding and handling dairy cattle, and the techniques needed for the proper care of horses. Women also made progress in the political arena. Margaret Burhans, for example, who was described by MSC's dean of women, Elisabeth Conrad, as "an able impromptu speaker and a young woman who the campus liked and respected," became the college's first female student council president. The formerly male-only MSC Concert Band discovered that it lacked enough musicians and began recruiting women. After the war ended, the women remained. One of the most obvious changes occurred at the *State News*, where women filled almost all the editorial positions.

Because most male graduates during this era went into military service, MSC concentrated on placing its graduating coeds. "Women are being called for types of industrial work not formerly considered to be women's work," Dean Emmons told the State Board of Agriculture in 1943. "Some organizations, such as Pratt-Whitney Air Craft Corporation, have set up scholarships here which pay the equivalent of about $1,000 a year to carefully chosen women who can complete their work in one year of specialized study and who will agree to take employment with the company upon graduation."

Many references during the war years downplayed the role women would have in winning the war. Though the first drafts of many of Hannah's wartime speeches (housed at the MSU Archives and Historical Collections) show that where his speechwriters originally wrote "men," the president added a handwritten "and women." In a 1942 speech to a group of women, he indicated that he saw them as important to the war effort, mostly in a supportive role. He encouraged women to pursue careers in fields such as teaching or home economics: "Women must be expected to do many things that were not formerly regarded as women's work. That does not mean, however, that every girl in college should immediately transfer to engineering. A wise young woman will fit herself for some occupation that is important in the war effort and that will provide an opportunity for her to earn a livelihood when the war is won. There are not likely to be jobs for too many women engineers in peace times. There is a great need for women trained in home economics, as dietitians and in the various sciences that have to do with homemaking, designing and merchandising. There is a great need for teachers, for medical technicians. There will always be room for trained women chemists and physicists and other women scientists." On another occasion, Hannah chided his female audience about behavior at the Student Union:

I have been very much disappointed by the activities of some of our college students during recent weeks and months—disappointed because I have been offended and because I have been very conscious of the offense caused in the minds of visitors to this campus. I refer particularly to the behavior of some couples on the campus and particularly in the Union Building. Some of this behavior has been such as to offend the rules of common decency. I recognize

Student Dick Charles was a member of the Michigan State College marching band in 1942. The combination of a large marching band and the thousands of young men and women receiving combat training gave the campus a very militaristic look during the early 1940s. *Courtesy of Michigan State University Museum Collections.*

Michigan State alumni, faculty, and students played a wide variety of roles during World War II. MSC graduate Burton Cargill went on to become a well-known combat photojournalist.

Courtesy of Michigan State University Museum Collections.

that it is only a very few offenders that have created the general bad impression. I now ask the cooperation of all the young women to see to it the situation is improved. I intend to ask Mr. Foster, the manager of the Union, to ask all couples that become offensive to leave . . . and am asking the college police department to get for me the names of those couples on the campus that behave in a manner to bring discredit upon the institution and the student body. After all, this college is publicly supported. The public has a right to expect reasonable conduct and behavior.

One woman involved in the college's war effort was Candace Appleton, head nurse at the college hospital. Addressing the shortage of staff at local hospitals, she began teaching students the intricacies of home health care. The idea was inspired by national Red Cross officials' belief that the training facilitated the treatment of minor health problems at home rather than in the hospitals. The course gave students an "elementary view of individual and community hygiene" and provided simple fundamentals in caring for illness in the home. Upon completion, students received Red Cross certificates.

While educational, political, and employment opportunities increased, housing posed a problem for MSC coeds. Military-related personnel were quartered in North Hall, Wells Hall, and in many fraternity houses. Because of strict policies that required men and women to live in distinctly separate units, the increased female population could not be moved into vacant men's dormitory rooms. The solution was to crowd three coeds into two-person dorm rooms and to place women in fraternity houses not used by the army. The served-meal system common in the women's dorms was converted to a cafeteria-style operation.

CAMPUS PATRIOTISM

The mood throughout the campus during the war outwardly appeared to be patriotic, promilitary, and much opposed to Germany and Japan. Deans' reports to the Board of Agriculture lauded the college's war efforts, while Hannah's speeches offered optimistic assurances that the United States would be the eventual victor. The war strongly influenced many campus activities: for example, a 1943 art exhibit in the Music Building was called War Posters Today and featured art from around the world. Wrote one reviewer, "Grim humor, pathos and satire are the theme elements. . . . Ferocious captions and caricatures urge complete defeat of fascism and denounce the methods of Axis leaders in carrying war to women and children." Many students contributed to the war effort. The twenty residents of 323 Ann Street in East Lansing, calling themselves Club 323, staged the first air-raid test by MSC students on 18 May 1942. Bill Johnston of the *State News* attended and described the test in detail:

> Situated in a central control room located in the basement of the large three-story boarding house, [test coordinator Bill] Lutz gave the air raid alarm through a broadcasting system which had two amplifiers on the second and third floors. Immediately, with a minimum of confusion, the students turned out their lights and shut their windows. They came quietly downstairs to the basement. The house was in complete darkness by then with only special blackout bulbs burning. . . . Special blackout paper was then put over the basement windows by an eight-man squad. Chairs were placed in a row along the walls, and the men sat down waiting for events to take place. . . . The fire warden on the third floor, armed with a fire hose, reported over the broadcasting outfit that an "incendiary bomb" had crashed through the roof and attic floor, setting fire to the attic and landing on the third story floor. Coordinator Lutz . . . immediately sent up a fire fighter with equipment for extinguishing the bomb.

At least two more "bombs" hit the house, but the men of Club 323 effectively handled the situation. A few minutes later, the "all clear" signal was given, and the owners of the boardinghouse, Mr. and Mrs. Garry MacDonald, served lunch to all the participants. The civil-defense officials in attendance declared the effort a success, and Lutz hoped that it would provide an incentive for other groups to carry out similar programs.

The student newspaper's editorial policy was characterized by a uniform patriotic enthusiasm. When students were observed ignoring pleas to conserve energy resources by driving their cars only for essential activities, the *State News* reacted. "It's quite plain to see that Michigan State students are still viewing the privilege of driving cars on campus as an undeniable pleasure," the paper commented in an 8 October 1942 editorial. "This is an unfortunate mistake, which is liable to have a very rude awakening for the guilty as well as innocent. While the number of registered cars on campus has been almost cut in half, public opinion is still against using cars to go from one class to another, for social activities, and for all purposes where walking can be substituted. For those students who do find it an absolute necessity to drive, it also should be remembered that every vacant seat is a Jap. How many Japs did you bring to school this morning?" When the Office of Defense Transportation asked colleges and universities to move vacation dates to avoid interfering with Christmastime troop movements, the newspaper applauded MSC when the college was one of the few to cooperate. "Once again it should be reiterated: Michigan State is not one of those 'typical' colleges which has failed to act," the *State News* stated in a 30 November 1942 editorial. "All of our students will be on their way home December 15."

The college's pro-American and sometimes anti-Japanese stance was not beneficial for all students. On 5 January 1942, just about a month after the attack on Pearl Harbor, Hannah wrote to registrar Robert Linton, "For the period of the war you should not register any students who are subjects of any of the Axis powers without authorization from this office," he ordered. "This includes the nations of Japan, Germany and Italy." Four months later, Linton wrote to Shizuko Higano of Seattle, Washington, turning down her admission application and explaining the college's position:

> I am sorry that it is going to be impossible to accept American born Japanese students at Michigan State College. I sincerely hope that proper arrangements will be made for you to continue your education in a college located farther away from our strictly industrial areas. While we feel you would be all right as a citizen in our college, we have been advised by our State Board of Agriculture and by our F.B.I. authorities in this area that it would create a bad situation to have you students out here. People in our towns and cities and in our war production industries would not have the opportunity to look over your credentials and realize you were all right. They

would be suspicious and would create embarrassing situations for you. . . . On purely Christian principles we realize that this is not the ideal way to deal with you since you are just the same as any other citizen and just as good a citizen. We sincerely hope that this action will not in any way prejudice you against America. . . . I feel that movements are under way for the government to assign certain colleges in a suitable area where you may continue your studies. May I urge you regardless of this necessary action to keep your belief that eventually we may come a little closer to our ideals of Christianity. We will work and hope and pray that peace will come soon even though at present it looks like a hard battle and a long one.

One student already feeling the effects of the country's anti-Japanese bias was Taiichi Thomas Asami. The only Japanese national on the Michigan State campus, he was just two months from completing his doctorate in chemistry when the war started. MSC's restrictions against Japanese students, like those at many U.S. colleges, prevented him from finishing. He was waiting out the war in a small basement room in East Lansing when a *State News* reporter found him. With little money to live on, he was grateful to the residents of the Elsworth Cooperative, who had invited him to eat the evening meal with them. He earned the food by helping out in the kitchen and said that other East Lansing residents had been "so kind" in giving him part-time jobs to pay his room rent. Asami had come to Michigan State in 1937 and began to study botany, but after discovering that most botanists worked for the government, he switched to chemistry because he thought that private companies would not discriminate against him because of his nationality. "I don't want to die for my country," he said, "but I would die for science."

Still, behind the scenes, not everyone was as promilitary and patriotic as appearances might indicate. Electrical engineering professor Ira Baccus remembered one administrator who had problems with the war:

President Hannah wanted the School of Engineering to participate in the war effort far more than Dean Dirks would permit. I thought Dr. Hannah should have "ordered" Dean Dirks to permit a Navy Electricians School to be established at MSC, but no other example

Electrical engineering professor Ira Baccus strongly supported the war, but he believed that other faculty members, including a prominent dean, did not. Courtesy of Michigan State University Archives and Historical Collections.

except this one should be necessary to show that Dr. Hannah was NOT autocratic. He did not order Dean Dirks to accept the school so it was established at Texas A&M—a college far less suitable than MSC. The E[lectrical]. E[ngineering]. staff was sorely disappointed. I have never understood why Dean Dirks was so completely opposed to the military services. I remember one occasion when members of the armed services spoke to all male students of the college. Dean Dirks was outspoken against the whole idea and reluctantly excused classes for the hour.

No one, however, seemed to question Hannah's support of the war effort. His speeches indicated a will to win but not blind patriotism. "We have dedicated ourselves, our possessions, and our lives if necessary, to winning this war in the least possible time," he told a meeting of the Howell Forum on 23 February 1944. "It is a war that might have been prevented. Shortsightedness and selfishness and greed have played a part in bringing it about. All of the possible causes of war are interesting subjects of research and conjecture, but there is no alternative now but for each one of us to dedicate ourselves to do our best so that it may be won in the least possible time."

Hannah's public pronouncements on the war blended both intellectual and practical elements. Speaking to the Rotary Club of Lansing on 13 November 1942, he began by quoting Abraham Lincoln's second inaugural address: "We are called upon to examine the issues before the country in critical times with calmness and moderation, and with all the powers of reason we can command. But even more important, we are called upon to examine them with integrity of purpose—with firmness in the right as God gives us to see the right. From such firmness springs the courage which in bleak days enables men to stand upright. Armed with firmness, men act on their convictions, make sacrifices if need be of their comforts, yield their erstwhile hopes and plans." Hannah then told the Rotarians about the personnel requirements for winning the war, stressing the educational component. "We can lose this total war on the battlefront as a direct result of losing it on the industrial front, on the home front or on the educational front. Education is the backbone of an Army. This was never more true than it is today. . . . Our Army today is one of specialists. Out of every 100 men inducted in the service, sixty-three are assigned to duties requiring specialized training. . . . We must have men who know the fundamentals of electricity, who know automotive, who can operate radios, or dismantle carburetors. Without them, your army would be an incongruous mass, incapable of attaining any objective." Hannah argued that these types of men were not available and that the educational community had to remedy the shortages. "Colleges and universities must insure a continual supply of technically trained men and women," he said. "Only through this insurance can this continual increase of our strength for war or peace be assured."

When the freshmen arrived on campus in the fall of 1942, Hannah told them of the nonmilitary side of the MSC campus. "You have selected Michigan State College to be your Alma Mater," he said. "Alma Mater, literally translated from Latin, means fostering mother. You will want to know more about the mother you have adopted." The president went on to describe the college as consisting of seventy buildings, more than 1,100 different varieties of trees and shrubs, and approximately 260 acres of lawn where the grass was cut by lawnmowers. A campus pool was home to a pair of wild swans and two Canadian geese caring for their six babies. And at the nearby Red Cedar River, two families of wood ducks had joined the hundreds of wild mallards already nesting on the river's banks. Hannah went on to talk about the sixty-five thousand Michigan children who were members of MSC-supported 4-H clubs. He described the friendliness of the campus and how "all of us will smile and say 'hello' without having to be formally introduced." He boasted of the eighty-five-year-old college tradition that students, faculty, and employees did not smoke on campus except in the Union Building or in designated dormitory rooms and encouraged students who saw someone smoking in nonsmoking areas to remind the offender of the tradition. And he talked about the high level of health care for students, including three physicians and twenty nurses and free hospitalization for up to sixty days. He stated his goal of wanting an opportunity to visit with each student individually to "learn from you something of your personal problems, your ambitions, your ideals, the goals toward which you strive."

Freshmen and other students suffered in ways that may have seemed trivial but nevertheless took away important parts of traditional college life. In early 1942, Union officials announced that because of the sugar shortage, Cokes would no longer be available in the grill, which according to employees' boasts, had previously been the Midwest's foremost distribution center for Cokes, serving fifty-six thousand glasses each year. Officials suggested that male students could still bring their dates to the grill for conversation over fruit juice. Dating would become even more difficult in 1942 as students began having trouble finding tires for their cars. The *State News*, convinced that dating might be a relic of the past, sent two reporters into the streets to find out how students were planning to cope. "I'll be alright as long as the rubber heels hold out," one said. "The tire shortage isn't going to affect me much," another commented. "I'm going to sell my car and go into the army at the end of the term." And a third didn't care at all, saying, "My old man won't let me have the car in the first place." No Cokes, no tires—and then, just a month later, women's dormitory dietitian Mildred Jones announced that every Tuesday would be "rations day" in the women's dormitories. Instead of choosing from a wide selection of food, coeds would all eat the same thing—food that was nutritious but not in short supply. Each woman would receive more than an adequate amount of protein, calcium, phosphorus, iron, and vitamins A, B, and C, according to Jones. A shortage of Vitamin D, derived from sunlight and butter, was unavoidable, she declared, because of Michigan's climate.

WARTIME ATHLETICS

Another casualty of the war was intercollegiate athletics. After fifty-nine consecutive years of football, MSC canceled its 1943 season because of the lack of both players and coaches: of the 135 men who had participated in 1942, 134 had gone into the military; only one remained on campus. All coaches were assigned full time to training soldiers. And even though the campus had thousands of soldier trainees, government regulations prevented them from participating in intercollegiate athletics. Hannah urged the continuation of the Saturday-afternoon football tradition at the stadium with games featuring intramural teams. Athletic director Ralph Young organized football doubleheaders as well as a winter basketball league. The

Intercollegiate sports were de-emphasized during World War II, but on 29 April 1944, John Hannah took the time to open the baseball season by throwing out the first pitch. MSC beat Wayne State 12-5. Courtesy of Michigan State University Museum Collections.

football league consisted of five teams, including the ROTC squad, the off-campus engineers, the on-campus engineers, the civilians, and the vets. The ROTC team won the championship with a 3-0-1 record.

When intercollegiate sports were reinstated, football coach Charlie Bachman faced a formidable challenge: he had only one returning letter-winner. Morgan Gingrass from Marquette, Michigan, had been a fullback on the Spartans' 1941 and 1942 teams and was the only player with any collegiate experience at the varsity level. Forty-five of the seventy-five players who came out for practice were seventeen-year-olds just out of high school. MSC publicists, however, tried to put a positive spin on the team's expectations. "Bachman and his aides are applying commando-like training tactics during the August workouts, even though the temperatures have been hitting around 90 degrees most of the time," the official press release stated. "As a result the men got into condition quickly and daily scrimmages have enabled the coaches to size up the most effective offensive and defensive combinations." Bachman was also optimistic. "Even though we have a young and unseasoned team there are a lot of potentially good men who may develop sooner than expected," he said. Perhaps because of the commando training and maybe because many other schools faced similar personnel shortages, MSC compiled a 6-1 record in the fall of 1944, losing only to Missouri and defeating Scranton, Kentucky, Kansas State, Wayne State, and Maryland (twice). One of the players to star on the team was Jackweir "Jack" Breslin, who reportedly received several lucrative offers to play professional football but chose to complete his education, even serving as president of the Class of 1946. He returned to campus in 1950 as assistant director of alumni relations and for many years served Hannah in a variety of top administrative positions.

ASSISTING THE WAR EFFORT

The MSC community participated in a variety of voluntary war-related activities. When the American Library Association and other organizations began the Victory Book Campaign, for example, MSC librarian Jackson Towne and East Lansing Public Library librarian Mrs. E. T. Crossman volunteered as local cochairs. The two asked the community to place donated books in campus and city receptacles. The books would then be sent to military installations around the world for service personnel to read during their leisure time. The effort sought books in good condition, including technical books with a copyright date of no earlier than 1935 as well as books on travel, photography, music, geography, biography, history, and poetry. Local residents responded by donating several thousand volumes. Another volunteer effort was the victory gardens that Frame remembered. One garden, off Harrison Road, was maintained by eight faculty members. "We call this wartime garden 'Harrison Heights,'" explained Emmons, one of the participants. "Eight of us own the 40 acres and about 14 garden plots are under cultivation." Several of the college's agricultural-related departments provided gardeners across the state with information about what to plant, when to plant, and how to can the harvest. Students also pitched in and by the end of 1942 had already sold more than two thousand dollars worth of produce at a booth in the Union. A 1942 Mardi Gras festival raised more than a thousand dollars for the purchase of war bonds that helped establish a loan fund for returning veterans. In early 1943, the student council voted to require 90 percent of the profits from all social events to be invested in war bonds.

Even the celebration of Christmas had the overtones of war. In December 1943, the front page of the *MSC Record* featured a holiday letter from Hannah bordered by a ring of Christmas holly:

These few words of greeting are directed primarily to the men and women of Michigan State College who are now serving in the armed forces. We are approaching Christmas and a new year. One suggests peace on earth and the other suggests a challenge. To hasten peace, Michigan State College has become an important military training center, with approximately 3,500 soldiers assigned to our campus for training in various fields. Our civilian students are emphasizing training that will fit them for useful places in the war effort. On the home front, the college through its graduates and former students is making immeasurable contributions in the fields of agriculture, science and industry. The college is doing research in many directions in the furtherance of the war effort. Our extension staff has assumed added responsibility in encouraging the maximum production and the efficient handling and utilization of food for victory. A living college or university must rise or fall upon its ability to serve. Today the service is war. Some day the war will be over and the world must be rebuilt. Whole devastated areas must be restored and great resources developed everywhere—resources of production, of transportation, of communication, of recreation and of education. There will be challenging opportunities for all intelligent young people to participate. The great challenge, however, will not be material. American democracy must become a beacon of fairness and opportunity for common people everywhere—a pattern the world will want to copy and make work for all the peoples of the world. It will be a meaningless victory if Germany and Japan are defeated by superior resources alone rather than by men who live in freedom for which they fight. Unless you who are fighting in this war do some thinking and planning for the kind of world you want in peacetime, your fighting may all have been in vain. No matter where you are this Christmas season, Michigan State College sends you warm personal greetings and hopes you will not lose sight of that brighter day when families again will be united and progress undisturbed in a society striving for a better world.

One of the servicemen on campus was Sergeant James Faulkner of Grosse Point. After graduating from high school in 1944, he had been ordered to report to MSC for the Army Specialized Training

Reserve Program. He described the wartime campus in a 1997 article that appeared in *Michigan History*:

> We reported and then were assigned to the barracks called Abbot Hall. (This was the finest barracks assignment I ever received during my military career). . . . Rooms were appointed, uniforms issued and we settled in. . . . Getting to class was easy—the entire dorm fell out in the uniform of the day on Bogue Street and marched off in sections to the appropriate buildings. We were rousted daily at 6:30 A.M. by whistles and a bugler for our first formation. . . . Roll was counted and then sounded off to platoon leaders and the company commander. I often wondered if the fraternity and sorority houses across the street appreciated the regular wake-up service we provided each morning. . . .
>
> It was a rigid environment for the young men in military training. All troops strictly followed class schedules that began at 8 A.M. We marched in formation to, from and between classes, ordered by our respective section leaders. Troops were dismissed to enter a building and head to the classroom. When an instructor entered the room or stood to begin class, the section leader called his men to attention until the instructor permitted us to sit. Socially it was still man meets woman, but a curfew was enforced for both sexes. Women had to be in by 10:30 P.M. weekdays and the men by 11 P.M. Women were expelled or their parents notified if they were late. The dorm housemother also notified the dean of women if any of her charges were late. If the men missed their curfew, they earned demerits. Too many demerits and you were out of the cadet program and off to the infantry. . . . We walked everywhere on campus, either in formation or on our own. We walked on dates or took the bus into Lansing. Cars were not permitted on campus. With gas rationing, no one could afford to bring a car from home even if he had one.

THE END OF THE WAR

Japan surrendered on 14 August 1945. Several hundred townspeople and students gathered at the corner of Grand River Avenue and

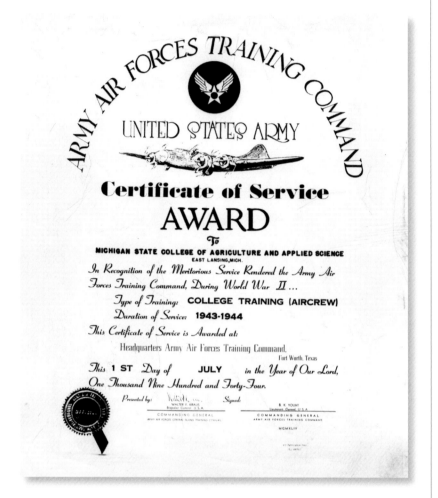

ARMY AIR FORCES TRAINING COMMAND
UNITED STATES ARMY
Certificate of Service
AWARD
To
MICHIGAN STATE COLLEGE OF AGRICULTURE AND APPLIED SCIENCE
EAST LANSING, MICH.
In Recognition of the Meritorious Service Rendered the Army Air Forces Training Command, During World War II...
Type of Training: **COLLEGE TRAINING (AIRCREW)**
Duration of Service: **1943-1944**
This Certificate of Service is Awarded at:
Headquarters Army Air Forces Training Command,
Fort Worth, Texas
This **1 ST** *Day of* **JULY** *in the Year of Our Lord,*
One Thousand Nine Hundred and Forty-Four.

Michigan State College received high grades for its efforts to help the United States and its allies achieve victory in World War II. The Army Air Forces Training Command presented the college with a special award in 1944. Courtesy of Michigan State University Archives and Historical Collections.

Abbott Road in celebration, building a bonfire and starting a small parade. "The majority, however, headed to downtown Lansing to join the bigger celebrations. East Lansingites left the city and could be seen streaming in cars and thumbing their way downtown to join Lansing multitudes in welcoming the arrival of peace," the *State Journal* reported. Hannah immediately issued a statement:

> The end of the war fills us with happiness and a feeling of profound appreciation to the members of the armed forces, to the workers at home and to our farmers for their great contributions in making victory possible. Jubilation in the victory is tempered with a deep sense of obligation to those men who have fought to make certain that the victory won at so great a cost is not to be lost through apathy, or selfish greed, or lack of understanding of the responsibilities

Harrison R. Hunt, R. P. Adams, and Jackson Towne, members of the Inter-University Committee on Post-War Problems, discussed educational issues before a WKAR radio audience in 1945. Courtesy of WKAR Radio.

of our nation and of our individual responsibilities within the nation if peace is going to be permanent. There has been no victory unless all the peoples of this world are assured political justice, social justice and economic justice regardless of race, or creed, or color, or the spot on the earth's surface where they live. Michigan State College, in common with all other educational agencies, has a grave and continuing responsibility in bringing about a maximum understanding of the problems that face us and all the peoples of the world. Only through education—and not the education of a few but the education of all our people and all the people of the rest of the world—is there any hope for the elimination of those conditions and situations which bring on wars.

PREPARING FOR THE POSTWAR EDUCATION BOOM

While Hannah and others had spent four years reacting to the ever-changing needs of a wartime campus, they had not neglected to plan for postwar challenges. "During the world war years of 1941 to 1945, President Hannah had requested the Administrative Group of the University to study and give consideration as to what the needs of the University would be in the immediate post war years," college secretary Karl McDonel later wrote. "This was to include personnel, services, buildings, classrooms, laboratories. . . . The deans of the various colleges appointed committees to make specific studies of the needs of their various colleges. . . . When the end of the war came, all the needed information was available to make firm and final plans for new buildings, and the operation of the University."

In December 1944 the college prepared a thirty-two-page report to support budgetary requests being made to the legislature:

It is expected that the end of the year will bring a great influx of college students, exclusive of the thousands of men and women now in the armed services who will avail themselves of the opportunities provided by the so-called G.I. Bill for college training at government expense. It is estimated that for each million service personnel going to college somewhere, at least 5,000 of them will attend Michigan State College. . . . It costs the state approximately $270 per year per student in addition to the fees paid by the students to provide the facilities and instructional staff and teaching materials that are required. Eighty-seven per cent of our students are residents of Michigan, less than 13 percent come from outside the state. Residents pay annual fees of about $120, and out-of-state residents pay $180. The average cost per student for the war veteran will be greater than the usual cost due to the additional counseling service required, and the large amount of refresher and sub-college work necessary to take care of the needs of some of these men in bringing them to the point where they can fit into a regular college program.

By 1943, Hannah had enticed University of Chicago educational guru Floyd Reeves to spend time on MSC's campus and make suggestions for improving the college's educational performance. Reeves recommended the creation of the Basic College, general education courses that would provide students with a well-rounded education before they picked a field of specialization. With Reeves's assistance, MSC reorganized its academic structure in 1944, with the new college officially opening on 19 September. The myriad of departments and offices were reorganized into six major schools—Agriculture, Engineering, Home Economics, Veterinary Medicine, Science and Arts, and Business and Public Service. Hannah also began programs that would evaluate current faculty, recruit new and talented teachers from around the country, and provide better facilities for scientific research.

Harry Stapler, founder of the *East Lansing Towne Courier*, described the Michigan State College of the 1930s as "a sleepy, agricultural institution that wanted to be great, but wasn't sure how to make it happen." He argued that the college began its quest to become a major educational institution with its successes in meeting the challenges presented by World War II and by not losing focus on the educational opportunities presented by the postwar era. That, Stapler believed, helped make Michigan State the university it would soon become.

3

Becoming Much More Than an Agricultural School

P ROFESSOR FLOYD REEVES REMEMBERED THAT JOHN HANNAH ONCE declared that he would read the one hundred great books selected by celebrated educator Mortimer J. Adler. In fact, Hannah had already read many of them by the time he made the statement. He also read five newspapers a day, including all the advertisements. Reeves not only was astounded that Hannah would have time for such efforts but also was puzzled by Hannah's insatiable curiosity. "Here was a man out of a highly specialized field of poultry," Reeves later wrote, "who had become president of an institution that was still an agricultural institution, but Hannah told me . . . this institution would have to become, sometime in the future, a different kind of institution. Not that it would get rid of agriculture as a major activity, but it would have to have other activities."

THE LAND-GRANT MISSION

On numerous occasions, Hannah expressed concern that colleges and universities "were graduating an alarming number of selfish little careerists who blindly believe they know something about how to earn a living, but make no pretense about knowing how to live." Each fall he would tell incoming freshmen that educated people should know how to write well; have a reasonable understanding of art, music, and literature; comprehend the laws of nature and society; and possess an appreciation of values, "without which no life is complete and adequate."

Even before Hannah became the school's president, MSC had begun to transform itself from a college with a strong agricultural focus into a multifaceted educational institution. On 4 December 1940, six months before assuming the presidency, Hannah addressed the Michigan State Horticultural Society in Grand Rapids. MSC was no longer just an agricultural school, he declared: "It is, in fact, a great university with some twenty courses leading toward college degrees in engineering, home economics, veterinary medicine, liberal arts, applied science, applied music, public school education, music, business administration, police administration, public administration, hotel administration, medical biology, as well as in the fields of agriculture, forestry and conservation." Moreover, he reminded his audience, agriculture students needed exposure to the broad spectrum of learning across the liberal arts and science curricula.

Hannah had promoted MSC's nonagricultural curriculum since becoming the college secretary in 1935, and he continued to push that agenda throughout his presidency. In the January 1965 edition of the *MSU Alumni Magazine*, Hannah described the "different kind" of institution he had helped create: "I would not have you think that Michigan State has become a university catering only to the intellectually elite. The majority of our students earn their solid B's and C's, and go forth into the world to become useful, productive citizens. They may not rival the academic geniuses, but they do become the school superintendents, principals and teachers, the bank presidents, the newspaper editors, the corporation executives, the productive engineers, the good fathers and mothers and the responsible citizens who make this country go. They are not forgotten in our striving for excellence, for they, too, deserve excellence in their educational preparation, and they continue to get it at East Lansing."

FOUNDATIONS FOR THE BASIC COLLEGE

Hannah's quest for a well-rounded curriculum at MSC received a boost when he recruited Floyd Reeves from the University of Chicago to come to the campus in 1943. Born in rural South Dakota, Reeves began a long career in education when he was seventeen years old, teaching in a one-room South Dakota school. According to Reeves's close friend, Opal David,

Boxing was never listed officially as a pre-requisite for teaching in the schools of South Dakota, but it was this "subject" that clinched his first teaching job for Dr. Floyd W. Reeves. . . . It was in a one-room school ten miles from his home, with a student body consisting primarily of the five large and unruly sons of the Chairman of the School Board. Three properly certified teachers had resigned in as many weeks—the last one, an aunt of the boys, after one of them had knocked her out with a stove poker and been sent to jail to cool off. The seventeen-year-old Reeves boy had no teacher's certificate but the school was offered to him anyway, with the understanding he was to get forty dollars for every month he stayed. He asked for two weeks to get ready and spent the time learning to box. When he rode over to take charge of the school, his gloves hung from the saddle-horn, and this variation on the birch-rod proved a complete success.

Floyd Reeves, a distinguished educator from the University of Chicago, played the key role in establishing MSC's Basic College in the 1940s and in several other important educational advancements. Courtesy of Michigan State University Archives and Historical Collections.

Reeves subsequently graduated from Huron College in South Dakota in 1912, receiving his bachelor's degree in just three years, and later earned his master's and doctoral degrees from the University of Chicago. He served as superintendent of three different South Dakota high schools before becoming dean and professor of education at Transylvania College in Lexington, Kentucky, and then professor of education at the University of Kentucky. In 1929 Reeves was appointed professor of education at the University of Chicago.

During his time in Chicago, Reeves developed an international reputation as an expert in public education, and thanks to the university's generous policy of granting leaves to its scholars, Reeves became a consultant to universities, U.S. presidents, and John Hannah. Hannah not only admired Reeves's educational background but also was attracted by his experiences in a wide range of political, social, and governmental arenas. His many activities included serving as an administrator with the Tennessee Valley Authority, as director of the American Youth Commission of the American Council on Education, as an associate of First Lady Eleanor Roosevelt in several youth-oriented projects, and as a member and sometimes chair of several education-related committees appointed by President Franklin Roosevelt.

In 1943, Hannah recruited Reeves to consult at MSC and to lead the effort to expand and improve MSC's curriculum. Reeves spent the

Paul Dressel, a member of the original committee that recommended the creation of the Basic College, wrote a book evaluating its success.

Courtesy of Michigan State University Archives and Historical Collections.

first six months of 1944 on the East Lansing campus, evaluating the education MSC students received. His experience at the University of Chicago had given Reeves firsthand knowledge of philosophies and approaches that might expose students to a rigorous general education. That university and its president, Robert Maynard Hutchins, were influential in presenting a case for a general education that led many colleges and universities to reexamine their approaches. According to Reeves, Hannah "wanted me to spend full time here and work in any way I pleased, and to recommend any reorganization of what was then Michigan State College, that I thought necessary. I went to work here and he never questioned me as I was going along as to what I was doing." Reeves asked students and faculty where they thought the college should be headed. During his informal interviews, he drank hundreds of cups of coffee at the Student Union and at East Lansing coffee shops, and on warm days he held his meetings on campus benches. By the end of the winter term, he had decided that MSC needed to broaden its educational scope by forming what became known as the Basic College. In his memoirs, Hannah declared, "If I were to identify a single individual to whom I think is due as much or more credit than any other single individual for his contribution to making Michigan State move from what it was in 1941 to the kind of institution it was in 1969, I would put Floyd Reeves at the head of the list."

The first official step in forming the Basic College came at a 9 March 1944 faculty meeting where Reeves outlined his plan. The faculty indicated an interest in pursuing the matter and approved the formation of a committee to explore the idea. The process moved rapidly, and on 22 May the committee submitted its final report to the full faculty. It was quickly approved, and the State Board of Agriculture accepted the Basic College plan on 1 July. While the Reeves plan had many supporters, not everyone was enthusiastic. Electrical engineering professor Ira Baccus later recalled that many scientists and engineers objected to the broad scope of the Basic College. According to Baccus, engineers and scientists were upset by the requirement that students in engineering and the sciences enroll in introductory science and engineering courses.

THE BASIC COLLEGE BECOMES A REALITY

The new two-year Basic College program was implemented on 19 September 1944, the first day of MSC's fall semester. Official explanations declared that the Basic College had been "developed by a committee of faculty members and approved by the faculty [and] designed to provide students with a sound foundation on which to build an intelligent interest in personal, family, vocational, social and civic problems, a better understanding of these problems, and a greater ability to cope with them." The seven required courses included written and spoken English, headed by Paul Bagwell; biological science, headed by Chester Lawson; social science, headed by Walter Fee; origin and development of civilization, headed by Harry Kimber; literature and fine arts, headed by Ben Euwema; physical science, headed by Stanard Bergquist; and effective living, headed by Leo Haak. Howard Rather became the dean of the new college. Before students were allowed to specialize in a specific field, they were required to pass a comprehensive exam covering the material found in the seven basic college courses.

The *Detroit News*, a paper that only occasionally provided in-depth coverage of educational issues at Michigan's colleges and universities, asked staff correspondent Allen Shoenfield to take a look at MSC's new Basic College. Shoenfield liked what he saw: "Breaking sharply with accepted pedagogical theory and practice, Michigan State College has staged a revolt of such significance and magnitude that it might influence the course of higher education in the United States for generations to come." Schuyler Marshall, editor and publisher of the nearby *Clinton County Republican-News*, read Shoenfield's analysis and felt compelled to add his own endorsement. Writing in a 27 July editorial, Marshall suggested that many U.S. educational institutions were not addressing their students' needs and then continued, "President John Hannah has led a reorganization designed to correct some of the ills mentioned. Regardless of results, it is refreshing to know that there is an educator who does not hesitate to openly and honestly state his convictions—and DO SOMETHING ABOUT IT."

Students—at least those producing the college yearbook—also were impressed. "Basic College is the most discussed, debated, and revolutionary change to date," enthused the 1946 *Wolverine*. "Because

Howard Rather was chosen as the first dean of the Basic College. A campus residence hall was later named in his honor. Courtesy of Michigan State University Archives and Historical Collections.

While Hannah and his staff were spending much of their time improving curriculum and upgrading the college faculty, students were finding ways to have fun. The Green Splash, MSC's women's swimming club, put on Cruising Down the River in 1949. Barbara Colvin and John MacDougall sit in the boat, while Barbara Busch, Flora Rowe, and Lois Vosburg look on. Courtesy of Michigan State University Archives and Historical Collections.

of its scope, the eyes of the nation's colleges are truly upon us and many have requested information about it. Some, in fact, have already begun a modified form of our plan in their own institution. To Michigan State, pioneering is nothing new. We have been pioneering since 1855. The change to a Basic College program is just another step up the ladder of our progress, another page in the annals of our already rich history."

Most observers at MSC concurred with the *Wolverine*'s assessment. In the first chapter of a 1955 book, *The Basic College of Michigan State*, dean of the college Thomas Hamilton wrote that despite much criticism and numerous attacks on its credibility, the Basic

Four of the ten 1948 Homecoming queen finalists: Joyce Wall, Jill Hubbard, Jean Cotter, and Joan Perry. Courtesy of Michigan State University Archives and Historical Collections.

College had become a critical part of the Michigan State curriculum. Eight years later, Thomas Goodrich, a professor in the counseling department, responded to an incoming freshman's question about why Michigan State had the Basic College requirement when many great universities did not by declaring that "many of our country's finest educational institutions have similar programs. They just call it something else." He then pointed out that a general education has been an important part of American history. He concluded by telling the student, "We believe that programs such as social science, humanities, natural science and American thought and language make you more informed about the world where you will eventually make a living and raise your family."

Another fan of the Basic College was Jack Bates, an East Lansing insurance executive, World War II veteran, and MSC student and varsity cheerleader in the late 1940s. As a child, Bates admitted, his view of the world had been quite narrow. Eventually, however, he developed keen and wide-ranging cultural interests. Asked years later where he had found his love of art, he responded without hesitation, "My first year of basic college." Bates also appreciated Hannah's open door policy for students. After having some academic problems, Bates decided to see if Hannah could help. Bates put on his cheerleading sweater, walked over to the president's office, went up to the secretary, and told her why he was there. Hannah motioned Bates into his office, listened to his story, and told him to see a certain administrator. When Bates replied that he had already done so, Hannah said to go back the following morning. Bates did as he was told, and the administrator said, "I got a call from President Hannah. I think we can take care of your problem." When Bates later thanked Hannah for his help, the president said, "We always try to help students."

A College President with an Open Door Policy

Many students were too busy trying to earn sufficient money to pay room, board, and tuition to spend much time thinking about philosophical approaches to a well-rounded college education. One was Hazel Shuttleworth Meyer, who described her campus experiences in a history prepared in 2000 for the MSU Museum:

> I enrolled as a freshman in what was then Michigan State College for the 1944–45 school year. That spring before leaving for summer break, I went to see Miss Mildred Jones, manager of the women's dormitories, to ask for a job that would pay my room and board my sophomore year. I wanted to leave the "cooperative house," where I lived with nine women students and a housemother, and move back to the Williams Hall dormitory. My mother had promised to pay my tuition if I could find a position to cover the cost of my room and board. I didn't know it then, but Miss Jones would become my mentor. A native of Louisville, Kentucky, who kept the southern custom of having 4 P.M. tea, Miss Jones invited me to join her and suggested we go into the kitchen to meet Mrs. Kathryn Gardner, food service supervisor. Mrs. Gardner explained the system of full-service meals, in which students were seated at tables of six each by a dining room hostess served by male waiters (usually fraternity or athletic

department students). In the background, women students dished the food on plates for the male students to serve. Besides eating, sleeping, working, and going to classes, I set aside study time from 7 to 9 P.M. Monday through Thursday. Friday night was date night. I attended ballroom dances, movies and athletic events, including all football games. Ten minutes left to play at football games signaled my departure. I would get out of the stadium fast by being first behind the marching band and return to Williams Hall to set out the cider, doughnuts, coffee and hot chocolate that were served to residents and alumni after every home game.

Student activities were well-attended. During my college years of 1944–48, students received with their tuition receipts a coupon book that allowed us to attend campus events free and we took advantage of the opportunity. Quarterly tuition cost $35 for an unlimited number of credit hours. During my junior and senior

Saturday football games were popular in the 1940s, as is evidenced by students lining up for tickets the night before the 1949 Notre Dame game. Courtesy of Michigan State University Archives and Historical Collections.

years, classes were scheduled from 6:30 A.M. to 10 P.M. and all day Saturday to accommodate the returning male students, out-of-state and foreign students who wanted to attend. A choice of all menu items was introduced in the cafeteria and strictly enforced as either/or selections. We kept records of the popularity of one item compared with another, e.g. the number of pork chops served vs. the chicken or roast beef. Servers refused to give seconds until the serving period had ended. Hamburgers, hot dogs and BLTs were favorite lunch menu items. Johnny Marzetti, an old-fashioned goulash, was the brunt of many jokes, but students ate it until it was taken off the menu permanently in the 1960s. Jello salads were common. . . . Male students flocked to the women's dormitories for food service jobs—which offered not only a paycheck, but a chance to meet girls. Social events became much more prevalent with the return of the GIs, and many dates and some marriages resulted.

SERVICE TO AGRICULTURE

While Hannah was continually approving changes in MSC's approach to education, he always insisted that he was remaining loyal to the original land-grant philosophy. He argued that land-grant colleges served agriculture almost exclusively in the nineteenth century because the United States was still an agricultural country. As the country became more industrial, land-grant colleges expanded their fields of service and began to offer programs in such areas as home economics, veterinary medicine, commerce, and public administration. On numerous occasions, Hannah insisted that land-grant colleges were "educating more young men and women in agricultural subjects than ever before, and devoting more effort and dollars to agriculture research than ever before. The land-grant colleges are remaining true to their obligation to serve agriculture."

But the creation of the Basic College was not the only change on the MSC campus in the mid-1940s. Floyd Reeves later recalled that faculty thought the "one thing . . . I did during that time was to set up the Basic College. They think that was the most important thing—that isn't the most important thing at all from my point of view. What is important is that I helped reorganize this entire

William Combs served in many capacities at MSC, including as dean of university services, as secretary of the faculties, and as the college's first archivist. Both John Hannah and Floyd Reeves considered Combs one of the college's most valuable administrators. Courtesy of Michigan State University Archives and Historical Collections.

University from top to bottom. We didn't leave any division of the Colleges completely unchanged—none. We changed departments into schools or divisions. . . . [W]e had an entirely different set up by June 30, 1944." Major changes included reorganizing and renaming six major divisions of the college into schools, creating the schools of Agriculture, Engineering, Home Economics, Veterinary Medicine, Science and Arts, and Business and Public Service. The former offices of the deans of men and women were placed under the direction of Professor Stanley Crowe, the new dean of students.

Reeves credited William Combs, dean of university services and secretary of faculties, for supplying much of the information that guided the college's programmatic modifications during the mid-1940s. Combs "had a leading part in a number of studies that were made in this university and in those studies I made in the early years . . . his were the facts I could depend on more than any other facts secured from any other persons."

But others also planted the seeds for the college's tremendous physical and academic growth over the next few decades. Horticulture department chair Harold Tukey had a favorite quote: "The future will favor those who possess that uncanny ability to stay on the leading edge of progress by accepting the new, but not too new, and by abandoning the old before it becomes too old." That phrase, in a sense, described Hannah's administrative team as Michigan State moved out of the war years into peacetime. Most of the team members were

Journalism professor Albert Applegate (*left*) interviews *Lansing State Journal* publisher Paul Martin on a WKAR Radio program in 1948. Photo courtesy of WKAR Radio.

white males in their fifties and early sixties, had extensive experience running a college, and were willing to accept change—but not too hastily. Journalism chair Albert Applegate, for example, had come to MSC in 1936 and would eventually be called the "dean of Michigan journalism educators" by the Michigan Journalism Hall of Fame. Agriculture dean Ernest Anthony had been a top MSC administrator since 1928 and had played an important role in the Extension Service. Veterinary medicine dean Ward Giltner would retire in 1947 but remained available for informal consultation. Science and arts dean Lloyd Emmons participated in a wide range of college decisions and served as faculty representative to the Big Ten Conference.

Hannah was aware, however, that quality education would not result simply from modernizing and reorganizing the curriculum; building a talented and competent faculty was also essential. Hannah's critics have suggested that he cared more about developing powerful football teams and creating massive buildings and parking lots than about quality teaching. Many who worked closely with Hannah would disagree. When Hannah retired in 1969, dairy professor G. Malcolm Trout wrote about his thirty-five-year relationship with the MSU president:

President Hannah's first four years of incumbency were during a war-administration period. Keeping a faculty intact, recruiting new staff, shifting responsibilities, providing facilities, were the minimum pressing academic chores of the day. Little time existed to lose oneself in the problems of curricular change and classroom performance. This was to come later. On a Monday afternoon, sometime after the 1945 armistice, my telephone rang. I answered and was surprised, if not startled, by what I heard:

"This is Hannah. . . ."

"Yes. . . ."

"I presume you read last Friday's *Staff Bulletin* about the coming Thursday's faculty meeting?"

"Yes, and I congratulate you on the subjects suggested for consideration."

"That's what I'm calling about. I'm asking two faculty members, you and Dr. [John] DeHaan [chair of the psychology department] to present your views on the questions listed, 'How can one evaluate a good teacher' and 'Are the teachers at Michigan State University properly recognized?' Be prepared. Goodbye."

One prepares for a command performance. As I recall, I reported on studies then just completed at a Big Ten university to the effect that, generally, academic promotion came through publication of research, not by excellence in the classroom; also that young instructors early become aware of the situation. Consequently, the quality of teaching suffered. Truth often hurts, for the allegation seemed apparent and significant. I pointed out also that good teachers at Michigan State [College] were taken for granted, were unheralded and unsung and, except for personal satisfaction, received little recognition for their dedication and efforts. Further, I emphasized that students and alumni, not the deans, could best evaluate teachers. I have always been grateful to President Hannah; first that he did not ask for my resignation and, second, that at once he set the wheels in motion to seek out excellence in the classroom and to screen the faculty for superb performers.

Upgrading the Faculty

Two surveys provided Hannah with the information he needed to make decisions related to upgrading the MSC faculty. First, as Trout and others had suggested, approximately eleven thousand graduates between 1930 and 1945 were surveyed about their educational experiences at MSC. More than fifty-four hundred questionnaires were returned, and the results were published in pamphlet form and in a 1947 issue of the *MSC Record*. "In analyzing the returns on the questionnaire, it is not the purpose of this study to make an exhibition of the rating of individual faculty members," the *Record* reported. "Rather, the study deals with groups of faculty members and with departments and schools." The final figures ranked the School of Agriculture first, followed by the Schools of Engineering, Business and Public Service, Science and Arts, Home Economics, and Veterinary Medicine. "As to the results of the questionnaires, suffice it to say here that the Deans were given the results, and the faculty members were told whether they were rated in the upper, middle or lower third of the group," Combs later reported. "If an individual faculty member insisted on knowing his exact rating, it was given to him. I'm not sure how the President and the Deans regarded the results of the questionnaire, nor do I know whether they used them in rewarding good teaching or in making promotions or giving salary increments, though they undoubtedly did."

Around 1970, Combs researched what had happened to the 351 staff members mentioned in the 1945 survey. "Of the 117 ranked in the top one-third as a result of the Survey, nine later served as deans, one as a vice president, and seven as directors of divisions or department heads," he wrote. "The fewest number of administrators came from those persons ranked in the middle third. One of these became an assistant dean, and four moved up to department headships or directorships, one of which became a Secretary to the Board of Trustees. Of those in the lowest third, three moved into top administrative posts; one went to a deanship and a central administrative office, one to a directorship, and one to a deanship and vice presidency. Six moved into department headships, or heads of agencies of the University. The great bulk of those who remained with the University until death or retirement continued in the teaching, research, or public service categories. All except some half dozen were given one or more promotions within the academic ranks before they retired from the University. Likewise, some of those who resigned from the University were promoted in rank while in service here."

Shortly after the alumni questionnaire was sent out, the accrediting body, the North Central Association, surveyed MSC's faculty credentials, such as number of earned degrees, faculty publication records, and memberships in professional societies as well as library adequacy and faculty-student ratio. The results showed that only about 35 percent of the academic staff held doctorates, 44 percent held master's degrees, and 20 percent had bachelor's degrees or less. The college was ranked at the sixty-first percentile among its peers, a rating barely qualifying MSC to offer master's degrees. Moreover, Combs pointed out, "If a survey to determine our adequacy to offer graduate work had been ordered, the institution might have been placed on probation."

Not surprisingly, the results did not please MSC officials. "In the vernacular of the streets, the President and others in the academic administration were 'all shook up' when the results were announced," Combs wrote. "At an early meeting of the Administrative Group where I related the results of the conference with officials of the N.C.A., I seem to recall that the President really 'laid it on the line,' so to speak. In effect, he said the College must never again be embarrassed in such a manner. The staff must be upgraded and other criteria must be met; and he called upon all the deans and department heads to cooperate." According to Combs, Hannah had little money to hire new faculty who had already earned national reputations and consequently decided to hire "bright young people" at the instructor and assistant professor levels, rewarding them for their progress in teaching and research. As the president later put it in his memoirs, "The best we could do was to hire good people, give them opportunities to grow, and reward those who did." New faculty received leaves of absence with pay to continue their education. All appointment recommendations had to be approved by Combs, and Hannah personally interviewed many candidates for full professorships and department head positions.

John Hannah's assistant, James Denison, believed that the improvements to MSC's faculty were largely overlooked as one of Hannah's achievements:

Much has been said and written about his leadership in acquiring new buildings and larger appropriations for Michigan State, and much of his current reputation rests upon accomplishments of

Paul Bagwell was one of the first department heads in MSC's new Basic College. Courtesy of Michigan State University Archives and Historical Collections.

Education professor Wilbur Brookover was one of the "white men" activist Robert Green would identify as being vital to local anti-discrimination efforts. Brookover also served as mayor of East Lansing. Courtesy of Michigan State University Archives and Historical Collections.

that kind. But little or nothing has been written or said about his great success in the academic area, specifically his upgrading of the quality of the faculty to provide a foundation for the great university that developed during his tenure. That accomplishment—possibly his greatest—has received too little publicity and recognition. I can explain that professionally: Neither he nor his close associates wanted to trumpet the inadequacies of the institution when he came into office; those who were induced to join the faculty in his first years did not want to talk about their decisions to join a college that had little academic prestige, and to publicize their coming would have been to call attention to the deficiencies everyone wanted to conceal. We had done so little to advertise the improving quality of the academic program and faculty that in the mid-fifties, when the question of changing the name of the college to "university" arose, there were many, many critics who could not or would not believe that Michigan State was truly qualified to elevation to that rank.

Paul Bagwell recalled being urged by Hannah to scour the country for young, bright talent to place in the classroom. "There was no real recruiting system to identify the best up-and-coming teachers, but many of us still had good contacts at the institutions where we graduated from or where we had our first teaching job," Bagwell said. "So we began contacting some of our former colleagues or professors and asked about the students and young instructors at those places. You've got to remember that this was right after the war and picking up the phone and calling someone was not always especially efficient. So, we often used the telegram. I'd send a telegram to a prospective teacher that I knew or had interviewed, asking him to come to the college, and I'd suggest a salary. He'd send me a telegram in return and give me a yes or no." Many of those newly hired for the MSC faculty in the years immediately after the war went on to have outstanding academic careers and helped to shape the college's and later university's development. Among those who arrived between 1946 and the early 1950s were John Winburne (university college), James Niblock (music), Benjamin Hickock (American thought and language), Louis Raynor (art), Edith Doty (foreign languages), John F. A. Taylor (philosophy), Rowland Pierson (counseling), Wilbur

Brookover (education), Virgil Scott (English), Ralph Turner (police administration), and Walter Adams (economics).

Talented administrators were also recruited. Leslie Scott, for example, was brought in from Chicago's Hotel Morrison to manage the MSC Union and then to head the department of hotel administration. Fred Stabley from the Associated Press's Baltimore office became a news editor in the department of public relations and then headed public relations functions for MSC sports. Philip May, a management analyst for the Reconstruction Finance Corporation in Washington, D.C., became college comptroller. Former MSC sports star Jack Breslin left an administrative job with Chrysler Corporation to become assistant director of alumni relations. And Denison, soon to become one of Hannah's most trusted advisers and a major spokesperson for the college, was lured from state government. Reeves also used his influence to attract people, especially his former students, who eventually had a huge impact on the college. Two of the most significant were Thomas H. Hamilton and Durward "Woody" Varner. Hamilton became vice president for academic affairs and later served as president of the State University of New York and the University of Hawaii. Varner became the youngest person ever to head a university Extension Service, the first chancellor of Oakland University, and eventually the chancellor of the University of Nebraska.

Walter Adams, Hannah's eventual successor as president, came to MSC in 1947 as an assistant professor of economics. At the time, he recalled,

> I was a typical Eastern snob . . . really a snob. I came from Yale where I got my Ph.D. degree. I didn't even know where East Lansing was, and I don't think I had ever heard of Michigan State College.
>
> The Yale employment office had presented us with a variety of possible places to teach. Before I made my decision I picked up a copy of *Time* magazine and, as always, I turned to the sports page first, and there was a story with a picture of Biggie Munn about his leaving Syracuse University to take over the Michigan State football program. So, I said to my wife, "What the hell, let's give it a try."

East Lansing at first seemed to Adams like "Indian country—the great unknown." But "either we succeeded in civilizing the barbarians, or

English professor Virgil Scott arrived at MSC after World War II and went on to become a celebrated novelist. Courtesy of Michigan State University Archives and Historical Collections.

Walter Adams was one of the young faculty members who arrived at MSC shortly after World War II. He later became president of Michigan State University. Courtesy of Michigan State University Archives and Historical Collections.

English professor Russel Nye gained nationwide prestige for MSC in the mid-1940s after his study of George Bancroft won the Pulitzer Prize.

Courtesy of Michigan State University Archives and Historical Collections.

we became part of the barbarians. . . . We fell in love with the place and I think primarily that was due to the personality of one man—John Hannah, who was an overpowering person as an educational leader."

MSC also recruited more experienced personnel for key upper-echelon academic positions. Egon Hiedemann, an international authority in acoustics and ultrasonic research, came from the U.S. government to head the department of physics and astronomy. Henry Leonard, chair of the philosophy department at Duke University, took the same position at MSC. East Lansing police chief Arthur Brandstatter left his city position to join the MSC police administration department and quickly became its chair. Wilson Paul, a Denver University speech professor, took over MSC's department of speech, dramatics, and radio education. And Oberlin College romance language professor Hermann Thornton became head of MSC's foreign language department. Hannah's decision to upgrade the faculty soon began to pay off. By 1956 the number of faculty had grown to about 1,250, while the percentage of faculty members holding doctorates increased from 35 to 56.5. Because of the rapidly expanding graduate programs, faculty members did a considerable amount of graduate teaching as well as research. Hannah's 1946 decision laid the groundwork for the development of a staff that was competent to undertake these tasks.

Still, while East Lansing was receiving an influx of talented new professors, veteran faculty members played vital roles in improving MSC's academic standing. English professor Russel Nye, for example, won a Pulitzer Prize in 1945 for his biography of George Bancroft. Nye had a special intellectual charisma that sparked an incredible loyalty among his many students, including Dale Herder, who later became a vice president at nearby Lansing Community College. At Nye's death in 1993, Herder wrote in the *MSU Alumni Magazine*,

Professor Nye taught me, as a student of history many, many years ago, about the connection between ideas and actions in our national experience. He instilled in me, through his teachings and his manners, an appreciation for the cultural roots we all share with George Washington, Thomas Jefferson, Abraham Lincoln, Chief Sitting Bull, Harriet Tubman, Booker T. Washington, Clare Boothe Luce, Duke Ellington, Martin Luther King, and Cesar Chavez. He also

instilled in me what it means to be a democrat in a republican form
of government—government built on the ideas of the Enlighten-
ment and the courage of men and women who died to establish
the freedom we now take for granted as if it were permanent and
secure. . . . Thank you, Professor Nye, and thank you to all the teachers like you. In our frantic lives we may not write or stop to visit
often enough. But be assured that we think about you more often
than you may know; we appreciate more than you can ever know,
your inspiration, the connections you help us make with new and
old ideas, and the mark you continue to make upon our lives.

Nye was an esteemed authority on popular culture, and his donation
to the MSU Library of items related to comic art, science fiction,
mysteries, and Western fiction form the basis of the world-renowned
Russel B. Nye Popular Culture Collection. Another faculty member,
Richard Dorson, was establishing an international reputation for his
work in folklore. Professor Trout became known for his pioneering
studies in dairy husbandry and food science and as the inventor of
homogenized milk. English professor Herbert Weisinger received a
three-year fellowship to the Warburg Institute of the University of
London to analyze key Renaissance philosophies through literature
and art. In 1949 Weisinger was both the first American and first
scholar of English literature to win a Warburg fellowship.

Strong cultural and artistic programs also played an essential part
in the college's establishment of itself as more than an agricultural institution. The new Music Building and William Thompson's success
in staging theatrical productions constituted important steps in the
late 1930s and early 1940s toward making MSC a more well-rounded
institution of higher learning. Three other programs furthered that
perception—Michigan State College Press, the University Archives,
and an increasingly respected art department.

MICHIGAN STATE COLLEGE PRESS

Michigan State College's press had its origins in a set of recommendations made by members of the Special Committee on Publications,
which had been instructed to find ways to relieve the college

bookstore of its responsibility for publishing course outlines, laboratory manuals, syllabi, and other material destined for classroom use.
In addition, the committee was told to devise a plan for publishing
MSC-generated research and distributing it to scholars and the general public. The committee's final report recommended the creation
of the Michigan State College Press to take on these responsibilities.
Acting on the committee's advice, Hannah established the fledgling
publishing house by executive fiat in mid-June 1947; the Board of
Agriculture approved the action a few days later. On 1 July the Michigan State College Press came into existence, with James Denison as
its first (part-time) director. In 1949, MSC Press became a nonprofit
corporation, and bylaws were created calling for a ten-member board.
Two years later, the press became a full member of the Association
of American University Presses.

The press's first books covered a wide range of subjects. The first
non-textbook title was *A Correlation of Some Physical Properties of
Alkane and Alkenes* by Ralph C. Huston, dean of the graduate school.
Another early book was Nye's *Fettered Freedom: Civil Liberties and
the Slavery Controversy*. Despite being an MSC English professor and
a Pulitzer Prize winner, Nye, like other faculty members, found that
the young press did not automatically accept his works for publication.
"One might expect that a newly established press would have eagerly
accepted the work of a college faculty member whose previous book
had won a prestigious national award," wrote Maurice Hungiville
in his fiftieth-anniversary history of the MSU Press, *From a Single
Window: Michigan State University and Its Press, 1947–1997*. "Instead,
Nye's manuscript was subjected to intense scrutiny. It was carefully
read by members of the Press's editorial board and then evaluated by
two outside readers, Professor Clement Eaton of the University of Kentucky and Arthur Schlesinger Jr. of Harvard University. Schlesinger
pronounced the study to be 'a valuable scholarly contribution both to
history and to the history of our tradition of civil rights.'"

In 1950, Denison brought in William Rutter, a former assistant to
the president of Oxford University Press, to serve as editor in chief.
In 1952, when Rutter left MSC to pursue a career in the U.S. State
Department, G. Lyle Blair, an Australian with a British publishing
background, took over; Blair would serve as press director for the
next quarter century. According to Hungiville, Blair was,

the kind of man who inspired myths. The details of his life were certainly dramatic, maybe even a bit melodramatic. Blair, it was rumored, had left his native Australia in 1935 under extraordinary circumstances—he had run off to England with an opera singer.

In London he served his apprenticeship in publishing under Jonathan Cape, the distinguished publisher of D. H. Lawrence, Robert Graves, and Malcolm Lowry. . . . During World War II [Blair] had been an RAF pilot and at some point engaged in top-secret, high-level espionage in the Middle East. After the war he served as diplomatic correspondent for the *London Graphic*, general manager of the British Publisher's Guild, and director of Pocket Books, G.R.

Despite some stumbles in its earliest days, the press soon developed a reputation for publishing quality work. Blair replaced Denison as director in 1955 and two years later spoke with *State Journal* reporter Neil Hunter about what was happening at the press. "New books by the press go from East Lansing to all corners of the globe," Hunter wrote. "They bring recognition to M.S.U. from their sales points in Europe, India, South Africa, Asia and in Mr. Blair's Australia." Blair said that "Our job is to publish the great minds of the world."

The tenth-anniversary celebration of the founding of the press attracted the attention of the *MSU Alumni Magazine*, which noted that "through the years the Press probably has received more favorable reviews than any other publishing house its size." Moreover, the piece continued, "Critics from coast to coast regard M.S.U. Press books favorably, commenting not only on the scholarship, but also on their popular appeal. The successes of the Press help focus attention on Michigan State University as a whole. One morning's mail brought reviews from the *Saturday Review*, the *New York Times*, and the *Washington Post* to the desk of Press Director Lyle Blair. . . . One of the most loyal friends of the Press since its beginning has been the head of the English Department, Dr. Russel B. Nye, a Pulitzer Prize winner. *Fettered Freedom*, the book Dr. Nye wrote after his prize-winning study of George Bancroft, was the second book to be published by the Press. Since then, the Press has published three books by Dr. Nye."

In 1957, the MSU Press edition of L. Frank Baum's *The Wizard of Oz and Who He Was* (edited by Russel Nye and Martin Gardner) sparked a national debate when, in an address to the American Library Association's annual meeting, the head of Detroit's public library system, Ralph Ulveling, declared the book subversive. Blair counterattacked with a blizzard of press releases defending free speech, scholarly publishing, and *The Wizard of Oz*. In particular, Blair took aim at pretentious public librarians who saw themselves as self-appointed defenders of the public good. Ulveling quickly retracted his remarks, claiming that he had been misquoted or at least misunderstood.

Blair must be considered one of the most remarkable individuals in Michigan State's 150-year history. He succeeded for many years in the difficult job of keeping the press financially afloat. He published many titles that met with literary success. And he was popular with both campus officials and international literary and publishing leaders. "Lyle Blair is an interesting fellow," Hannah once wrote. "You will never know anyone quite like him but you can count on him to get his job done quite well. He came to East Lansing with all the usual prejudices of a British educated person and has become one of the best salesmen in the world for land grant education." Blair always stated that he had great support from Hannah's office.

THE UNIVERSITY'S HISTORICAL COLLECTIONS

While the press was building a literary reputation for Michigan State, the college was also recognizing the importance of its own history and traditions. MSC historical records were kept in early years by such administrators as Theophilus Abbot, Robert Clark Kedzie, William James Beal, Frank Kedzie, and Elida Yakeley. Around 1950, the museum, under the directorship of Joseph Stack, established a historical collections program, specializing in historical artifacts and manuscript materials related to agricultural and rural life. It would eventually expand the collection to all aspects of Michigan State College history. In 1967, the college historical records were detached from the museum and placed under the supervision of the university provost. Dean William Combs was appointed Michigan State's first archivist. Combs traveled to many other university archives before making recommendations to the Board of Trustees about how the MSU archives should be structured. On 21 November

1969, the board formally established a university archives that was "responsible for collecting and preserving inactive records for all units in the University which have legal, administrative, fiscal or historical value. It is also a repository for the personal papers of faculty, administrators and alumni." In a Summer 2004 article in the *MSU Alumni Magazine*, emeritus director of the MSU Archives Fred Honhart described some of the highlights of the collection. "25,000 cubic feet of materials, including more than 700 Historical Collections, 50,000-plus photographs and more than half a million negatives, movie film, video, sound records, maps and digital materials tell MSU's story, and more." Honhart mentioned the records of Michigan State's Semi-Centennial and Centennial celebrations, the 140 boxes of John Hannah papers, the two hundred collections of faculty papers, the personal papers of automobile pioneer Ransom E. Olds, and extensive materials related to the U.S. Civil War as just a few highlights of the archives' collections.

A. G. Scheele joined the college art department in 1918 and eventually became its chair. Courtesy of Michigan State University Archives and Historical Collections.

THE ART DEPARTMENT

While the establishment of a college press moved MSC closer to the standard of other major educational institutions, the art department was making slower but definitely steady progress in creating programs and attracting personnel that were more like those of a major university than a midwestern agricultural college. Under the leadership of A. G. Scheele and later Howard Church, the art department was attracting excellent professors who provided greater artistic and cultural sophistication. Scheele came to MSC in 1918 after earning bachelor's and master's degrees from Oberlin College. He had originally enrolled in the Johns Hopkins School of Medicine but quickly decided that painting was more attractive than surgery. Called "Dad" by his friends and colleagues, he was especially known for his marine and landscape paintings. "The beauty of the campus is one of the things that brought me here," he told the *Michigan State News* in 1934. "I have never seen a more beautiful campus and I have seen them from the Atlantic to the Pacific." For many years, Scheele chaired the art department and organized frequent faculty exhibits at the Union or the library. In 1937, for example, he displayed his work

Edith Butler, a member of the art faculty since 1919, was well known for her Christmas and other greeting cards. Courtesy of Thomas Collection.

Edith Butler, who had been teaching in the college art department since 1919, also used her artistic talents on the other side of Grand River Avenue. She sculpted a bust of Peoples Church minister Martin Luther Fox that is still displayed near the church entrance. Courtesy of David Olds.

at the library along with pieces by Edith Butler, Alma Goetsch, and Katherine Winkler.

Despite his accomplishments as a painter, Howard Church may have been best known for his skills as an educator and administrator. Serving as art department chair from 1945 through 1960, he worked closely with architect Ralph Calder in the design of Kresge Art Gallery, provided commentary about the visual arts for television and radio, served as a member of the Governor's Art Commission, and frequently appeared at local high schools to talk to students about art careers. "Both art students and art faculty can at times become excitable, depressed, passionate, angry or maybe even reclusive," he once said. "I tried to be the person who provided some stability, always trying to assure everyone that everything would eventually work out for the best."

Butler had begun teaching at the art department in 1919. She too had impressive credentials: she had attended the Art Institute of Chicago and held a bachelor's degree from the University of Southern California and a master's degree from Columbia University. She specialized in landscapes in both oils and watercolors, and her bust of Peoples Church minister Martin Luther Fox continues to be displayed at the church entrance. According to Church, during the early 1920s, "the art division had in its studios many antique plaster casts—heads

Art faculty members Alma Goetsch (*pictured*) and Katherine Winkler commissioned a Frank Lloyd Wright home in Okemos in the 1930s.
Courtesy of Michigan State University Archives and Historical Collections.

and busts of old Greek gods and senators, the Venus de Milo, etc. Students were expected to become proficient in copying such works, before imaginative drawing and painting was encouraged." On one occasion, Butler and Scheele were asked to perform for a college-sponsored film by pretending to criticize some students' work. But as Church related, just before filming started, the cameraman asked to have an "old wreck" moved out of the way. The "old wreck" was

Erling Brauner, chair of the art department, also built a house in Okemos designed by Frank Lloyd Wright. Author's collection.

a replica of the Venus de Milo. Said Church, "It just wouldn't do in those days to have in the background of a college film to be shown to farmers, a plaster cast of a nude."

Other members of the art department faculty excelled in other media. Goetsch was known for her silk-screen paintings, while Winkler was known for both her paintings and ceramics. In the late 1930s, the two women commissioned a Frank Lloyd Wright house in Okemos that became their home for many years. The original plans called for an entire Wright-built Usonian community with seven houses and a caretaker's cottage, but financing could not be secured, and the Goetsch-Winkler home was the only one built. Another member of the art faculty, Erling Brauner, who served as department chair from 1962 to 1970, also built a Wright-designed home nearby.

John deMartelly arrived at MSC in 1943 and was named artist in residence in 1946. DeMartelly had extensive international training

and soon developed a worldwide reputation as a teacher and practicing artist. He had studied at the Pennsylvania Academy of Fine Arts
and the Carnegie Institute of Technology, the Academia delle Arte in
Florence, and the Royal College of Design at the Victoria and Albert
Museum School in London. His work was eventually displayed
at New York's Metropolitan Museum and Whitney Museum of
American Art and the Tel Aviv Museum in Israel. Appearing gruff to
people who did not know him well, he was extremely popular with
his students. "Just being around him was an inspiration," wrote Ann
Scott, one of his graduate assistants. "He was always trying to help
his students seek out something inside of themselves that would
help in their artistic creation. He taught them how to enhance their
work, helping them think things through, to achieve more artistic expression. He was a real artist." MSU art professor Roger Funk agreed.
"He taught with love and he drew out the best in each student with

Charles Pollock served on the art department
faculty from 1942 to 1967 and is best known for
his murals at the entrance to the Auditorium.
Photo byDavid Olds.

The audience awaits the unveiling of Leonard Jungwirth's *Sparty* on 9 June 1945. Courtesy of Michigan State University Archives and Historical Collections.

friendliness and warmth," Funk said. "He was a friend and a teacher at the same time."

Charles Pollock, the oldest brother of famed American abstractionist Jackson Pollock, visited MSC in 1942 for a mural commission and spent the next twenty-five years on the MSC faculty. He had studied under Thomas Hart Benton at the Art Students League in New York City in 1926, and from 1938 to 1942 he lived in Michigan, supervising mural painting for the Works Progress Administration and working for the United Auto Workers. Pollock's greatest campus legacies are the murals at the entrance to the Auditorium.

Four other art department faculty members who arrived between 1945 and 1950—Irwin Whitaker, James McConnell, Louis Raynor, and William Gamble—also helped MSC establish a solid reputation in the visual arts. But perhaps the artist who left the biggest legacy on the college campus was Leonard Jungwirth. On 9 June 1945, Jungwirth's terra-cotta statue, *Sparty*, was dedicated. Hannah described the work as an "exemplification of the youth and spirit of Michigan State College." Although many modern observers consider *Sparty* the symbol of Spartan sports, Hannah did not mention the word "sports" in his dedication remarks; instead, the president extolled the statue's artistic merits:

> One of the possessions of all educated persons should be an appreciation for the beautiful and for the arts. . . . A little appreciation for good music, for good painting, for sculpture can make life more interesting for all of us. The real function of the Art Department at this college is not only to train a few artists but to bring . . . us at least a little understanding and appreciation of the artistic. We are proud of the Art Department's ability to create worthwhile work. DeMartelly and some of his fine paintings and etchings, Pollock and the fine murals in the auditorium, and Jungwirth and this figure we are dedicating this morning. It has been interesting for me to see this great figure grow from a few wooden laths tied together to the clay model—the clay figures ready to be fired and this finished figure. It reminds me that his quotation from Emerson is certainly true: "There is no way to success in art but to take off your coat, grind paint, and work like a digger on the railroad, all day and every day." Jungwirth has truly worked like a digger on the railroad, and worked hard and long. He can well be proud of this accomplishment. We are proud of it for him. In the years ahead, this Spartan Warrior in this beautiful and proper setting will become one of the distinguishing marks of this campus that all students and visitors will associate with this college and this campus in much the same way that Beaumont Tower is now generally recognized as the proper symbol of Michigan State College.

Defining Academic Boundaries

While Hannah took pride in MSC's many artistic and cultural developments during the 1940s, he especially enjoyed bragging about the

Most of the post–World War II faculty additions were white men, but Gertrude Nygren was an exception. Nygren came to MSC in 1945 and eventually became a full professor in the Cooperative Extension Service. Courtesy of Michigan State University Archives and Historical Collections.

continuation of the land-grant philosophy and how it was helping the citizens of Michigan. In a 1945 series of Sunday-afternoon radio addresses on WKAR, he often discussed the college's Agricultural Extension Service. "The county agricultural agents, the home demonstration agents, the 4-H club agents are all a part of Michigan State College as are the faculty members on the campus at East Lansing," he explained on 21 January. "Their salaries are paid by the college; the program which they are part of is operated by the School of Agriculture. There are some 60,000 boys and girls enrolled in the 4-H clubs of Michigan. There are some 30,000 farm women enrolled in the classes in home economics studying human nutrition, food preservation, the making of clothing, home furnishing, the care of children and all those other arts that go into rural home making and family life. Some three million bulletins were distributed by the Extension Service last year. More than 50,000 different Michigan farmers visited the county agricultural agents in the various counties of the state."

On 4 February, Hannah argued that the state constitution's establishment of the Board of Regents at the University of Michigan and the State Board of Agriculture at MSC had been a blessing: "This is a most fortunate situation and has allowed [both schools] to be preeminent in their fields and to be free from the sort of political domination that has sometimes handicapped state institutions of higher learning." In his 11 February talk, he said that the college's total operating budget was almost $5.5 million and came from the state legislature, subsidies from the federal government, student fees, and income from the sale of farm land. On 18 February, Hannah explained that returning veterans should be quickly assimilated into the total student body: "We do not believe it is desirable to segregate veterans. From our experience with the men and women who are now here, we are sure that they want to be treated exactly like all other men and women. They want no sympathy. They want no special treatment. They deserve the assistance we are able to give, but it is best for them and the college to regard them as regular college students." And on 25 March, he praised the college's students:

Michigan State College is proud of its student body. They are the best crop of young men and young women that the state has ever produced, and they are getting better. It was a popular pastime a few years ago for older people to be critical of young men and women of college age. They were accused of being soft, frivolous, unthinking, selfish individuals. Their contribution in the armed services has effectively answered those critics. There is not much wrong with our young people that is not traceable to the faults or flaws for which older people are responsible. They have intelligence and ability, and have shown conclusively that when the 'chips are down' they can do their part better than there is any reason to expect their parents could have done at the same age.

As the 1950s arrived, Michigan State continued to expand its physical and academic boundaries beyond those that had formerly defined a small agricultural college. It now boasted talented teachers in history, literature, chemistry, education, and economics, among many other areas. Its concept of a well-rounded education—the Basic College—was catching the attention of colleges and universities around the world. It was gaining a reputation for enlightened cultural programs in art, music, theater, and academic publishing. Its students, according to President Hannah, were top-notch. Perhaps most important, however, many in the college community believed that the best was yet to come. The years immediately following the war had been the catalyst for the world-class university MSC would become in the 1950s and 1960s.

4

Building a University

THROUGHOUT HIS CAREER, JOHN HANNAH KEPT HIS FINGER ON THE pulse of every aspect of Michigan State College's (and later Michigan State University's) operations: academic departments, athletic programs, legislative relationships, and especially the monumental task of transforming the campus from a small agricultural college to a major international university. Both as secretary of the State Board of Agriculture and later as the school's president, Hannah would rise early in the morning, stroll through the awakening campus, check on the progress of new buildings, and speculate about those structures that were still only dreams. Even in the middle of the day, he sometimes left his office to make sure that construction was proceeding as planned.

ARCHITECT OF THE FUTURE

Hannah's interest in building construction was not merely curiosity. Shortly after Hannah became secretary of the college and secretary of the State Board of Agriculture in 1935, Michigan State President Robert Sidey Shaw gave him the daunting new task of overseeing the repair and modification of buildings and grounds as well as the construction of new buildings. Hannah wrote in his memoirs, "I made it a practice every morning to walk over much of the campus to see what was going on. If construction was taking place, either of new buildings or substantial alterations, I made it a point to check its progress practically every day." Sometimes he would be accompanied by Edward Kinney, head of the physical plant department. "On many occasions, when spotting new buildings, he would dig his heel in the ground and say, 'Here is where it should go,'" Kinney remembered. "Well do I recall the cold, wintry day when he pointed out a twelve-foot error in our stakes for the new wing of the ancient Administrative Bld. He was especially concerned about the location of Power Plant No. 2. It had to be adjacent to the railroad spur, not too far from the river (for cooling water) and yet should not cast cinders and fly-ash on North Campus."

Lansing State Journal sports editor George Alderton also remembered Hannah's great interest in new construction. "When the Jenison gymnasium and field house building was being constructed, I was thrilled and two or three times a week I would go over during the evening and see how the work was advancing," he wrote. "I was down in the basement peering around and I found Dr. Hannah there too. We joined up and took the tour together. At one point he stopped and turned to me and said, 'You know, they can fire me tomorrow but they can't tear this building down.'" But Hannah scrutinized more than new buildings on his walks. He also paid attention to the environment surrounding both new and old structures and even the wildlife. On 25 February 1947, he wrote to police administrator Arthur Brandstatter regarding the alarming growth of the campus's red squirrel population:

> These creatures are increasing in numbers and unless drastic steps are taken to reduce their population they will drive off the fox squirrels; and what is much more important seriously decrease the population of song birds. Red squirrels are very destructive of birds' nests and birds' eggs. As long as Mr. Shaw lived on campus, he kept them under control. May I again suggest that you assign one of your police officers the job of shooting these squirrels early in the morning before pedestrians begin moving and when the squirrels are in evidence and during the spring vacation when there will be few pedestrians about. It is much easier to shoot these creatures when there are no leaves on the trees. There is an additional reason for destroying them in that they get into building partitions and attics. I have a colony of them now in the attic and partitions in the President's house on the campus.

In 1948, Hannah wrote to several of his top administrators to express concern about the landscaping around the women's residence halls:

Since the opening of the fall quarter, I have had an opportunity to walk around the campus in the evening. I have been interested in traveling about alone and unannounced to make some first-hand observations. I am convinced that it is necessary that we proceed at once to install additional outdoor lighting about the women's dormitories and that some of the brush and shrubbery be radically trimmed about the older women's dormitories. . . . The tall shrubbery makes the area about Mayo and Williams very romantic but certainly does not improve the behavior of our students in these areas. I am impressed that in the planting about the new dormitories shrubbery should be low growing, and I think that radical changes must be made either in the lighting or the shrubbery about the older dormitories. I should like to see this work undertaken at once with the observation and location of the lights determined before the leaves fall off the trees and shrubs.

Herman H. Halladay, a former livestock commissioner, served as secretary of the Board of Agriculture from 1921 to 1935. Halladay was succeeded by John Hannah. Courtesy of MSU Archives and Historical Collections.

Toward the end of World War II, college administrators began to prepare for the influx of returning veterans, which officials knew would affect every facet of East Lansing life. According to Hannah, "Every effort was made for the emergency. It was realized that tremendous new demands for student enrollments would arise. These would call for an enlarged faculty and more extensive physical facilities." Marie Mercier, who worked as secretary to both Herman Halladay and Hannah when they were secretaries of the State Board of Agriculture, credits Hannah alone for anticipating and preparing for the dramatic increase in postwar enrollment.

PREPARING FOR GI JOE AND THE GI BILL

Well before the end of World War II, President Hannah discussed the newly enacted Servicemen's Bill of Rights of 1944 (the GI Bill) with the board. He predicted that the legislation would inspire large numbers of returning war veterans to enroll in the nation's colleges and universities. Among a variety of benefits, such as one-year's unemployment compensation, low-interest home loans, and low-interest loans to start businesses, the GI Bill provided all returning World War II veterans with funds for college and vocational education. MSC had to be prepared. Most veterans would be married, Hannah believed, and the college would need to provide suitable married-student housing as well as more dormitories for single students. He also saw the need for additional faculty and faculty housing. Before the end of hostilities, Hannah received the board's approval to request surplus barracks housing from the federal government. Michigan State took possession of these units soon after the war ended. As Mercier recalled, "We received more than any other institution simply because of President Hannah's foresight. . . . Also because of his foresight, architects were instructed to prepare plans for faculty housing with the result that the day after the war ended in 1945, President Hannah ordered ground broken for these apartment buildings and they were ready for renting when they were needed."

NEW CONSTRUCTION

The combination of returning veterans and a lack of state funding for new construction in the 1930s and early 1940s created enormous pressures. "The state has provided not a single building for instructional purposes at Michigan State College since 1929, and during that period the college has grown from a little college into a great university," Hannah told the Michigan State Horticultural Society on 5 December 1945. Any new building was financed either on a self-liquidating basis or largely with alumni donations. MSC had become accustomed to financing new construction with little or no help from the state legislature. The MSU Union Building (1925) was constructed with money raised by the MSC Alumni Association, although the legislature later provided some assistance. Beaumont Tower (1928) was constructed with funds donated by alumnus John Beaumont. Student fees—often dormitory rentals—paid off the construction debt of dormitories such as Snyder-Phillips Hall for men and Campbell, Mayo, and Williams dormitories for women. A combination of Public Works Administration money and student fees financed the building of the Auditorium, Jenison Field House, Olin Health Center, and the power plant.

One example of MSC's self-liquidating approach was Sarah Langdon Williams Hall, named after the wife of the college's first president, Joseph R. Williams. Dedicated on 31 October 1937,

it provided housing for 258 women and included living rooms, sunrooms, recreation facilities, and bedrooms. The total cost was $477,000, and it was financed by a bond issue sold by the Ann Arbor Trust Company at 3.3 percent interest. The bond would be paid off in fifteen years using a portion of the money students paid for room and board. But MSC could not expect to continue meeting its enormous building needs through self-liquidating efforts or alumni generosity. The state of Michigan would have to become involved. Some argued that increasing enrollment meant large increases in income from tuition and other student fees, making outside financial help unnecessary. "Too few recognize that when the enrollment of the college increases by 1000 students the income from student fees is increased

Dedicated on 12 March 1940 by First Lady Eleanor Roosevelt, the Auditorium was partially financed by Public Works Administration funds. It provided space for a wide range of performing arts and served as the new home of the MSC Museum. Courtesy of Michigan State University Archives and Historical Collections.

New buildings such as Jenison Field House (*above*) and the Auditorium allowed an increasing number of audiences to watch sports and cultural activities on the MSC campus. Courtesy of Michigan State University Archives and Historical Collections.

by $120,000 but the overhead cost of operation is increased by more than $400,000," Hannah responded. "Every time the enrollment increases by a thousand, it is necessary for us to spend for operation at least $280,000 from some other source."

James Denison was one of the key players in the college's efforts to attract state monies. A former *Detroit Free Press* correspondent in Lansing, director of information for the Michigan War Council, and an administrative assistant to Michigan governor Harry F. Kelly, Denison knew the ins and outs of Lansing politics. "One of my first assignments [from Kelly] was to help plan for and gain public acceptance of the Governor's 'Victory Building Program,'" Denison wrote. "During the war, at the Governor's insistence, the State of Michigan had hoarded its income surpluses in a 'Veterans Trust Fund,' amounting to some $50,000,000, as I now recall. A portion—I believe $25 million—was to be set aside to aid indigent veterans and

Olin Memorial Hospital was built in the late 1930s and named for Richard Milo Olin, MSC's first full-time physician. The "Constructed without Expense to the Public" sign was common on campus during the Shaw and Hannah years, informing visitors that tax dollars were not being spent for building projects. Courtesy of Michigan State University Archives and Historical Collections.

their families, and the remainder was to underwrite a substantial State building program to meet the accumulated and anticipated needs for educational buildings and for State-operated facilities, such as hospitals."

Kelly asked colleges and universities to submit a "want list" of new buildings and their approximate cost. State officials then approved future construction on an institution-by-institution basis. In MSU's case, a classroom building (Berkey Hall), a science building, an agricultural engineering building, a physics building, and additions to the power plant were approved. Hannah directed that construction start simultaneously on all approved buildings, a strategy that eventually met with great success. Not surprisingly, soon after

John Hannah hired James Denison, an administrative assistant to Michigan governor Harry F. Kelly, for a number of key assignments, including helping to obtain money from the legislature for building projects to meet the needs of veterans returning from World War II. Courtesy of Michigan State University Archives and Historical Collections.

Hannah hired Denison, the president asked the former gubernatorial aide to make certain that MSC's building program would succeed despite legislative opposition. As planning moved forward, Denison recalled, "The Legislature began to have second thoughts and the ultra-conservative instincts of some of the leaders began to assert themselves. . . . One, Senator Otto Bishop, of Alpena, chairman of the Senate Finance Committee, demanded a halt in the educational building program. Figuratively pointing to the unfinished skeletons of academic buildings on the MSC campus, he predicted that there would never be a need for them, and said they would never be more than 'ghost buildings.'" Muddy Waters, a student in the late 1940s and later the Michigan State football coach, remembered walking around campus seeing unfinished basements where major structures were to be built. "It was intentional," Waters said. "Once the building was started, somehow it would have to be finished." Denison agreed. "My personal judgment is that the needed buildings would not have been financed had not President Hannah got them all started in good time, for the argument that it would be a waste not to complete them was persuasive in the end," he wrote. "We could argue practicality, not debate philosophy and theory this time around, and the buildings were completed on schedule." That was exactly Hannah's strategy. MSC administrators put together a publication, *Schools and the Means of Education*, that included photographs of the unfinished buildings with text arguing that it would be wasteful not to finish them. The small brochure, which received wide distribution throughout Michigan, undoubtedly helped to convince legislators that MSC's skeleton structures should be completed.

Even more convincing than *Schools and the Means of Education* was a stroll around the MSC campus. By the 1946 winter quarter, two thousand returning World War II veterans were already enrolled. Thirty percent were married, and many had families with them. Under the terms of the GI Bill, married students received ninety dollars a month and single students received sixty-five dollars for room and board. But even with a monthly check, finding housing on or near the East Lansing campus proved a challenge. Single women who had been living in Abbot Hall were doubled up with coeds living in Mary Mayo, Campbell, Mason, and Williams dormitories, freeing up 650 spaces for male veterans. Bunk beds were installed in Jenison Field

House, and the third and fourth floors of the Union were converted to sleeping spaces. Clergy in Lansing and East Lansing appealed to their congregations for help, resulting in 250 rooms. The Women's Society of the Peoples Church systematically canvassed East Lansing in search of rooms. Four hundred mobile home trailers were set up on a thirty-acre tract near the corner of Kalamazoo Street and South Harrison Road. Another fifty veterans and their families occupied trailers in Lansing. The future looked to contain even greater challenges. Each day, between forty and fifty applications arrived at the admissions office.

Dealing with returning veterans, many of whom had fought heroically in Europe and the South Pacific, proved to be far different than managing kids just out of high school. As Frederick Mueller, a member of the State Board of Agriculture and a Grand Rapids businessman, recalled, "Because of their maturity and war experience, they resented a long-time rule that alcoholic beverages were not allowed on campus. In the trailer village we simply ignored the beer consumption we knew was going on." MSC finally had to restrict enrollment. "These restrictions bore most heavily upon young women," wrote Edna Brookover, who has chronicled the history of temporary housing at MSC in the years immediately after World War II. "Because of inadequate housing, the college was forced to deny admission to all new women students except those who could provide housing for themselves in Lansing or East Lansing."

Some critics believed that all the new dormitories would stand empty after the wave of World War II veterans passed through the college. President Hannah responded by declaring that when "occupancy is reduced to normal—two in a room, instead of three—we will have capacity in our dormitories for fewer than 5,000 students. If our enrollment continues to hold around present figures (and there is every reason to believe that it will), we will then have room to house fewer than one-third of our students on the campus." But enrollments did not continue "to hold around present figures." They grew. In 1947, Michigan State College became the country's thirteenth-largest institution of higher learning, with 12,412 full-time students. MSC trailed only the University of California, the University of Minnesota, Ohio State University, Columbia University, New York University, the University of Michigan, the University of Wisconsin, the University

The Brody Residence Hall Complex was named for Clark L. Brody, a member of the Class of 1904 who served as a county agricultural agent and as a member and two-time chair of the State Board of Agriculture (later the Michigan State Board of Trustees). Courtesy of Michigan State University Archives and Historical Collections.

of Texas, the University of Washington, the University of Southern California, and Indiana University. Harvard occupied fourteenth place.

The state-funded building projects undertaken during the second half of the 1940s included Berkey Hall; buildings for general science, physics and mathematics, agricultural engineering, and electrical engineering; and the steam-generating plant. The self-liquidating projects comprised seven dormitories, including Yakeley Hall and Gilchrist Hall; living quarters for faculty and married students; and additions to the Student Union and stadium. The stadium project added twenty-one rows of seating on the sides and from eleven to forty-six rows in the end zones, increasing capacity from twenty-seven thousand to fifty-one thousand, making Macklin Field the sixth-largest football stadium in the country, behind the facilities at Michigan, Ohio State, Illinois, Minnesota, and Notre Dame.

NEW POSTWAR HOUSING

The Faculty Village, located south of what is now the Breslin Center and north of Shaw Lane, was among the first of MSC's postwar construction projects. It would eventually consist of eighteen British Empire flat-topped prefabricated houses and thirty-two Quonset huts. Many married students moved into nearby brick apartments. Six of the units were named in honor of former MSC students who had lost their lives in World War II. Arthur Jon Howland from East Lansing was a captain of artillery in the U.S. Army and received the Legion of Merit, the Air Medal with clusters, and the Purple Heart. Killed in action in France on 27 August 1944, he was a 1941 MSC graduate who had majored in hotel administration. John Allshouse Pelton of Pontiac was a lieutenant colonel in Third Army headquarters who received the Legion of Merit and the Bronze Star. The 1936 liberal arts graduate was killed in action in France on 25 August 1944. First Lieutenant William Thomas Rafferty of Fremont, Ohio, served in the Ninetieth Infantry Division of the Third Army and received the Oak Leaf cluster and the Purple Heart. Enrolled in the forestry department during 1938–39, he was killed in action in Germany on 26 November 1944. Robert Lionel French of Dearborn, who studied applied science

Spartan football stadiums have increased in capacity from 24,750 to 75,005. In 1957 the upper decks were added to Macklin Field and the name was changed to Spartan Stadium. Courtesy of Michigan State University Archives and Historical Collections.

at MSC, served as a first lieutenant in the armored infantry and received the Silver Star with the Oak Leaf cluster. He was killed in action in Germany on 28 February 1945. Robert Parker of Lansing was a first lieutenant in the Army Air Forces who received the Air Medal with the Distinguished Flying Cross and the Silver Star. He was enrolled in business administration during 1939–41 and was lost over New Guinea on 15 November 1943. Infantry First Lieutenant Arthur Kenneth Ungren of Lansing received the Bronze Star, Silver Star, and the Purple Heart. The 1932 graduate in business administration was killed in action in Belgium on 10 January 1945.

Edna Brookover and her husband, education professor Wilbur Brookover, chose the Quonsets. When they arrived in the late summer of 1946, they found "just a pile of dirt" with no trees or grass. However, the Brookovers were assured that their new home would be ready when the college term started two months later. Edna Brookover was dismayed. "I was in tears all the way back to Huntington, Indiana, where we were spending a few months with my parents. Not only did I feel it was a disgrace to live in a Quonset Hut (which we had chosen to do), but there was not even a Quonset Hut to move

The Quonset huts were constructed to house faculty members and veterans arriving on campus at the end of World War II. Courtesy of Michigan State University Archives and Historical Collections.

into, and there was none to see." Wilbur Brookover moved into the unfinished Quonset on 21 September to begin the fall term; Edna arrived with the couple's two children on 16 October. "During the Depression Wilbur had worked his way through college by working on construction gangs, so he felt he knew how to talk to the building crew," Edna wrote. "He hunted up one of the plumbers and told him he had a bottle of scotch for him if he would come over on Sunday to connect the bathroom. The plumber came."

The Quonsets were organized like typical five-room houses but tended to be hot in the winter because each structure featured eight radiators and heavy insulation, according to Brookover. But the insulation also kept the rooms cool in the summer. "We rapidly became a very cosmopolitan community," she wrote. "We were quite self-sufficient. There were engineers, economists, journalists, music and art faculty, scientists, mathematicians, sociologists, English and language faculty, horticulturists and political scientists. People with children were mixed with people without children. One of the most important things we learned was to cooperate with each other. There was always a friend around and a pot of coffee ready at most neighbors' homes. One could always borrow an egg, a cup of sugar, or whatever. We learned to share. We formed carpools, baby-sitting leagues, etc."

In 1977, the *MSU Alumni Magazine* asked several former residents of the Quonset huts about their "special memories." Social science professor Arthur Vener, who lived in one of the huts in the mid-1950s, recalled thinking that "they were absolutely marvelous. They were cheap and we had trees outside. . . . The walls were metallic, and if you slept with your head against the wall, you woke up with your hair frozen to it." George Trumball, a 1952 graduate, remembered, "In the winter there were only two ways to control the heat. You could turn it off, which meant you froze—or open your window, which meant you caught cold from the draft." Army veterans had a unique point of view: "There was very little studying done in that madhouse. But talk? There seemed to be endless bull sessions," Clarence Zeno remembered. "After a term or two in the Quonsets, we Army guys moved into Mason Hall, which had been vacated by the women. It was like moving from a sleazy hotel to a ritzy one. All we had to do was clean the powder out of the drawers and take the doors off the potties."

During the early 1970s, East Lansing screenwriter and MSU graduate Jim Cash worked in Quonset 101 on the edge of the campus as a producer at MSU's public television station. In 1995, he remembered one night when Jim Adams and Terry Braverman, the "Voices of MSU Sports," inadvertently failed to lock the door to their storage room. "I pushed the door open and . . . then reached carefully inside for the light cord. A dangling, naked bulb revealed the incredible cult secret that Adams and Braverman had protected for years. . . . The storage room contained something that gave me endless hours of tremendous pleasure for the next several years—hundreds of silent reels of MSU game films that went all the way back to the 1930s." Cash spent hours in the old Quonset hut watching long-ago football stars such as Dennis Mendyk, Lynn Chandnois, Blanche Martin, John "Thunder" Lewis, and, of course, Dave Kaiser kicking the winning field goal in the Rose Bowl. Much to Cash's dismay, Quonset 101 burned down during the 1980s.

As Cash's reminiscence highlights, the Quonsets long outlived their originally planned five-year life span and served a wide variety of purposes for the campus community. In 1982, *Lansing State Journal* staff writer Mark Nixon wrote their unofficial obituary: "For nearly 20 years they were known as eyesores on the Michigan State University campus, like giant tin cans sliced in half and plopped down unceremoniously on a vacant lot. As far back as 1964, one MSU official vowed to get rid of them 'as fast as we can.' It wasn't that easy. The austere-looking Quonset huts on the western fringe of MSU's campus dwindled with each passing year, but always managed to avoid extinction. Until now. The last of the post-war Quonsets will soon fall before the wrecking ball. The last tenants of the Quonsets have left, and were to make a formal good bye to the Quonsets at a flag-lowering ceremony at 11 A.M. today."

Alma Routsong, a 1949 MSC graduate, eventually became one of the world's most famous lesbian writers, frequently using Isabel Miller as her pen name. Her first novel, *A Gradual Joy* (1953), told the story of a young married couple at MSU. The beginning of the work offers an unflattering description of one of the temporary trailers: "He unlocked the padlock on the trailer door and they went in, stooping to save their heads. The first thing noticed was the musty, mildewed smell, which he later identified as the floor rotting under the linoleum where the icebox had leaked. There were two couches, one at each end of the trailer, a drop-leaf table, and four folding chairs. The walls were covered with flaked, drab varnish, and the linoleum was a neuter, mottled insipidity. There was no color or freshness anywhere, and Jim felt very depressed, as though he had gone to live in the belly of a whale."

PRESERVING THE CAMPUS CORE

Of course, new construction did take its toll on the college's historic landscape. Old buildings had to come down to make way for the new structures. The Old President's Home, which had housed the college's second chief executive, T. C. Abbot, as well as subsequent presidents through 1915, was razed on 20 March 1946. Designed by Michigan Capitol architect Elijah Myers in the early 1870s and originally known as Faculty Row No. 1, the building subsequently served as a dormitory for senior women, as a hospital, and as a practice house for home economics students. Four other Faculty Row houses were also destroyed to create space for new construction. Three more college landmarks—the old Union Literary Society (built in 1890), the former home of landscaper and horticulture professor Thomas Gunson, and the Old Chemical Fort—fell in the early 1950s, when construction began on the new library. The Chemical Fort, nicknamed because of its architectural style, was built in 1871 as a chemical laboratory and later housed the physics and chemistry departments before the Kedzie Chemistry Building was constructed.

Hannah and others worked hard to avoid intruding on the campus's gently rolling landscape, preserving many of the trees, grassy spaces, and ivy-covered buildings that had long been the hallmark of the college campus north of the Red Cedar River. Professors such as John C. Holmes, William James Beal, Liberty Hyde Bailey, and Levi Rawson Taft had played prominent roles in designing the open park areas where Linton Hall, the Horticultural Laboratory, the Botany Laboratory, Cowles House, and the old library (now the museum) still stand. In fact, when Frederick Law Olmstead Jr. proposed a plan that would change the campus from a meandering flow of trees and brick buildings to a series of quadrangles similar to campuses at the University of Michigan and Ohio State University, students, faculty, and alumni strongly objected. The State Board of Agriculture apparently listened, rejecting the plan, and the college soon cut its ties with Olmstead. Titus Glen Phillips, the first student to take landscape architecture at the college, replaced Olmstead as designer and in 1926 produced a campus plan that left the hallowed grounds making up the old campus mostly untouched and became the bible of MSC landscape architecture for the next quarter century.

Acutely aware of MSC's history, Hannah undoubtedly knew of the love those connected with MSC had for the existing campus. Consequently, new construction left the original campus largely intact, as the post–World War II buildings arose on the fringes of Circle Drive and on land south of the river. When students returned to classes in the fall of 1947, the importance of the new South Campus became obvious. The area had previously been frequented mostly by those who lived in the new housing. Now it was home to eleven temporary buildings designed to serve as both faculty offices and classrooms. Fewer students had to make the trek across the newly built bridge to attend classes or consult with faculty advisers.

CONSTRUCTION CONTINUES

Still, the temporary offices and classrooms could not be a final solution. Classes began before the sun came up and continued until it went down. Classrooms were crowded, making both teaching and learning difficult. More buildings were needed. "Faculty might speak of an edifice complex or of an empire where the cement never sets; but few would go back to classes running from seven in the morning to ten at night in the steel army-surplus halls that pioneered 'south campus' in 1946–47," campus historian Madison Kuhn later wrote. "So, the construction continued. Within the next decade students and faculty had many more reasons for crossing the river into the south part of campus. Shaw Hall, Van Hoosen Hall, Kellogg Center, Anthony Hall, etc." The changes were obvious. The 1946 *Wolverine* devoted several pages to construction. "State is growing. Evidence of this is to be seen all over the campus. Where green lawns and trees formerly greeted the eye, huge cranes and excavators are burrowing deep holes from which new brick structures soon will rise. Heavy dump trucks piled high with clay and sand rumble along campus roads to disgorge their contents in some secluded area scheduled for a face-lifting treatment. Contractor's sheds, piles of lumber, brick and stone line roads and walks." The *MSC Record* said that an "alumnus returning to the Spartan campus after an absence of five or ten years would hardly recognize the old 'camping grounds.' Expansion has taken place on all sides of the central units, paralleling the rise of student enrollment from 3,272 in 1932 to 14,979 in the fall term of 1947."

Even though squeezing construction money from the legislature was not an easy task, Hannah refused to cut corners. "I recall also that in a number of discussions with him about building plans he always emphasized the importance of having a good architect, and provision for proper facilities even if it did cost a little more at the time," wrote Arthur W. Farrall, chair of the agricultural engineering department. "He stated that people will remember you for the quality of the building and not for the fact it cost a little more."

Heavy rains causing massive flooding swept through the MSC campus on 7 April 1947, forcing delays in construction and damaging existing buildings. The worst on-campus flood disaster since 1904

Giltner Hall, housing the School of Veterinary Medicine, was named after Ward Giltner, who served as dean of veterinary medicine from 1923 until 1947. Courtesy of Michigan State University Archives and Historical Collections.

cut off heat, electricity, and hot water from the Quonset village and forced the cancellation of classes. The Jenison Field House basement filled with twelve feet of water, and its floor sank three to four feet at the north end. A green and white campus bus made its way through the flooding to rescue stranded students and faculty. While the new building sites received little damage, time was lost while construction workers, especially those using heavy equipment, waited for the land to dry. Nevertheless, new structures kept rising.

Some of the new buildings quickly boosted MSC from having some of the worst facilities in a certain discipline to some of the very best. The decision to build a veterinary building, for example, was really no decision at all: the American Veterinary Medicine Association had threatened to remove the college from its accredited list because of the inadequate facilities. MSC officials lobbied hard, convincing

Giltner Hall was constructed in 1913 and expanded on several occasions, the last time in 1952. The architect for this remodeling project was O. J. Munson, and the builder was the Christman Company, a team that produced several campus buildings during the Hannah Administration. Courtesy of Michigan State University Archives and Historical Collections.

Michigan legislators that veterinarians did not just treat sick dogs and cats but also constituted the front line in the battle against diseases that affected cattle, hogs, and poultry—businesses essential to the Michigan economy. The legislature appropriated the money in 1949, and in the fall of 1952 the $2.4 million Giltner Hall opened its doors. Department head Chester Clark immediately proclaimed the new building "second to none" in the nation.

Other new buildings generated national attention. In 1950, when Robert S. Shaw Hall opened its doors to house sixteen hundred male students, it was immediately anointed as the world's largest dormitory, and an estimated ten thousand people attended the 3 June open house. Five years later, *Lansing State Journal* reporter Jack Grenard hailed Shaw Hall as "the most modern structure of its kind" and took his readers on a tour of the facility. Grenard focused not on the dorm's size but on MSC students' creativity in "improving" on the architects' work. Facing a fifty-cent fine for each mark left on the walls of their rooms, students quickly discovered a tape that left no marks, and everything from "navigation maps to the pin-ups lovingly referred to as 'pictures of Mom,' adorn[ed] those pristine walls." Metal coat hangers were bent into the shape of tie racks; in another room, hats could be stored on a huge rack of deer antlers. "Maintenance men patrol the halls five days a week, insuring clean living," Grenard wrote. "When the room is uninhabited during vacations, they wax floors, paint walls and ceilings, generally preparing what has been called the 'East Lansing Country Club' for a fresh wave of residents."

Anthony Hall, which opened in 1956, gave MSC a $4 million teaching and research center that added to the school's already excellent reputation in agriculture. Located at Farm and South Shaw lanes, Anthony housed the three animal industries departments—animal husbandry, dairy, and poultry. The editors of the *Quarterly Record of Michigan State University* were impressed. "Magnificent new buildings, completely equipped new laboratories, latest technological advances, finest facilities obtainable—all these have become familiar sights to Michigan State students and alumni alike," the publication reported in 1956. "But the most blasé of them all, whether old grad or undergrad, scientist, researcher or layman, stares in wonderment when, for the first time, he sees Anthony Hall."

Over the years, some observers have criticized Hannah for paying too much attention to new buildings and not enough to academics. But as his successor, Walter Adams, pointed out, "We had thousands of veterans arriving on campus. Many of them were married and had children. New faculty was being hired. What choice did John Hannah have except to provide classrooms for them to teach and learn, and housing for them to live? If we were only constructing new buildings and not providing students with a good education, I would have gone elsewhere."

THE NEW LIBRARY

Hannah knew of the criticism that he was wasting tax dollars on unnecessary construction. When a structure was built using alumni donations or student fees, he would post a sign that announced, "This

Constructed in 1964, Akers Hall was named after Chrysler Corporation vice president Forest H. Akers and his wife, Alice. Forest Akers served on the State Board of Agriculture for eighteen years and donated the land for the Forest Akers golf courses. Courtesy of Michigan State University Archives and Historical Collections.

building was built without cost to the taxpayer." When speaking before outside organizations, he highlighted new buildings constructed without state funding. He also argued, however, that still more facilities were needed. In a 1947 address to alumni, he told his audience,

> As local officers in our alumni organization, you are interested in having Michigan State College maintain its position. Therefore, you should know we may be rather seriously embarrassed because of our library. This library was planned to take care of 3,000 students; now we have 15,000. Moreover, we have students of a different kind. For example, we now have 800 graduate students, and within the next decade we will have a graduate enrollment of more than 2,500. Many of them will be people working for Ph.D. degrees, not in the technical fields of engineering, economics, alone, but in the humanities as well. We have the poorest library of any school of our size in America. Something has to be done about it. It isn't a matter of adding a little addition to the library and a few books. . . . Whether we have 15,000 students or 7,000, we must have an adequate library.

Hannah's public relations efforts eventually paid off, and in 1953 MSC announced that it would build the new library. When it opened in 1956, it was the nation's fifth-largest university library in terms of floor space under a single roof. During the first year of its operation, circulation increased by more than ten thousand volumes. The library was admitted for membership in the Association of Research Libraries. Funding increased, and twenty-two new full-time staff positions were added. Perhaps the most important aspect of the new and bigger library, however, was the positive publicity it generated. *College and Research Libraries* published a six-page article by MSC librarian Jackson Towne describing his new quarters; the facility was also featured in *Library Journal*, the *Pioneer*, and the *Wilson Library Bulletin*. A retired expert in public library planning wrote to Towne, "There is a lot to be studied and learned from what you have done there, and having been interested in college as well as public library buildings for a good many years, I thought I would tell you I think it is swell. . . . [W]hen I see something good I can't help getting up and cheering."

Towne was the driving force behind the continually improving library facilities in the early years of the Hannah Administration. When Towne retired in 1959, his successor, Richard Chapin, spoke about Towne's achievements, pointing out that a research library can expect to double in size about every sixteen years. "Give or take a few years this would indicate that the library you inherited, Mr. Towne—some 90,000 volumes—should have increased to 180,000 and then 360,000 during your tenure. As you know, Mr. Towne, and most of the others present here tonight know, the library now has in the neighborhood of 900,000 volumes. . . . [Y]ou have accomplished 50 years' work in about half that time." Chapin also praised Towne's work in establishing significant collections in such fields as the biological sciences and horticulture. In veterinary medicine, Chapin said, "we have a good working library and the best library in the country for research into the history of the subject." Chapin also

MSU's library was constructed in 1955–56, providing students and faculty with a world-class facility. Students, here shown checking out books in 1958, gained both an expanded book collection and increased study space. Courtesy of Michigan State University Archives and Historical Collections.

acknowledged the importance of Towne's efforts to establish the collection of books related to printing history and announced that it would be named the Jackson E. Towne Collection of the History of Printing in America.

THE KELLOGG CENTER

Completed in 1951 with the help of a $1.4 million grant from the W. K. Kellogg Foundation, the Kellogg Center provided another boost to the college's academic status. The "foremost building of its type in the nation," according to MSU administrators, the facility featured fifteen conference rooms, an auditorium seating 350, and 193 hotel-type double rooms. Its main purpose was adult training, consistent with the land-grant philosophy of providing education to a broad sector of Michigan residents. If people utilizing Kellogg's facilities "are helped in doing their jobs better, in becoming better citizens, or in learning to employ their leisure time more wisely, then MSC will feel it is doing its job well," the *MSC Record* explained. An added benefit of the Kellogg Center was the opportunity it offered MSC students to learn the hotel and restaurant profession. They served as bellhops, elevator operators, room clerks, waitstaff, cooks, and assistant managers in a state-of-the-art laboratory, receiving both student wages and college credit. The concept proved successful, and the Kellogg Center remains part of the School of Hospitality Business training program in the twenty-first century.

In 2002, writer Jan Reed looked back at the Kellogg Center's fifty-year history in the *MSU Alumni Magazine*:

Imagine . . . room rates were $5 per night for a single and $7.50 for a double. A tenderloin steak dinner in the State Room cost $1.75, and a piece of apple pie to top off your dinner cost a whopping 20 cents. The year was 1951, when the Kellogg Center just opened its doors. . . . MSU's Kellogg Center was the first of 11 Kellogg Centers nationwide established via a major grant from the W. K. Kellogg Foundation of Battle Creek. The original concept was to create a facility that could house, feed and conduct educational conferences and meetings, under one roof at the lowest possible cost. . . .

In 50 years, there have been just five general managers. The first four were graduates of The School of Hospitality Business at MSU. Weldon "Bill" Garrison was just 27 when he took the reins as the first manager of the Kellogg Center. A 1946 graduate of what was then called the Hotel, Restaurant & Institutional Management (HRIM) program, he steered the course for five years. Next came Bob Emerson, a 1947 graduate of MSU's HRIM program who served for nearly two decades as manager from 1956–74. George Fritz, another MSU grad, served as manager until 1984. Fritz had previously opened another Kellogg Center in Nigeria. Jack Burns, a 1968 HRIM graduate, rose through the ranks after starting as a night manager in 1970. He served as manager from 1984 until his untimely death in 1992. Joel Heberlein, a 20-year veteran of the hospitality industry, has been manager since 1993. . . . Guests to the Center come from every country in the world. Distinguished visitors read like a Who's Who in the world of education, science, politics, and the arts. President Gerald Ford, Gen. Douglas

Opened in 1951, the Kellogg Center has provided a permanent home for Michigan State's continuing education program as well as a hands-on workshop for students in the hospitality school.
Courtesy of Michigan State University Archives and Historical Collections.

MacArthur, Ralph Bunche, singer Marian Anderson, Van Cliburn, Walter Cronkite, Martin Luther King, Robert Kennedy, Ralph Nader, Margaret Mead, Roberta Peters, Tyrone Power, Nelson Rockefeller, Carl Sandberg, Adlai Stevenson and Canadian Prime Minister Jean Chretien are among the famous people who have visited.

Hannah's top educational adviser, Floyd Reeves, believed that building projects such as the new library and the Kellogg Center were a physical means to an educational end. "I know I differ possibly from the majority on this campus. . . . I also am egotistical enough to feel perfectly sure that I am right on this point. [Hannah's] greatest contribution was not in building buildings. It was not in making a beautiful campus. It was in developing a great institution that would be outstanding in research, outstanding in teaching, outstanding in providing educational leadership and political leadership for people of this state."

NAMING THE NEW CONSTRUCTION

All of the new buildings required names, of course. On 6 September 1960, Hannah sent a memo to key university administrators: "At an early meeting of the Breakfast Group I should like to initiate discussion with reference to possible names for the classroom building and for the office building on South Harrison Road. Mr. Denison has suggested the office building be named for Manly Miles, and I certainly have no objection to that proposal. . . . Of the names listed in the first category, I think Dr. Bessey should be given first consideration. An added factor here is the fact that his widow has recently given $3000 to the Development Fund to be used toward a memorial for her husband." College historian Madison Kuhn declined to recommend contemporaries for the honor of having a building named after them but made numerous suggestions of people in the university's past, including two women—home economics dean Marie Dye and home management expert Irma Gross. Others suggested included longtime Extension Service director Robert Baldwin, chemist Ralph Huston, horticulturist Harry

Eustace, economist Harold Patton, former college president Edwin Willits, art professor William Holdsworth, entomologist Albert J. Cook, ornithologist Walter Barrows, and education professor Walter French. Kuhn also added the name of Kolia San Thabue, an 1891 graduate "whose work as importer, preacher, photographer and mission teacher in Burma would give his name a certain fitness for an international student center." Michigan State eventually adopted several of these suggestions: the South Harrison Road structure became the Manly Miles Building; the classroom building on Farm Lane was named Bessey Hall; the old entomology building was dubbed Cook Hall; and in 1961, Liberty Hyde Bailey's horticultural laboratory was named Eustace Hall. A dormitory in the East Complex became Holmes Hall, while the old bacteriology building later became Marshall Hall.

HANNAH'S 1940s VISION FOR THE FUTURE

Expansion was essential for MSC to emerge as a respected leader in education. The building of a new library contributed to a more positive academic reputation. The belief that MSC had more than adequate athletic and academic facilities contributed to its admittance into the Big Ten. And there was, of course, Hannah's belief in the land-grant philosophy, which stated that MSC existed to serve all Michigan residents, not just an intellectual elite. "The business men among you know that machines cannot be worked beyond their capabilities indefinitely, nor can human beings," he told the Detroit Economic Club in 1948. "Eventually comes the time when either the load must be cut back or the machines break down. It would be unthinkable to establish an arbitrary limit on enrollments, thereby selecting a comparative few to attend our public colleges and saying to those we shut out: 'We're sorry, there is no room for you in college. It is too bad your parents can't afford to pay all your expenses and send you to some private institution but we just can't afford to educate at public expense everyone of intelligence and ability.' If we did that, there would eventually be no democracy under which to educate anyone." The postwar boom in enrollment eventually forced Michigan State to limit admissions, but Hannah remained committed to the idea that education should be available to everyone. He did not believe that the state's existing colleges should carry the entire burden, and he favored the establishment of junior colleges to provide training for students who wanted just a year or two of education beyond high school. The "more complex and expensive institutions" would thus remain "free to train those who require four and five and six years of higher education—the engineers, the lawyers, the doctors, the dentists, the veterinarians, the agriculturists, the physicists, the home economists, the teachers, and others."

THE MEMORIAL CHAPEL

The postwar construction boom also included the Alumni Memorial Chapel, which Hannah dedicated on 7 June 1952 in honor of the approximately 6,800 alumni who had defended the United States in wartime. "I know the alumni who built it had strongly in their mind their intention to promote the cause of universal peace by making young people increasingly aware of the realities of human brotherhood," Hannah said in his dedication speech. Many of the phrases Hannah spoke that day would later be etched on the windows located at the chapel's entrance. "Though Episcopal in design, the chapel remains interdenominational, serving as a spiritual center for all religions and faiths," *MSU Alumni Association Magazine* editor Robert Bao wrote on the chapel's fiftieth anniversary.

> MSU accepted more than 30 gracious gifts from generous alumni, mostly stones from European cathedrals, to underscore this non-sectarianism. Some of the stones are over 500 years old, and some were from bombed out churches. Stones hailed from St. Paul's Cathedral and Westminster Abbey in London, from the Notre Dame Cathedral in Paris and even from the White House. Stones also came from the ruins of a cathedral built by the Crusaders in Caesarea, the Roman capital of Palestine, and from a synagogue from Capernaum, where Jesus Christ reportedly preached. . . . Carved into the chapel's entrance wall are 487 names of those who

served in wars and perished. The oldest names are from the Class of 1861, students who died in the Civil War. . . . Seen together, much like the names on the Vietnam War Memorial in Washington, D.C., the list evokes a powerful response and remains a grim reminder of the human cost of wars.

Since its construction, the chapel has hosted hundreds of weddings and funerals. Visitors immediately notice the thirty-eight stained-glass windows given by alumni, friends, and graduating classes. Made by the Willet Stained Glass Studios in Philadelphia, ten depict events in Michigan State history, such as President Abraham Lincoln signing the Morrill Act of 1862, which gave land to states to establish colleges, and the admission of women to the college in 1870.

THE KRESGE ART CENTER

Next door to the chapel, the $1.5 million Kresge Art Center was dedicated on 9 May 1959. A gift from the Kresge Foundation, the building quickly became the campus arts mecca, providing a base for the visual arts and complementing the performing arts focus of the nearby Auditorium. "The concept of a great university as distinguished from a technical and professional school invariably emphasizes leadership in the realm of the cultural and humanistic," Hannah said. "Michigan State was founded in the new scientific tradition, and has made a name for itself in that area of intellectual activity. But it has always placed a strong emphasis upon the liberal arts and general education. . . . When Michigan State serves both the liberal and practical educational needs of the people of Michigan and the United States, it is doing no more than expected from a university. That it will be able to perform far more effectively in the future because of the generous gift is beyond any question." Artists exhibited in the first year of operation included Picasso, Rembrandt, Miró, Constable, and Daumier. Pieces by MSU faculty members Charles Pollock, Murray Jones, Louis Raynor, and Alma Goetsch were also featured.

The Issue of "Bigness"

With Michigan State's explosive growth in the aftermath of World War II came questions about the effectiveness of large educational institutions. Hannah addressed the bigness issue in a 1966 interview with William T. Noble of the *Detroit News*, stating, "A university must be big if it is to undertake the large and complicated research assignments, to insure high quality education in scientific fields. Small universities cannot afford the comprehensive library and tremendously expensive equipment today's teaching and research demand."

But what was "big" doing to the small-college atmosphere and rolling campus that alumni from early days still cherished? Were the traditions of the past quickly disappearing as new buildings rose and the numbers of students and faculty skyrocketed? Historian Kuhn's answer was yes. In a 1973 interview for the *MSU Alumni Magazine*, however, he suggested that Michigan State's traditions had begun to fade long before John Hannah assumed the presidency:

> The unity on campus began to disappear after 1900. It used to be that students one generation apart would take the same courses from the same professors, and that created a common bond which helped keep tradition intact. In the early 1920s we added many, many vocations—police administration, journalism and so on. This was a good thing, but it acted to sever the ties of tradition. As the university grew in the 1950s and 1960s President Hannah sought to preserve the tradition of a friendly campus by keeping class sizes down to a minimum. The huge lecture halls, so common to other universities, were seldom used other than for conventions. As enrollment increased, the number of classes multiplied, further fragmenting the campus. In consequence fewer and fewer students, for example, shared the same professors. . . . It used to be that everybody walked the same sidewalks. By the sixties, however, say a chemistry major may have never crossed the river in a year. We decentralized by pushing our residence halls out, by pushing our snack bars out, all of which is good, but we've lost unity and a coherent tradition.

Kuhn often argued that a strong university tradition attracted talented students and faculty, generated prestige, formed a basis for solid academic programs, and even made legislators more willing to give money. No matter how many more buildings were erected and no matter how scattered the campus became, he suggested, the university had to find ways both to preserve old traditions and to create new ones.

5

A Decade of Academic Achievement

EWLY ELECTED U.S. PRESIDENT DWIGHT D. EISENHOWER NEEDED a favor. On 31 December 1952, he telegraphed the Michigan State Board of Agriculture and asked to borrow John Hannah: Secretary of State designate Charles E. Wilson "and I have requested John A. Hannah to undertake the heavy responsibilities of Assistant Secretary of Defense for Manpower and Personnel. While I appreciate the importance of the commitment to you, I believe it would be most beneficial to the nation if you grant him sabbatical leave for one year while he assists in the difficult tasks of organization which lie ahead. I shall be personally grateful to be able to count on his support."

Hannah was willing to accept the president's offer. "I was too young for World War I and too old for World War II," dairy professor Malcolm Trout remembered Hannah saying. "I longed to do something for my country and President Eisenhower's invitation afforded me that opportunity." Hannah immediately contacted the board, informing them of his proposed federal responsibilities and recommending a new but temporary administrative structure for the college. He suggested that he continue as president, spending several days each month on campus and attending appropriation hearings and other key meetings, and that his salary be reduced to half the regular sabbatical rate. If his absence were to become detrimental to the college, he offered to return permanently to campus after giving reasonable notice to the secretary of defense and the president. Hannah suggested that the arrangement could benefit MSC by bringing the college worldwide attention and making him an even more qualified administrator. The board approved Hannah's proposal. Media rumors suggested that Hannah had originally been offered the post of secretary of agriculture but that he had declined because the

On 8 October 1953, while on leave from Michigan State and serving as an assistant secretary of defense, John Hannah received full honors on an official visit to the U.S. Naval Training Center in Bainbridge, Maryland. Courtesy of MSU Archives and Historical Collections.

job would have required at least a four-year commitment and he did not want to be away from MSC for that long.

Hannah was not allowed to leave East Lansing quietly. On 21 January 1953, more than 200 faculty members treated him to lunch in the Kellogg Center. Trout presented the president with a Spartan paperweight, while Faculty Women's Association president and communications skills instructor Beatrice Hartman gave two dozen roses to Sarah Hannah, the president's wife. A day later, students staged an even more elaborate send-off. "Goodbye Uncle John," the *State News* declared. "That was the sincere message in the hearts of more than 3,000 Michigan State College students who streamed into the Auditorium Wednesday evening for a 'surprise party' in honor of Pres. John Hannah." Hannah seemed genuinely shocked. "I was completely taken aback this evening when I was interrupted from my newspaper by the young men who called at the house to tell me of the surprise rally. I'm still amazed that anything so big as this could be planned with me on the campus and not be aware of it." Earlier that day, the MSC student body had received a telegram: "Please extend our best wishes to John Hannah, the new assistant secretary of defense designate. I regret taking him from you, but our country needs his services. Dwight Eisenhower, President of the United States."

RUNNING THE COLLEGE FROM WASHINGTON, D.C.

MSU education professor Richard Niehoff conducted extensive research related to Hannah's off-campus work, detailing his findings in a 1989 book, *John A. Hannah: Versatile Administrator and Distinguished Public Servant.* "During his eighteen months in Washington, Hannah did get back to the campus on most weekends and for Board meetings, graduation convocations and other special student and faculty events, a few 'critical' football games, and for other special events in which his participation was particularly important," Niehoff wrote. "He also arranged to have a special telephone hook-up to have almost instant access to the campus on his initiative or with one of his key colleagues to whom he had delegated broad responsibility for actions in his absence and to Board members who wished to consult with him. He also was visited in Washington by members of the Board and faculty to consult with him about University matters. He also responded to a large number of letters on University matters."

Hannah picked a five-member board of MSC administrators to run the college on a day-to-day basis during his sabbatical. Karl McDonel, James Denison, Tom King, William Combs, and Philip May were talented individuals and were also unquestionably loyal to the president. The head of the team, McDonel, was a graduate of Michigan Agricultural College, had joined the college's staff in 1916 as a farm extension specialist, had become assistant to the director of Extension Services in 1921, had earned a master's degree in 1931, and had succeeded Hannah as secretary to the board in 1941. "He was a faithful and loyal assistant to the President, who depended upon him for many services," Denison wrote. "His loyalty may have been more rigid than one might prescribe for an administrative staff member. He once told me that when he was appointed Secretary, he resolved

Education professor Richard Niehoff's 1989 book, *John A. Hannah: Versatile Administrator and Distinguished Public Servant*, is the most detailed look at Hannah's service with the Defense Department in the early 1950s. Courtesy of MSU Archives and Historical Collections.

When John Hannah briefly left MSC to become assistant secretary of defense, Board of Agriculture secretary Karl McDonel headed a five-member board of administrators that operated the college on a daily basis. Courtesy of MSU Archives and Historical Collections.

that he would never object to anything Mr. Hannah wanted to do. For many years, he was the university's 'lobbyist' in the Legislature, and was highly respected."

Denison had joined MSC in 1947 after working for the *Detroit Free Press* and as an assistant to Michigan governor Harry F. Kelly. Born in Mount Sterling, Ohio, he worked in the mechanical department of the *Mount Sterling Press* before learning the printing trade. Denison, Hannah's personal assistant and chief speechwriter, was protective of his boss, often lashing out against those who he believed offered unwarranted criticism. Hannah consultant Floyd Reeves once said of Denison, "No one did more educating of John Hannah than Jim Denison."

King, MSC's dean of students, had originally come to the school as an assistant football coach, and he later headed the police administration department and served as director of alumni relations and director of the placement and personnel service. "Tom King, probably because of his football background, could be tough as hell and sometimes would really scare a student who had broken university rules," former MSC football player Ed Klewicki once said. "But he also had lots of compassion for both students and his colleagues. He knew how to use the compassion and the toughness at just the right times and that made him a very effective administrator."

William Combs, Hannah's administrative assistant, served the university in many capacities, eventually becoming a dean and secretary of the faculties. According to Reeves, Combs was "called on to do many things he didn't want to do, many things when he was sick and could hardly stand. . . . He [was always] loyal to the University. He never hesitated to tell Hannah what he thought whether he liked it or not. . . . Combs was one of Hannah's greatest friends and greatest helpers."

Philip May had been an MSC administrator since 1947, specializing in financial matters. Earlier in his career, he was the auditor general of South Dakota, and during World War II he had been in charge of the army's overseas accounts division. Reeves's opinion of May differed sharply from the strong endorsements he gave Denison and Combs: said Reeves, May was "a man with whom I disagreed on almost everything. He did make a major contribution and yet history will tell whether he did more harm than good to this University. I just do not know. I am not able to judge—my guess is, he probably did more good than harm." Hannah apparently did not share Reeves's negative views of May, regularly consulting him on a wide range of financial issues.

PANTY RAIDS AND STUDENT UNREST

The team of five was quickly tested on the evening of 11 May 1953, when hundreds of students celebrated the arrival of spring with an eight-hour campus riot. What started out as a panty raid at Mason Hall soon became a rock-throwing melee that included stealing cows from university barns, tipping over canoes and their passengers in the Red Cedar River, and storming downtown East Lansing. More than thirty students were arrested. King quickly began expelling students involved in the mayhem, an action that would likely cost male students their student draft deferments. College administrators had previously kept the names of expelled students confidential but changed their policy this time. "We will release to the press the names of all men expelled from college because of this riot," King announced. Hannah paused from his duties as assistant secretary of defense and issued a statement condemning the riots. The *State News* also reacted negatively, running an unusual front-page editorial the next day under the headline "Mob Action Gives College Black Eye." Said the paper, "Doubtless, a number of Michigan men and women are wondering today just what kind of future citizens their state university is preparing." Panty raids and spring riots were not uncommon during the early 1950s. The same night that the MSC students rioted, one thousand Ohio State University students broke windows in women's dorms, pulled trolleys from buses, opened fire hydrants to flood the streets, and snake-danced down the aisles of a local theater.

Hannah returned to Lansing to address a student government banquet on 16 May and strongly voiced his frustrations and declared his embarrassment. He reminded students that the people of the state of Michigan spent millions of dollars supporting Michigan State. Such an incident "makes them doubt their investment. It creates a sour taste for those unfriendly critics not close to young people."

Tom King held many key posts at Michigan State, including assistant football coach, head of police administration, director of alumni relations, dean of students, and member of the board of administrators who ran the college when John Hannah was on leave to the U.S. Department of Defense in the early 1950s. Courtesy of MSU Archives and Collections.

Many of the college's administrators and faculty were also upset
by the students' behavior, particularly because state legislators would
undoubtedly remember the events when the time for appropriations
hearings arrived. Hannah and his staff often went out of their way
to project a positive image; their strategies ranged from providing
Michigan apples to guests in the stadium press box to making themselves available as speakers to hundreds of organizations throughout
the state. Addressing problems at both the college and the Defense
Department took its toll at times. Veteran journalist Elmer E. White
saw an exhausted Hannah at a Michigan Press Association dinner: "I
remember how ashen he was and how tired he looked. In fact, I was
afraid he would put his head on the table and go to sleep. I felt a deep
feeling of respect for the substantial effort and energy this man was
expending for the people of the state and the people of the nation. I
was delighted to see that once he was called upon, he became invigo-
rated and quite lively. Nonetheless, I always remember how terribly
tired he looked earlier in the evening." Hannah's Defense Department
assignment was extended an additional six months, and he returned
to campus full time at the end of July 1954.

Journalist White knew Hannah from 1937 to 1940, when White
was a student, and later when he served as executive secretary of the
Michigan Press Association. "Dr. Hannah was always extremely careful never to ask for anything which could remotely be considered a
favor from MPA or any member newspaper," he would recall. "Even
though he was sometimes grieved, or I suspect, angered at stories
in some of the state's newspapers, there was never any specific
effort to deal with the situation through our office. I suspect he was
uneasy working with newspaper people, which I always thought
was a shame, although I could understand why he had the feelings
he did. Most of Dr. Hannah's efforts were positive and gentle. I
believe he was appreciative of the opportunity MSC had to present
its accomplishments and its best points to newspaper leaders of
Michigan as they gathered at MPA meetings which were frequently
held on campus." Hannah sometimes consulted journalists about
what should be done to improve journalism training at Michigan
State. "In one of these personal talks with him, I cautioned Dr. Hannah that much work would be involved and perhaps university staff
members might not be willing to undertake the effort. I ventured the

thought that not all staff members worked hard. Dr. Hannah heaved a sigh and said something to this effect: 'I know about the workload of some college professors. A substantial number arrive late, leave early, take long lunch periods between frequent coffee breaks, and complain much of the rest of the time. And, if you quote me, I'll have to call you a liar.'"

THE NURSING PROGRAM

For the first year of the MSC nursing department, the program had only one faculty member, Florence Kempf, who according to the department's official history served as a teacher, counselor, administrator, admissions officer, publications director, and clinical supervisor. In September 1951, the college added an instructor in nursing arts and skills. Success came quickly: the first graduating class of ten students—Barbara Anderson, Patricia Bakke, Joyce Carlson, Marilynn Grigg, Mildred Heslip, Sara Johnson, Betty Klingelsmith, Margaret Morgan, Mildred Small, and Patricia Watkins—received the highest scores on the State Board Licensure Examination in that year. In 1964, when Kempf retired, forty-six students received their diplomas, the nursing department had become the School of Nursing, and the National League for Nursing Education had accredited the school.

Florence Kempf headed the college nursing department. Courtesy of MSU Archives and Historical Collections.

THE EVENING COLLEGE

The year 1951 also saw the MSC Evening College open, offering classes to anyone in the Lansing area who was interested in learning. Although the college had previously offered sporadic evening classes, the creation of the Evening College represented the first organized attempt to offer night classes. College officials had surveyed various Lansing industries for suggestions regarding community interests and consequently offered courses such as psychology of human behavior, hydraulics, public speaking, accounting, business methods, and engineering. Since many of the survey respondents worked in assembly plants such as Oldsmobile, Motor Wheel, Fisher Body, and

REO, the college at first featured numerous industry-related courses, although the offerings gradually became more recreational and intellectually oriented.

EXTENSION IN THE 1950s

While the Evening College was in its infancy, the Extension Service continued its longtime involvement with Michigan communities. According to the April 1952 *Michigan Courthouse Review*, "Michigan State College started an extension program prior to 1900 with 'Farmer's Institutes' and by 1914, when the Smith-Lever Act passed Congress establishing the cooperative extension program, the college had its program well-rooted." The Extension Service's Earl Richardson went on to explain the variety of services offered to more than 125,000 rural and urban adults and youth per year in the fields of agriculture and home economics. "The 4-H Club program is one of the most important phases of the Cooperative Extension Service. It serves more than 60,000 rural and urban youth from 10 to 21 years of age and provides education and incentives for learning better practices to 'Make The Best Better.' . . . [W]ork in home economics helps provide better nutrition and more home comfort and enjoyment for thousands of Michigan families. . . . [W]ork among farmers, which interprets the latest results of experimental work done by the Michigan Agricultural Experiment Stations, is responsible for millions of dollars of added income in the state."

WKAR TELEVISION

On 15 January 1954, WKAR-TV went on the air. The station was the third educational television station in the United States and the first east of the Mississippi River. The station was not the first in mid-Michigan, but WKAR offered a new type of programming, featuring detailed coverage of campus social life, news programs conducted by MSU faculty members, programs designed for farmers and agricultural educators, and credit courses such as salesmanship and interpretation of dramatic literature. At least one program, Don

Buell's *Curtain Going Up*, perhaps the country's first theater news show, piggybacked off a similar program on WKAR Radio.

The *State Journal* described the new station's facilities for its readers:

Armand L. Hunter (*left*), the first director of WKAR-TV, and Les Hareus (*center*), producer-director of the *MSU Medical Forum*, receive a certificate for meritorious service from the president of the Ingham County Medical Society.
Courtesy of WKAR Television.

> Operating on ultra-high frequency channel 60, the station is expected to cover an area of 13,000 square miles in the central Michigan area. Programs originate in the campus studios located on Kalamazoo st. just east of Harrison rd. in the old quonset cafeteria building. The old cafeteria has been converted into a modern studio in the past several months and now houses two large (40 by 50 feet) studios and a medium sized (20 by 25 feet) studio, control rooms, 10 staff offices, conference rooms and various special facilities for film, editing and projection, art work and set construction. From the elaborate studios the program is carried by micro-wave to the station transmitter located on Dobey rd. near Okemos where the WKAR-TV antenna is

Key members of WKAR's radio team pose for a photo in 1952: (*back row, standing*) J. Kenneth Richards, Howard Hass, Robert Shackleton, John Chandler, and William Finucan; (*front row, sitting*) Robert Coleman, Mary Collopy, and Lawrence Frymire. Courtesy of WKAR Radio.

located. The new transmitter has an output of 243 kilowatts, which combined with the 1,034-foot height of the antenna gives the station an operating radius of 65 miles from the tower.

Belying such bold rhetoric, however, few people could receive the station's signal: most television sets of the day lacked UHF tuners. According to Bob Page, an early worker at the station and later WKAR's general manager, staffers joked about the fact that even President Hannah could not receive the signal at his official residence, Cowles House. Moreover, despite being housed in converted Quonset huts that had previously served as a cafeteria, the station was considered a state-of-the-art facility—the National Association of Educational Broadcasters held workshops there, using WKAR as a model for nascent stations. Recalled Page, "Believe it or not, when the stations in the Quonsets first opened, it was considered phenomenal for the university to provide this elaborate building with three studios."

The new station's director was Armand L. Hunter, a television industry pioneer who had already been at work on the station for nearly
three years. He had previously been the radio and television coordinator at Temple University and had served as educational director of
Philadelphia's WFIL-AM and -FM radio. The impressive staff that
Hunter assembled for the new station included operations manager
James Davis, an assistant professor in the speech department known
for his work in the college's summer high school speech institute;
chief engineer Linn P. Towsley, who had received extensive training
in technical communications as a radio engineer with WKAR Radio;
production manager James B. Tintera, who brought experience as a
speech instructor, had been a radio station manager for the armed
forces during World War II, and had done Ford Foundation research
in television production; and program manager J. Kenneth Richards,
an employee of WKAR Radio for twelve years who had attended the
NBC Radio and Television Institute in Chicago and had served as
radio chair for Michigan's Congress of Parents and Teachers.

THE HIGHWAY TRAFFIC CENTER

Another pioneering effort began in 1955 when the legislature appropriated $177,500 to Michigan State to open a Highway Traffic
Center. Legislators had become concerned about the high death rate
on the state's highways—an estimated two thousand in 1955—and
were responding to a 1951–53 MSC study regarding colleges' and
universities' role in promoting traffic safety. The study proposed a
variety of measures, including preparing more students for careers
in traffic administration and increased training of driver-education
teachers in public schools. The new program was billed as the most
comprehensive in the country, taking a multifaceted approach to
traffic safety rather than offering only isolated solutions to the
problem. "Naturally, our prime objective is to educate motor vehicle
drivers," said Gordon Sheehe, the center's first director, a nationally
respected traffic-safety expert who had taught political science at
the University of Washington and had served as a Vermont state
highway officer. "If we can, through any one or all of the various
programs we have available, educate individual drivers and change

Ralph Turner had a degree in chemistry from the University of Southern California and had worked as a criminalist for the Kansas City Police Department. Turner and other respected faculty members helped to provide international prestige to Arthur Brandstatter's police administration department. Courtesy of MSU Archives and Historical Collections.

the mental attitude of those drivers usually found, after thorough investigation, to be at fault in accidents, we will be able to bring the number of traffic accidents down substantially." The center opened in January 1956 with five staff members, ten graduate student research assistants, and adjunct faculty from such departments as urban planning, police administration, mechanical engineering, political science, and radio and television. The traffic center and WKAR Radio collaborated in 1957 on *You Are the Jury*, a fifteen-minute weekly program dedicated to promoting traffic safety. Thirty-four Michigan radio stations carried the program, which earned WKAR a Peabody Award for broadcasting excellence, the first university radio station to receive such an award since 1942.

THE POLICE ADMINISTRATION DEPARTMENT

Sheehe was not the only talented faculty member that Arthur Brandstatter, chair of the police administration department, recruited to Michigan State. Ralph Turner held a degree in chemistry from the University of Southern California and had worked as a criminalist and laboratory technician for the Kansas City Police Department. Attorney Robert Scott had served as a judge in the state of New York. Albert Germann had earned his doctorate while serving as an officer with the Los Angeles Police Department. And Louis Radelet taught at the University of Notre Dame, conducted research for a welfare department, and worked as an administrator for the National Council of Christians and Jews. Because of the leadership of these five men and others in his department, Brandstatter believed police administration at Michigan State enjoyed both a national and international reputation by the 1950s. He cited the development of the undergraduate security curriculum in 1955, the sponsoring of police-community relations institutes in 1955, the establishment of the Highway Traffic Safety Center, international efforts such as the development of a training program for German police officers that began in the early 1950s, the establishment of a statewide training program for Michigan police officers, and the approval in 1956 of a master's degree program. Brandstatter also liked to point out that Daisy Kim of Honolulu became the department's first woman graduate in 1951.

THE HONORS COLLEGE

In 1955, the State Board of Agriculture approved the establishment of an Honors College at Michigan State, the first such program in the country. "The danger has grown, since the advent of mass university education, that the talents of the superior student will become lost in the vast educational process," academic vice president Thomas Hamilton said in announcing the new concept. Students who completed their freshman or sophomore year with a 3.5 average would be relieved of all graduation requirements except for total credit hours and would be permitted to work with an adviser to create a special program of study. Opportunities included earning course credit by examination only and by independent study, the waiving of prerequisites for advanced courses, enrollment in graduate courses and special seminars, graduate- and faculty-level library privileges, and even an Honors College lounge. Michigan State's Honors College opened in the fall of 1957 under the direction of Professor Stanley Idzerda. Only 9 of the 319 eligible students chose not to join. Idzerda stressed that honors students would not be separated from other classmates as an elite group and should not be stereotyped as bookworms. They would continue to live in dormitories, fraternities, and sororities and would lead normal student lives. "It is assumed that the Honors College graduate will have mastered on graduation more subject matter both within and without his field of specialization than will other graduates," Hamilton told the *Michigan State University Magazine.* "He will be more alive to intellectual concerns, more skilled in analysis, more comprehensive in judgment, and more cognizant of the responsibility of talent."

The concept met with success. When Hannah wrote his memoirs in the late 1970s, he praised the Honors College. "This program did much to enhance the reputation of Michigan State as a distinguished educational institution. The Honors College did not in any way derogate or denigrate other programs designed for students proceeding in the regular curricula at the average rate. The presence on the campus of numbers of extremely bright students not only did much to raise internal morale, but served notice beyond the campus that the university in East Lansing was indeed a high quality university, one whose graduates could compete effectively with any from the

Stanley Idzerda served as the first director of Michigan State's Honors College. Courtesy of MSU Archives and Historical Collections.

best universities of the world." Two decades later, Provost Lou Anna K. Simon expressed similar sentiments to the *MSU Alumni Magazine* when she stated, "The Honors College historically has contributed greatly to the distinction and distinctiveness of Michigan State."

THE LABOR AND INDUSTRIAL RELATIONS CENTER

The idea of a Labor and Industrial Relations Center was also proposed in 1955. At the recommendation of Vice President Durward Varner, who had chaired a special committee to investigate the possibilities for such a center, the State Board of Agriculture directed the university to begin operations on 1 January 1956. Charles Killingsworth became the center's first director and set about hiring faculty members. One of the first men hired was Daniel Kruger, a young University of Alabama scholar who came to Michigan State's attention when he gave a talk on "Business, Ethics, and Economics" at the Harvard Business School. Recalled Kruger,

> When I got through with the talk, a man came up to the podium named Dalton McFarland, a professor of management at Michigan State University. He said, "I was impressed with your remarks. You belong at Michigan State University because we are starting a labor and industrial center. You'd be a very valuable addition." I thanked him very much and told him I couldn't possibly leave the University of Alabama since the fall term was to begin shortly. I was relatively content at the University of Alabama, except for an important event. An able black woman, Autherine Lucy, wanted to enroll at the University of Alabama in Tuscaloosa, but then Governor George Wallace said that no blacks could ever attend the University of Alabama. To me that was devastating. It made me mad. Here was a major conflict between my personal values and the organizational values of the University of Alabama. I said to myself, "I can't stay here."

In October 1956, Kruger accepted Killingsworth's offer of a job and soon became one of the country's most respected authorities in the field of labor and industrial relations.

The institute initially faced challenges from conservative legislators and business leaders who accused Michigan State of favoring labor over management. One of the most dramatic confrontations came on 20 September 1961, when Hannah appeared before the Special Senate Committee to Investigate the Labor and Industrial Relations Center at Michigan State University. Hannah pointed out that the institute had been unanimously approved by the State Board of Agriculture, which included businessmen such as retired Chrysler Corporation chair Forest Akers, furniture manufacturer Frederick Mueller, and merchant Arthur Rouse. Michigan State's president argued that university schools such as education, engineering, and agriculture offered both undergraduate and graduate courses for leaders of business and industry. And he concluded that establishing the Labor and Industrial Relations Center was consistent with providing educational services to "all of the people of Michigan, rich and poor alike, farmers, factory workers, businessmen, shopkeepers, teachers—all of those who go to make up our complex society." The university's services to management, he added, "far outweigh services to labor unions." The institute survived.

Michigan State's agricultural heritage remained strong in the 1950s. In a decade that saw more and more Americans leaving farms and declining enrollments at agricultural schools, Michigan State's College of Agriculture was growing. By 1956, 1,573 undergraduate students had enrolled, making it the nation's fourth-largest agricultural school, trailing only Iowa State University, Cornell University, and Ohio State University. Agriculture remained a growth industry— according to one estimate, 15,000 agriculture-related jobs awaited college graduates every year, even though the nation's agricultural schools produced only 8,500 graduates annually. Most of these opportunities, however, were not in direct farming. A 1953 study of more than 5,000 Michigan State graduates in agriculture indicated that 25 percent were employed in agricultural business or industry, 24 percent worked in public agricultural service, 13 percent taught, 11 percent farmed, and 3 percent conducted agricultural research. Another 24 percent served in the armed forces or worked in fields not related to agriculture. "The trend is toward fewer on the farms but more in the business of serving agriculture," the *Michigan State University Magazine* reported in 1957. "This has increased interest in

Harry Kimber overcame doubters in his efforts to establish a religion department. Courtesy of MSU Archives and Historical Collections.

business training in the agricultural programs. Likewise, there is increased concern at Michigan State with the building up of courses in food technology, agricultural marketing, food storage and handling, and packaging. For today, the cost of packaging some food items is greater than for the raw product as purchased from the farmer."

RELIGIOUS STUDIES

Another growing area of study at Michigan State was religion. Although religion classes had been taught for many years at Michigan State, a specific academic department was not established until 1948. Skeptics at first nicknamed the department "Kimber's Folly," doubting that Professor Harry Kimber's idea would attract many students. But the naysayers were wrong: more than five hundred men and women enrolled in the department's offerings during the first year. The early classes were taught by local religious leaders (usually unpaid), such as Catholic priests Cecil Winters and Jerome MacEachin, Protestant ministers Newell McCune and Gordon Jones, and Rabbi Philip Frankel. By 1957, enrollment in religious department classes had increased to nearly two thousand students. Two other changes were also apparent. The curriculum was broadened from an emphasis on Christianity and Judaism to include courses from religions around the world. In addition, regular faculty members gradually replaced unpaid lecturers.

ALUMNI RELATIONS

With enrollment increasing each year and consequently larger graduating classes, the Office of Alumni Relations faced continuing pressure to increase its services. Between 1948 and 1958, the number of active alumni clubs had grown from thirty to more than one hundred. Opened around 1915, the alumni organization had first been located in a trolley shack opposite the Abbott Road entrance to campus. The office was then relocated to Barrows House on Faculty Row before moving to the Union in 1925. When the Student Services Building was constructed in 1957, alumni association director Starr Keesler and his staff moved into the new structure. Keesler thought the expanded space would provide improved services to all alumni, but he was especially excited about the new mailing room in the basement. The alumni office had fifty-seven thousand names on its mailing list in 1958, and Keesler saw a state-of-the-art mailing center as essential to communicating with members who lived all over the world.

FACULTY CHANGES

Beginning in 1951, the college presented annual Distinguished Faculty Awards to faculty members who had made outstanding contributions in teaching or research. Winners in the 1950s included English professor David Dickson, engineering professor Oscar Fairbanks, physical education professor King McCristal, agriculture professor Boyd Churchill, mechanical engineering professor James Anderson, speech professor Donald Buell, history professor Arthur Adams, education professor John Hanson, and humanities professor Austin Moore.

During the 1950s, Michigan State saw the retirements of many of its longtime faculty members and administrators—men and women who had worked side by side with John Hannah in transforming the institution. In 1987, former East Lansing Historical Society president Robert Gianettino wrote about one of the most important of the retiring college leaders, Lloyd Emmons. "He came to wear his title of 'Dean' as imperiously as any ruling monarch. He was termed 'arrogant' in his convictions that his goals, beliefs, and decisions were right as they affected his college, his church, his community, and his family. A granddaughter once said, 'He had an ego the size of Rhode Island.' Yet, despite such pomposity, a valid argument can be made that he was more influential than any single individual in the developments on both sides of Grand River Avenue during his lifetime." Pompous or not, Emmons bore responsibility for many of Hannah's key academic, athletic, and administrative projects. Emmons had been named dean of liberal arts in 1934, had chaired the Athletic Council from 1945 to 1952, had developed the college's registration system, had served as acting director of the museum, and had even authored an advanced algebra textbook.

History professor Arthur Adams received a Distinguished Faculty Award in the 1950s for his outstanding work in the classroom. Courtesy of MSU Archives and Historical Collections.

Well-respected soil science professor George Bouyoucous numbered among the numerous long-serving faculty members who retired during the 1950s. Courtesy of MSU Archives and Historical Collections.

Another dean, Ernest Anthony, ended four decades of service to the college in 1953. He had arrived at MSC in 1928 and had served as dean of agriculture since 1933, playing prominent roles in almost all aspects of agricultural education and overseeing tremendous growth, especially in the faculty, which had increased from one hundred to five hundred members. "The outstanding experience in my life has been helping this growing institution for a quarter of a century," Anthony told the *Michigan State News.*

George Bouyoucous had served on Michigan State's faculty since 1911, becoming the school's longest-serving full-time employee before retiring as a research professor in soil science in 1957. A native of Likohia, Greece, with an international reputation for his research in automatic moisture control, Bouyoucous had invented a device for the automatic control of irrigation systems that was used in thirty countries. He did extensive agricultural work in Greece and was awarded the Cross of our Savior by the country's king. Retiring at the same time was Nevels Pearson, a faculty member since 1922 who had served for many years as the director of the horse and dairy programs of the state 4-H clubs. He also was a leader in the formation of the junior livestock show in Detroit as well as a popular speaker who often served as a goodwill ambassador between MSU and the Michigan farming community.

Shao Chang Lee retired from the faculty in 1959. A native of Kwantung Province, China, Lee had arrived at MSC in 1943 to head its international studies program. "He created a two-way understanding that benefited both students from abroad and students in this country who learned about each other's ways," Dean Glen Taggart said of Lee. With Lee's arrival, Taggart continued, "the university started taking on a new global significance." A voracious reader, a book collector, and the writer of a Chinese-language history of the United States, Lee donated his collection of history books to the Michigan State library. "I think the extensive international make-up of our faculty and of our students is a strength of our university," English professor Russel Nye once said. "Lots of people like to take credit for that. But, I think it was all started years ago by a man named S. C. Lee."

Margaret Harris, an associate professor in the Extension Service, also retired in the late 1950s. A 1923 MAC graduate, she joined the extension faculty in 1926 and was known for her leadership in home economics in Michigan's Upper Peninsula. Other Extension Service staff who retired at the same time included Leona MacLeod, who had come to MSC in 1934 and had served as assistant director in charge of home economics programs, and H. D. Hootman, a member of the extension staff since 1917 and former superintendent of the campus orchards and gardens.

E. E. Kinney said good-bye to the university after twenty-four years on the electrical engineering faculty and twelve as superintendent of buildings. On one occasion, according to the *MSU Reporter*, "an officer in the M.S.U. Military Department once issued an order that if the flag was flying from the pole in front of Demonstration Hall the following morning, all cadets were to report for a parade. During the night the flag rope was cut. That might have been the end of the parade—but the officer made a phone call and a little while later a wiry man was scaling the 120-foot pole to attach a new rope. 'Didn't have time to wait for a professional,' said Kinney. 'You might say I reached the top at Michigan State.'" Kinney apparently approached most of his assignments with similar dedication and a good sense of humor—describing the wild animals that made their way into the campus's buildings, he listed bats, squirrels, raccoons, "and, of course, . . . the wolves that get into the girls' dormitories."

Stanley Crowe joined the faculty in 1909 as an instructor in mathematics, becoming dean of students in the 1940s. He was most famous, however, as the longtime head of the Lecture-Concert Series, a position in which he was responsible for bringing a wide range of world-class entertainers to the campus. Many newspapers covered his retirement in 1956, and he talked to the *State Journal* about television's effect on live performances on the Michigan State campus. "People often are interested in seeing stars or artists in person whom they have seen on television," he said. "But at the same time, a major TV production can cut into attendance of a live performance if both take place the same night." Crowe told the *Grand Rapids Herald* about the time a prominent maestro became infuriated when someone took his photograph during a live performance. The program had to be halted until the film was surrendered. Crowe also remembered the time lecturer Lowell Thomas requested that his campus appearance be scheduled for the same day as the Michigan–Michigan State football game so that Thomas could attend. Other retirees in the late

Stanley Crowe's tenure included stints as a mathematics instructor, as dean of students, and as director of the Lecture-Concert Series, a position that left him with numerous anecdotes regarding the celebrities who had performed on campus. Courtesy of Michigan State University Archives and Historical Collections.

Liberty Hyde Bailey became famous as a scientist at Cornell University but always remained loyal to MSC, from which he had graduated, visiting campus, donating books to the library, and taking time to advise younger faculty. Courtesy of Michigan State University Archives and Historical Collections.

1950s included Robert Linton, who served as registrar from 1939 to 1956 when he became secretary of the faculties; Ralph Tenny, who had been head of short courses for thirty-five years and had served as director of Farmer's Week; mechanical engineering department chair Leonard Price; and longtime athletic trainer Jack Heppinstall.

The 1950s also saw the death of a number of other veteran faculty members. Museum director Joseph Stack died in 1954. He had joined the college faculty as a zoology instructor, becoming a museum curator in 1924 and museum director in 1941. Stack was known for his creations of groupings of wild animals placed in their natural settings and for starting one of the nation's first bird-banding stations. He was also recognized for his articles about birds and their importance to agriculture.

In early 1958, Harold Tukey traveled to Cornell University in Ithaca, New York, to honor another famous horticulturist, Liberty Hyde Bailey, on the one-hundredth anniversary of his birth. Bailey, who had died three years earlier and was often referred to as the dean of American horticulture, had graduated from State in 1882 and taught there for several years before leaving for Cornell to become the chair of the practical and experimental horticulture department. Tukey, who still used Bailey's old desk, said of his old friend, "Those in the fruit culture think of him as a fruit man. Amateur horticulturists think of him as their special leader. Agricultural administrators think of him as a dean. Taxonomic botanists think of him as the great authority on palms and the classification and nomenclature of horticultural crops. Nurserymen think of him as plant propagator. In short, his interests were so great, and his coverage so broad, that he stood as a dozen men—helpful, interested, and a marvelous friend to all."

Some refused to leave. Ernst A. Bessey, for example, had officially retired in 1944 as head of the botany department and dean of the graduate school, but into his eighties he could still be found at his desk in Berkey Hall. First at the U.S. Department of Agriculture and later at Michigan State, Bessey's career had combined both adventure and academics. He conducted agricultural studies in both the Caucasus and Turkistan and in 1903 traveled to Russia on an agricultural expedition with his father, Charles Bessey, an 1869 State Agricultural College graduate. He was instrumental in organizing the graduate school and was proficient in French, Latin, Italian, Dutch, Spanish, and Russian. He even read agricultural papers in Romanian, Bulgarian, and Afrikaans. After Bessey's death in 1957 at the age of eighty, a group of MSU faculty members wrote to Hannah to urge that the natural science building be named in Bessey's honor, describing him as "known both nationally and internationally as an outstanding botanist and an authority in his special field of mycology" and as having "the respect and affection of all who knew him as a man of integrity and large humanity." The Bessey name did not go on the natural science building, but the 1961 classroom and office structure built on Farm Lane across from the Auditorium was named Bessey Hall.

The departure of so many faculty members opened the way for new professors who came to play prominent roles. Thelma Porter succeeded College of Home Economics dean Marie Dye in 1956. A 1921 MAC graduate and a national nutrition expert, Porter had headed the home economics department at the University of Chicago before being appointed head of the same department at MSC in 1944. In 1947, MSC conferred on Porter an honorary doctorate of science degree. In 1955, Frances DeLisle was appointed the first director of the women's division of the Dean of Students' Office, a position in which she bore responsibility for all campus women's activities, including residence hall programs, sororities, and the Associated Women Students organization. She had joined the faculty as a guidance counselor in 1947 and had earned her doctorate in 1953. Clifford Erickson, who had been serving as dean of the Basic College, became the first full-time dean of the new College of Education in 1953. Fifty years later, education professor Walter Johnson described Erickson as "the most important person in the history of the College of Education," with "tremendous energy and ideas." Erickson subsequently served as provost from 1961 until his death in 1963. Erickson's widow, Mildred, later became an authority on the education of older students while serving as assistant dean of lifelong-education programs at MSU.

Gordon A. Sabine arrived in East Lansing in 1955, becoming dean of the newly created College of Communication Arts. Sabine possessed an extensive background in classroom, administrative, and practical experiences. He had earned his doctorate from the University of Minnesota; had taught journalism at the University of Wisconsin, the University of Kansas, and the University of

Thelma Porter became dean of the College of Home Economics in 1956. Courtesy of MSU Archives and Historical Collections.

The last remaining dean to predate John Hannah's assumption of the Michigan State presidency, Marie Dye, retired in 1956. Courtesy of MSU Archives and Historical Collections.

A tough but fair and innovative administrator, Gordon A. Sabine arrived on the Michigan State campus in 1955 and remained until 1972. Courtesy of MSU Archives and Historical Collections.

Minnesota; and had served as dean of the University of Oregon's journalism school since 1950. He also had worked as a reporter for several newspapers; had written articles for the *Saturday Evening Post*, *Better Homes and Gardens*, and *Esquire*; and had served as editor of *Wisconsin Wildlife*. While at Michigan State, Sabine received several key assignments from Hannah and the school's other presidents. Gordon Guyer joined Michigan State's entomology faculty in 1953 and ten years later became the department's chair. He subsequently served as director of the Extension Service, associate dean of the College of Agriculture and Natural Resources, and president of Michigan State University.

Another newcomer during the 1950s was Thomas Hale Hamilton, who had worked his way through DePauw University in a variety of jobs, including soda jerk, part-time accountant, dance-band drummer, and operator of a dry-cleaning business. While at graduate school at the University of Chicago in the early 1940s, he worked as a linotype estimator for Lakeside Press and as an inspector for the Chicago Better Business Bureau. Hamilton earned his doctorate in 1947 and served as vice president of Chatham College before accepting Hannah's offer to become assistant dean of the Basic College in 1953. An "academic dynamo," Hamilton wrote numerous books and articles related to education. He became dean of the Basic College in 1954 and Michigan State's vice president for academic affairs in 1956.

A TRAINING GROUND FOR COLLEGE AND UNIVERSITY PRESIDENTS

Many people came to Michigan State as students or educators and left to assume presidencies at other educational institutions. In 1953, for example, Gus Turbeville, who had earned a doctorate at Michigan State, became president of Northland College in Ashland, Wisconsin. Although Northland had only 228 students, a far cry from the 21,000 students on the East Lansing campus, Turbeville saw similarities between the two schools: "To me the most remarkable thing about Michigan State University is that in spite of its enormous size it still has much of the friendly smaller college atmosphere," he told the *Michigan State University Magazine* in 1956. "I hope that Michigan State will never lose that priceless asset."

Arthur Knoblauch received a master's degree from MSC in 1929 before going on to earn a master's degree from the University of Michigan in 1933 and a doctorate in education from Harvard University in 1942. He became superintendent of schools in Cassopolis, Michigan, before joining the faculty of the University of Connecticut. He became president of Moorhead State Teachers College in Minnesota in 1955 and then assumed the presidency of Western Illinois University three years later. According to the Western Illinois Web site, "President Knoblauch took the university through the turbulent times with a spurt of construction, growth and development, expanding the institution's foundation from a teachers college into a comprehensive public university." He received Michigan State's Distinguished Alumni Award in 1960.

Clifford Hardin came to MSC in 1944 to teach agricultural economics and became director of the Agricultural Experiment Station in 1949 and dean of agriculture in 1953. A year later, he left the college to serve as chancellor of the University of Nebraska, and he subsequently served as President Richard Nixon's secretary of labor. Hardin's colleague in the agricultural economics department, Robert C. Kramer, earned a doctorate at MSC in 1952 and subsequently held several key agricultural positions at Michigan State before leaving in 1965 to become vice president of California State Poly Tech College, eventually becoming its president. Harold E. Sponberg, who earned a doctorate at MSC in 1952, headed the college's Extension Service before becoming vice president of Northern Michigan University in 1956. He later served as president of Washburn University and of Eastern Michigan University.

Edgar Harden joined the Michigan State College faculty in 1946 as an associate professor at the Institute of Counseling, Testing, and Guidance. He later was dean of continuing education, and in 1956 he became the sixth president of Northern Michigan University, serving until 1967. In 1977 he became Michigan State's interim president, filling the job until the university selected a permanent successor to Clifton Wharton. According to Northern Michigan University historian Russell Magnaghi, "In the legislature [Harden] out-did his mentor, Dr. John Hannah, the president of Michigan State University, with his budgets. When questioned about their size, he said he was merely seeking what was best for the people of the Upper Peninsula. . . .

Edgar Harden joined the MSC faculty in 1946 before becoming president of Northern Michigan University. Courtesy of MSU Archives and Historical Collections.

"Academic dynamo" Thomas Hamilton served as dean of the Basic College then academic vice president before becoming president of the University of Hawaii. Courtesy of MSU Archives and Historical Collections.

[D]uring his tenure the budget went from $914,376 to $5,140,342. . . . Harden was open to students and faculty. His office was on the first floor of Kaye Hall, and anyone could see him. He knew every faculty member and what they were doing. One time when the state could not meet the payroll, Harden took out a personal loan and the staff and students got paid."

Paul Miller served as a professor of sociology and anthropology and subsequently as Michigan State's provost during the 1950s before assuming the presidency of his alma mater, West Virginia University, in 1961, where he deserves credit for much of the university's modern development. James W. Miller (no relation to Paul) came to Michigan State as a political science instructor in 1940 and later served as secretary of the Board of Trustees before becoming president of Western Michigan University in 1961, serving for thirteen years and establishing a reputation as a champion of the arts.

Michigan State vice president Thomas Hamilton left to become chancellor of the State University of New York system in 1959 before moving on four years later to serve as president of the University of Hawaii. According to Susan Kreifels of the *Honolulu Star-Bulletin*, Hamilton "led UH through the boom years of higher education across the nation. Under his 1963–1968 leadership, new buildings soared and enrollment doubled." Hamilton was a Hannah favorite who often described the University of Hawaii with a phrase also used in reference to Michigan State: "an empire on which the concrete never set." Hamilton later became head of the Hawaii Visitors Bureau.

Lawrence Boger received his doctorate from MSC in 1950, served as chair of the agricultural economics department, and later became dean of the College of Agricultural and Natural Resources. For nearly twenty years, other universities found Boger an attractive presidential candidate, but Michigan State retained him until 1977, when he became the fourteenth president of Oklahoma State University, a position he held until his retirement in 1988. According to his official OSU biography, under Boger's administration, "more than a dozen new buildings were constructed, student enrollments peaked at more than 23,000 and capital expenditures exceeded $200 million. . . . He is credited with preparing OSU for the information age. . . . Dr. Lawrence Boger was a gentle, caring, generous, compassionate individual. He was a calm and effective leader. He commanded great respect and loyalty from his staff. . . . He was a university president in the classical sense. . . . The world is a better place for his having stopped here."

THE FIFTIES, A DECADE OF MEMORIES

The 1950s produced fond student memories of Michigan State. Patricia Foster, for example, a graduate of East Lansing High School, did not have to go far to earn her bachelor's degree in education in 1952. She loved education and eventually did her student teaching in Lansing and DeWitt. "We had a university bus that would pick us up on campus," she recalled in the Spring 2002 issue of the *New Educator*, published by Michigan State's College of Education. "I remember that my father would drive me in early, like at 6:30 in the morning, to catch the bus, which didn't make him too happy. But we had to get an early start and get to school by 8:00." Another student, Sally Jackson, arrived on campus in 1948 with the dream of becoming an actress but soon switched to elementary education. "Michigan State was a great experience and I had a lot of wonderful teachers," she said. "The class sizes were small and it was a very happy time." In a sign of the times, however, Jackson was required to swear that she was not a communist before she was permitted to graduate. Max Raines had come to Michigan State in 1948 to work on his doctorate and study under education professor Walter F. Johnson. Raines left but returned to MSU in 1965, serving on the education faculty until his retirement in 1993. He recalled Johnson and other faculty members, including Wilbur Brookover, Clyde Campbell, and Clifford Erickson, as "brilliant." In contrast, what Joanne Wheaton remembered about Michigan State during the early 1950s was the significant amount of construction. As a freshman, Wheaton lived in Gilchrist Hall, which "was great because it was brand new." In addition, she and her friends were impressed by the World War II veterans on campus: "That was a big deal for us little freshmen at the time. None of us wanted to go out with guys our age. We wanted to date the veterans—and one of them turned out to be my husband, Paul."

Tom and Julie Ruhala were also students in the early 1950s. Tom, who later would become a member of MSU's social work faculty, chose Michigan State over the University of Michigan because "the

Lawrence Boger, a key agricultural administrator at Michigan State from the mid-1950s until the mid-1970s, went on to become president of Oklahoma State University. Courtesy of MSU Archives and Historical Collections.

A male student helps a coed with her coat at a 1950 dance. Courtesy of MSU Archives and Historical Collections.

campus was so beautiful." He then talked his future wife, a friend since the seventh grade, into also attending. "We virtually lived in the Union, eating in the grill, playing cards on the third floor and attending dances in the ballroom," Tom remembered. The Ruhalas were socially active, dancing and partying at places such as the Deer Head and the Coral Gables. Tom said that men wanting to impress their dates might splurge and take them to Dines Restaurant in Lansing, but parents were more likely to be entertained at East Lansing's Mary Lee Tea Room. "Everybody seemed to have fake IDs in those days," Tom said. "Students also sneaked beers into dorm rooms by putting them in the bushes and then passing them though the windows. I can also remember students renting nearby farmers' fields and then building fires for their parties." Other common student activities of the time included attending the Water Carnival, warming themselves in front of bonfires at rallies at Landon Field or Demonstration Hall before football games, and hanging out at the Union grill. Julie Ruhala, who later became director of Lutheran Social Services in

Campus activities could be elaborate events in the 1950s, as evidenced by this photograph of students decorating for a 1959 dance. Courtesy of MSU Archives and Historical Collections.

Lansing, remembered some of the old campus legends. "For example, you were not officially an MSC coed until you were kissed in the shadows of Beaumont Tower at midnight," she said. "I also remember that it was said that the tallest piece on the spire on Beaumont Tower represented the only virgin on campus." One of Tom Ruhala's favorite memories was the time a fake plane crash at his fraternity, Delta Psi of Kappa Sigma, became the talk of the college. Ruhala and his fraternity brothers discovered a two-seat engineless World War II plane owned by a local bar owner, who had planned to install the plane on the bar's roof and call it the Crash Bar but had never done so. The fraternity bought the plane for forty dollars and placed it in front of the fraternity house to make it look like it had crashed into the structure. They then placed a dummy in the pilot's seat, sprinkled it with ketchup, and added a sign that read, "He rushed Kappa Sigma but didn't quite make it."

Picnics such as this one in 1957 were frequently held on campus during warm weather. Courtesy of MSU Archives and Historical Collections.

THE KELLOGG BIOLOGICAL RESEARCH STATION AND OAKLAND UNIVERSITY

The Kellogg Foundation and Matilda and Alfred G. Wilson made significant donations to Michigan State during the early 1950s. In 1953, Kellogg presented MSC with a thirty-two-acre estate that had formerly been the summer home of cereal magnate W. K. Kellogg. Located twelve miles from Battle Creek, the property included a thirty-nine-room manor house, a guesthouse, a six-car garage, chauffeur's quarters, and a greenhouse, providing the college with extensive new facilities for both education and research. The foundation also granted the school forty-five thousand dollars to purchase equipment and remodel the buildings. The property adjoined a fifteen-hundred-acre tract of land that Kellogg had given the college in 1930. The

Pep rallies remained popular during most of the Hannah era, as at this gathering the night before the 1957 football game against Purdue. Courtesy of MSU Archives and Historical Collections.

site eventually became the university's largest off-campus education complex and today houses a bird sanctuary, biological laboratories, and a conference center.

In 1957, the Wilsons gave the university two million dollars in cash and a fourteen-hundred-acre Oakland County estate, Meadow Brook Farms, valued at more than $8 million. Discussions immediately began about creating a four-year branch college on the property. On 8 October 1958, Hannah outlined his thoughts on the future Oakland University in a letter to Ford Foundation president Henry T. Heald:

It seems to me that this is one of the greatest educational opportunities available anywhere in the country. This property is mid-point between the west boundary of Oakland County and

John Hannah and Matilda Wilson participate in the groundbreaking ceremony for Oakland University on 2 May 1958. Matilda Wilson and her husband, Alfred G. Wilson, had donated their fourteen-hundred-acre estate for the new school.
Courtesy of MSU Archives and Historical Collections.

the west boundary of Macomb County, both of which are located immediately adjacent to Wayne County (Detroit) on the north. Both counties are caught up in the great population move out of Detroit to the north, and currently the combined population is around one million. By 1970 it is estimated this figure shall move very close to two million. . . . [I]n neither of the two counties is there a single educational institution beyond high school except for a very small community college which began two years ago in southeast Macomb County. . . . Our population experts estimate that within a

15-mile radius of the new campus we now have 50,000 college-age
youngsters, and that this figure shall be practically doubled within
the next 10 years.

The budding university had a program-development committee that
included what Hannah described as some of the "best thinking"
in America—committee chair James Zeder, the vice president of
Chrysler; General Motors president John Gordon; Ford Motor Company vice president Theodore Yntema; and Elizabeth Gossett, wife
of Ford's legal vice president. Hannah pointed out that educational
programs would be developed with the "full realization that we are
not hampered by tradition, nor alumni, nor faculty, nor tenure—nor
even a student body yet." Emory Foster, who was in charge of MSU's
physical plant when Meadow Brook was donated, wrote in 1972 of
his "early impression that one of the accomplishments that Oakland
was to strive for was to give the Pontiac area . . . an opportunity to
extend some of Michigan State University's advantages to the poorer
student who would be able to commute with little expense for the
first couple of years and then move to Michigan State for more
specialized education."

Michigan State vice president Durward "Woody" Varner, a native of Cottonwood, Texas, became the first chancellor of the new
branch. Woody Varner sometimes played the country bumpkin,
lulling people with his slight Texas drawl, but in reality he was one
of the country's sharpest educational administrators. A graduate of
Texas A&M, he arrived at MSC in 1949 as an extension specialist in
agricultural economics. In 1952 he was appointed extension director,
the youngest director among the forty-eight extension services in
the United States, and three years later he became Michigan State's
first-ever vice president.

After Varner took over as Oakland's chancellor, he stressed hiring
quality faculty at the new institution. "Young teachers of the highest
ability, vigor and motivation were selected," the *Michigan State
University Magazine* reported in its November 1959 issue. "Most of
them share a desire to get away from standard college curriculums."
Varner received 250 applications for the 25 faculty positions and
bragged that Oakland had "the youngest faculty with the highest
percentage of earned doctoral degrees of any university in America,

Durward "Woody" Varner became Michigan State's first vice president in 1955 and later became the first chancellor of Oakland University. Courtesy of MSU Archives and Historical Collections.

and . . . the faculty with the greatest amount of enthusiasm in the land." The new faculty members averaged thirty-three years old and came to Oakland from such universities as Harvard, Yale, Princeton, Columbia, Michigan, and of course Michigan State. The new dean was Robert Hoopes, who had earned his doctorate at Harvard and had left his position as vice president of the American Council of Learned Societies to come to Oakland. Gerald Straka signed on as a history instructor after completing his doctorate at a British university while on a Fulbright scholarship. "The chance to become a part of a growing university comes once in a lifetime," he said. "This school is not tradition-bound and it is one that encourages initiative." Foreign-language instructor Nadine Popluiko had graduated from the Moscow Pedagogical Institute of Modern Language and had attended the University of Hamburg and the Sorbonne. Colleague Helen Kovach was born in Russia, knew eight languages, and had earned a law degree and a doctorate in political science and public administration. And from MSU's East Lansing campus came assistant English professor William Schwab, who had earned his doctorate from the University of Wisconsin but had also studied at the University of London, the University of the Philippines, and the University of Michigan.

The first MSU–Oakland class of 570 entered in the fall of 1959, enrolled in such programs as engineering science, teacher education, business administration, and liberal arts. Students were required to take half their work in the liberal arts and to acquire a command of a foreign language as well as to become proficient in English rhetoric and English literature. The "program is the result of asking 40 of the nation's leading citizens and educators—top men and women in business, the professions, and the liberal arts—to design an 'ideal' nuclear age university from a fresh start," the *State Journal* reported. "They recommended immediately that the ivy-covered traditions that bind many of the nation's large universities be thrown out."

In its first few years, undoubtedly because of its highly educated faculty and its liberal arts and classical curriculum, MSU-O was called such names as "Egghead U" and the "Dartmouth of the West." According to *Detroit News* reporter George Bullard, the school vowed to have no athletics, no fraternities and sororities, and no frills. Oakland University gained independence from MSU in 1970, by which time Oakland had developed into a good state university with a solid program of career-oriented studies and a dedication to serving the educational needs of Oakland County.

Mobile Homes, Curriculum, and Controversy

While some observers criticized MSU and its Oakland branch as being too elitist, others blasted a different program, one they found to be an embarrassment to a major university. In 1957, MSU established the nation's first university curriculum in mobile-home park management, manufacturing, and marketing. The new venture was financed by a forty-five-thousand-dollar grant from two large mobile-home associations that anticipated major demands for mobile-home professionals. Critics contended that MSU should be concentrating on such courses as history, mathematics, philosophy, and anthropology, not mobile homes. Former University of Chicago president Robert Hutchins called the program a good example of the "service station" approach to education and charged that it had been instituted because of "crude pressure and bribery" by the mobile-home industry. Despite such criticism, the program survived until late 1961, when officials closed it as a result of student disinterest. On 2 January 1962, Hannah gave some insight into his educational philosophy in his response to a correspondent who had quoted Hutchins in asking about the program's rationale:

> We are not inclined to apologize for offering the course leading to a B.S. degree for those interested in the mobile homes industry in Michigan, but Dr. Hutchins has seemingly failed to take into account the factors which led to the original decision to add it to our program. The mobile homes manufacturing industry is an important one in Michigan, and when representatives came here to offer some special work to prepare graduates to serve in that industry, we felt some obligation to do so. . . . I venture to say that the program was as rigorous academically as any other in that general area; students were of course required to complete the curriculum of the University College (general education) and hence were generously exposed to the kind of liberal education which Dr. Hutchins loves to espouse. . . . In our public reply to the criticism of Dr. Hutchins,

we have pointed out that it is the proper mission of the University, as a land-grant institution, to serve the needs of society as they are identified, and that institutions such as this came into being because the kind of education of which Dr. Hutchins is enamored plainly did not serve the needs of the American people.

HANNAH AND THE U.S. CIVIL RIGHTS COMMISSION

In sharp contrast to the criticism Hannah faced regarding the mobile home program was the almost universal praise he received for his appointment as chair of the U.S. Civil Rights Commission. On 24 December 1957, a *New York Times* reporter wrote, "A clue to Dr. Hannah's attitude on race relations is found in some of his first actions as president of Michigan State. He integrated dormitories, ordered racial designations struck from students' records, and refused to allow athletic teams—of which he is an enthusiastic fan—to play in places where Negro players might be deprived of equal rights." Hannah continued as the commission's chair under Presidents Eisenhower, Kennedy, and Johnson until 1969, proving himself an effective leader and a champion of civil rights during a time of great change in U.S. race relations.

THE NEW BOARD

In 1959, the name of Michigan State's governing body was changed from the State Board of Agriculture to the Michigan State Board of Trustees. Hannah had always seemed to get along well with the university's governing body, whatever its name. In a 30 December 1958 letter to new board member C. Allen Harlan, Hannah described his historical relationship with the board:

> I was secretary of the board for 7 years, and am now finishing 18 years as President of this University. During most of this time we have had an excellent Board. There have been many changes in the faces that have met around our board table. In the early years, the majority of the Board members were Democrats; in the middle

years, the majority of the board members were Republicans; and now again, the majority of the board members are Democrats. But always, and almost without exception, the Board membership was made up of dedicated, responsible, objective persons sincerely interested in making this a good University rendering the maximum of service both in quality and quantity to the people of this state. One of the consistent objectives is to make certain that we have on our Board at least some Board members that have had a considerable amount of experience in business enterprises of some magnitude and who are accustomed to doing business in a business like way. For many years leadership in that area came from Fritz Mueller of Grand Rapids and Forest Akers of Detroit, and prior to that from Ben Halstead of Petoskey. Mr. Halstead was a lawyer from a small town, but he had very sound judgment and at one time served as chairman of our board.

Frederick "Fritz" Mueller, a 1914 MAC graduate and a partner in the Mueller Furniture Company of Grand Rapids, served on the board

John Hannah stands beside President Dwight Eisenhower in a 1959 photo of the U.S. Civil Rights Commission. Courtesy of MSU Archives and Historical Collections.

from 1944 to 1957. In 1959 he was sworn in as an undersecretary of commerce in the Eisenhower administration, at that time the highest government position ever held by a Michigan State alumnus. Other prominent board members at the time included Clark Brody, the executive vice president of the Michigan Farm Bureau; C. Allen Harlan, president of the Harlan Electric Company in Detroit and president or director of ten affiliated companies; Connor Smith, who had received his doctorate in veterinary medicine from MSC in 1930 and had a veterinary practice in Pinconning; Arthur Rouse, a 1935 MSC graduate who owned and operated service stations in Northern Michigan and served as president of the Boyne City Chamber of Commerce; Don Stevens, educational director and member of the board of the Michigan CIO Council; and Jan Vanderploeg, a North Muskegon nurseryman, member of the North Muskegon city council, and activist in the state Congregational Church organization.

Hannah worked hard to maintain cordial relations with board members, recognizing important dates in their lives and even sending them gifts. In 1959, Brody thanked Hannah for recognizing the Brodys' wedding anniversary. That same year, Vanderploeg wrote to Hannah that "each day that I live is different because I am privileged to be a member of the Board of Trustees of M.S.U. I greatly enjoy the feeling of satisfaction it gives me. Beside the satisfaction there are the little instances of thoughtfulness from you—the blue berries, the commencement picture, the Easter lilies and the maple syrup." Many board members addressed Hannah by his first name, an extremely uncommon practice among members of the Michigan State community.

One issue that consistently threatened Hannah's relationship with his board was the desire of certain faculty members to bypass Hannah and communicate directly with board members. In 1959, for example, chemistry professor Harold Hart invited Brody to discuss various faculty-related issues with the MSU executive chapter of the American Association of University Professors. "You would be supplied in advance with a short list of some of the problems which several of our faculty feel might profit from open discussion," Hart wrote. "Your comments on your personal conception of the relationship between the faculty and the board would be welcome." Brody quickly declined. "Though I have long enjoyed personal friendships with many of the faculty, I feel it would be improper for me to participate in the type of meeting indicated by your letter. My conception of my duties as a member of the Board of Trustees is that official relationships should be handled through the President's office. Conversely, I believe strongly in members of the faculty having every opportunity to express their views and interests through the regular channels of the administration. I feel that President Hannah's administration is providing every practical opportunity for you to do this."

Grady L. Mullennix, president of the MSU Federation of Teachers, apparently was more aggressive than Hart. After Connor Smith, the board president, denied Mullennix's request for access to the board, Mullennix pointed out that board policy limited the body to dealings only with "administrative officials" of the university, with the result that no direct communication took place between the faculty and the board. "We are hopeful that the present Board will see fit to change this practice. We are convinced that you will find the faculty of Michigan State more intimately aware of the problems of the university than any other group or individual and therefore helpful in ways of improving it. . . . We feel that a publicly elected body like the Board will in the long run better serve its institution and the citizens of the state by opening channels of communication rather than closing them." After receiving a copy of the Mullennix letter, Hannah immediately responded with his own letter to Smith. "The content of the letter from Mr. Mullennix disturbs me a great deal," Hannah wrote. "As I indicated to you, I fear that we will be in line for very serious trouble if the Board should decide to permit direct communication from employees of the University without coming first through the central administration. This battle was fought and won in the early days of President Shaw's administration. . . . I hope that you will handle this one with any of the new Board members who may be inclined to comply with suggestions like those made by Mullennix."

Some board members disagreed with Hannah's approach. Don Stevens, for example, made himself accessible to faculty members and sometimes passed on their concerns to university officials. On 9 March 1959, Stevens wrote to Hannah that he had learned of a "situation in the College of Engineering that not only is very serious, but in my opinion has been aggravated by a somewhat arrogant attitude displayed by Dean Ryder. This was brought to my attention completely accidentally on the night of February 24, when I observed some of the faculty of the College of Engineering leaving a meeting at the Union Building. Sometime when it is convenient, I would like to discuss this matter further with you."

When Thomas Hamilton resigned to become chancellor of the New York university system, various people lobbied the board on behalf of specific candidates. Writing to Hannah on 21 May 1959, C. Allen Harlan probably expressed the entire board's position:

> In the end, the broad and heavy responsibility for choosing a successor for Tom Hamilton is yours. If you make a wise choice, it is to your credit. If you make a poor choice, it will reflect upon your stature as a great university administrator. In arriving at that decision, the opinion of many people may be sought but, however well intended, the full responsibility is yours. As a matter of basic philosophy, I do not feel that in a great university the administration or governing body should put itself in a position that would seem to give advantage to a pressure group. . . . This seems to be another of those suggested popularity contests in which, if they get their man nominated, he would owe loyalties to them, and both management and the board would be put in a position that is untenable. It is hoped that, in your decision, the pressures of a minority segment do not outweigh what is best for the university.

When Hannah retired in 1969, Frederick Mueller wrote of his service on the board from 1945 to 1956, "The members of the Board during my term of service were dedicated men and women, people of judgment and vision and with ideas for the betterment of MSU. They were responsive to the philosophy and programs of President Hannah and implemented his suggestions and ideas for the future of MSU. We functioned as a Board of Directors of a large corporation—directing policy matters and exercising statutory responsibilities only, leaving administrative and management functions to the officers of the institution. We did not propose to interfere in the everyday operations, but did not shirk from formulating policy that enabled university authorities to function firmly and properly." Hannah concurred with Mueller's positive assessment of the board, lauding in his memoirs the service of Akers, Brody, Harlan, Win Armstrong, and Warren Huff.

The *Michigan State News*

As the 1950s came to a close, the *Michigan State News* celebrated its fiftieth anniversary. Begun in 1909 as the *Holcad*, the newspaper became the *Michigan State News* at the same time the college became Michigan State College in 1925. "The State News is printed by Campus Press, a privately owned East Lansing printing firm which recently installed a rotary press once used by the *Christian Science Monitor*," *Lansing State Journal* reporter Larry Gustin wrote in 1959. "The new press cuts printing for the 17,000 copies of each issue from six hours formerly required to 45 minutes and allows the use of color printing. Prof. A. A. Applegate, former M.S.U. journalism department head and advisor to the *State News* for 20 years, is credited with a leading role in the development of the paper. Applegate developed standards for the newspaper and otherwise directed a program of improvement that was to bring All-American ratings to the student newspaper year after year." Coverage of the 1937 labor holiday in Lansing and East Lansing, the college's acceptance into the Big Ten Conference in 1948, and Michigan State's second trip to the Rose Bowl in 1956 were identified as three highlights in the newspaper's history.

Gordon Sabine, director of the Office of Admissions and Scholarships, made a presentation to the MSU Men's Club about the strengths of the university. A synopsis was later sent to all faculty members.

Journalism professor Albert A. Applegate played a key role in developing the *Michigan State News* into an award-winning newspaper. Courtesy of MSU Archives and Historical Collections.

> What is there to say about Michigan State University to prove its worth to a high-ranking high school senior who is wondering whether to come here or go to any one of a half dozen other major institutions? There is this to say:
>
> We have the broadest, most faithful approach to general education of any institution our size in America.
>
> We have a Kresge Art Center second to none.
>
> A member of our botany department and plant pathology faculty is one of only 20 in the world invited to a distinguished professional conference in Japan.

Rollin H. Baker became director of the MSU Museum in 1955 and served in that position until 1982. Photo courtesy of the Michigan State University Museum.

We have a Pulitzer Prize winner who continues to produce top-ranking books in addition to his work as an English professor.

From an old-fashioned high-ceilinged ill-lighted and over-heated room in one of the oldest buildings on campus, we created a language learning laboratory whose 32 booths permit a student to do two years of language work in just one year.

Our chemistry department alone operates roughly a quarter of a million dollars a year in research projects.

The graduates of our nursing curriculum have the advantage of a student-centered program that takes each of them into several different hospitals for specialized training, and that results in their scoring above both the state and national averages in their certification exams.

We have an Honors College that is unique in all America.

To our teaching, research, and extension work, we have added the entirely new dimension of international involvement to an extent equaled nowhere.

Our Gull Lake biological station is probably the finest of its kind.

Our School of Music presents more than 100 free performances a year to enrich the cultural offerings of the campus.

Our College of Home Economics is considered among the top three in the United States in the quality of its research.

6

A City-Campus Partnership

I N EARLY 1950, A GROUP OF FACULTY FAMILIES APPROACHED JOHN Hannah about purchasing college land to build a "cooperative" subdivision. Hannah refused to grant the request, telling them that after presiding over many faculty meetings, he found it inconceivable that a group of faculty members could agree on anything, much less stay in agreement long enough to complete a major housing project. As political science professor Alan Grimes wrote in his 1999 history of the beginnings of Lantern Hill, "The future members of the Lantern Hill community were for the most part in their thirties, with young children, who had joined the faculty in 1947 or soon after. All desired to own their own homes, but at the prevailing prices for building or buying they found that goal out of reach. A further pressure on these young faculty members was a college rule that they would have to vacate college housing after two years of residence." Many of these "young faculty members" became Michigan State's leaders over the next few decades, including President Walter Adams, Vice President Durward Varner, economics professor Leonard Rall, Provost Lawrence Boger, psychology professor Milton Rokeach, natural science professor Clarence Schloemer, and Grimes.

LANTERN HILL

The Lantern Hill project unofficially began in February 1950 when landscape architecture and urban planning professor Myles Boylan gave a talk on "Helpful Housing Hints" to the college Newcomers Club. Described by Grimes as a "tall, lean ruddy faced Bostonian with a commanding presence," Boylan told the group about other communities in which people had met their housing needs through

Psychology professor Milton Rokeach was one of the pioneer residents of Lantern Hill. Courtesy of MSU Archives and Historical Collections.

Landscape architecture and urban planning professor Myles Boylan's talk to the college Newcomers Club in 1950 provided the impetus for the creation of the Lantern Hill project. Courtesy of MSU Archives and Historical Collections.

a cooperative enterprise, joining together to buy land and construct homes. Many of Boylan's listeners liked the idea, and a cooperative corporation was soon established at Michigan State. The corporation found land north of Burcham Drive in Meridian Township, just outside the East Lansing city limits (the city later annexed the area in 1958). Boylan drew up a site plan, which eventually consisted of forty-one roughly half-acre lots, and the corporation invited Hugh Stebbins of Harvard University (later the architect of the Ronald Reagan Presidential Library) to East Lansing to talk about designing homes that faculty members, then earning about forty-eight hundred dollars per year, could afford. Grimes remembered Stebbins as "an amiable, soft-spoken man who made an impressive presentation. He showed attractive drawings of low roofed houses with light and airy rooms, lots of glass, and indoor-outdoor living areas. They were in the style of what were then called California or ranch type houses, built on a slab for economic reasons. He showed how there could be variations in living arrangements, yet by keeping the same over-all design, one could achieve great economies in construction."

The original forty-one families eventually subdivided themselves into two groups, with twenty-four contracting with Stebbins and seventeen making their own arrangements. The corporation's members included trained surveyors, who laid out the new subdivision's roads and water and sewer lines. Approximately two years after Boylan suggested the cooperative approach, the new Lantern Hill residents moved into their homes. Nearly fifty years later when Grimes wrote his history, thirteen of the original families remained in residence, and what had once been a muddy field boasted "tall pines and spruces . . . maples and . . . locusts and . . . ornamental crabs . . . put there as slender saplings by the first generation of owners of the Lantern Hill subdivision." Hannah had most definitely been proven wrong on this issue.

East Lansing's Expansion

As Michigan State grew, so did the city of East Lansing, desperately trying to meet the housing, business, and social needs of the expanding campus population. The city had been founded in 1907 because of the college, and college staff, alumni, and students played major roles in its development. The first subdivision was developed around 1887 by professors William James Beal and Rolla Carpenter. The first church, Peoples Church, had its origins in the ideas of faculty members Thomas Blaisdell, Chace Newman, and Jesse Myers and college president Jonathan Snyder. And the first mayor was Clinton DeWitt Smith, an agriculture professor. Other men with Michigan State connections who served as East Lansing's mayor included Richard Lyman, dean of the veterinary school; Max Strother, who worked in the college's business office; communications professor Gordon Thomas; and education professor Wilbur Brookover.

An undated and unsigned document found in one of Hannah's files at the MSU Archives and Historical Collections describes the early relationship between the college and the city:

John Hannah was active in a wide range of community activities. He urged all Michigan State employees to do the same, and the city of East Lansing flourished as a consequence of the university community's contributions. Courtesy of MSU Information Services.

> Thirty years ago East Lansing did not exist save for a few small houses opposite the extreme west entrance to the campus. As the town started and grew and for many years thereafter the community was made up almost solely of people on the payroll of the College. There was virtually no one else from which to select the school board, mayor and council and officials of the bank and church which were later organized. College officials had to take the initiative in providing safe water and suitable water supply, sewage disposal system and protective health regulations. In all these endeavors they performed a valuable service to the city, frequently involving self sacrifice without any direct adequate money reward. It is not surprising, therefore, that the East Lansing Council, bank, church, school and the various private business organizations became officered by college people.

The Hannah era saw significant changes in the city's physical appearance. Because of an ever-increasing university population, nonuniversity families deciding to make East Lansing their home, and the annexation of residential areas such as the Marble and Carl communities, building occurred almost as heavily in the city as on the nearby campus during the 1950s and 1960s, with the addition of a new high school (1957), an expansion of city hall (1963), a new library (1963), a new water-treatment plant (1965), a new middle school (1968), a new post office (1969), and several new elementary

Economics professor Leonard Rall was both a popular teacher and a frequent volunteer for East Lansing community projects. Courtesy of MSU Archives and Historical Collections.

MSU library director Richard Chapin served on both the city's human relations commission and on the school board. Courtesy of MSU Archives and Historical Collections.

schools. Many of the same people who were responsible for the growth on campus played major roles in the city's development. Lloyd Emmons, the dean of the School of Science and Arts, for example, lived in East Lansing during virtually the entire period from 1909 until his death in 1957. He helped to establish MSC's Basic College, became the college's first athletic representative to the Big Ten Conference, and served for a time as assistant director of the MSC Museum. He also was one of East Lansing's leading citizens, serving as president of the school board during the 1920s, volunteering at Peoples Church, mentoring many teachers in the local school system, and eagerly welcoming foreign students and faculty. Just prior to his death, Emmons wrote *The Story of East Lansing* for the city's fiftieth-birthday celebrations.

Other Michigan State faculty who served on East Lansing's school board during the Hannah years included agricultural economics professor James Shaffer and librarian Richard Chapin. Many university staffers contributed to the city's betterment in a variety of ways. For example, David Milstein of the department of hotel, restaurant, and institutional management headed the Joint Downtown Redevelopment Committee; Hannah assistant James Denison, social science professor Douglas Dunham, and MSC landscaper Harold Lautner served long terms on the planning commission; urban affairs professor Robert Green, social work professor Dozier Thornton, communications professor David Berlo, and Chapin, among others, participated as members of East Lansing's Human Relations Commission; and parks and recreation professor Louis Twardzith, landscape architecture professor Dean Glick, and horticulture professor Harold Davidson contributed to city aesthetics through the Grand River Beautification Committee. Stanley K. Ries earned a bachelor's degree from MSC in 1950 and graduate degrees from Cornell University before returning to East Lansing in 1953 as a professor of horticulture. In addition to his numerous professional accomplishments, he created a beautiful garden at his home in East Lansing's Cahill subdivision, one of the neighborhood's highlights. Other longtime faculty members who made major commitments to the city's neighborhoods included Charles Press (political science), James Niblock (music), Maurice Crane (humanities), Jeremy Mattson (social science), and Leonard Rall (economics). Rall explained his perspective on the connection

Myra Bogue, wife of forestry professor Ernest Bogue, worked in the bulletin department at the college, taught Sunday school at Peoples Church, and ran a boardinghouse at her home on Grove Street. Courtesy of MSU Archives and Historical Collections.

between Michigan State and East Lansing: "I've got a great job at the university where I'm able to help students learn and then see them make successes of themselves as adults. Then, the rest of the time I spend with my family and in community projects, hopefully making East Lansing a better place to live. It's a good life."

Another Spartan with strong East Lansing ties was Myra Bogue, wife of forestry professor Ernest Bogue. After her husband's death in 1907, Myra Bogue not only took a job at the college bulletin department but also spent the next five decades participating in the city's social and civic organizations. She served as longtime historian of the East Lansing Women's Club, taught Sunday school at Peoples Church, and served on the school board. But her favorite activity was taking care of "her boys," male college students who rented rooms in her home on Grove Street.

Emily Frame, wife of math professor J. Sutherland Frame, became concerned about the safety of her children and of others who had to walk to Marble School along the side of Hagadorn Road, particularly after a child was hit by a car in 1955. After the school board rejected appeals to build a sidewalk because such a construction project fell outside of the board's area of responsibility, Frame suggested to the Marble Community Association that residents build the sidewalk themselves using private contributions. The group did so, raising eleven thousand dollars for the project.

Emily Frame was a longtime East Lansing community activist. Courtesy of the Frame family.

Dora Stockman served on the State Board of Agriculture as well as in the state legislature. She worked with both John Hannah and East Lansing city manager Jack Patriarche on issues that affected the campus and the city. Courtesy of MSU Archives and Historical Collections.

Dora Stockman, a resident of rural Ingham County, won election to the State Board of Agriculture (MSC's governing board) in 1919, becoming the first woman elected to statewide office in Michigan. She moved to East Lansing in 1925 and was elected to the state legislature in 1938. She worked with both Hannah and East Lansing city manager Jack Patriarche in the late 1930s and 1940s on a variety of issues, specializing in health care, liquor control, and wartime policy.

Michigan State professor and renowned glacial geologist Stanard Gustaf Bergquist served as president of the American Association of Geology Teachers as well as on the East Lansing City Council and as president of the East Lansing School Board. In 1943, he served on the committee that revised the city charter. He played active roles in the local American Legion Post and Peoples Church, and was a supporter of local reading and literary groups. In the late 1930s and 1940s, said a colleague, "Dr. Bergquist epitomized everything that was good about both the college and the city."

Some Michigan State faculty and staff became involved in local and state politics. Speech department chair and East Lansing resident Paul Bagwell, for example, became a leader in the state's Republican Party during the 1950s and 1960s, running unsuccessfully against G. Mennen Williams and John Swainson for the governor's office. Bagwell also was active in numerous local organizations, including the Chamber of Commerce and Rotary Club, and served on Michigan State's Board of Trustees, as president of the U.S. Junior Chamber of Commerce, and as chair of the state March of Dimes campaign. He was even featured on the cover of *Time* magazine. Leroy Augenstein, the chair of Michigan State's biophysics department and a local activist, was a rising star in Michigan's Republican Party and was considering a 1970 run against Michigan senator Philip Hart when he was killed in a 1969 plane crash.

Other members of the Michigan State community became active in the Democratic Party. In 1954, speech professor Don Hayworth won election to the U.S. Congress, beating incumbent Kit Clardy to represent Michigan's Sixth District. A few years later, Hayworth's office mate and fellow Democrat, Gordon Thomas, was elected to the city council; he eventually became mayor. His successor as mayor in 1971, MSU education professor Wilbur Brookover, was also a Democrat. These electoral achievements demonstrated that the Democratic

Party, which prior to 1920 had been a tiny minority in East Lansing, had achieved political acceptability in the city.

Spanish professor Edith Doty volunteered with a variety of organizations as well as opened her home to visiting musicians and other artists. Doty gave her guests a private room, cooked their breakfasts, and provided guide services and transportation, developing many lifelong friendships in the process. In one instance, two opera singers whom Doty had befriended gave her a kitten, which a delighted Doty named Don Giovanni in honor of the production in which the singers were appearing. "Life for many performers is not especially glamorous but, because of the constant traveling, can be very lonely," she later remembered. "I always tried to give them someone they could talk to."

But Sarah Hannah may have most clearly demonstrated the strong ties between the campus and city. The daughter of college president Robert Shaw, Sarah grew up living on campus and attended East Lansing High School. "East Lansing was 100 percent a college community until the expansion started around 1930," she told the *Towne Courier* in 1963. "My family had a 160-acre farm centered by the Saginaw and Harrison intersection, and it was necessary to subdivide it for sale because the area was beginning to be built up and taxes were prohibitive. Around this time, faculty families could live off campus and professional people from Lansing were beginning to come out here because they found it a pleasant place to live." After marrying John Hannah, Sarah continued to consider both the campus and East Lansing her home, and she was active in both the American Association of University Women and the East Lansing Women's Club.

Among the alumni who particularly strongly influenced East Lansing's development were Albert White and Jack Patriarche. White studied business and economics at Michigan State before graduating in 1940 and taking a job with Montgomery Ward. He eventually became interested in construction and began building subdivisions, including some of the city's most exclusive homes. White also donated land for city and school projects, supported mentoring programs at local high schools, contributed to a wide range of arts groups, and was active in the local Rotary Club. In recognition of White's contributions to East Lansing's physical development, a park in the north part of the

Stanard Bergquist was a renowned geologist at Michigan State, but he also served as a member of the East Lansing City Council and was president of the East Lansing School Board. Courtesy of Michigan State University Archives and Historical Collections.

Leroy Augenstein, chair of MSU's biophysics department, was active in East Lansing community projects and the Republican Party prior to his death in a 1969 plane crash. Courtesy of MSU Information Services.

Sarah Shaw Hannah was comfortable both on campus and in the city of East Lansing. Courtesy of MSU Archives and Historical Collections.

city was named in his honor. Patriarche graduated from MSC in 1938 and took a job as operator of the new East Lansing sewage plant. In 1947, he became city manager, remaining in that position until 1976. Throughout his tenure, he maintained a positive relationship with college officials, particularly presidential assistants Karl McDonel and Philip May, and through them with President Hannah. Patriarche recalled that Hannah firmly believed that he should not interfere with city government: "He would cooperate and work with us, but he would not interfere." Another MSC graduate, Charles Pegg, joined city government the same year as Patriarche and served more than thirty years in the police department, becoming chief in 1946.

The presence of Michigan State gave East Lansing's community organizations and media ready access to experts on almost every subject imaginable. When the *East Lansing Towne Courier* wanted more in-depth coverage of the news, editors sometimes asked faculty members to write opinion columns. In 1969, for example, the paper provided in-depth coverage of proposals for state funding of non-public schools by having faculty members James Shaffer and Donald Hillman write columns opposing and supporting the idea, respectively. Other Michigan State faculty who were frequently consulted on issues important to the East Lansing community during the 1950s and 1960s included economics professors Walter Adams and Charles "Lash" Larrowe; history professors Wesley Fishel, Charles Press, and Madison Kuhn; communications professors David Berlo and Hideya Kumata; art professor Paul Love; physical education professor Wayne Van Huss; home management and child development professor Alice Thorpe; social work professor Lucille Barber; and labor and industrial relations faculty members Charles Killingsworth and Daniel Kruger. The East Lansing community also sought opinions on world events from faculty involved in Michigan State's international programs, including S. C. Lee, George Axinn, Ralph Smuckler, Homer Higbee, and Glen Taggart.

MICHIGAN STATE'S TIES TO COMMUNITY RELIGIOUS GROUPS

Accomplishments such as the creation of Lantern Hill often resulted from coordinated efforts between the Peoples Church and the college.

During the Hannah years, the list of church leaders read like a who's who of MSC faculty and administration, including professors Walter Fee, Kenneth Hance, Milo Tesar, H. T. Darlington, William Gamble, Malcolm Trout, and Roland Pierson. The leaders of the church's Woman's Society included many faculty wives, and college students always constituted an important part of the congregation. "For many years, until the college enrollment became too large for such a purpose, Peoples Church folk took all freshmen home for Sunday dinner on what was known as 'Freshman Sunday,'" the Reverend Newell Avery McCune wrote in his history of the church. "Also, each student was given a postcard of a picture of Peoples Church with the request that the card be sent home to their parents stating where they had attended church that Sunday. Students were elected to the Board of Elders and Trustees of the church as it was the policy of the church that Peoples Church should be a real home church while they were attending college. Many students taught church school classes or were of service to the church in other ways."

East Lansing's Catholic community also had strong ties to the college. Monsignor Jerome V. MacEachin, known popularly as Father Mac, taught at MSU for twenty-three years, founded the St. John's Student Center, and served as pastor at St. Thomas Aquinas Church from 1943 to 1978. An ardent fan of MSU football, he served as the Spartans' team chaplain for many years, accompanying the team on many road trips, especially those to South Bend, Indiana, for games against Notre Dame. His Sunday-morning masses the week before MSU's annual contest against the Fighting Irish always included calls for a Michigan State victory, and at the pregame pep rallies he opened his coat to flash his green S sweater. "I'm a firm believer in the separation of church and state—except in football," he liked to say.

Father Mac's good friend and fellow Michigan State football fan, Rabbi Philip Frankel, was a leader in mid-Michigan's Jewish community. He liked to tell the story of the time he and Father Mac took a group to the 1956 Rose Bowl game. "That was the year Dave Kaiser won the game for MSU with his field goal in the last seconds," Frankel said. "Afterwards, Father Mac and I argued about whose prayer it was that helped the ball over the goal posts. We finally agreed that it was probably a combination of both prayers that did it." Frankel taught religion at MSU for many years; spoke to numerous civic, social, and

History professor Walter Fee was a respected member of the faculty who was involved in a variety of community activities, including East Lansing's Peoples Church. Courtesy of MSU Archives and Historical Collections.

Bill Yeoman was a Michigan State assistant football coach in the 1950s who taught Sunday school at East Lansing's Edgewood United Church. If the young men in his class paid close attention to their lessons, Yeoman would diagram football plays on the blackboard as a reward. Courtesy of MSU Archives and Historical Collections.

religious groups, teaching Christians about Jews; and stood at the forefront of many civil rights causes. But more than anything else, he worked to help others get along. "If I were a ditch digger instead of a rabbi, I think I would still want to help others," Frankel said. "I don't play golf or have hobbies like many others have. I guess my hobby is my relationships with people."

John Hannah believed that MSC should reach out to the entire population of Michigan by educating people of all ages and backgrounds through its Cooperative Extension Service, its continuing education programs, and its sponsorships of many campus events for both students and nonstudents. He also believed in personal service to the community, whether that community was local, national, or international. This point of view led to Hannah's service as chair of the U.S. Civil Rights Commission, as head of the U.S. section of the Permanent Joint Canadian-American Defense Board, and as president of the Rotary Club of Lansing. Hannah often participated in East Lansing events, frequently giving the main address at the official dedication ceremonies for important new community buildings, including the new high school, which opened in 1957. "The community can take pride in what has been accomplished through working, planning and building together," he said. "The university city has a new landmark, emblematic of its progressive attitude and representing its appreciation of the values of education." When the new Michigan Education Association building was dedicated in 1964, Hannah again gave the opening address. And when groups of mid-Michigan YMCA youngsters met for an awards ceremony at East Lansing Junior High School in the mid-1960s, Hannah took time from his busy schedule to thank the boys for their efforts in making the community a better place to live.

Assistant football coach Bill Yeoman, who later became head football coach at the University of Houston, combined his religious faith and sports expertise. Teaching a Sunday school class at Edgewood United Church, Yeoman promised to diagram football plays on the blackboard after class if the young men paid close attention to their religious lessons. Not surprisingly, many of Edgewood's early members, including James Porter, Chester Clark, King McCristal, Lawrence Boger, and Durward Varner, were MSC faculty.

THE ARTS

Many university employees became involved in the East Lansing community through artistic endeavors. German teacher Margot Evans was also one of the most honored painters in mid-Michigan, and she donated countless hours of her time to share her artistic insights with a wide range of nonprofit organizations. When Evans had a retrospective exhibit of her tapestries at the Kresge Art Museum in the 1980s, Lydia Woodruff of MSU's humanities department wrote,

> Margot Evans is widely recognized and admired as a prolific water-colorist whose love of nature bursts forth in her designs filled with flowers, birds and animals, all radiating color and light. But the stitched and woven tapestries of Mrs. Evans are less well known to the general public. In these she "paints" with colored wool the memories of her native Germany, as well as scenes from the Bible, giving expression again to her love of nature and the world of her youth. After arriving from Germany in 1936 as a refugee with only $5.00 in her purse, Margot Evans won a scholarship to Cornell University which enabled her to become qualified as a dietician. "In America," she was told, "a poor girl should have a bread and butter profession." However, it was not long before she earned a master's degree in French, and, in 1959, she was invited to join the Michigan State University faculty where she taught French and later German. . . . A Vienna critic called her art work "a cosmic vision alive with glowing colors." A Parisian writer described her creations as belonging to a "Fairy-like universe."

One of Evans's tapestries is permanently displayed on a wall at the East Lansing Public Library. Another is found on a wall of Edgewood United Church, and many more hang in East Lansing homes.

Dirk Gringhuis, a former curator at the MSU Museum, also wrote and illustrated children's history books, produced murals for Fort Mackinac and Fort Michilimackinac, and produced *Open Door to Michigan*, a weekly television show that began in 1964 on MSU's WMSB and taught elementary school children about their state. His most lasting local legacy is the mural at the entrance of the East Lansing Public Library, which Gringhuis painted in 1962 when the

The 1964 MSU Museum team that gathered materials for a moose habitat exhibit included Leslie Drew, Dirk Gringhuis, Charles Smith, and Val Berryman. Courtesy of the MSU Museum.

library opened. The mural ties together several of Michigan's most famous legends, including the story of the ghost ship *Griffon* that was lost at sea and now is seen only as an apparition skirting the shores at full mast; the famous Chippewa footrace between Nanabojo and his evil brother, Peepaukawis; Paul Bunyan and Babe, the blue ox; and the excursions of the famous Johnny Appleseed. "As an author of children's books, I have a great interest in the library," he said when he finished the mural. "By doing this mural, I may be able to repay libraries for the important roles they play in my career."

Both art professor Martin Soria, a specialist in Latin American and Spanish art, and his wife, Marion, were major contributors to the East Lansing and MSU communities. After Martin Soria was killed in a 1961 plane crash, his widow remained involved in the local arts scene. Soon after the 1963 assassination of President John F. Kennedy, MSU art student John T. Scott created a sculpture modeled after a newspaper photograph of Jacqueline Kennedy holding the president's head in her lap. The work, *Pietà,* was later cast in bronze and placed on the grounds of East Lansing's Edgewood United Church in honor of Martin Soria.

THE BUSINESS COMMUNITY

Downtown businesses had always catered to both students and faculty, who in the college's first years had few other options close by and consequently did their day-to-day shopping at East Lansing's stores. Prior to the 1970s, when shopping malls and subdivisions in Okemos, Haslett, and other surrounding communities were constructed, large numbers of faculty members still lived near downtown, and area businesses were patronized by a fairly even mix of students and faculty. East Lansing's businesses had a wide range of semicaptive customers from the college residence halls, rented rooms, fraternity and sorority houses, and several hundred faculty homes situated within walking distance of the corner of Abbott Road and Grand River Avenue. Residents visited Hicks Hardware for hammers, nails, and other items needed to fix up their homes or dorm rooms, while Prince Brothers Meat Market and Hauers Grocery Store sold food and cleaning supplies to large numbers of loyal customers.

Downtown also offered recreational and dining opportunities. The State and the Lucon theaters often showed movies to full houses, and both faculty and students enjoyed dining at Hunt's Food Shop on Grand River Avenue. Sisters Ada Hunt Whitehouse and Clara Hunt Vedder (who was married to engineering professor H. K. Vedder) had opened the business in 1922, and it remained an East Lansing landmark until 1944. The cafeteria-style restaurant's offerings included veal loaf, sliced tongue, sliced ham, creamed potatoes, lemon cream pie, and chocolate cake.

Students ate out less during the 1940s and 1950s than in later years, choosing to take meals in dormitory cafeterias or with landlords, or to cook on hot plates in rented rooms. East Lansing was a dry town until 1968, so students in search of an evening at a bar had to leave the city limits to enjoy the hospitality of such establishments as Dagwood's, Coral Gables, Paul Revere's, or the Gay Bar, located at the northwest corner of Hagadorn Road and Grand River Avenue. Faculty wanting wine with their meal often chose Poplars, a classy restaurant just east of Coral Gables. But the place to be seen during the 1950s was the basement cafeteria in the Union Building on a Sunday afternoon. Faculty, staff, and other townspeople and their families would congregate after church, eating old-fashioned family dinners and visiting with friends at other tables.

Charles Washburn graduated from MAC in 1917 and opened the Smoke Shop on MAC Avenue, specializing "in pipes and cigarettes and tobacco at first, and we had the biggest line of smoking tobacco anywhere around, as well as the biggest line of magazines and newspapers." Washburn remained in business through 1960, expanding his establishment with "pool tables and a soda fountain and sandwich grill [where he] sold all sorts of Heinz soups [and] cold meat sandwiches." As Washburn recalled in an interview conducted by dairy professor Malcolm Trout for *At the Campus Gate: A History of East Lansing*, "During and right after World War II, there was a great shortage of eating places here in town, and we had so many customers we just couldn't take care of them fast enough. I remember there would usually be anywhere from one to four people standing behind each place, trying to get a seat during rush hour." Washburn's shop did not allow women and "was the mecca of the men students of the college. . . . Up until after World War II, I used to know all the football and basketball players, most of whom used to make my store their headquarters."

Other notable patrons included longtime college groundskeeper and East Lansing mayor Thomas Gunson and several Michigan State presidents. Recalled Washburn, "President Shaw used to stop in regularly. I'll always remember one time when he and Secretary [Herman] Halladay were in, and one of the quite prominent faculty members went by. The secretary said to President Shaw, 'I don't know what they'll think, seeing the president and the secretary in the Smoke Shop.' And Shaw said, 'Well, I don't know about the secretary, but the president's going to do about as he dum pleases.'"

INTELLECTUAL LIFE IN EAST LANSING

The Michigan State community's involvement in East Lansing sometimes took the form of intellectual pursuits. In 1934, MSC librarian Jackson Towne founded a club that brought together faculty members and their wives to read plays and eat gourmet meals. By the 1960s, group members included philosophy professor John F. A. Taylor, sociology professor E. B. Harper, and Dean John Winburne, and the works read included Noel Coward's *Tonight at 8:30*, Thornton Wilder's *The Merchant of Yonkers*, and Eugene O'Neill's *A Long Day's Journey into Night*.

Katherine Towne, Jackson Towne's wife, was involved in the city in a variety of ways, most notably through the East Lansing Garden Club, which was founded in 1951. In her history of the group's first ten years, Towne listed horticulture professor Paul Krone, zoology professor Joseph Stack, urban planning professor Myles Boylan, and extension specialist Joseph Cox among the club's featured speakers. Special programs included a workshop on dried arrangements, one on Christmas decorations, sessions on wild birds, and the creation of a Junior Garden Club consisting of members of Brownie troops at Marble School. Conservation was important to club members, and they financed trips for local teachers to the Higgins Lake Conservation Training School to increase "their conservation education so they can better integrate that knowledge into their regular classroom programs."

During the 1950s, Michigan State alumnus William McCann turned his home into what former MSC student and professor Russell Kirk dubbed "East Lansing's cultural center." McCann was a bibliophile, a writer, an authority on the Civil War, and a supporter of the local visual arts scene, whose library "overflowed his house; and he was ready to talk at length about everything, but especially matters literary." Maury Crane, who as a young married man moved into the house next door to McCann's, remembered his neighbor as "a voracious reader, an eclectic writer, a great thinker, a fabulous wit, and one of the world's most generous human beings. I was immediately welcomed into his home where I met intellectual giants of all persuasions, from the conservative Russell Kirk to the liberal Russ Nye, with many positions in-between, and it was in that heady atmosphere that I decided that Michigan State was where I would like to stay."

Michigan State head librarian Jackson Towne started a play-reading club, while his wife, Katherine, was active in the East Lansing Garden Club. Courtesy of MSU Archives and Historical Collections.

In addition to such private entertainments, Michigan State offered after-hours intellectual and cultural diversions for faculty and area residents through two major institutions. The first of these, the State College Club, was founded in 1929 with Robert Shaw as its first president and with a membership consisting of 184 faculty members and 8 local businessmen. The club initially met for lunches in the Union, with the goal of encouraging "improved communications among all members of the faculty," as Hannah wrote in the 1982 history of the club, which by then had been renamed the University Club. The club became a major social gathering center, and its presidents included such Michigan State leaders as chemistry professor and marching band leader A. J. Clark, veterinary science dean Ward Giltner, economics professor W. O. Hedrick, and general college dean Stanley Crowe. Its programs featured such impressive speakers as Chicago Board of Trade director Clarence Henry, Big Ten commissioner Tug Wilson, rocket scientist Werner von Braun, and English actor Richard Carey. The University Club also provided its patrons with cultural programs, such as readings from *The Iceman Cometh* and *Cyrano de Bergerac* by speech professor Joe Callaway and musical entertainment by WKAR director and pianist Robert Coleman and by some of East Lansing's high school students. The club also frequently joined with the Faculty Folk Club to sponsor dinner dances and other special functions.

Second, and probably more important, the college's Lecture-Concert Series offered faculty, students, and area residents sophisticated entertainment. Inaugurated in 1912 and permanently housed in the Auditorium after 1940, the series brought to East Lansing such world-renowned speakers and entertainers as soprano Lily Pons (1945), actress Lillian Gish (1948), pianist Vladimir Horowitz (1950), writer Ogden Nash (1952), violinist Isaac Stern (1955), poet Carl Sandburg (1959), the National Ballet of Canada (1961), baritone Robert Merrill (1964), the Martha Graham Dance Company (1966), pianists Ferrante and Teicher (1968), and numerous symphony orchestras. Starting in 1961, the university also offered the Summer Circle Theatre, which brought such productions as *Blithe Spirit* and *A Thurber Carnival* to Demonstration Hall.

In some cases, faculty spouses played key roles in enriching local culture. For example, painter Carolyn Hoagland, who was married to business professor John Hoagland, participated in many activities that supported art education, and Wilma Dressel, the wife of education professor Paul Dressel, taught local children how to ice skate.

MSU art professor Leonard Jungwirth was married to noted mid-Michigan painter Irene Jungwirth, and both husband and wife contributed to East Lansing's iconography. Leonard Jungwirth created a three-ton ceramic sculpture of Sparty in 1945; twelve years later, the East Lansing City Council adopted an official city seal based on a painting by Irene. The design shows a background of university buildings, churches, schools, homes, the Red Cedar River, and an apple tree symbolizing promise and fulfillment. Both Sparty and the city seal remained as important symbols for school and city as they entered the twenty-first century.

TOWN-GOWN TENSIONS

Inevitably, clashes sometimes arose between East Lansing homeowners and the thousands of young men and women who attended Michigan State and who wanted to take advantage of the freedom offered by what was generally their first taste of life away from parental supervision. Michigan State administrators walked a fine line, negotiating the tensions among local residents who wanted the school to take responsibility for the actions of students who lived in off-campus housing, parents who wanted the school to protect their children (especially their daughters) from whatever evils the mid-Michigan community might harbor, and students, most of whom apparently wanted the school to exercise minimal control over their behavior. In 1964, a local physician and his wife became disturbed by the "filth and suggestive movies our young people are seeing in East Lansing." After complaining unsuccessfully to both the East Lansing police department and the manager of the State Theatre, the couple wrote to Sarah Hannah, asking for her suggestions about ways to combat the problem: "So much filth has been shown our young folks, they cannot tell which is evil anymore. . . . We feel there is a concerted effort of Communism to demoralize our younger generation, as well as the bad literature that still stares at us from the news stands. . . . We will do anything to fight this creeping evil in our city . . . I pray this will mean as much to you as a family and leaders of our University as it does to all of us." Sarah Hannah passed the letter along to her husband, who explained to the couple that although he understood their concerns, the university could do little to remedy the situation:

> As long-time residents of East Lansing, you probably know that the University tries very hard not to intrude itself directly into the affairs of the community. . . . Of course it has an active interest in what goes on there, and many of its faculty members are active in community life, but the University itself feels that it has enough to do to handle matters south of Grand River Avenue. Beyond that, I am sure you appreciate that it is very difficult to challenge matters of taste, particularly in the entertainment field. Doing so is often interpreted as censorship. I think we often go too far in the direction of bad and perverted taste in literature, motion pictures, and even popular music, but it would be next to impossible for the University to impose a higher set of standards and values on the East Lansing community. . . . The University will do and is doing its part in offering cultural and entertainment features of high quality as alternatives to events of lesser quality, and this, it seems to me, is about all it can be expected to do.

While some locals questioned the appropriateness of the entertainment, others objected to students being treated as full-fledged residents of the city. In 1966, a Lansing television station ran an editorial pointing out that students were not real "citizens of East Lansing." Editorial writers at the *State News* vehemently disagreed, however, urging students to respond by taking their business back to their hometowns. A few months later, when the city raised parking rates by twenty-five cents an hour, the *State News* claimed the action was directed specifically at students, and again pointed out the students' contributions to East Lansing's economy. "It is difficult to imagine why the store owners would want to make things hard for the very people who do the shopping in their stores—the people who spend $25 million each term in the Lansing–East Lansing area. It is possible that some students will simply forget about browsing in East Lansing stores, because it just isn't worth the trouble. It is also possible that some students will forget about buying in East Lansing stores, where they feel their money isn't fully appreciated. If antagonism continues to be heaped upon insult, East Lansing businesses could eventually be hurt. It wouldn't be unjust."

In an attempt to defuse the tensions between the city and students, local leaders sponsored a City-Student Relations Banquet on 14 November 1966. Those in attendance included police chief Charles Pegg, city manager Jack Patriarche, John Cote of the Chamber of Commerce, members of the city council, student leaders, and MSU administrators John Fuzak and Eldon Nonnamaker. Participants discussed such topics as parking problems, student behavior, and garbage pickup, maintaining lively but civil and sometimes even friendly conversation throughout the meal. Mayor Thomas said of the banquet, "I'm not sure how much we actually accomplished, but I think we demonstrated all members of our community could sit down and discuss issues in a rational and productive manner."

RACE RELATIONS

Since its founding in 1907, East Lansing had consisted almost exclusively of white residents. Thousands of students graduated from the city's high school without ever having a black, Hispanic, or Asian classmate. The typical resident usually encountered minorities only at sports competitions against other high schools, at international programs on campus, at Spartan football games, or while traveling in foreign countries.

In early 1963, the *State News* launched an investigation of housing practices in East Lansing and uncovered some disturbing results:

A phone canvas by a *State News* reporter of 22 off-campus residences revealed that 13 of the owners were unwilling to rent rooms to Negroes under any circumstances. . . . Discrimination was more prevalent in women's houses, with seven out of ten owners saying they would not rent to Negroes. Landlords in men's residences were less positive with only six out of 12 definitely refusing to take Negroes. Several owners of women's residences said they didn't rent to Negroes because "the rest of the girls wouldn't like it." One landlady said that, "all the girls are white and I really don't think a Negro girl would be happy here." Another said she took some foreign students but "wouldn't take Negroes at the present time."

Thelma Evans, the first black member to serve on the city council, recalled that when she moved to East Lansing in July 1962, "We ran into difficulty finding housing. We checked the papers every day and contacted realtors, but to no avail. . . . Every day I bought the *State Journal* and called all the places with apartments for rent. On the phone I was told, 'Yes, it is available.' But when we got there an expression of shocked amazement came over the face of the person who answered the door. We were told that 'Negroes just don't live in East Lansing,' or that 'I really would rent it to you but I don't know what my neighbors would say.' Other reasons we were given were, 'You know, my husband didn't know that you were coming and he rented it before you got here,' or 'I'll have to ask my husband and I'll call you back.' We never got any calls. This continued for three and a half weeks. It was a great surprise to me because in the South you always hear about the liberal North." The Evanses finally were able to rent a home but ran into problems when they subsequently tried to buy a house: "I called a couple of realtors and they told me that they were very sorry but they could not show [a house off Whitehills Drive] to me because I was black. Then I called one man, whose name I don't recall, and he said, 'Yes I will show you that house. But I'll probably get in trouble for doing it.' He showed us the house and we liked it very much, but the owners would not agree to sell it to us. But because he had shown us the house, this man did lose his job." Dozier Thornton, a black professor who joined the university in 1965, also had difficulty buying a house. He finally bought a home from another professor in the late 1960s, without going through a real estate agent.

As was the case elsewhere in the United States, racial attitudes in mid-Michigan began to change during the 1950s and early 1960s. East Lansing religious leaders Gordon Jones, Truman Morrison, John Duly, Philip Frankel, and Wallace Robinson began to work to make East Lansing more hospitable for minorities. In part as a result of Jones's efforts, David Dickson, a professor, became the first black homeowner in the city, and the Evans family also eventually bought a home, partially through the work of real estate agent Art Boettcher.

Gordon Thomas, an MSU speech professor, served as East Lansing's mayor for a decade starting in 1961 and favored greater racial acceptance, especially in housing. The cautious Thomas, however, hoped to avoid the confrontations that were erupting between civil rights activists and municipalities elsewhere in the country. In the fall of 1963, acting on the suggestion of Thomas and other community leaders, the city council formed a Human Relations Commission, a group of citizens who would listen to civil rights complaints, encourage local input, and advise the city council on specific actions. The Human Relations Commission brought added attention to the race issue and thereby created significant turmoil in East Lansing, although the commission was effective in the long run.

The Human Relations Commission's original members included MSU zoology researcher Stephanie Barch, Peoples Church pastor Wallace Robertson, attorney Dan Learned, banker Thomas Schepers, real estate executive James Ehinger, psychiatrist H. C. Tien, homemaker Mary Sharp, MSU student Robert Morgan, and Michigan State education professor Robert Green. Sharp later served on the city council, where she voted consistently in favor of civil rights measures, and Green, a black Detroit native who held bachelor's and master's degrees from San Francisco State College as well as a doctorate from MSU, quickly became the area's most outspoken and perhaps most effective civil rights advocate.

Shortly after the council created the commission, the editors of the *State News* outlined the situation in East Lansing:

> For many of the 27,000 students the city of East Lansing provides a room or an apartment and is therefore home. . . . Some who make this city home are from Detroit, while others are from Bombay, Lagos and Hong Kong. And while most are white, some are black or yellow or brown. . . . Most of them pay for the privilege of living in East Lansing and thus have a right to expect this community to extend to them certain opportunities. But this has not always been the case in East Lansing, a city which prides itself on being a proper and select community. . . . There are serious problems in East Lansing and those problems must involve all of us attending the University. We commend the concern which prompted the establishment of this commission. It was long overdue and we can

Robert Green led civil rights marches both on campus and in East Lansing during the 1960s. He also served as an aide to Martin Luther King Jr. Courtesy of MSU Archives and Historical Collections.

only hope it was indicative of a similar sentiment on the campus at large and in East Lansing itself. Our students are a diverse lot, but they all share the common desire to study and learn. We hope they will soon be able to learn how an American community can eradicate an unjust bias. The prolongation of the present situation is a continuing source of shame. It smacks of an ugly hypocrisy. While East Lansing may pride itself on the presence of the University as a neighbor, the opposite may unfortunately become true for us if nothing is done soon.

After more than a year's work, the commission issued two recommendations: an open-housing ordinance with punitive measures for violators, and an official procedure for handling complaints of housing discrimination. The city council turned down both recommendations by a three-to-two vote. Council member Max Strother, a former East Lansing mayor and one of the three votes against the recommendations, defended his position by saying, "There is nothing wrong with integration, but legislation to enforce it is entirely out of place." The *State News* editors disagreed, arguing that "an open housing ordinance is not legislation to enforce integration, but to prevent enforced segregation of minority group members." The editorial continued by pointing out that those who had opposed the proposals had "ignored the wishes of East Lansing Mayor Gordon L. Thomas, who strongly favors an open housing ordinance. The council has ignored the mayor, the Human Relations Commission, and the minority group members of the community who deserve an end to discriminatory practices in the City of East Lansing."

The council's actions precipitated some of East Lansing's first demonstrations in favor of racial equality. On 2 June 1964, more than one hundred students picketed MSU's Administration Building and East Lansing City Hall. The protest, led by Green and the president of the campus chapter of the National Association for the Advancement of Colored People, Melvin Moore, was directed at the three East Lansing councilors who had voted against the commission's recommendations—Strother, local businessman Kenneth Dillinger, and realtor Tod Kintner. The protesters carried signs that compared Strother to Alabama governor George Wallace and suggested that Dillinger and Kintner were Ku Klux Klan loyalists. Compared with the demonstrations that followed, however, the protest was relatively dignified.

By the end of 1964, the commission had established procedures for handling racial-discrimination complaints. When a written complaint of discrimination was filed, commission members would interview all parties involved. If the commissioners determined that the complaint was valid, they would attempt to mediate a settlement. If mediation failed, the case would be referred to the Michigan Civil Rights Commission. Although this procedure represented a step forward, it did not solve the problem, and sit-ins and protests continued into 1965, with demonstrators forcibly removed from city property; some were jailed. Much of the demonstrators' displeasure was directed at the city council for its failure to approve the commission's recommendations. Other protesters criticized Hannah's failure to become more involved in pressing for an ordinance. In a 2003 interview, for example, Green stated, "On one hand you could never call [Hannah] a racist, but there were times when I became perplexed by his unwillingness to tackle the racial problems in open housing in East Lansing. John Hannah could deal with specific acts of racial discrimination but he couldn't deal with the broader policy issues." The editors of the *State News* concurred with Green's view, criticizing both university officials and students for what seemed to be racial ambivalence: "Unfortunately, a singular silence has permeated the atmosphere on this side of Grand River. One would think that a University as embodied with the philosophy of racial equality as Michigan State would exert itself to right an apparent injustice. But such has not been the case. And MSU students have never taken more than a casual interest. Last year a group of dedicated students picketed an elderly lady's home and later staged a sit-down demonstration in the middle of Abbott Road for the cause of open housing. Since then, there has been nothing. Not a whimper out of student government, or from protestors or from other student publications."

Meanwhile, the council claimed to be doing everything it could to further civil rights, and city officials sought both to promote civil rights and to maintain order despite the increasingly obvious differences within the community. In 1965, the council passed a resolution declaring "its long-standing support of efforts to assure equal housing opportunity for all its citizens regardless of race, color, religion or national origin"; condemning discrimination; and endorsing "the effort of the State Civil Rights Commission to assure the fullest implementation of the civil rights provisions of the state constitution." Once again, another step forward had been taken, but the city still had no ordinance requiring equal opportunity in housing.

Some council members opposed the passage of an open-housing ordinance because Michigan attorney general Frank Kelley had ruled that only the state had the authority to legislate in the area of civil rights and they consequently feared that the passage of such a measure would result in a series of expensive lawsuits. In June 1965, however, East Lansing city attorney Ray Campbell informed the council that he believed an open-housing ordinance would be legal and constitutional. Rather than taking Campbell's opinion as an opportunity to enact the legislation, the commission decided that an open-housing ordinance was not needed, stating in March 1966, "There is increasing evidence that the citizens of the community are putting their houses in order, that progress is being made," and that "equal opportunity can be achieved without legal measures." Not until 15 April 1968 did the city council amend the housing ordinance to bring discrimination under the city's penal code, with penalties of a fine of up to five hundred dollars and/or ninety days in jail.

East Lansing Gets Wet

Since its creation in 1907, East Lansing had been a dry community, with the sale of liquor strictly forbidden. The city's voters defeated measures to legalize alcohol in 1958 and 1962, but yet another referendum appeared on the ballot in November 1968. Proponents of legalization touted the possibility of the construction of a major hotel complex and the likelihood of attracting other liquor-related businesses, winning the support of city councilors, other city officials, and members of the Greater East Lansing Chamber of Commerce. Opponents countered by forming the Best for East Lansing Committee, which put out pamphlets arguing not only that liquor should not be legalized but also that the convention center should not be built: "Have you ever attempted to drive near the Abbott-Albert intersection at mid-day on a busy Saturday? How would you like to try it if right then 300 cars were seeking to leave the area just after a convention ended? Supposing about half the 300 drivers had taken 'a few for the road' before starting out? Traffic would be a dangerous snarl. . . . Tax money from a large downtown apartment-hotel would NOT be worth the problems such an establishment would create." The committee also urged students to vote no: "East Lansing has been a blessing to the students who attend MSU for helping them go out into the world with the know-how to earn a living and raise a family," committee representative W. D. Baten wrote to the *State News.* "They should think twice before leaving East Lansing worse than it was when they came here by allowing intoxicating liquors to be sold in our city. As soon as our present charter, that has been in force for so long, is changed to allow intoxicating liquor to be sold here there will be other places, besides the tall hotel that is anticipated, where liquor can be sold."

But such arguments failed to carry the day, and voters overwhelmingly approved the sale of liquor, 7,271 to 3,935. Nearly eleven months passed before the opening of East Lansing's first bar selling liquor by the glass. In addition to the members of the Best for East Lansing Committee, others who were not pleased by the vote included merchants in neighboring communities: said Patriarche, "Surrounding areas would have been most happy to see the liquor question defeated because they would have gained commercial developments that will now locate in East Lansing."

On 1 October 1969, the Pickwick Pub, located in the Albert Pick Motor Hotel, hosted a special celebratory opening attended by local business and civic leaders. Pub manager Al Kelling said that the "hotel business operates with three things. First is service, 2nd is rooms and 3rd is liquor. It becomes a necessary part of the business." Other establishments selling liquor soon followed—Cave of the Candles, which served gourmet dinners, beer, liquor, and quality bottles of wine at its basement location at the corner of Abbott Road and Grand River Avenue; the Lizard's; the Old World Bread and Ale House; the Best Steak House; the restaurant at the top of Jacobson's Department Store; and the Pretzel Bell. Jacobson's offered impressive views of the Michigan State campus, and the Pretzel Bell decorated its

An International University

CLINTON DEWITT SMITH WAS ONE OF MID-MICHIGAN'S MOST PROMI-
nent early-twentieth-century civic leaders. Smith became a
professor of agriculture at State in 1893 and subsequently
filled key academic roles and earned a reputation for being
honest, kind, efficient, and smart—going out of his way to help area
farmers solve problems that were threatening to damage their crops.
In 1907, he became the new city of East Lansing's first mayor, on
several occasions paying city bills out of his own pocket when the
municipal bank account was empty. But a year later, he surprised the
local farming community and East Lansing's residents by suddenly
leaving Michigan. Smith departed because he had been offered the
presidency of Brazil's agricultural college, located in São Paulo. He
remained there for five years and then returned to his family farm
in New York.

In 1941, MSC student Margaret Smith, a freshman from Royal
Oak, Michigan, accompanied her father, businessman and collector
James Smith, on his annual trip to South America, traveling "farther
into the jungles of Dutch and French Guiana than any other white
woman," in the words of the *Michigan State News*. The Smiths visited
tribes of cannibals, as well as the famous French prison Devil's Island, carrying nothing more lethal than a movie camera. At one point,
seven prisoners escaping from the penal colony tried to seize the
Smith party's boat, although they were eventually frightened away.

Such travels were not unusual in the early days of the institution.
The land-grant mission of extending educational services to people
far from the campus proved a consistent and ongoing theme and
was put into practice with fervor. College professors' and researchers'
agricultural expertise was a natural by-product that could be exported
to other communities, near and far. College personnel, like Clinton

MAC professor of agriculture Clinton DeWitt Smith served as the first mayor of East Lansing before becoming president of Brazil's agricultural college. Courtesy of MSU Archives and Historical Collections.

DeWitt Smith, at times took permanent jobs at institutions outside the United States; on other occasions, they traveled to local farms to solve problems in cornfields. But with the advent of commercial airline travel, international projects became commonplace at what is now Michigan State University.

The Institute of Foreign Studies

MSC's approach to international programs had many facets. One of the more sophisticated of these revolved around the efforts of professor of Chinese history and language Shao Chang Lee. Lee, who had previously served as professor of Chinese and head of the Oriental studies department at the University of Hawaii, arrived in East Lansing in 1943 to take over the newly created Institute of Foreign Studies. "In the kind of world in which we are now living it is important that our college students have an opportunity to be reliably informed on the cultures, political philosophies, economics and other matters pertaining to those portions of the world with which I think we will be particularly concerned when the war is over," Michigan State president John Hannah wrote to Lee before he left Hawaii. "We have been thinking about this proposed program in foreign studies with particular emphasis on the Orient, South America and all of the Pacific areas. The many changes that have been necessary to accommodate to war have prevented as careful thinking as might otherwise have been possible as to specific proceedings. . . . For this first year of our Institute of Foreign Studies the program will be an experiment while we decide just how to proceed." When the two men first met, Hannah graciously greeted Lee and told him to "look after the Institute as if it were a new-born babe."

Lee arrived with an impressive international reputation. In a 26 August 1943 editorial, the *Honolulu Advertiser* lamented his impending move away from the islands, declaring, "The departure of Prof. Shao Chang Lee from the post he has held brilliantly at the University of Hawaii during the past two decades is an occasion for community regret. In Hawaii, Professor Lee has been more than a talented educator. He has been an envoy extraordinary of mutual understanding between the American and Chinese people and their governments.

International Center director Shao Chang Lee (*far right*) talks to students during United Nations Week in 1947. Students include (*left to right, standing*) Jean le Junter of France, Orlando Rodriguez of Nicaragua, Wilma Pinch of Lansing, and George Vayionis of Greece; (*seated*) John Wats of Trinidad. Courtesy of MSU Information Services.

He has been the personification of what Chinese friendship may mean to Americans, and at the same time has lost no opportunity to bring before his own people an understandable conception of Western ideals. Professor Lee will leave Hawaii with the appreciative aloha of the community."

During the 1943–44 school year, the institute's curriculum included nine courses, six related to the Far East and three to Latin America. Special lectures were common and featured such scholars as MSC sociologist Paul Honigsheim and Chilean journalist Ernesto Montenegro, who addressed Latin American issues, and Hindu scholar A. T. Raman, who presented a lecture series, India: Past and Present. A total of 306 students enrolled in the nine courses. "Students showed their interests in foreign studies by doing something," Lee later wrote. "For example, during the winter term, those who studied Oriental

history and culture set up an attractive and thought-provoking display of Chinese books and art objects in the College Library. During
the spring term the 49 students in the Oriental religion class and
the 46 in the Oriental art class gathered together enough pieces of
Chinese embroidery, pottery, porcelain, etc., of aesthetic value and
religious significance to encourage them to give an exhibit in the
College Museum."

Lee and other MSC faculty promoted the importance of understanding foreign culture and history outside the classroom as well.
From 15 October 1943 to 30 April 1944, Lee estimated that he gave 176
talks about China, Japan, and Sino-American and Japanese-American
relationships to a variety of groups—28 on campus, 38 in greater Lansing, and 110 in thirty-one other Michigan cities. E. B. Clement, vice
president of the Industrial Executives Club of Grand Rapids, wrote
to Hannah to express appreciation. "Professor Lee's presentation . . .
was everything you said it would be. . . . The fame of Michigan State
College will grow immensely through being represented by such men
and we hope to obtain another speaker from you for our next season
which starts in October." Lee reached still more areas of Michigan by
speaking about China and Japan on WKAR Radio.

Hannah always seemed to be thinking about the future, and the
Institute of Foreign Studies fit into his plans for MSC when the war
ended, just as he envisioned a need for more teachers, classrooms, and
dormitories. "It is expected that the facilities of the Institute will be
greatly expanded with the end of the war," he said. "The field of this
Institute is not limited to the campus of Michigan State College. . . .
There is an old Chinese proverb that says: 'If you are planning for
one year, grow grain, If you are planning for ten years, grow trees, If
you are planning for a hundred years, grow man!' All of us Americans
must not only plan for a hundred years, but must widen our horizons
to encompass the best interests of all good people of the world.
Yellow people, black people, brown people and red people must be
assured of those reasonable wants and freedoms that must be assured
all decent people if there is any likelihood of an enduring peace. The
Institute of Foreign Studies at Michigan State College may in a small
way contribute to widening those horizons."

Lee's duties at MSC quickly grew to encompass a variety of responses he had not originally envisioned. On 8 July 1944, he received

John Hannah aggressively promoted the world-wide expansion of Michigan State's educational role. Courtesy of MSU Archives and Historical Collections.

a note from Dean Lloyd Emmons offering free housing on campus in exchange for serving as the official adviser for the college's foreign students. Lee accepted and moved into the house known as Faculty Row No. 3 the following October. Renamed the International Center, it was declared the headquarters for all foreign students on campus, their home away from home in East Lansing. In 1944, Michigan State's foreign students came from Panama, Brazil, Puerto Rico, Costa Rica, Peru, Colombia, Cuba, Canada, and China as well as other countries. On 16 March 1946, the center moved to Faculty Row No. 6, a more spacious house located directly across the street from the Hannah residence, Cowles House.

By the 1957–58 school year, four instructors offered a total of thirty-six courses in foreign studies, and the institute sponsored many special events, such as International Students Day in 1958 and the annual Summer Institute on Asia in the late 1950s. Years later, English professor Russel Nye commented that "the extensive international make-up of [Michigan State's] faculty and of our students is a strength of this university. . . . Lots of people like to take credit for that. But, I think it was all started years ago by a man named S. C. Lee."

Perhaps partly as a result of Lee's influence, Hannah developed in-depth philosophies about the importance of international relations and its role in education. On 25 February 1945, Hannah shared his thoughts on the subject in a Sunday-afternoon broadcast on WKAR Radio.

> From where I sit, as an ordinary American, not an expert on international affairs, it seems obvious that the welfare and best permanent interests of the people of the United States and the people of Michigan are virtually intertwined with the interests and the welfare of Latin America and all the Pacific areas. In the world in which we live, with no point on the globe more than 60 hours away from our nearest airport, with the young men we knew as boys a few years ago not giving a second thought to stepping into a plane and taking off for Europe, India or Australia, no longer can the people of America or the people of Michigan, or you and I be concerned only with our selfish, best interests. It seems to me that it is a function of our educational institutions, and particularly of our colleges and universities, to make available to our students more adequate information than has formerly been possible about these people of the world with whom we must cooperate. . . . We are told that the United States is badly misunderstood in the nations in South and Central America, largely due to the attitudes of the representatives of our business and commercial houses that have gone to those areas to further the interests of the organizations for which they work. They have gone into the Latin American countries, not with the idea of becoming a part of them or trying to understand them, but solely for the purpose of financial exploitation, making what money could be made and returning to the United States in the least possible time. . . . The good will and civic intelligence which can deal with international questions wisely and humanly will have to be developed, not only in the schools and colleges of America but in the schools and colleges of all the nations of the world. . . . Michigan State College as a public institution financed by the people of Michigan has a responsibility to provide some leadership in this direction.

Hannah was correct that airplanes would force Americans to take a strong interest in foreign affairs. The convenience of air travel enabled professors in many disciplines to add a touch of Indiana Jones to their academic lives. Botany and plant pathology professor G. W.

John Hannah was equally comfortable conversing with college freshmen or with world leaders, including India's Indira Gandhi. Courtesy of MSU Archives and Historical Collections.

Prescott traveled to Ecuador in 1953 on a trip, financed by the National Science Foundation, to plan a longer research expedition. Five years later, he returned for a twenty-four-week exploration sponsored by the National Science Foundation and the Atomic Energy Commission. The Prescott party studied aquatic life and gathered more than one thousand specimens of plants for the MSU herbarium. It traveled by airplane, station wagon, and mule to collect plant, animal, soil, and bone specimens for a survey of radioactive fallout, avoiding headhunters and spending time with the Colorado Indians who lived on the western slopes of the Andes.

Assistant professor of social science John Messenger and his wife, Betty, spent part of 1958 with the Anang of Nigeria, visiting

The 1970 participants in the MSU Museum–sponsored annual expedition to Mexico to study insects included Rollin Baker, Richard Fitzner, Julia Allen, Gary Dawson, Robert Webb, and James Koschmann. Courtesy of MSU Museum Collections.

more than forty villages to study the impact of Christianity. The Messengers discovered that the young people had merged Christianity with the indigenous Anang religion, accepting parts of both faiths, although older men had completely rejected the new religion. The Messengers also encountered poisonous snakes and a group of large red and white lizards that ran around their house. "At first the lizards were shocking," Betty reported. "But we learned to love them. They killed ants and mosquitoes and scurried around all the time. We could hear them on the roof. When the lizards left and everything became quiet, we knew a snake was somewhere on the roof."

Students often accompanied their professors on these adventures. Geology professor Bennett Sandefur took his students to British Columbia, Labrador, Quebec, and Venezuela. "Out in the bush country where the going is toughest, the boys decide whether they want to be geologists or not," he told the *Michigan State University Magazine*. "If the boys still like geology after three months in an isolated area, living off the land, 700 miles from the nearest bathtub . . . they probably will make good geologists." The groups sometimes shaded the truth when encountering indigenous populations: recounted Sandefur, "For some reason the public thinks grown men who go looking for rocks are mentally unbalanced. To avoid the job of explaining the valuable work of a geologist, our researchers told their hosts they were taking an animal survey. A little white fib frequently saved us from numerous questions."

THE FOUR-POINT PROGRAM

In his 1949 inaugural address, President Harry Truman called for a "bold new program for making the benefits of our scientific advances and industrial progress available for the improvement and growth of underdeveloped nations." On 4 February, Hannah, writing in his capacity as president of the Association of Land-Grant Colleges, responded by offering "the full cooperation of the members of the Association of Land-Grant Colleges and Universities in carrying out the [proposed plan], which gave new inspiration to many of us who have long been convinced that such a program is basic to progress toward the stable, democratic, peaceful world which we all want. My own travels in Europe last summer . . . led me to think that bringing American know-how to bear on the problem of taking the resources of science, technology, and education generally onto the farms, into the factories, and into the homes of peoples abroad is essential to the rehabilitation of the post-war world economy. As institutions and in-dividuals, and collectively, the Land-Grant institutions and their staff will welcome an opportunity to do their part in realizing the program you have outlined." Truman's initiative, dubbed the Four-Point Pro-gram because it was the fourth point in the speech, eventually sent millions of dollars and many experts to underdeveloped countries throughout the world.

According to Ralph Smuckler's 2003 work, *A University Turns to the World*, "Michigan State was among the first to commit its talents to the newly defined national goal. It was a natural response for MSU, the university that took pride in having served as a model in congressional debates leading to the Morrill Land Grant College Act in 1862. The land-grant philosophy defined the mission of some

Homer Higbee filled many roles in MSU's international relations efforts but was perhaps best known for his work with the overseas study programs. Courtesy of MSU Archives and Historical Collections.

higher-education institutions to be that of serving the needs of society. At Michigan State, it applied to agricultural and also to other fields. Research, education, and extension programs were designed to meet the needs of the people. All were thought to be of high quality, and all were to address societal needs. Truman's Point IV represented an extension of the same populist educational philosophy to the broader world." Many of the international projects MSU undertook over the next decade were stimulated by or at least consistent with Truman's philosophy. MSU took a giant step in increasing its international presence in 1956, when it created a formal Office of International Programs under the direction of sociology professor Glen L. Taggart, who had started his international career when he traveled to Czechoslovakia as an eighteen-year-old Mormon missionary. He had also worked as an administrator in the U.S. Office of Foreign Agricultural Relations and had served as the Agriculture Department's key representative in the federal government's Point Four assistance program. The State Board of Agriculture charged Taggart with developing international-related research, education, and training programs for MSU students; providing consulting services and other technical assistance to the U.S. government, the United Nations, foundations, and other nonprofit agencies; and providing educational programs for students, business leaders, and government officials from other nations. He would report directly to Hannah. Over the next several decades, Taggart; Smuckler, who had become an assistant dean; and others, including George Axinn and Homer Higbee, helped MSU establish a worldwide reputation for its international programs.

According to Smuckler, both he and Taggart were

firmly committed to building a well-educated citizenry, that is, university graduates who carried with them adequate understanding of the international trends and forces they would live with or confront in the decades ahead. Forces within international economics and politics were important parts of the mix, as were influences of ethnicity and cultural diversity. We agreed that "international understanding," the popular phrase of the time, did not necessarily lead to world peace. Knowing one another better might actually incline one nation to take a stand against another more quickly or effectively. Nor were we trying to impose our values on people of the underdeveloped world. We were offering to strengthen institutions and introduce modern technologies that could, in their view and ours, contribute to their own progress. . . . We talked of working ourselves out of a job, about getting back to teaching and research in sociology and political science. If we could build international interests and commitment throughout the university, a central office such as ours would no longer be needed, at least not in its initial form. By then, each department and college would move internationally as appropriate to individual disciplines and fields, without the need for the help or encouragement of an international dean's office.

University-Building Projects

In 1951, Michigan State embarked on its first major overseas project, assisting Okinawa in the development of a new university. The University of the Ryukyus had been started in 1949 but encountered major problems in growing from a stone administration building and nine wooden classrooms into a legitimate university. MSC was asked to assist in an advisory capacity, furnishing four to six professors on two-year assignments to help in administration, curriculum development, instructional procedures, academic standards, research, and extension services. The consulting professors did little teaching but rather trained Ryukyuan faculty in a wide variety of functions needed in a quality university. More than 130,000 Okinawan civilians had died as a consequence of the invasion by U.S. and Allied troops during World War II, so island residents did not always welcome Americans—especially the very visible soldiers still stationed on the island. Nevertheless, Ferris Hartman of the Worldwide News Service reported in 1959, "Perhaps the most appreciated American activity here is the help of Michigan State University to establish Okinawa on the site of old Shuri castle." When the project concluded in 1968, fifty-eight MSU faculty members had participated, and the University of the Ryukyus had grown from being almost invisible to four colleges, twenty-eight departments, 219 faculty members, and 3,413 students.

Also in 1951, MSU became involved in Colombia, establishing a program, financed by the U.S. Technical Cooperation Administration, for an exchange of professors with the Colombian colleges of agriculture in Medellín and Palmira. On 1 January 1952, seven MSU professors departed for Colombia, while staff members and students from Colombia came to East Lansing for advanced training. The Michigan State staff members took the land-grant philosophy with them, and it appeared to catch on with the Colombians. "Faculty and students are now conducting field demonstrations in cooperation with neighboring farmers and are working more closely with experiment station staff," the *MSU Reporter* explained in 1957. MSU also helped establish a forestry institute at Medellín, introduced students and faculty to the concept of the short course, and worked with the W. K. Kellogg Foundation to provide needed physical facilities. "It is these professors and those they train who will provide the technical leadership essential to the future development of agriculture in Colombia," said John Stone, one of the MSU participants.

Similarly, four MSU professors journeyed to Brazil in 1954 to help establish the country's first school of business administration. And in 1959, MSU personnel helped in the establishment of the University of Nigeria. "Fifteen months ago there was nothing here except the village of Nsukka, a drab collection of mud houses with rusted tin roofs, surrounded by innumerable little plots where farmers patiently tilled their yams beneath the African sun," Paul Conklin reported in the *Detroit News* in 1961. "Before the spring of 1960 nothing had disturbed life in the valley for centuries. Today it has been transformed into a modern university campus and Nsukka has become the scene of an educational experiment of importance for all of West Africa." When MSU faculty members arrived in Nigeria, many of the students had been concentrating on subjects such as English literature and medieval history rather than on more practical areas such as sanitary engineering, agronomy, and industrial chemistry, skills the country desperately needed. MSU experts began stressing farming's importance to Nigeria's economy. "Most of our students come from rural areas and they want to get as far away from their past as possible," said Kirk Lawson, an MSU soil science professor. "Even those who do get degrees are above field work. This is a holdover from the old Africa where the white man never got his hands dirty. So, part of our program will be to get students back into the fields and get their hands into the earth." According to Alfred

Edwards, an MSU economic adviser, "Most of [the MSU personnel] do our own odd jobs, such as digging in the garden or putting up a radio aerial," he said. "It is good for the students to see that even though a man has a Ph.D. he can enjoy working with his hands."

THE VIETNAM PROJECT

In 1955, Michigan State launched what was perhaps its most ambitious international effort, the Vietnam Project. The most notorious of the project's many participants was Wesley R. Fishel, a Cleveland native who held a bachelor's degree in international relations from Northwestern University and a doctorate from the University of Chicago. Fishel had worked for naval intelligence during the early stages of World War II and as an intelligence analyst and language officer later in the conflict. He began his academic career in 1948 as a political science instructor at the University of California and came to Michigan State in 1951 as an associate professor of political science. In addition to his impressive background in international relations, Fishel brought with him a friendship with Ngo Dinh Diem, who became prime minister of South Vietnam in 1954 and hired Fishel as an adviser. As a result of this close relationship, Diem asked Michigan State to provide technical assistance to his country, and Hannah sent four staff members—Arthur Brandstatter of the department of police administration, public relations specialist James Denison, political scientist Edward Weidner, and economist Charles Killingsworth. They recommended four technical-assistance programs: public administration, police administration, assistance in establishing a constituent assembly, and help in writing a constitution. With Fishel's help, these agreements were finalized in 1955; thirty Michigan State personnel were authorized to work on the various programs after Diem was elected president of South Vietnam in 1955.

The Michigan State University Group (MSUG), especially Fishel, became intricately involved in the affairs of Diem's government, using both Michigan State's presence in Vietnam and the MSU campus to leverage that influence. In the fall of 1956, for example, thirty-two MSU staffers were stationed in Saigon and twenty Vietnamese government officials traveled to East Lansing for nine months of concentrated study in public administration, political science, economics, and police administration. In 1957, Diem traveled to MSU, where he was greeted warmly by Hannah and many university and state officials. Hannah met Diem at the airport, and a long procession of brand-new Oldsmobiles led by a police escort took the presidential party to the campus, where Diem addressed more than four thousand people. The *State Journal* reported that Michigan governor G. Mennen Williams presented Diem with a green-and-white polka-dot bow tie, saying, "This has been a good luck symbol for me through a number of political elections. I hope it will bring good luck to some of your campaigns." The Vietnamese president replied, "I do not know that political good luck is such good luck in my country. . . . Three weeks ago I was very fortunate to escape an assassin's attempt on my life."

By 1956, MSU officials were touting the Vietnam effort as a success. According to Vietnam Project economist Stanley K. Sheinbaum, "The State is our Campus. . . . For many years this has been the proud slogan of President John Hannah and Michigan State University. . . . Today, however, this slogan is being replaced by another and more engaging one: The World is our Campus. Today in South Vietnam, in Okinawa and in Brazil, Michigan State is serving the peoples of the free world." Sheinbaum went on to explain how the project was geared toward creating economic and political stability in South Vietnam, how instruction was not provided directly to the Vietnamese people but to native personnel who would directly interact with Vietnamese citizens, and how MSU faculty members' experiences would help them become better teachers when they returned to their East Lansing classrooms. "The communist threat remains, but South Vietnam is increasingly able to deal on equal terms with that threat," he concluded. "Michigan State can be proud of having extended its services and helped in bringing about the necessary stability to Vietnam."

Just six years later, however, MSU terminated the Vietnam Project. Smuckler told the *State Journal* that the Diem government had begun to insist that MSU prevent its faculty from publishing research that offered a negative or neutral analysis of the regime. Criticism of Diem's leadership had begun to grow, with no small amount of it emanating from the pens of MSU scholars. The *State*

Journal nonetheless reported significant successes for the MSU team, including helping to modernize the Vietnamese budget process, creating in-service training programs for public officials, developing police training institutes, assisting in reforming the civil service system, and helping to reestablish refugees.

Although MSU had departed South Vietnam before the Kennedy and Johnson administrations began to expand America's military presence, the school's early role in the country would not be forgotten. In 1965, three years after the Vietnam Project ended, Robert Scigliano and Guy Fox, two members of the MSUG, wrote a book, *Technical Assistance in Vietnam: The Michigan State University Experience*. The book offered broader and deeper criticism of the Vietnam Project than had been found in most previous newspaper and magazine stories, although the authors stated that "many of MSUG's weaknesses were corrected with the progress of time" and admitted that because of their personal involvement, they were reserving an overall judgment on the MSU project. Scigliano and Fox suggested that MSU faculty had benefited little from the project, with many opting not to return to the university after their stays in Vietnam or returning only briefly before leaving for other positions. The instructors who remained on campus showed little interest in the project, as evidenced by a 1958 campus survey showing that a mere 14 percent of faculty members indicated an interest in learning more about Southeast Asia and that none had expressed an interest in becoming proficient in Vietnamese. Scigliano and Fox also believed that the number of MSU participants became "seriously bloated" at times and that the university had given insufficient thought to the problems it would encounter in South Vietnam.

Few people outside the world of international relations ever read *Technical Assistance in Vietnam*; in fact, the extent of MSU's role in Southeast Asia was not common knowledge. That, however, would soon change. A 1966 article in *Ramparts* magazine, "Michigan State: The University on the Make," severely criticized Hannah, Fishel, and the entire university for abandoning academic integrity and replacing it with an unquestioning loyalty to U.S. foreign policy. Written by staff writer Warren Hinckle with an introduction by Sheinbaum, the article questioned both the university's role in Vietnam and its lack of honesty regarding the project. Sheinbaum, who had written the

Robert Scigliano was a member of MSU's team that consulted in Vietnam, as well as a co-author of one of the first sustained criticisms of the project, a 1965 book, *Technical Assistance in Vietnam: The Michigan State University Experience*.
Courtesy of MSU Archives and Historical Collections.

glowing article about Vietnam that appeared in the *Michigan State University Magazine* in 1956, wrote in *Ramparts* that the project had "become a CIA front" and that MSU might have been used to set up a potential assassination of a South Vietnamese leader. Hinckle then detailed all aspects of the project, dramatically linking the university to the law enforcement community. Hinckle suggested that MSU team members even bought guns for Vietnam's police and security training programs. "MSU is still big on police," he wrote. "There are, literally, policemen all over the campus, almost beyond the wildest expansion of the human retina. There is the campus police—a complement of roughly 35 men in blue uniforms. Then there are the professors and visiting firemen at the school of Police Administration. Finally, it is hard to find a parking spot on campus since so many police cars are occupying the stalls; state police headquarters adjoins MSU."

Hinckle's article broke little new ground. An earlier pamphlet produced by another *Ramparts* writer, Robert Scheer, had also accused MSU of having worked closely with the CIA in Vietnam. In 1966, *State News* staffer Tom Segal had approached Fishel about the accusations and had been told that Scheer's information was "without basis." Fishel explained that neither he nor the program was involved at any time in undercover work. "Although Fishel has been connected with Vietnam for many years and has done much valuable work there, it doesn't appear as if any of his work will ever be the basis for a James Bond novel," Segal wrote.

Michigan State initially decided to ignore the charges, even though spokesperson Jim Denison called the *Ramparts* article "scurrilous" and filled with "half-truths, distortions, misinterpretations and outright lies." He also pointed out some minor factual errors in the article—Hannah was not the son of an Iowa chicken farmer, and parking spaces could be found on campus. MSU soon began to alter its stance, however. The front page of the 15 April 1966 *State News* quoted Hannah as admitting, "There is some truth to the content of the *Ramparts* article," and Denison admitted that "CIA men worked on the MSU Vietnam Project."

One of the first major discussions of the *Ramparts* charges took place on 20 April at a panel discussion sponsored by Delta Phi Epsilon National Professional Foreign Service Honorary. More than one thousand people filed into the Union ballroom to hear Smuckler, Fishel, and English professor Adrian Jaffe, a critic of the Vietnam Project, talk about "whether the Central Intelligence Agency should attempt to penetrate American university projects abroad." The moderator was Charles Adrian, chair of the political science department, who announced that he had been selected because he was "the only person on this campus who has never seen a James Bond movie." Smuckler said that relationships with the CIA were inappropriate, and that in the future, Michigan State would have "no relationship with the CIA or with people known to be part of the CIA." Jaffe said that overseas projects should always be subordinate to the primary obligations of the student and faculty at home, and that MSU had become involved in something "unworthy and it forgot its primary obligation." And Fishel, when asked why the university had been buying guns, flatly denied the accusation: "At no time did MSU buy guns or any other weapons for the Vietnam government. Magazines sell by these statements and the reputations of universities and individuals rise or fall by them." *State News* staff writer Joan Solomon reported that most of the audience, "a mixture of gray-suited faculty members, madras-skirted coeds and bearded 'activists,'" took the side of Jaffe and opposed Fishel.

MSU's decision to ignore the charges was not working. At Hannah's regular Friday press conference on 25 April, he apparently anticipated that most of the questions would be about Vietnam and consequently prepared a lengthy statement. The university, he said, "did not have CIA people operating under cover provided by the university or in secret from the Vietnamese government," but he admitted that officials had begun to suspect that the project had been infiltrated. Hannah also said that MSU had learned from the effort, and that in other international projects, four out of every five team members now came from the MSU campus. In the future, he said, the university would avoid situations of great political sensitivity.

The debate nevertheless continued. *Ramparts* staff and MSU administrators confronted each other before a state House Ways and Means committee; *Ramparts* representatives appeared at a meeting of the Students for a Democratic Society and argued MSU actions with Vietnam Project participant and police administration professor Ralph Turner; and Hannah and Denison continually responded to questions from the media about past actions in Vietnam.

The more MSU defended itself, the more criticism it seemed to generate. After the 25 April press conference, the *Detroit Free Press* ran an editorial, "He Doth Protest Too Much":

Ramparts magazine might have overstated the case against MSU's involvement in Vietnam over a seven-year period, but MSU President John A. Hannah certainly overstated his denial. . . . We will accept Hannah's explanation that he didn't know about the CIA involvement, but the fact is that members of MSUG did. Wesley Fishel, MSU professor and buddy of Diem, knew about it. Stanley K. Sheinbaum was a coordinator for the project as an MSU faculty member and he helped write the article. Ralph H. Smuckler, acting dean in charge of MSU's international programs, said just the other day that Washington, Saigon and MSU all knew about it. . . . Hannah's 4,400-word statement, it seems to us, would have been more convincing if he'd just copped a plea and said MSU learned a lesson—which it apparently did.

Also in April 1966, Smuckler prepared a *Report on the MSU-Vietnam Project,* beginning the document with the words, "In some respects reviewing the Michigan State–Vietnam Project is like delving into old history." Smuckler went on to list some of the lessons MSU had indeed learned in Vietnam: international programs should provide more "feedback" to the academic programs in East Lansing; projects such as Vietnam were too large for the university to staff appropriately; if people suggested by government agencies were considered for employment, the university should be "completely sure" of their background; and a university should stress the building of academic institutions, concentrating on its expertise—teaching, educational research, and strengthening the curriculum. "The important point which we hope would also come through clearly in such a future analysis would be that the University learned important lessons from the experience and went on to wiser, more effective, more valuable endeavors," Smuckler said.

The *State News* had carefully followed both *Ramparts*'s and the university's sides of the controversy and eventually launched an investigation of the *Ramparts* allegations. Campus editor Joe Bumbarger and his assistant, Joan Solomon, traveled to San Francisco over the 1966 Labor Day weekend, visiting *Ramparts*'s "nondescript" office located "in the heart of San Francisco's 'topless' district. . . . The staff asked whether we knew President Hannah and Wesley Fishel, professor of political science, and were amazed that two coeds at a school overrun with police actually would have been allowed to see the two men. They also seemed to have real suspicions that we had been sent by the University on an official fact-finding mission."

Analysis of and speculation regarding MSU's role in South Vietnam continued for many years. In 1997, for example, the University of North Carolina Press published Joseph G. Morgan's *The Vietnam Lobby: The American Friends of Vietnam, 1955–1975*, in which Fishel is one of the featured characters. According to Morgan, Fishel might "have been involved in the decision to appoint Diem. At least one account states that Fishel 'worked for or with the CIA' at the time he first encountered Diem in Japan. It is not clear if this is true, although embassy reports from Tokyo state that Diem . . . spoke to an 'American source' during their stay in Japan. Fishel nevertheless acted as an intermediary between Diem and the State Department after Diem took up residence in the United States, and one Foreign Service officer thought that Fishel served as 'a sort of press agent and advisor' for Diem. The nature of Fishel's activities nonetheless remains obscure because his name does not appear in State Department archives until the month after Diem became premier, and Fishel's personal papers contain little information from the early 1950s."

In 1998, the MSU Press published John Ernst's *Forging a Fateful Alliance: Michigan State University and the Vietnam War.* Agreeing with many of the earlier assessments of the project, Ernst also offered some insights into the motives and personalities of many of the key players. He called *Ramparts* a muckraking journal that "often sensationalized the truth to sell copies, and at times the accuracy of its reporting was questionable. Using 'color, gloss and flamboyance,' Warren Hinckle, the magazine's young editor, set out to 'make *Ramparts* pay.' He considered the Michigan State story their biggest exposé." Hannah, Ernst wrote, "enthusiastically endorsed the MSUG because it combined his love of institution building and dislike of communism." He described Fischel as "part of a new breed of intellectual surfacing after the Second World War. The philosopher and historian Garry Wills appropriately dubbed them 'Bogart professors,'

Wesley Fishel was popular among Michigan State students but also became a target for much of the criticism of the Vietnam Project.
Courtesy of MSU Archives and Historical Collections.

the get-tough, take-action liberal academics of the cold war. Similar to actor Humphrey Bogart's character in the movie *Casablanca*, they were idealists with an edge, individuals with a job to do: stop the communist menace at whatever cost. . . . As a result of the *Ramparts* exposé on the MSUG, Fishel was singled out by anti-war demonstrators and suffered more than other Michigan State faculty. In 1955, the first year of the Vietnam contract, he was voted 'Teacher of the Year' by Excalibur, Michigan State's senior men's society. Just more than a decade later, students disrupted his classes and referred to him as a butcher."

OTHER INTERNATIONAL EFFORTS

In 1948, the national 4-H Club Foundation created the International Farm Youth Program, and MSU was involved in the effort from the beginning. The program sent young people to other nations to live with farm families, while foreign youth came to the United States to live with American farm families. Russell Mawby, an assistant director of MSU's 4-H Cooperative Extension Service, later explained, "The participants are between twenty and thirty years of age, may or may not be college graduates, and must show ability to adjust, communicate, and learn the language of their host country. In the end, the young people come to understand other ways of life and develop an international scope to their thinking." Mawby, who later served as president of the W. K. Kellogg Foundation and as a member of the MSU Board of Trustees, was a pioneer in the program. He went to England and Wales between his junior and senior years as a horticulture major at Michigan State. "The program was different then; we were guinea pigs," he said. "I lived with 50 families—never stayed anywhere more than four days. I never really got to know anyone and get into the routine of life there."

In 1954, Michigan State received a Carnegie Foundation grant of $150,000 to address the international floodplain along the U.S.-Mexican border and suggest technical improvements that could improve living conditions on both sides of the border. In 1957, eight professors and eight graduate students left for South America to help establish research, extension, and short-course programs and to work to improve farming processes and teaching methods—further efforts that connected to the school's long-standing land-grant philosophy. In October of the same year, two deans from a Colombian agricultural college arrived in East Lansing to begin work on master's degrees. Involvement in Africa and with the 4-H youth exchange program led to MSU's 1961 selection as the training center for Nigeria-bound Peace Corps volunteers. "Michigan State University is uniquely qualified to conduct the training program and be the administering agent for the Peace Corps in the overseas portion of the project," Peace Corps director Sargent Shriver said. Thirty-three volunteers lived in Butterfield Hall that fall and put in fifteen-hour days learning about Nigeria, both from MSU professors connected to the University of Nigeria and from Nigerian students studying on the East Lansing campus.

MSU faculty periodically traveled to a lodge outside of Washington, D.C., to conduct communication seminars for groups of government, social, and business leaders from dozens of nations throughout the world. Sponsored by the International Cooperation Administration (ICA), the professors attempted to help participants learn in a week communication skills that the average American college student learned in a term. An article in the May 1959 *MSU Reporter* described the process:

> From the minute they get to the lodge until they leave, the professors work. They answer questions at breakfast, discuss problems with participants over coffee and constantly try to anticipate the communication problems the men and women will face. The challenge of meeting a new problem every few minutes and tailoring an entire course to fit a particular group involves intense intellectual effort. Because the demands on the professor are so great, few staff members are asked to stay for more than one week at a time. When the professors return to their campuses two things seem to happen. First, they notice the slowed pace because their students have four years to find the answers to many of the communication problems the professors and ICA participants have had to solve in a week. "It's like getting off an educational turnpike onto a country road," was the way one professor who had taught at a seminar explained it. The second thing that happens is that the professor no longer perceives the world the way he did before he left his campus. He

MSU teams of consultants who traveled to other countries to provide assistance often employed a multidisciplinary approach. Campus landscaper Harold Lautner, for example, traveled to Nigeria to help plan the new university because officials believed that the physical look of a university greatly influenced its academic development.

Courtesy of MSU Archives and Historical Collections.

has lived with people from many different lands and things have changed for him.

MSU's faculty participants included James Page of education, Iwao Ishino of sociology and anthropology, Hideya Kumata of the Communications Research Center, Wilfred Veenendaal of the Audiovisual Center, and Theodore Kennedy of communication arts. David Berlo, assistant professor of communication arts, served as director of the seminars.

MSU's international programs almost always involved multidisciplinary teams that brought together faculty members from fields such as economics, languages, agriculture, management, forestry, horticulture, and education. For example, Harold Lautner, MSU's head of urban planning and landscape architecture, consulted in the planning of the University of Nigeria because program administrators believed that a university's physical appearance greatly influenced its academic development.

Many other MSU faculty members were not part of MSU's official international efforts but made the exploration of other cultures and languages a key part of their lives. Oscar Tosi, an Italian physicist fluent in Spanish, French, German, Romanian, and English as well as his native tongue, joined the speech department in the mid-1960s to teach and conduct research in psychological and physiological acoustics, involving a combination of electronics, acoustics, psychology, and physiology.

Irwin Whitaker, an artist known for his pottery and for his enamels on copper, arrived at MSC in 1950 along with his wife, Emily, a writer and photographer who specialized in Latin America. The Whitakers eventually combined their interests and began an in-depth study of Mexican pottery. "The 1960s were a time at MSU when faculty was encouraged to travel, to learn and teach in other cultures," they subsequently wrote. "At times, President Hannah seemed almost preoccupied with international issues." By 1971 the Whitakers had begun taking field trips to Mexican villages, traveling by car, by bus, on foot, and even by oxcart. They interviewed practicing potters, took hundreds of photos, and described pottery traditions that would soon be extinct. The Whitakers secured funding from the Ford Foundation, the MSU Foundation, MSU's Latin American Studies Center, the art department, and the College of Arts and Letters and in 1976 published their in-depth study, *A Potter's Mexico*, which offered more than just descriptions of the Mexican creations: "The real issue is human life," the Whitakers wrote. "The Mexican potter can no longer afford to contribute his gifts to society when his only reward is an empty stomach. Ultimately, if Mexican pottery is to survive in any form, ways must be found to assure the potter will earn a living wage, and that his product will meet contemporary technical standards. It may well be that, for a time, as in Scandinavia, his government will have to subsidize him. Both of us feel that unless efforts are begun immediately to solve the potter's dire economic dilemma, the end of the 20th century may well witness the death of a cultural heritage which once belonged to us all."

Like the Whitakers, humanities professor Austin Moore published an account of his travels. In 1963, Moore spent two months traveling in Africa, visiting "Egypt, Ethiopia, Kenya, Zanzibar, Tanganyika, the Rhodesias, South Africa, Mozambique, and Uganda." He wrote in *Knight Errant in Africa*, "We traveled 12,000 miles by plane, rail, bus, and car, and for added zest rode camels, an ostrich, and a tamed Grevy's zebra. However exciting we found Zanzibar, aromatic with cloves, wide-spanned Victoria Falls, and the Kimberley diamond mines, we were most stirred by our contacts with vestiges of primitive tribalism and the wild animals which we saw in seven great parks and reserves."

PRESIDENT HANNAH AND INTERNATIONAL PROGRAMS

John Hannah probably took a more direct interest in the university's international projects than in any other academic area. When the idea of a new college in Nigeria was proposed in 1958, Hannah flew to Africa to make a preliminary inspection trip. In 1960, accompanied during portions of the trip by Taggart and business college dean Alfred Seelye, Hannah spent three weeks in South America visiting the MSU projects in Brazil and Colombia. He also delivered an address at a U.S.-Brazil technical cooperation conference. Hannah often talked about his belief that his university should serve the populations of the world as it had always served the citizens of Michigan. In talking about international aid, his words frequently resembled those he used to describe the university's Extension Service: "One of the greatest contributions America can make to the improvement of living standards, elimination of hunger, and fostering of peace in certain parts of the world is by encouraging education in food production, food handling, food utilization and better homemaking and family life among rural and urban people."

Hannah's travels to MSU's international projects often resulted in memos to top administrators suggesting changes or additions to the university's existing programs, especially those academic areas that directly affected students. In early 1964, the president wrote to the dean of the College of Arts and Letters, Paul Varg,

> I returned from the recent trip to Nigeria, Pakistan, Taiwan, and Okinawa with an even greater conviction of the requirement that we put more emphasis into the teaching of languages on this campus than we have been doing in the past. . . . I have an increasingly strong conviction that this University must move in the direction of expanding its offerings in Chinese language, Chinese history, Chinese culture, a study of Chinese traditions, mores and the rest. . . . Beyond that, we are very shortsighted if we continue to ignore the Arabic world. When I travel all the way from sub-equatorial Africa across the Middle East into Pakistan and recognize that the Arabic world extends on up into Afghanistan and over a substantial fraction of Russia and a part of Red China, and then on to the south covering all of Indonesia and some of the intermediate areas, it appears to me that we act as though we do not understand the world in which we live.

Varg quickly responded:

> In your letter you refer to the importance of Chinese studies. We are by no means wholly backward in this area. The Department of History offers some fine work in both Chinese and Japanese history and the Department of Political Science offers courses in Contemporary China, Japan and Southeast Asia. . . . May I say that these offerings are by no means adequate. We should have a qualified professor in Oriental Philosophy and in Oriental Art to supplement

John Hannah spent much of his professional career traveling to foreign lands, including the My Long hamlet in Vietnam. Courtesy of MSU Archives and Historical Collections.

the work being done in Oriental Religions. . . . We are not in nearly as good shape in the field of Arabic and Middle East Studies. Here our work is almost wholly limited to what is being done by Professor [Fauzi] Najjar. Professor Najjar gives most of his time to the Social Science division of the University College but he also teaches a course or two in the Department of History. Mr. Najjar is from Lebanon, a Ph.D. from the University of Chicago, a first-rate scholar, and a highly attractive person. . . . In my opinion it would be wiser to begin by building where we already have considerable strength, namely, Far Eastern studies. I assume that financial resources will play a considerable part in determining our first moves.

Historian Madison Kuhn described the extent of Hannah's commitment to international programs:

Each winter he took off by air for a month or two, usually accompanied by Mrs. Hannah or by their daughter or one of their sons. But there was time to study only a few programs with the intensity he wished. Often these inspections were combined with responsibilities to one or another of the dozen international-oriented bodies on whose boards he served at various times. These range from the Foundation for European Educational Centers to the Public Advisory Committee for Trade Negotiation. One year he studied American aid to Korea for the United States Senate. By 1965 he had flown more than a million miles on university and federal matters; but the world campus had grown to twenty-two institutions. He was beginning to ask whether one university could afford to spread itself much thinner. For several years no other American school sent so many of its staff on overseas assignment. This was maintained at substantial cost—not in dollars, for governments and foundations provided them—but in the loss to the campus of so many of its best people for a year or two at a time. Yet President Hannah insisted that it send its own rather than outsiders, and the best rather than the expendable. Whatever the cost, he saw in this missionary work a "hidden overhead" that accrued to the university in knowledge of other peoples and cultures. It enriched teaching, broadened research, and strengthened the new foundation-supported institutes of African, Asian and Latin American studies. And it contributed the training of young people who, like the contingents of Peace Corps trainees, would soon go overseas themselves.

When Hannah could not personally visit MSU's international projects, he sent trusted staff and had them prepare detailed reports when they returned. While some of these emissaries produced glowing reports about overseas projects, College of Agriculture dean Thomas Cowden did not, frequently criticizing programs that were at least partially his responsibility, proposing solutions, and then informing Hannah that changes were already under way. After a 1963 trip to Okinawa, Cowden wrote,

Considerable progress appeared to be made by the university. I have the feeling, however, that the big contribution of the university is probably in the field of teacher training and education. . . . I am very much concerned about faculty members at the University of the Ryukyus who have been students in the College of Agriculture at Michigan State University. They have been back long enough that some of them should be assuming roles of responsibility. It appears to me that many of them have settled in a rather comfortable groove and do not really have enough drive to implement the philosophy of service of the land-grant college. If we are going to spend public money in bringing foreign students to our campus, we must take steps here to supercharge them with a philosophy of service so that they will carry it back and use it in their home country. Steps are being taken to improve this situation in the College of Agriculture. . . . It is my feeling that from the standpoint of oriental agriculture Japan has more to offer than the United States. Consideration should be given to using Japanese in our contracts even if we have to subcontract with some universities. Japanese are more familiar with rice and also the type of farming practiced in much of the orient.

Hannah was also fascinated by university faculty members' experiences in distant lands. He always sought to provide timely responses to anyone who wrote to him concerning an issue relevant to MSU, but his quickest responses often were related to international topics. Museum curator and anthropologist Moreau Maxwell, for example, wrote about his fieldwork in a late 1962 letter to the president:

In the period from July 2 to September 9, I conducted archeological field investigations along the southern coast of Baffin Island in the Canadian Arctic. The field members of this expedition included six persons. The field phase of the research and subsequent laboratory analysis will be financed in large part by a grant from the National Science Foundation. Our field work this season was extremely successful. We were fortunate in finding twelve additional early sites which should encompass the period 4000 B.C. to the beginning of the Christian era. We located one valley approximately $11\frac{1}{2}$ miles long and $\frac{1}{2}$ of a mile wide which was intensively occupied over a period of at least 4,000 years. Cultural materials in this valley were covered by a thick layer of sod which was so insulated in the soil that it has remained permanently frozen through this period. We recovered

MSU Museum curator Moreau Maxwell traveled to foreign countries, his trips frequently financed by grants from scientific and governmental institutions. Courtesy of MSU Archives and Historical Collections.

5,000 artifacts in this valley and in other sites that included in the recovery material specimens such as wooden knife handles, seal skin and caribou skin clothing and carved ivory specimens which had not been hitherto reported from the eastern Arctic. I feel that the scientific results of the summer are unusually significant and that our research was most satisfactory in every respect.

Two days after receiving the Maxwell letter, Hannah responded: "I am delighted with the fact that you and this University have acquired an interest in the Arctic. You may recall that many years ago I tried to convince some of our researchers, including the Museum staff, that this is a much more fertile area for our interest than Mexico or elsewhere in the world where we will be competing with many universities. No American university can more appropriately be interested in the Far North than this one. I hope that your work marks the continuance of a significant interest on the part of not only our Museum, but of all the departments and disciplines with an appropriate interest in this area."

CRITICISM OF MICHIGAN STATE'S INTERNATIONAL PROGRAMS

In the spring of 1962, the *Michigan State News* reprinted critical articles from the *New Republic*, including one titled "Professors Serving Overseas Live Life of Diplomat." The authors, MSU professor of economics Milton Taylor and MSU associate professor of English Adrian Jaffe, suggested that professors from U.S. colleges and universities involved in overseas projects often ignored intellectual pursuits in favor of the exciting life of quasi-diplomats. Taylor and Jaffe quoted from Walter Adams and John Garraty's *Is the World Our Campus?*, citing the testimony of a former political science dean in Turkey that the American personnel he encountered "were not the first-rate scholars New York University had promised us. With possibly one exception, they were mediocrities. They were not the kind of specialists we needed most. . . . They seemed more concerned with getting diplomatic license plates for their cars, buying scotch at bargain-counter commissary prices, and joining the social whirl of the cocktail circuit than with helping Turkey. They were status-starved and power-hungry. They treated us not like colleagues and equals, but like benighted souls to be saved from intellectual backwardness."

According to Taylor and Jaffe, the "hybrid professor-diplomat rarely fulfills either of his functions satisfactorily. The qualities of a good foreign service officer—loyalty to directives from above, industrious and tactful obedience to the requirements of the establishment—are not the qualities of a good teacher. And the qualities of a professor—independence, detachment, intellectual integrity, freedom of thought—are not of very much practical value to a foreign service officer. Consequently, neither the government nor the university derive much benefit from the cross-breeding." Of more direct concern to the readers of the *Michigan State News*, however, was the authors' charge that the "former chief of the Michigan State University Group in South Vietnam, in civil life a professor of political science, was a close competitor in prestige, duties and influence with the U.S. Ambassador himself and on one occasion, when he arrived at the Saigon airport was offered a motorcycle escort. He set the tone for the entire establishment." The unnamed professor was clearly Wesley Fishel.

The *State News* printed a letter from Taggart alongside Taylor and Jaffe's piece. Not surprisingly, MSU's dean of international programs strongly disagreed with their assessment: "The article . . . will justifiably be taken as an affront to a large proportion of university professors who have participated in programs abroad," he wrote. "Their conditions of work and motivations are so different from those described in the article." Taggart argued that MSU's programs were helping people in other lands "to lift themselves out of ignorance, poverty and despair." He pointed out that MSU's growing foreign experience would be a valuable tool in addressing U.S. problems in international relations. "I am convinced that there is nothing this country is doing abroad that will have a more fundamental effect for betterment than our educational efforts. When history records this era, one of its more significant developments will be the spread of education to all people and classes in the less developed countries."

Management professor Stanley Bryan, working in Brazil, also responded to Taylor and Jaffe's article: "The authors swung their tar brush with little consideration for on whom they dripped tar. . . . I am writing this letter at home [in Brazil]. Outside, in our postage-stamp-sized yard and in the street in front, there are about forty children playing, chatting in Portuguese. Of the forty children two are Americans (ours) and the rest are Brazilian. My older son is getting ready to play basketball tonight with a Brazilian team. My wife and I are going to have dinner with a Brazilian family. Is there any better way to widen a person's horizon than to learn a foreign language, to experience something different in life? This is part of the attraction of becoming an 'overseas professor.' There are wonderful relationships developed." Bryan also rebutted the charges regarding the alleged extravagant lifestyles enjoyed by overseas professors: his family had no maid, unlike many other residents of his middle-class Brazilian neighborhood; he had been to the commissary only once during his two years in Brazil; he traveled to work by bus or streetcar; he and his wife attended cocktail parties about as frequently as when they lived in East Lansing; and his house lacked screens on the windows and central heating. Bryan concluded, "Everyone at Michigan State University can justifiably be proud of the dedicated group of MSU professors who over the years have participated in the MSU Brazil Project, and of the wonderful Brazilians who are carrying on the successful institution created to help Brazil achieve its rising expectations of greatness."

Agricultural economics professor Harold Riley's description of his stint in Colombia in the early 1960s echoed Bryan's positive assessment. "We taught Colombia's future leaders how to make their food system work better," he later said. The Rileys had to pasteurize their own milk and wash their vegetables in special water; nevertheless, all the members of the family got hepatitis. The Rileys remembered not driving around in cars with diplomatic license plates or attending frequent cocktail parties but instead watching fireworks during celebrations at the Catholic church across the street from their house. The professor's wife, Dorothy, took pleasure in painting the country's market scenes, and their children learned much more than reading and math at their multicultural school. Riley returned to Colombia in 1972, during which time he hosted John Hannah, by then the director of the U.S. Agency for International Development, and showed him the successes of MSU's Colombian project.

Despite the sporadic criticisms, the overseas projects overwhelmingly brought positive publicity to the Michigan State campus. In 1957, the *Michigan State University Magazine* reprinted an article

In 1972, John Hannah visited Colombia, where agricultural economics professor Harold Riley (*far left*) highlighted the successes of MSU programs. Courtesy of the Riley family.

by William H. Stoneman that had previously appeared "in 45 of the largest newspapers in America, with a total circulation of more than 12,300,000," noting that the piece provided "conclusive proof that the eyes of the world are on M.S.U.":

> From Maine to California most Americans think of mighty Michigan State University as a first-class menace. . . . Coach Hugh Duffy Daugherty's six-decker team of high-velocity behemoths has spread terror and apprehension throughout the land. . . . Outside the continental United States, from Saigon to Okinawa, to São Paolo, Brazil and back again via Colombia, Costa Rica, Mexico and distant Pakistan, another set of teams have won a different sort of reputation. The stars who make up these outfits are fighting and winning against the toughest opposition of them all—the misery, ignorance, poverty and malorganization which hamstrings the underdeveloped countries of the world. In the football world, M.S.U. ranks with Oklahoma as one of the two greatest powerhouses in the land.

In the application of academics to the assistance of underdeveloped
countries of the world, M.S.U. is in a class almost by itself.

Other journalists also wrote eloquently about MSU's international efforts. "In the last eight years, M.S.U. has reached out to the lives of . . .
the farmer in Pakistan, the student in Okinawa and the businessman
in Brazil," Bob Voges of the Associated Press editorialized in 1959. "It
has brought these diverse people skills harnessing their immediate
environment—what might be called practical education, American
know-how." Closer to home, the *State News* frequently covered MSU's
overseas programs, including a 12 November 1962 article that
credited faculty with helping the University of the Ryukyus increase
its enrollment from 560 in 1957 to 2,700 in 1961, building a library
containing thirty-thousand volumes, and providing extensive training
to new librarians.

The stories usually focused on the efforts of men; the only
women usually mentioned were the international specialists' wives.
But female MSU faculty members, especially those in the home economics department, made significant contributions. The department
had developed a reputation for providing Michigan women with quality homemaking services, but home economics officials also believed
that a home filled with love and peace extended those feelings into the
rest of the world and that homemaking skills were just as important
to a peaceful world as were agricultural production, academics, or national defense. Women from thirty-six countries, including Thailand,
Pakistan, Greece, Peru, Argentina, Lebanon, Egypt, and China, visited
the East Lansing campus during the 1950s and 1960s, studying a
wide range of subjects related to improving home life and children's
welfare. Home economics faculty traveled overseas, helping to teach
about nutrition, among many other subjects. In 1959, for example,
Faye Kinder, an associate professor of foods and nutrition, consulted
with MSU's project at the University of the Ryukyus.

FOREIGN STUDENTS ON THE EAST LANSING CAMPUS

MSU's international effort emphasized providing students from
foreign countries with the skills needed to better conditions in their

The Adventure in World Understanding program brought foreign students from all over the United States to the Michigan State campus during the Christmas season to experience American holiday traditions. Courtesy of MSU Information Services.

native countries. In 1963, for example, five individuals received the Roman Magsaysay Award, given to persons in Asia in recognition of "greatness of spirit shown in service to the public." Two of the award winners were former MSU students. Verghese Kurien of India had taken classes in dairy engineering and had earned a master's degree in mechanical engineering in 1948. After graduation, he returned to India as an engineer in the dairy department of the national government, and he later became manager of the Kaira District Cooperative Producers Union. Under Kurien's leadership, the cooperative increased its production of pasteurized milk from five thousand gallons in 1950 to 111 million gallons in 1963. Enormous improvements in the physical and financial health of the villages where the milk was produced were also realized. Kurien singled out MSU professors Howard Womochel and A. W. Farrell as instrumental to his professional success. The other winner, Akhter Hameed Khan, studied at MSU in 1958 to prepare to become director of the new Pakistan Academy for Rural Development at Comilla, which opened on 27 May 1959. The academy quickly began providing banking and credit facilities, machinery service and repair, information about up-to-date farming

During the 1950s, Michigan State students participated in an annual international festival in Jenison Field House that featured music, dancing, and folk art from dozens of different countries. Courtesy of MSU Information Services.

practices, and education and health programs for children and adults in isolated villages. Kahn was recognized for his inspiring personal commitment of experience, erudition, and energy to scientific testing and application of a workable formula for rural emancipation among his people.

Students from throughout the world were frequent visitors on campus. Beginning in the early 1950s, the Adventure in World Understanding became an annual December event. Dozens of foreign students from colleges and universities across the country came to live in Michigan State's dorms and later at the Kellogg Center during their schools' holiday break. They toured Michigan automobile plants, participated in cross-cultural discussions, and spent Christmas Eve and Christmas Day with mid-Michigan host families. The program's coordinator was Louise Carpenter, who also served as a counselor to international students. In 1954, she took a sabbatical, visiting many of the students with whom she had worked on the East Lansing campus. In her seven months of travel, she met with seventy-five former students in the Near, Far, and Middle East. In Baghdad, eight Iraqi Spartans held a Michigan State Night for her in Baghdad: "Every one of our former Iraqi students is working in the job for which he was trained," she told the *MSC Record*. "I am convinced that it is important to remain in contact with our former students after they leave the United States. It proves to them we are interested in their problems and are ready to help them just as we would our next-door neighbor. Then too, they can give us valuable information about their countries, which will help us understand their culture and which may eventually lead the way to peace." Despite such lofty goals, the program occasionally ran into real-world problems: in 1963, Arab and Israeli students physically threatened each other when a discussion became heated, and they had to be separated by university staff.

That Remarkable Year, 1955

I N THE 1940S, WHEN MICHIGAN STATE COLLEGE PRESSURED THE BIG
Ten Conference for membership, many suggested that nearby
University of Michigan posed the biggest obstacle. UM officials
denied that they stood in the way, and when MSC was admitted
in 1948, Wolverine athletic director Fritz Crisler extended his congratulations. Six years later, it was a different story.

MSC Becomes MSU

On 15 January 1954, the State Board of Agriculture sent a request
both to the state legislature and to Michigan governor G. Mennen
Williams asking that the school's name be changed from Michigan
State College of Agriculture and Applied Science to Michigan State
University of Agriculture and Applied Science. "We thought of
changing it as early as 20 years ago," board member Sarah Van
Hoosen told the *Michigan State News.* "I think we have grown and
reached the status now where we should be called a university." John
Hannah, then on leave from the college to serve as assistant secretary
of defense, agreed. "We have been a university in every sense since
1930," he said, pointing out that most of the country's land-grant
institutions now carried the title of university. Why not Michigan
State? College officials had previously attempted to change the
school's name in 1949 and 1951, but those efforts had failed. Hannah and others thought, however, that 1954 might be different. The
building program begun immediately after World War II had given
the East Lansing campus the physical look of a university. Biggie
Munn's football teams had met with remarkable success, registering
wins over many of the country's top universities. And 1955 would

represent the college's one-hundredth birthday, prompting celebrations that officials hoped would garner international attention for the school's academic and athletic successes.

The *State News* enthusiastically supported the change, and in an 18 January editorial urged students to support it by writing letters to the editor. Two days later, however, the editors took a more pessimistic view: "A number of persons consider the proposed name changing of Michigan State College an important issue. Unfortunately the student body of this institution does not seem to be in this select group." The paper had received only four letters on the subject, with two of them written by faculty. "It is this general apathy that is most distressing," the paper complained. "Students apparently do not care. Or, perhaps they have stopped only to view the superficial aspects of the question."

In addition to this apathy among students, opposition to the name change soon arose from other quarters. After a 27 January meeting of the University of Michigan Board of Regents, UM president Harlan Hatcher wrote a letter to the speaker of the Michigan House, Wade Van Valkenburg, summarizing the board's position: "The Regents of the University of Michigan view with deep concern any action which would give the Michigan State College of Agriculture and Applied Science any other name similar to that of the University of Michigan." Hatcher pointed out that a name change would confuse the identity of the two institutions, that it would probably be unconstitutional because both the University of Michigan and Michigan State College were embedded in the Michigan constitution, and that it would eventually lead to wasteful duplication of academic programs. Hatcher concluded, "Michigan State College of Agriculture and Applied Science is the first of these institutions in the nation to attempt to violate the long established relationship between sister institutions in the states which separated them by taking the name of the state university. If the college wishes to take on a new name not in conflict with that of the University of Michigan, the Regents of the University of Michigan would have no objection."

The university's opposition carried weight with both legislators and public opinion, and the bill might have immediately died except that MSC students suddenly became involved, circulating petitions requesting the legislature to give the bill more time for discussion.

And Senator Harry Hittle of Lansing introduced a bill changing the name to Michigan State University of Agriculture and Applied Science. Neither move, however, seemed likely to break the MSC-UM deadlock.

Wishing to avoid another defeat, Hannah and members of the Board of Agriculture requested that "the attempt to procure legislative action approving the change in name of Michigan State College should not be pursued further at this time." In a 15 February letter to legislators, Hannah and board chair Clark Brody pointed out, "There was no desire or intention to borrow the prestige or reputation of any institution. Michigan State College has achieved a world-wide reputation in its own right during the ninety-nine years of its existence. It will celebrate its 100th birthday next February. . . . It appears, however, that officials of the University of Michigan are apprehensive that confusion might result and that in some way the prestige of the University of Michigan might be affected. While we do not think that there is any reason for apprehension, it is our desire and purpose to avoid any action that might cause further controversy. . . . This is not a matter requiring hasty action." In response, the legislators tabled discussion of the name change.

A year later, another effort to change Michigan State College's name began, but this time MSC students and state legislators provided the impetus. A 15 February 1955 United Press International story identified Hittle and various other legislators as being willing to introduce name-change legislation. One of those legislators, Lansing Representative Willard Bowerman, held degrees from both UM and MSC and was optimistic about the chances of passage for such a measure: "There'll be a few die-hards from Michigan in the Legislature who will oppose the change for sentimental reasons, but I think we can get it through this year," he told a reporter. On 16 February, the MSC Student Congress passed a resolution favoring the change. Student government president Bill Hurst said, "The present effort to have MSC's name changed is a move initiated by students and will be followed through by students." While Hannah denied the State Board of Agriculture's involvement in the new effort, board members quickly lined up in support. On 18 February, the board passed a resolution indicating that "it would welcome enactment by the Legislature of a law authorizing the name change." Three days later, Representative John

McCune, an East Lansing Republican, introduced a name-change bill, stating, "If logic and good reason prevail, the bill will pass."

The UM Regents quickly reacted, voicing the same concerns they had expressed in 1954. "It is the duty of this board to protect the name of the University of Michigan as such because I believe every graduate of this institution has a vested interest in the name 'University of Michigan,'" Regent Roscoe O. Bonisteel told the *Ann Arbor News*. The paper also reported that the UM regents continued to believe that the name change would cause confusion and would probably be unconstitutional. Hannah and Hatcher, hoping to avoid the animosity of the 1954 battles, quickly formed trustee committees from both colleges, led by Bonisteel and State Board of Agriculture member Frederick Mueller. The two sides met at the Hotel Olds in Lansing on 17 March, but it quickly became apparent that no compromise would be reached. Mueller charged that the UM representatives were acting on an emotional rather than a factual basis. The UM's Otto Eckert accused the State Board of Agriculture of having a closed mind. Both sides agreed, however, that settling the controversy was impossible. The University of Michigan regents then passed a resolution directing that letters be sent to every legislator protesting the name change. The UM Alumni Association supplied its members with promotional materials, urging them to contact legislators to oppose the proposed change.

MSC also actively lobbied the legislators. Supporters of the name change presented a 250-foot-long petition with eleven thousand student signatures to the Michigan legislature, and students and alumni combined to publish a pamphlet titled *Michigan State College or University?* that concluded, "The people of Michigan will be the principal beneficiaries. Students and alumni will derive the most immediate benefit for they will have the advantage of bearing diplomas from a university in name as well as fact. In the long run, however, all the people of Michigan will share the benefits. Freed of needless handicaps, their university at East Lansing will be strengthened and better qualified to serve them. In this manner, Michigan State will reflect increasing credit upon the State of Michigan to which so much credit already belongs for having established a pioneer institution of higher learning dedicated to the service of all the people."

While the confrontations between the two educational institutions at times became nasty, one of the healthiest exchanges occurred

on 15 March when WJIM-TV in Lansing televised a half-hour debate
between students from both schools. Representing UM were football
player Fred Baer; Eugene Hartwig, managing editor of UM's student
newspaper, the *Michigan Daily*; and Michigan Union secretary
Richard Pinkerton. The MSC team consisted of Dave Hyman, chief
justice of the student traffic court; *Michigan State News* editor in chief
Jack Kole; and student government president Bill Hurst. UM students
echoed the regents' arguments, insisting that both the likelihood of
confusion and constitutional issues made a name change inappropriate. MSC students declared that since the institution functioned as a
university, it should be called a university.

The MSC cause received help from two sources that legislators
could not help but notice. First, despite Hartwig's role in the debate,
the *Michigan Daily* came out in support of MSC: "Out in Pennsylvania
at the proud University of Pennsylvania they may be snickering a
little. No one yelled when Penn State College switched to Penn State
University. . . . The fact of the matter was that Penn State has become
a university and deserved the title. That is the only fact that need
concern us in Michigan and no one denies that Michigan State is
now qualified." Second, Michigan attorney general Thomas M. Ka-
vannaugh ruled that the constitution did not prevent the legislature
from changing Michigan State's name. "There is no constitutional
reservation of a name for these institutions by use of proper nouns,"
he stated. "The people have recognized this fact by changing the reference to 'agricultural school' in the constitution of 1850 to 'agricultural
college' in the constitution of 1908. I do not find any constitutional
prohibition to the change of name proposal."

UM appeared to have an advantage, since the legislature had
twenty-nine UM alumni and only twenty members who had attended
MSC. Moreover, only four legislators had graduated from Michigan
State: the other sixteen had taken special courses or had enrolled in
short-course programs. Four legislators had attended both schools.
Politics, however, "make strange bedfellows," the *Ann Arbor News*
pointed out, identifying McCune, the sponsor of the House bill, and
Louis Crampton, "the bill's most vocal proponent on the floor," as
graduates of the University of Michigan Law School. On 22 March,
however, the Michigan House overwhelmingly approved the name
change. The bill would move on to the Senate. *Ann Arbor News*

reporter William Kulsea compared the battle to football, admitting that the Spartans led at halftime but pointing out that the end result might be different: "The first half—fought in the House the last two days—ended with MSC coming out on top by a vote of 88-14. . . . It chopped up a traditional rival, the University of Michigan, as its adherents pushed back attempts to send the bill back to committee for a hearing. . . . But better U of M blocking and tackling is promised in the Senate, where the bill must be approved before it goes to the governor for his signature, and most senators concede the Spartans have a 50-50 chance of getting through."

On 13 April 1955, the Michigan Senate voted 23-2 in favor of the name change. On 21 April, Lieutenant Governor Philip Hart— replacing Williams, who was out of the state—signed the bill into law

The smokestacks by the campus power plant reflected the school's progression from MAC to MSC and finally to MSU. Courtesy of MSU Archives and Historical Collections.

before the approving eyes of Hannah, MSC vice president Durward Varner, McCune, East Lansing mayor Max Strother, and Lansing mayor Ralph Crego.

The *Detroit Free Press* described Michigan State's students as "stoical" about the name change. "Several jubilant students painted '23 to 2' and 'MSU' in large green letters on the door of the Union grill," one reporter observed. "But otherwise, students greeted the news with conservative applause and sighs of relief." Hannah, not wanting to appear smug in his triumph over UM, issued a statement:

> On behalf of the State Board of Agriculture, the faculty, students, alumni and friends of Michigan State College, we are grateful to the legislature for this action making possible another forward step in

the progress of Michigan State. We assure them that the institution will make every effort to measure up to this new responsibility through a continual improvement of our educational programs on the campus and through the services rendered the people of the state through the Agricultural Experiment Station, Agricultural Extension, Continuing Education, research, and public service. We assure our friends and colleagues at the University of Michigan that every effort will be extended in the direction of associating our new name with our location in East Lansing, so as to overcome their often-expressed concern over confusion between our two fine institutions. Higher education faces more difficult problems and at the same time greater opportunities in the years ahead than anything we have seen in the past. If all our public and private institutions devote all of their energies to constructive work, we shall probably fall short of the demands to be made upon us. Michigan State University of Agriculture and Applied Science pledges itself to carry its full weight in cooperating constructively and unselfishly with all educational agencies, public and private, in carrying forward the important work we all face.

The bill would take effect on 1 July, which led to the question of what name would appear on the diplomas of those scheduled to receive degrees at the end of the spring 1955 semester. The members of the Class of 1955 voted 343-9 to delay receiving their diplomas and to have them bear the name "University." One confused or possibly sarcastic voter requested a diploma bearing the name of Michigan Agricultural College.

Changing the name from college to university presented some other practical challenges. New stationery would have to be printed, new signs would have to be erected throughout campus, and the initials on campus smokestacks would have to be repainted. Both the fight song and the alma mater, "MSC Shadows," also needed some tweaking. And of course, the local bookstores had to unload their MSC T-shirts and hats and order the new MSU variety. The Associated Press reported that in East Lansing on 1 July, "The name change went practically unnoticed with no ceremonies or fanfare. . . . Townspeople, students, faculty and alumni agreed the name change was a good thing—but a bit anticlimactic. They insisted, as they had when the name change was a bitterly contested issue in the Legislature, that the college had for years been a university in fact—if not in name."

MSU's Semi-Centennial

The Centennial was not the first time that State had held a major celebration of its heritage. The fiftieth anniversary celebration, held in 1907, had concentrated on the college's tremendous role in furthering agricultural education and its continuing loyalty to the land-grant philosophy. Congratulatory letters and resolutions had poured into East Lansing from all over the world. "The University of Wisconsin extends congratulations to its sister institution in the completion of a half-century of service to the state, and to the cause of agricultural education," President Charles R. Van Hise wrote. "Not only in time of establishment, but in molding the agricultural thought of the nation, the Michigan State Agricultural College has been the pioneer." Robert Gibbons, the retired editor of *Michigan Farmer*, wrote that "the Michigan Agricultural College is the Plymouth Rock of American Agriculture, and as inspiring in its history as that famous rock has been in the history of free government. Its pioneers had as arduous a task before them as the Pilgrim Fathers, and did their duty as they saw it, as faithfully as the Puritans. Long after we have passed into oblivion the agricultural colleges of the United States will be the beacon lights along the stream of progress which will warn voyagers from the rocks of ignorance and prejudice, and guide them into the harbors of success and advancement." Other congratulatory correspondence came from President Charles C. Thach of Alabama Polytechnic Institute, President Edwin H. Hughes of DePauw University, President Ira Remsen of Johns Hopkins University, President Woodrow Wilson of Princeton University, President James B. Angell of the University of Michigan, and Hungarian minister of agriculture Darangi I. Royal.

While the 1907 celebration had emphasized agricultural education, a few hints indicated that times might be changing for both the college and the nation. Speakers pointed out that the number of farmers was shrinking, that agricultural education would have to become more science oriented, and that as much emphasis needed to be placed on marketing as on growing. Other hints, not quite as strong, showed that students might need more than a purely agricultural education to become truly good citizens and productive members of society. Michigan governor Fred Warner, in his opening address to Semi-Centennial attendees, suggested that the college had allowed "common school" graduates an opportunity to learn not only about agriculture but also about other sciences and arts that directly affected agricultural pursuits. "This broad foundation, established by our farseeing predecessors, has enabled this College to keep pace with advancing thought and take advantage of opportunities as they presented themselves for broadening its courses and thus increasing its usefulness."

Distinguished alumnus Ray Stannard Baker went a step further:

We need two different things. In the first place the individual man must be trained not only in money-making, but he must be given knowledge of how money should be used in something beside fine houses, fine clothes and wasteful eating and drinking. There must be training in how to get the best things out of life—in literature, art, music, travel. Unless surplus wealth widens our opportunities for development and happiness along those higher lines, of what real use is it to anyone? . . . We need in our colleges a broader and more careful training of boys and girls in what may be called the human sciences. . . . I mean the science of sociology, economics, political economy—those subjects which treat of the relationships of men and the duties and responsibilities which grow out of them. In most schools these subjects, which are in many ways more important to the citizens of a democracy than anything else, are commonly neglected. We produce excellent farmers, doctors, lawyers, chemists, engineers, and we train each of them to make money from his calling, but we fail dismally in training our boys and girls for citizenship. We make little or no attempt to develop that social sympathy and responsibility upon which, after all, every free government must rest.

And U.S. President Theodore Roosevelt declared at the 1907 Commencement, "The fiftieth anniversary of the founding of this College is an event of national significance, for Michigan was the first state in the Union to found this, the first agricultural college in America. Agricultural colleges and farmer's institutes have done much in instruction and inspiration; they have stood for the nobility of labor and the necessity of keeping the muscles and the brain in training for industry."

GETTING READY FOR THE CENTENNIAL

According to college historian Madison Kuhn, John Hannah had planned for the Centennial celebration "from the day he accepted the presidency." Even while on leave from the college and serving as assistant secretary of defense, Hannah worked to put the celebrations in motion, writing numerous letters to dignitaries nationwide. In a 22 July 1953 letter written on Department of Defense stationery, for example, he invited President Dwight D. Eisenhower to come to East Lansing in October 1955 to "mark more than the Centennial of an institution—the birth of a basic education philosophy that has played a very major role in the development of our country." On 19 April 1954, Hannah addressed the Economic Club of Detroit at the Sheraton-Cadillac Hotel and hinted at the school's big plans. "Perhaps, in view of the contributions made by Michigan State College to the building of our state's economy, it would not be presumptuous to remind you that Michigan State will be celebrating its centennial in 1955, beginning February, and that we hope for the interested cooperation of Michigan business and industry in the observance. All of you will be most welcome as visitors one or more times in the course of the centennial year, for which a great many interesting events have been planned, including what we hope will be a really significant industrial exposition."

In early 1953, Alvie L. Smith, who had previously served as news editor of the college's public relations department, became Centennial director. Smith had been a member of the college's information staff since 1948 and held bachelor's and master's degrees from the University of Wisconsin. His best qualification for his new job may have been his 1947–48 service as director of Wisconsin's state centennial program. Another key administrator was Centennial Office manager Hilda Mitchell, who bore responsibility for coordinating the events that would bring a half-million people to the campus.

Music professor Owen Reed coauthored and directed *Michigan Dream* in honor of Michigan State's Centennial. It opened in the Auditorium to favorable reviews on 13 May. Courtesy of MSU Archives and Historical Collections.

On 30 May 1954, Smith announced the official Centennial plans. The highlights would include the formal opening on 12 February, which marked both the anniversary of the school's founding and the birthday of President Abraham Lincoln; a series of academic symposiums that would attract scholars and scientists from all over the world; and the hosting of the annual conventions of fourteen national associations. The Centennial's theme, chosen from among more than four hundred submissions by alumni, students, and staff members, would be a quotation from Lincoln's Gettysburg Address, "It is for us the living . . . to be dedicated here to the unfinished work," suggested by Henry Stafseth, director of the college's division of biological sciences. Barbara Brown, staff artist for the information services department, designed a Centennial seal featuring Beaumont Tower. Among the faculty committees formed were groups to prepare a movie about the history of the college, to work with local hotels and restaurants to insure that visitors would receive quality accommodations, to develop a master list of important guests to invite, and even to plan security for those guests. A legislative committee, including the lieutenant governor and speaker of the House, was also established to help with statewide coordination. The All-College Centennial Committee, chaired by Hannah assistant James Denison, included Kuhn, Stafseth, physics and astronomy head Thomas Osgood, farm management director Elton B. Hill, and administrator Leslie Scott. Roy Rider chaired a corresponding student government planning committee.

A month later, administrators mailed 3,500 formal Centennial announcements to "colleges, universities and learned societies of the world; alumni leaders; major foundations of the U.S.; trade associations; business and industrial concerns; and other important persons and organizations." Signed by Hannah and State Board of Agriculture chair Clark Brody, the announcement stated that because of the traditions of the land-grant philosophy, "the heritage of Michigan State College . . . has manifested itself in the broadening of all higher education in America, a heritage of responsibility to serve not a few, but all of the people of this nation." On 8 November, Smith reported to Hannah that preparations were proceeding well in almost all areas. Professors John Jennings and Owen Reed were writing a "Centennial Folk Opera" that would be a "light musical, something on the order of *Oklahoma!*, except the locale is rural Michigan in the 1870s." Professor Paul Herbert's Centennial Tree Project Committee was making thirty-seven hundred white pine trees available to municipalities, schools, and sporting and garden clubs for planting in the spring. Each tree would carry a plastic label stating, "WHITE PINE: The Michigan Tree of the Century Presented by Michigan State College in Its Centennial Year, 1955."

Rider's Student Government Centennial Commission worked to identify top student entertainers to help with special events, established an information booth in the Union Building, and encouraged each student to be "a courteous and helpful ambassador of good will for the college during 1955." Emery Foster's Centennial Housing and Food Committee reserved one wing of Butterfield Hall for special Centennial guests, combining with the Kellogg Center to free approximately six hundred rooms. Speech professor Gordon Thomas's Program Service Committee identified speakers from each department who could present special Centennial programs to groups and organizations throughout the state. And public relations administrator Lowell Treaster's Public Information Committee prepared a special packet of Centennial materials for the State Department to distribute to seventy-seven foreign countries and sponsored two trips to New York to meet with the media for the purpose of selling the MSC story.

With the beginning of the new year, anticipation of the Centennial shifted into high gear, and the college's public relations efforts began to bear fruit nationally. On 26 January, Associated Press writer Robert E. Voges explained the event's importance: "A revolutionary notion was stirring in the minds of those interested in education about 100 years ago," he wrote in an article that appeared in newspapers throughout Michigan:

> This was the idea that a farmer—a plain dirt farmer, not just a
> gentleman farmer—should and could go to college. The new phi-
> losophy of education for the common man led to the establishment
> of Michigan State College, now busily preparing for its centennial
> as the nation's first agricultural college. Farmers made up more than
> 85 percent of the population 100 years ago. But the colleges and uni-
> versities followed the European tradition of devoting their teaching
> to the education of doctors, lawyers, clergymen and "gentlemen."
> Then, in 1862, Abraham Lincoln signed the Morrill Act creating a

Public relations specialist Lowell Treaster played a significant role in generating a positive image for Michigan State, helping the school both achieve university status and put on a successful one hundredth anniversary celebration. Courtesy of MSU Archives and Historical Collections.

nation-wide system of land-grant colleges to be financed by the sale
of public lands. The system was patterned after Michigan State College, which Congressman Justin Morrill, author of the act, declared
"was in full tide of successful experiment."

Newsweek magazine echoed these sentiments in its 28 February
edition: "At 100, Michigan State College (originally, the Agricultural
College of Michigan) is observing more than a birthday. It is celebrating the triumph of an educational idea. When it was founded
in 1855, colleges were for gentlemen, and few gentlemen sullied
themselves with the study of such practical matters as agriculture
and engineering. In moving away from the traditional classical curriculum, Michigan State and its fellow land-grants opened a new era
for American colleges." The 5 February *Saturday Evening Post* gave
equal praise, using the occasion to point out that "by teaming science
and technology with agriculture, the land-grant college services were
a key factor in the revolutionary increase that has occurred in farm
productivity." But perhaps the 11 February *Detroit Times* best reiterated what Baker had suggested in 1907:

> It is difficult to realize Michigan State College is celebrating its
> 100th birthday; difficult to appreciate the lusty East Lansing institu-
> tion is beginning a second century of service. MSC seems so young.
> It has avoided the sedateness of an ivied cloister and often strikes us
> as a delightfully impudent stripling, making faces at older brothers
> and sisters. Much of this youthful spirit stems from a willingness
> by faculty and students alike to rub elbows with all of Michigan
> and with the entire world. MSC welcomes with equal hospitality
> the farmer who seeks a new milking machine and the engineer who
> seeks a new turbine. And much of MSC is young. A small, so-called
> cow college through much of its life, its great expansions are those
> of the new generation. In both buildings and curricula there are
> broad and deep windows, to let in today's light. With attention
> focused on tomorrow, it teaches the ways of living as well as book
> knowledge.

The local daily, the *State Journal*, was also celebrating its one
hundredth birthday, and on 28 April 1955, the paper devoted an

entire section to college history. Articles discussed chemistry professor Robert Kedzie, the fire that destroyed the engineering building in 1916, the creation of Peoples Church, MSC's admission to the Big Ten, and the first women to attend what was then Michigan Agricultural College. The special section also included a variety of advertisements wishing Michigan State a happy one hundredth birthday. Michigan Supply Company extended its congratulations. The Fox Hole PX in East Lansing paid for a "Growing with Michigan State College" advertisement. The Smoke Shop saluted "Michigan State College and . . . the thousands of students who have been our friends through the years." The Pig 'n Whistle Shop, a longtime East Lansing business, pointed out that it had been supplying the campus with trophies for more than twenty years. Hicks Hardware noted that although it had only been located in East Lansing for a short time, the store still was proud to extend its congratulations to the college. And the Lucon Theater, celebrating the fiftieth anniversary of the motion picture industry, also offered its best wishes to MSC and to the *State Journal*: "We are proud to be part of a community that has seen the growth of these two great institutions."

THE BIG PARTY

Appropriately enough, when 12 February 1955 arrived, Detroit's Awrey Bakeries (owned by Robert Awrey, MSC Class of 1947) presented the college with a three-and-a-half-foot birthday cake with six tiers decorated to honor special events in the college's history—the establishment of the veterinary school, the first football win over UM in 1913, the first Farmer's Week in 1914, Hannah's assumption of the presidency in 1941, and the football team's 1952 national championship. The tiers also included transportation typical of each era, ranging from the buckboard wagon to the automobile. Founders' Day featured a keynote address by James B. Conant, former president of Harvard University and at the time the U.S. high commissioner of Germany. Other distinguished guests included Milton S. Eisenhower, brother of the U.S. president and the head of Pennsylvania State University, which was also celebrating its centennial as a land-grant college, and the presidents of the five other land-grant colleges in the

MSU president John Hannah and Michigan governor G. Mennen Williams celebrate the university's one hundredth anniversary in 1955.
Courtesy of MSU Archives and Historical Collections.

original Northwest Territory: Howard Landis Bevis of Ohio State, E. B. Fred of the University of Wisconsin, Frederick L. Hovde of Purdue University, Lloyd Morey of the University of Illinois, and James L. Morrill of the University of Minnesota. All of these men received honorary doctorates of law, as did U.S. Secretary of Agriculture Ezra T. Benson; Michigan governor G. Mennen Williams; U.S. Secretary of Labor James P. Mitchell; General Motors president Harlow M. Curtice; University of Michigan president Harlan Hatcher; the Canadian ambassador to the United States, Arnold D. P. Heeney; and Albion College president William W. Whitehouse. The media estimated that seven thousand visitors were on campus, with one thousand of them attending the official Founders' Day program in the Auditorium. Mutual Broadcasting System, the country's largest radio network, provided coverage. The U.S. Post Office issued a commemorative stamp honoring the one hundredth anniversaries of the founding of both MSC and Penn State, printing 110 million of the green three-cent stamps. The East Lansing Post Office estimated that preorders and first-day sales would total 2 million stamps, and the university sent first-day covers to all alumni.

Other commemorative events continued throughout the rest of the year. The staff of the college yearbook, the *Wolverine*, put out a 700-page edition thought to be the largest ever produced on a college campus. The publication featured two hundred old photos as well as color reproductions of artist John S. Copin's paintings commissioned especially for the Centennial. The *Michigan State News* ran a series of historical articles describing the college's earlier days, frequently featuring early photos of the campus. The *State News*, the *State Journal*, and many other Michigan newspapers gave the Centennial events extensive coverage.

The *Michigan State News* dubbed the 1,859 men and women who graduated in June 1955—the first to receive their degrees from Michigan State University—the "Centennial graduating class." The Commencement speaker was Admiral Arthur W. Radford, chair of the U.S. Joint Chiefs of Staff. Graduates met at Power Plant Road and marched in unison into Macklin Field as WKAR Television and WKAR Radio carried the ceremonies live.

To coincide with the Centennial, Michigan State University Press published history professor Madison's Kuhn exhaustive 501-page work, *Michigan State: The First Hundred Years*. (Kuhn's volume constituted the second in-depth history of the university, following on William James Beal's 1915 *History of the Michigan Agricultural College and Biographical Sketches of Trustees and Professors*.) Kuhn spent a week with former botany professor Liberty Hyde Bailey at Cornell University in Ithaca, New York. He also talked to the widows and descendants of early college presidents and faculty, longtime professors, and many alumni who had played an important part in Michigan State's development. On 13 May, the special Centennial folk opera, *Michigan Dream*, opened in the college auditorium to what *State Journal* reviewer Hayden R. Palmer called a "large, appreciative audience." Set in the 1870s, the musical told the story of the sale of public lands under the Morrill Land Grant College Act. "'Michigan Dream' differs from the usual musical show in many respects," reported Palmer. "At times it becomes almost grand opera in its scope and at others it borders upon the old-fashioned melodrama. Prof. Reed directs an orchestra of 52 musicians who provide accompaniment for

Michigan State historian Madison Kuhn made enormous contributions to the university's successes. In 1955, he provided key background information that helped convince legislators to bestow the name *university* on Michigan State and published his book, *Michigan State: The First Hundred Years*. Courtesy of MSU Archives and Historical Collections.

some of the 20 song numbers of the production, all of which Mr. Reed composed."

The biggest event of 1955 took place during the summer, after many students and faculty had left town. Between 15 August and 20 August, 250,000 people attended the Centennial of Farm Mechanization, which featured six hundred exhibits with a total value of $200,000. Sponsored by the College of Agriculture, the exposition occupied more than one hundred acres near the intersection of Farm Lane and Mount Hope Road, as well as Macklin Field, Jenison Field House, the Auditorium, and Demonstration Hall. Both the new and the old shared the spotlight. The old was represented by a plow built in 1797, a 1902 John Deere tractor that was the first to drive backward as well as forward, and many other types of farm machinery that had played an important part in Michigan's agricultural history. The new included examples of the latest in kitchen designs, models of Detroit's latest automobiles, and of course, state-of-the-art farm machinery. There were also demonstrations of such skills as pole construction, the mechanical removal of stones and boulders from fields, tractor

The Centennial of Farm Mechanization was the biggest Michigan State event of 1955. The arch was designed by James S. Boyd of the agricultural engineering department. Courtesy of the MSU Museum Collections.

safety, and the tricks of irrigation. This world's fair of farming featured more than metal and mechanization, however—including concerts in the band shell, tug-of-war competitions, special sound-and-light shows, and an appearance by Mrs. America (Mrs. Ramon Deitemeyer of Nebraska). Arthur Farrall, chair of the agricultural engineering department, later recalled that "each morning before the crowd arrived," President Hannah and athletic director Biggie Munn "walked down through the exhibits and personally inspected the toilet and service facilities to see they were clean and in good shape." Even CBS commentator Lowell Thomas visited campus, doing one of his national radio broadcasts from East Lansing.

When students and faculty returned to campus in the fall, the *State News* greeted them with the headline, "Centennial Construction Greets Visitors; Building Boom in High Gear." According to staff writer Jack Berry, the "biggest building boom to hit Michigan State since the

Above: Wagons pulled by tractors provided transportation for visitors attending the Centennial of Farm Mechanization. Courtesy of the MSU Museum Collections.

Right: Early Michigan farming is reenacted at the Centennial of Farm Mechanization in 1955. Courtesy of the MSU Museum Collections.

early post-war years" included a $4 million library, more than three hundred apartments for married students, the expansion of Kellogg Center, the construction of a new bridge over the Red Cedar River (running toward Macklin Field from Wells Hall), and additional parking spaces throughout the campus. The new construction was needed to help the university deal with the more than seventeen thousand students who would be attending classes, an all-time MSU high.

The biggest campus weekend of 1955 was probably 21–22 October. Approximately twenty-six thousand alumni arrived on campus for the Centennial Homecoming. Thousands of people lined Grand River Avenue from downtown East Lansing to the campus on Saturday morning for a celebratory parade led by one-hundred-year-old Milton M. Marble, an 1881 student and MSU's oldest living alumnus. The grand marshal was Robin Roberts, who had starred on Michigan State's baseball and basketball teams during the 1940s and had gone on to become a top pitcher for the Philadelphia Phillies. The procession included antique buggies from the MSU Museum, former Miss Big Ten and Miss Michigan winners riding in convertibles, teams of horses, bands, and thirty-four student-constructed floats featuring the university's history—"an illustrated biography of MSU's 100 years," according to the *Michigan State News*.

The Spartan footballers rose to the occasion, defeating the University of Illinois 21-7. Quarterback Earl Morrall completed five of eight passes for 136 yards and two touchdowns, catching a pass, recording an interception, kicking off, and punting to lead MSU. Homecoming and most Centennial activities concluded that evening with a banquet at Shaw Hall and a dance in the Auditorium. Hannah was delighted by the day as a whole and by the efforts of MSU's students in particular. In an open letter to the *State News*, he wrote, "On many occasions, the students at Michigan State University have given me reason to be proud of them, but never have they given me greater reason for pride than last Saturday when they presented the magnificent parade-banquet in observance of our Centennial. The planning of the event and the execution of those plans displayed intelligence, resourcefulness and ingenuity of the highest quality. To everyone connected with the affair . . . my sincere personal thanks and those of the University. Experiences like these strengthen my great confidence in the often-abused 'younger generation' and confirm my

Former Spartan baseball and basketball star and Philadelphia Phillies Hall of Famer Robin Roberts served as the grand marshal of the Centennial parade. Courtesy of MSU Archives and Historical Collections.

belief that this is the finest group of men and women Michigan State has had as students in its history."

MSU in the Public Eye

The Centennial brought Michigan State enormous attention. As the *MSU Alumni Magazine* reported in February 1956, "M.S.U. definitely is news—news of a national and international nature." Summing up the Centennial, the magazine continued, "If there is a person in America who hasn't heard of Michigan State University, he must lead an extremely lonely life, for he is far beyond the range of newspapers, magazines, radio, television and all other types of mass communications. It can be said conservatively that the M.S.U. Centennial brought more national attention to this institution than any other series of events in the history of the University. The name, reputation and objectives of Michigan State are much more familiar to millions of persons throughout the nation and the world because of the vast amount of newspaper and magazine space and the huge number of hours of radio and television time based on our Centennial. . . . M.S.U. was in the public eye on a scale that probably has not been surpassed by any other university." And even after the Centennial celebrations officially ended, the news stories kept appearing. Much of the attention resulted from the Spartans' football success, including their appearance in the 1956 Rose Bowl, but the university's strengths outside the athletic arena also gained notice.

On 30 December 1955, the *Escanaba Daily Press* told its readers that 17,200 men and women had attended classes during 1955; that students had come from almost every state in the union and from fifty foreign countries; that limited use of the new library had begun in the fall; that a team of approximately forty was beginning to train governmental employees in Vietnam; and that Olin Health Center was being expanded. The article ended with a quote from Kuhn's new book: "Secure in the knowledge that to the genius of the land-grant college movement it had contributed substantially, Michigan State entered its second century aware that its opportunities were as great as those which faced it in 1855 as the first agricultural college in the land."

Opposite: A parade down Grand River Avenue honored both the Centennial and Homecoming, with floats depicting many of the important events in Michigan State history. Courtesy of Gordon Thomas.

Furthermore, as Kuhn later pointed out, 1955 had seen other changes that strengthened the university:

> To meet the impending scarcity of professors, the depression-born retirement age of 65 was advanced to 68 and 70. The rather unwieldy monthly faculty meeting became a quarterly Senate; while much of its legislative power was given to an Academic Council. The Michigan State University Press, under its new name, published its fifth novel by R. K. Narayan: *Waiting for the Mahatma*. Plans were begun for a scholarly quarterly that appeared in 1957 as the *Centennial Review*. A new college of communication arts realized the president's desire for a common curricular core in journalism, radio and television. The university television station, on a rather inaccessible UHF channel, was replaced by WMSB that shared channel 10 in a unique arrangement with a commercial station. And that year a new venture sent teachers out to live in Michigan cities as members of the community for a term rather than for half-days.

When Treaster retired in 1973, he reflected back on his time at Michigan State and identified 1955 as a turning point for the school: "After the Centennial, MSU really took off in national prominence."

The Man Named "Biggie"

Professors are often caricatured as forgetful, but at Michigan State College in the 1940s, the football coach assumed the role of absent-minded professor. George Alderton, longtime sports editor at the *Lansing State Journal*, recalled that coach Charlie Bachman "had a weakness, and it was his memory. He lost coats and hats and even forgot some days that he had his lunch. . . . It was said that Charlie was walking across the campus one day and met one of the professors. Friendly, always, he would talk at length with anybody who would engage him in conversation—mostly about football. When Charlie and the professor parted, Charlie called back to the professor and asked him, 'Which way was I going when I met you?' The professor replied, 'You were going the way you are headed now.' Charlie said, 'OK, Prof, then I have had my lunch.'"

Bachman Departs

But Bachman's memory did not cost him his job in 1947; rather, according to some observers, he departed East Lansing because of his lack of imagination. Bachman, a teammate of Knute Rockne's at Notre Dame, had arrived at MSC in 1933 after a successful stint as head coach at the University of Florida. In his thirteen years as Spartan head coach, he had compiled an impressive 70-34-10 record, including four straight wins over Michigan as well as victories over Purdue, Penn State, and Kentucky. His 1937 team went 8-1 and concluded the season with a 6-0 loss to Auburn in the Orange Bowl. John Hannah and Bachman had been friends since Hannah's days as a poultry specialist. "One evening John invited me to attend a movie in Lansing," Bachman remembered. "Between the change in reels he started talking about the college. He said, 'Michigan State College is like a diamond in the rough; all it needs is a football victory over Michigan—no, two victories, so people will not say it was a fluke—and the college will become a great educational institution.' We fulfilled that wish in 1934 and made the string four instead of two."

In 1945 and 1946, however, Bachman's teams had lost to Michigan by scores of 40-0 and 55-7. The squad's 5-5 record in 1946 had been especially disappointing since the team, made up of older returning war veterans, had been expected to be a big winner. After the season, there were rumors that Hannah would announce Bachman's firing at the football banquet on 6 December. Two days before the banquet, Bachman said, "I've heard all the reports, but know nothing about them. I'm doing my job as always and will go right on until somebody officially notifies me that there's been a change. . . . President Hannah has not discussed the matter with me."

Hannah made no announcement at the Friday banquet, but Bachman used the occasion to declare that he was resigning because "I don't think I can do as good a job as someone else can." Bachman claimed that he had tendered his resignation on the previous Sunday but that Hannah had refused to accept it. According to the coach, "I thought the matter over all week and, Thursday night after talking to my friends and family, I finally decided to make the resignation stick." Hannah responded by praising Bachman as a man and as a coach. "I know Charlie Bachman well and never in almost fourteen years has there been a single incident when Bachman was not decent and ethical and honorable. There were never any worries about any embarrassment to MSC because of his personal behavior or his attitudes. He is always decent and clean and honorable."

Hannah insisted that Bachman's resignation had not been forced, but writers for both Detroit papers believed that the coach had been pushed out the door: Lyall Smith of the *Free Press* claimed that influential alumni had pressured Hannah and athletic director Ralph Young to get rid of Bachman, and Harry LeDue of the *News* wrote, "Bachman wasn't resigning at all. Figuratively, he had been handed a gun and told: 'Go out and shoot yourself.'" Writing many years later about his experiences at Michigan State, Bachman did not mention his resignation and wrote only positive things about the school and its president.

Assessing Bachman's departure, Alderton wrote, "Football was changing rapidly. New formations and new defenses were springing up. Charlie was almost angry over the new [trends] and even suggested that the national rules committee should put a rule in the book that would hold seven players on a defensive line and only four in the secondary defenses. But the changes kept coming. The alumni and business segment . . . were unhappy." Muddy Waters, one of Bachman's players and the Spartans' head coach in the early 1980s, agreed. "The [players] made fun of Charlie because his football was out-of-style. He was still using the old Notre Dame box even though the T [formation] was becoming popular. I think the game had passed him by."

Enter Biggie

The game had definitely not passed by Clarence L. "Biggie" Munn. The former Minnesota All-American lineman had learned the coaching profession at the University of Michigan, spending ten years as line coach for Fritz Crisler before moving on to spend two years as Syracuse University's head coach. Immediately after Bachman's resignation, the media quickly anointed former Cornell and Notre Dame coach Ed McKeever as Bachman's probable successor. Munn was not mentioned. Within a few days, however, Munn had become the odds-on favorite, and on 14 December, just over a week after Bachman's departure, Munn accepted the offer to become the Spartans' new head coach. Alderton claimed that Munn had been the only person considered for the MSC job, although Hannah later identified three candidates—Munn, future Oklahoma coach Bud Wilkinson, and Wesley Fesler, later head coach at Ohio State. Munn met in Detroit with Hannah and a three-person committee from the Board of Trustees and was offered the job. He immediately accepted. According to Hannah, "if [Munn] accepted the job and came, that would be that. If he did not, we would interview the next man on the list."

Veteran Detroit sportswriter Joe Falls recalled that Hannah had high expectations for Munn: "Build me a football team. Build me the best football team in the land," the Michigan State president supposedly demanded. Others have suggested that Hannah saw becoming a

Biggie Munn compiled a 54-9-2 record as head football coach at MSC. Courtesy of Michigan State University Archives and Historical Collections.

national football power as the key to Michigan State's membership in the Big Ten, also called the Western Conference. Hannah, however, always denied that winning football games was more important than other college successes. When asked whether he and the trustees "calculated coldly that improvement in the football program would benefit Michigan State in other ways," he replied, "No. We certainly did not. We considered football as part of the total university. We did not foresee that the new athletic program would become as successful as it turned out to be, or as soon. We certainly hoped that the football program would be successful, and that it would be something all the faculty, students, alumni and friends of the university as well as the public might approve of."

MSC FOOTBALL ON THE RISE

Football at MSC was on the rise even before Munn arrived in East Lansing. On 17 October 1946, the college announced that it would increase the capacity of Macklin Field from twenty-three thousand to around fifty thousand and that it was resuming its football rivalry with Notre Dame after a twenty-seven-year lapse. The two-pronged announcement was no coincidence: the Spartans were well aware that scheduling top teams at home was extremely difficult because of their small stadium. With the promise of larger crowds in East Lansing, Notre Dame agreed to an extended home-and-home arrangement. Also influencing the decision to enlarge Macklin Field's seating was the prospect that MSC might someday enter the Big Ten, a development that would probably not take place with a facility that seated fewer than twenty-five thousand fans.

Munn arrived in East Lansing knowing that he would have a refurbished stadium in just one year, but he knew little else about the town or the school. The Munns were strangers to MSC. Biggie had never even coached a game there during his ten years as a University of Michigan assistant coach. "I'd been near East Lansing when we were on our way somewhere else," Vera Munn, the coach's wife, remembered. "But I don't believe I ever set foot on the campus." On 11 March 1947, Biggie Munn wrote to a colleague describing his initial experiences in mid-Michigan: "Ever since the end of last football season things have been sort of in a mess as far as we are concerned. We took the new job and had to sell our home in Syracuse, find a house in East Lansing, which is no small job. We have rented a house in Lansing for the time being but are looking for one to buy— something that is in our reach. Real estate prices are way out of sight and the competition for houses keen inasmuch as the officials of the Oldsmobile plant make money that is unheard of as far as the Munn family is concerned. . . . We do like it here and the college is certainly growing . . . with 13,500 students and a $20,000,000 building project going on now. I do feel that this is an excellent opportunity and, in fact, one of the best in the country."

Munn and Hannah would become close friends. Hannah was a frequent summer visitor to the Munns' lakeside Canadian cottage. At work, however, Munn was respectful of his boss's authority but was not afraid to challenge the MSC president on certain issues. Vera Munn remembered an early Munn-Hannah confrontation: "Soon after we came to East Lansing, we were going to live in campus housing until we found a home," she said. "We had a dog that was very close to the family. There was a rule that you couldn't have dogs in college housing. Mr. Hannah said there were no exceptions. Biggie replied, 'No dog, no Biggie.'" The Munns kept their dog.

The media, the MSC sports family, and football fans across the country responded positively to Munn's hiring. MSC sports information director Nick Kerbaway wrote that the new Spartan coach "has enhanced his position in coaching by his amiable personality, his ability to teach and direct players and the aggressive spirit he imparts to his boys." Fritz Crisler was not as enthusiastic. The University of Michigan football coach had been Munn's boss for ten years and was not thrilled by his employee's return. "I think Crisler saw Munn as a much tougher opponent in both recruiting and coaching than Charlie Bachman had been," said Ed Klewicki, the most valuable player on Bachman's 1934 team and a longtime observer of MSC football. "Crisler believed Michigan football was king. He didn't want that to change." Alderton agreed: "Crisler was unhappy to have his old sidekick come out into the same football pasture. Biggie told me that the first time he met Crisler face to face after the announcement, Fritz said: 'What the hell are you doing back in the state of Michigan, Munn?' Biggie told me that he replied that he was back in the state of Michigan to make a living for his family. The hostility between the two was heated all the time they headed their football jobs."

Crisler could also not have been happy that two of the three assistants Munn brought with him from Syracuse were Michigan men. Forest "Evy" Evashevski was All-American Tom Harmon's chief blocker and captained the Wolverine football team during his senior season. Laverne "Kip" Taylor was known for scoring the first touchdown in Michigan Stadium and served in various capacities

at the UM athletic department during the early 1940s. The third assistant was Hugh "Stubby" Daugherty, later known as Duffy Daugherty.

Munn's first encounter with the Wolverines—his initial game as MSC's football coach—was not a pleasant experience. The Spartans lost the game 55-0 and then returned to their locker room at Michigan Stadium to find that the drains were stopped up, forcing them to wade through water and sewage. According to Muddy Waters, Munn stood on a bench, tears in his eyes, and said, "I've been humiliated. We've been humiliated. But if you're the kind of guys I think you are, we'll be back and have our day." Were the blocked drains

Biggie Munn (*wearing hat*) and Duffy Daugherty (*standing behind a table*) brought fame to Michigan State with their winning football teams.

Courtesy of Michigan State University Archives and Historical Collections.

intentionally plugged on Crisler's orders? "No doubt about it," Waters said. Concurred Vera Munn, "Biggie knew it was no accident."

The one-sided loss discouraged few Spartans. Bill Marsh, the reporter who covered UM football for the *Ann Arbor News* and who thus was hardly inclined to write positively about Michigan State, noted, "There is one thing you can say for Biggie Munn's boys. Although outclassed, they never quit fighting with what they had to fight with. At times the Spartans looked plenty good and they were still giving their all right up to the final gun. There are other years ahead and Michigan isn't always going to roll over State as it did today." Marsh was right. The games became closer, with MSC losing 13-7 in 1948 and just 7-3 in 1949. Finally, in 1950, the Spartans beat the Wolverines 25-0 in Ann Arbor, following up with victories over UM the next three seasons.

A Player's Coach

Despite having lost their first game under the new coach, players immediately noticed a difference between Bachman's casual coaching style and Munn's more intense approach. "Biggie was a disciplinarian and a motivator," said Waters, who played for both men. "He was always for his players. He really had it all together." Klewicki agreed: "Biggie took complete control of MSC football the day he arrived. He was a real hands-on coach. If he saw a player who was not doing something right, Biggie would jump in and demonstrate the proper way. He was tough but he was also a player's coach. He really supported his kids." George Guerre, a star halfback on Munn's early teams who remained among the Spartans' top offensive producers for decades until great running backs such as Eric Allen, Clinton Jones, and Lorenzo White ran up big yardage totals, recalled Munn as "an outstanding coach . . . a great, great motivator. He was the kind of coach who could look at his talent and develop a whole system or systems around that talent. He had some players who were proficient at quick kicking so he developed a whole series of plays around those individuals." Guerre also fondly remembered assistant coach Evashevski: "Evy was a punter in college and I did the punting for our team, so we would stay after practice and have a little punting contest.

We would play for malteds over at the Union Building. I was losing a little weight at that time and needed to beef up. . . . I did pretty well in the malted area and gained a few pounds as a result of punting against Evashevski."

Munn had to be an enthusiastic and effective motivator to beat the bigger teams MSC often faced. When not teaching players on the football field or talking with them on walks across campus, he often wrote letters and stuffed them in his players' lockers. The messages emphasized hard work, attention to detail, and the importance of learning life lessons. "I heard a story the other day about a man sitting down at a counter and he told a waitress standing nearby that he would like to be waited on," he wrote in one letter. "She said that she couldn't wait on him because it wasn't her station. You may be playing an end, guard or tackle and it would be a pretty sad state of affairs if you could not make the tackle because it wasn't your station." Sometimes, he chastised his players about a lack of dedication. "As in the past years of coaching, I have seen a few players whose love life has been their downfall. I am not mentioning any names but there are a few players at whom this is aimed. If the shoe fits, put it on." Other times, Munn spelled out what he expected of his players: "During practice no one will be excused unless there is an emergency. Don't plan to be best man at anybody's wedding on weekends."

In a 20 July 1950 letter to his players, Munn explained that he had given the team members their football shoes in the summer "so you will become accustomed to them and will not have any blisters or foot trouble. WEAR THEM AT LEAST TWO TIMES A WEEK." He then reminded the players of the need for secrecy: "Keep in mind at all times that any information given out to the team in the field or in chalk talks belongs wholly to the Michigan State football team of 1950 and it would not be right for you to reveal any of our secret information. Do not tell anyone what is going on pertaining to offense and defense." He concluded with a statement about work ethic: "Those who are the first ones out to practice are the ones who are the best football players and those who lag and drag are the ones who wind up being the third string men. In other words, THE DIFFERENCE BETWEEN GOOD AND GREAT IS A LITTLE EXTRA EFFORT. All of your coaches have had a lot of experience in big time football and I would suggest that you start out listening closely to what they have to say. If we all add to the 1950 team 100%, we should be in good shape even though we meet some of the top teams in the Nation."

Munn also often stressed playing by the rules. On 11 December 1952 he wrote, "I would like to call your attention to the fact that you cannot play in any basketball games where admission is charged and you cannot lend your name to any advertising or appear on any commercial program. I am giving all of you this warning so you will be able to retain your eligibility at Michigan State. I am very, very proud of every one of you for the wonderful record you made. Now don't let anything happen to you in the future because the tradition has been set and every one of you will be expected to do an outstanding job. I am counting on you—Biggie." More frequently, Munn's advice stressed the nitty-gritty of winning football: "I would suggest right now if you are serious about your football that you start taking some sprints," Munn wrote on one occasion. "I would recommend that you start out slowly and then increase the number and the speed. Football is a game of movement and consists of short sprints. Each man should be able to go at top speed at least 60 yards either to make a long run or to cover a punt or the kickoff." Sometimes the messages were personal. Before the 1952 season began, Munn wrote to quarterback Tom Yewcic, "Even though I do not want to put the pressure on you, I want you to realize how much I am counting on you this fall. I am sure that you have shoes and a ball and I hope you will soon start doing some passing and kicking."

Academic success also remained a concern. Munn told his players that professors rarely flunked students but that students usually flunked themselves by missing classes, failing to pay attention, not handing in homework, having a poor attitude, and not taking good notes. "After every class review the lecture as a whole and then pick it apart in detail and remember definitions and dates," Munn urged. "You are here for a college education. Remember there have been more potential All Americans who have flunked out of school than there have been actual All Americans." Whatever Munn was doing, he was doing it right. The Spartans rebounded after the Michigan loss to post a 7-2 record in 1947, losing only one more game, 7-0 to Kentucky. Individual standouts on that first Munn team included center Robert McCurry; running backs Guerre, Waters, and Lynn Chandnois; and end Warren Huey.

The team inaugurated its expanded stadium on 25 September 1948 with a game against Michigan, a team MSC had played only four times in East Lansing, most recently in 1924, the day of the initial dedication of Macklin Field. Special guests at the 1948 ceremonies included State Board of Agriculture chair Clark Brody, UM president Alexander Ruthven, UM athletic director Fritz Crisler, MSC athletic director Ralph Young, and the facility's namesake, John Farrell Macklin. "There remains only for me to say that this stadium is dedicated to good sportsmanship and fair competition," President Hannah told the crowd. "It was built and will be maintained in the abiding belief that intercollegiate athletics, properly conducted, are of great benefit to those who participate in them actively on the playing field, and to those who participate by observation." The only disappointment that day was the 13-7 loss to the Wolverines, and the rest of the season turned out much better for the Spartans, who finished at 6-2-2. A 6-3 record followed in 1949, but bigger things were in store over the next four years.

Running back Lynn Chandnois was one of Biggie Munn's star players, achieving All-American status in 1949. Courtesy of Michigan State University Archives and Historical Collections.

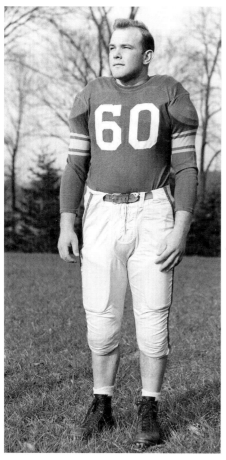

Guard Don Mason was named an All-American for the 1949 football season. Courtesy of Michigan State University Archives and Historical Collections.

Munn's Multiple Offense

Munn had started out at Michigan State using the T formation (three backs behind the quarterback) and an unbalanced line (more men on one side of the center than on the other). Munn later added many variations to this formation—the winged T, the single wing with the deep wing back, the single wing with the up wing—to develop what became known as the multiple offense. When teams figured out how to defend against a certain formation, Munn would simply devise a new one. Munn was not the only coach using the multiple offense, but many observers considered him its best practitioner, and his teams racked up some impressive scores in 1948 and 1949, recording 58 and 68 points against Hawaii, 61 and 75 against Arizona, 62 against Temple, 48 against Marquette, and 42 against William and Mary. In 1953, Munn published *Michigan State Multiple Offense*, a 211-page book devoted entirely to his coaching philosophy. College and high school coaches frequently asked Munn for details of his system, and the coach responded by suggesting that anyone interested buy a copy of his book.

Joining the Big Ten

As the Spartan football program continued to improve, college officials continued their attempts to join the Big Ten. Michigan Agricultural College had sought to join the prestigious conference as early as 1924, and efforts continued over the next two decades.

Despite Michigan State College's football success during the 1930s—including records of 7-1 in 1932, 8-1 in 1934, 6-2 in 1935, 6-1-2 in 1936, and 8-2 in 1937—the Spartan squad received little attention and respect. Hannah believed that the problem was weak schedules—beating Grinnell, Carnegie Tech, Wayne State, and Alma created little excitement in national football circles. And, of course, potential recruits tended to choose colleges that scheduled games against elite programs. Moreover, the top schools that agreed to play MSC often insisted on playing the games at home, forcing the Spartans continually to play in front of hostile crowds. Prior to 1947, for example, twenty-nine of Michigan State's thirty-three varsity games against the University of Michigan took place in Ann Arbor. The logical way to upgrade the quality of the Spartans' opponents was for the school to join the Big Ten, but the conference was full and did not seem disposed to add another team.

Hannah's assistant, James Denison, believed that Hannah began lobbying for Big Ten membership soon after assuming the Michigan State presidency, writing, "The growing strength of the Presidents in control of the Big Ten worked to the advantage of Michigan State with the advent of President Hannah and his developing friendship with the other Presidents and their growing respect for him and his institution." On 13 December 1942, H. G. Salsinger of the *Detroit News* wrote a column arguing in favor of MSC's admittance to the conference. "If any college is qualified for membership in the Western Conference it is Michigan State. Under the direction of President John A. Hannah the college has grown into one of the country's most important educational institutions and one of the most progressive. Athletically, Michigan State is on a par with a majority of Western Conference members. The college is located in Western Conference territory. There is no sound reason for withholding an invitation to join."

Hannah wasted no time in taking advantage of Salsinger's endorsement. Two days later, he wrote to each Big Ten president, enclosing a copy of the column and making additional arguments for eventual admission. The responses were favorable, and even Ruthven voiced no outward opposition. "I have your letter of December 15," he replied. "I know that you have long wanted Michigan State College in the Western Conference. You know, I am sure, that the presidents have absolutely no voice in determining the policies of the conference except as we may occasionally insist that we will not go along with some policy. It is a matter of irritation to members of boards of trustees that the Conference representatives are so independent that if anyone else expresses an opinion they are more likely than not to turn it down on general principles."

World War II eclipsed college football over the next few years. "It is very evident now that at least at this college, intercollegiate athletics are going to be of very little importance for the duration [of the war] due to the fact there will be no adequate number of civilian men to make up competitive teams," Hannah wrote to Ralph Aigler, UM's conference representative, in 1943. "We now have 2,000 Army men in uniform on the campus and accepted several hundred more, and all of them are prohibited from participation, being assigned schedules of activities that provide no free time for practice or competition." Still, anticipating times more conducive to athletic competition, Hannah added three paragraphs arguing MSC's cause for eventual conference admittance. And on 25 November 1945, just a few months after the war's conclusion, Hannah wrote to the Big Ten requesting admission.

Shortly thereafter, Michigan State received its opening: early in 1946, the University of Chicago dropped its intercollegiate sports programs and withdrew from the Big Ten. The conference began considering three replacements: the University of Pittsburgh, the University of Nebraska, and MSC. Hannah and MSC went to work. In a confidential 21 March 1946 letter, Floyd Reeves of the University of Chicago, who had been instrumental in establishing MSC's Basic College and who had also consulted at Pitt and Nebraska, wrote to Hannah that he considered Michigan State the most worthy candidate and had presented that opinion to University of Chicago dean L. A. Kimpton. Reeves continued, "My opinion is that Dean Kimpton will have some influence in the selection of the new Conference member institution and that he will be inclined to favor Michigan State College." Sports and editorial writers throughout the Midwest also tended to back the Spartans. In a 12 March 1946 editorial, "Why Not Michigan State?" the *Pontiac Daily Press* stated, "Michigan State has made tremendous strides in the last decade or two and is now one of the big and important educational institutions in America. It has a magnificent plant and equipment and professors who place it among the nation's leaders." Despite Ruthven's apparent support a few years earlier, the University of Michigan opposed having an in-state school join the conference, believing that the UM's intrastate dominance would be curtailed. Officials from the University of Illinois and Indiana University also expressed apprehension, fearing that an annual MSC-UM Big Ten rivalry would diminish their profitable and prestigious annual games against the Wolverines. Iowa favored adding its regional rival, Nebraska. Leaders of other conference schools, however, believed that MSC's entry into the Big Ten might dilute Michigan's dominance in football, making a more balanced sports conference.

UM supporters soon began to change their views. In late April, the president of the University of Michigan Alumni Club of Lansing, Dr. Maurice C. Loree, wrote to Hannah that his group "heartily endorse[d] Michigan State College as a Member of the Big Ten Conference and as evidence of that support we are attaching hereto a copy of a formal resolution we have sent to the officials of the University of Michigan." The resolution praised MSC's curriculum, faculty, and student body; stated that its athletic facilities were worthy of conference competition; lauded the quality of the coaching staff; pointed out the college's athletic success against conference teams in past years; and suggested that precedent existed for more than one institution in a state to be a conference member. "Therefore," the resolution stated, "be it resolved that it is the sentiment of the Board of Governors of the University of Michigan Club of Lansing that Michigan State College be admitted to membership in the Western Conference."

Nevertheless, Hannah later recalled, "We knew from the beginning that there would be no friendly consideration of Michigan State's cause by the Big Ten if the University of Michigan had its way. We anticipated that Ann Arbor would be unfriendly and critical and obstructive, and that is exactly what they were. . . . But several other universities, particularly the University of Minnesota, helped us a great deal." Especially important was Hannah's friendship with University of Minnesota President James Lewis Morrill. Wrote Tommy Devine in a 16 June 1949 *Sports Illustrated* article, "This was a coalition of two young college presidents with intimate knowledge of athletics and deep personal concern over the hypocrisy, double-talk and shady deals big-time intercollegiate athletics spawn. Morrill did not give lip-service to Michigan State's application. He was the greatest single factor inside the conference in Michigan State's election last December. For the first time in modern annals a campaign, athletic in nature, had been waged at the college president's level. The fact shocked and jolted Big Ten athletic directors, who reside in and rule a little world of their own in dictatorial fashion. They did not take kindly to the encroachment on their authority. The campaign's significance was all too clear to them, for it may mark the beginning of a trend." Morrill, however, may have had other motives for supporting MSC. According to Denison, Morrill "had at one time been an alumni executive at Ohio State U. where there was no love for the University of

Michigan, and he had said frankly that the people at Minnesota were convinced that they would have better success in their traditional games with Michigan if Michigan State were in a position to compete with Michigan for athletes and athletic support."

Denison and University of Minnesota public relations head William L. Nunn convinced *Minneapolis Star* sports editor Charles Johnson that the Spartans should be admitted, and Johnson agreed to plead MSC's case to his fellow Big Ten sportswriters. Johnson also suggested to Denison that Dean Lloyd C. Emmons, the chair of MSC's Athletic Council, should meet with his Big Ten counterparts to advance the MSC cause. "Almost simultaneously," Denison remembered, "we began to get favorable mention in sports pages all over the area."

On 25 May 1946, Hannah wrote to Aigler, summarizing MSC's actions and expressing the hope that the University of Michigan would support Michigan's State's application for admission. "We have tried to be ethical and have not contacted the faculty advisers of the various universities. Some months ago I wrote to the presidents of each of them and received very favorable replies from all of them. Most of them were of course noncommittal, but at least three of the presidents indicated that their schools are enthusiastically favorable to our cause which of course means nothing." Aigler's reply told Hannah what had occurred at a Big Ten meeting held a week earlier:

> There was . . . no definite vote on your application. When the matter came before the Faculty Representatives, I made a statement to the effect that I hoped the Conference would see its way clear to elect Michigan State, but I did not press for a vote, realizing that the temper of the group was to approve the Directors' recommendation [that no change be made in membership]. I thought it was better to leave the matter more or less in suspense. What, if anything, it may have had to do with the general attitude, I cannot say, but it was not uncommon to hear a remark to the effect that a man or woman ought not to remarry until a decent interval has elapsed after the spouse's death. . . . After a little more time has gone by, one will be able to tell better what the long range disposition of the group is.

To influence that disposition in a positive direction, Michigan State dropped one of its traditions, the Jenison Awards. Since 1942, the college had provided Spartan athletes with scholarships that covered tuition, fees, and books, funded by a bequest from longtime supporter Frederick Cowles Jenison. Although other conferences commonly offered athletic scholarships, the Big Ten frowned on the practice. On 29 May 1947, Hannah appeared at a Big Ten meeting in Highland Park, Illinois, to discuss the Jenison Awards. "We gave great thought to the plan before the awards were inaugurated," Hannah explained. "We thought it preferable to be open and above board in our aid to athletes rather than to follow the methods we'd seen used elsewhere. There is convenience to point to the absence of scholarships as a sign of purity. These schools merely are dealing from the bottom of the deck. I think it better to list in the college catalog what you are doing. That is our method." Nevertheless, MSC dropped the Jenison Awards.

The Big Ten convened three days of meetings in December 1948 with conference members still undecided about whether to invite MSC to join. MSC assembled a ten-person delegation to attend, including Young, Munn, assistant athletic director Lyman Frimodig, track coach Karl Schlademan, tennis coach Frank Beaman, baseball coach John Kobs, wrestling coach Fendley Collins, and sports information director Fred Stabley. "What will be the vote?" asked Alderton in the *Lansing State Journal*. "If there is a vote taken and it's favorable, you can be very sure that it will be announced as a unanimous one. There will be some kind words spoken. If there is a negative result (and we have no way of knowing if the case will actually be voted upon at all!) there will be no comment. The announcement will say that the conference did not 'get around' to Michigan State's case, or that it was delayed for further consideration. The conference, unable to help the Spartans, will not embarrass them, either."

The media seemed to be in the Spartans' corner. *Detroit Free Press* writer Lyall Smith wrote, "The Free Press has learned that State is the ONLY school being considered for membership to the most elite athletic conference in the land. A simple 5-4 majority is all that is needed to decide the issue. The Spartans have not overplayed their hand. They made a formal written application to join the conference two years ago. They have made no other direct overtures and actually have leaned over backward to avoid any accusation of pressing for a decision in their favor." The *Pontiac Press* argued, "State has

S P A R T A N   A L U M N I   M A G A Z I N E

THE *Record*

JANUARY 1949

STATE MAKES BIG 10

Michigan State News | EXTRA

EXTRA | Michigan State News | EXTRA

Wilson Voices Invitation

President's New Era | MSC Had Blessing
Statement | Of Sports Writers

MICHIGAN STATE
COLLEGE

The Michigan State College *Record* featured the college's acceptance to the Big Ten in its January 1949 issue. Courtesy of Michigan State University Archives and Historical Collections.

become one of the biggest and most important universities in the nation. Under President John Hannah, the East Lansing institution has acquired a new stature and a new breadth. Physically the plant has expanded. . . . It is difficult to think of any reason for refusing State admission. She has the faculty, the students and the plant. She has a new football stadium and while it isn't equal in size to many in the Big Nine, it is adequate. Michigan State is a big, fine outstanding college in the United States and in the Midwest. She is every bit as deserving as others. Merely because her importance is comparatively recent is no objection." Even legendary sportswriter Grantland Rice joined the cause. Referring to the possibility of MSC's admission, he wrote, "And why not? Michigan State today has more than 15,000 students. It also has one of the best football layouts in the game, a new stadium that can handle 55,000 spectators, the most modern one yet built. Beaten only by Michigan and Notre Dame, Michigan State has known one of its best seasons this fall. It has a better team than several members of the Big Nine."

On 12 December 1948, the *Michigan State News* blared in an unusual Sunday edition, "State Makes Big 10." As Alderton had predicted, the vote for admission was announced as nine schools in favor, none opposed, and Big Ten commissioner Kenneth L. "Tug" Wilson indeed had "kind words" for Michigan State: "I am very happy. MSC is a fine institution. We are happy to have them with us."

More than six thousand students—including some men in coats and ties—took to the streets, parading through the campus and downtown East Lansing after the decision was announced. One of the triumphant procession's first stops was President Hannah's home. "We have waited for this . . . for so many, many years," Hannah told the crowd. According to longtime Michigan State faculty member Roland Pierson, quite a few faculty members joined in the celebration: "We had an enormous number of young faculty just beginning their academic careers. Many looked so young that it was sometimes hard to tell the difference between teacher and student." Despite the decision's importance on the MSC campus, however, Wilson gave it only part of a paragraph in his 496-page history of the Big Ten, merely listing it among the other conference highlights of 1948.

Hannah downplayed his role in convincing the Big Ten to eventually extend an invitation to MSC to join, and instead credited the people and the institution: "Munn's teams were well coached and he was respected by all who knew him. Ralph Young and his entire staff kept our athletic programs on a high plane. Certainly the quality of the university and its athletic programs were main factors in our invitation into the Big Ten. This was an important step forward for Michigan State, not only athletically, but academically." Deflecting praise by *Detroit Free Press* editor Malcolm Bingay, Hannah wrote, "Michigan State College is what it is today and where it is today only because a great many persons have worked hard in her behalf. The institution is larger than any one of us. To my mind, the greatest benefactor of Michigan State was the unknown genius who first established the tradition of service to the public on this campus, knowing that an institution of this kind can grow and succeed only so long as it serves the best interests of those who support it with their tax dollars."

Hannah frequently argued that sports were important to a university and that if entrance into the Big Ten enhanced the athletic program, the entire university community would benefit. "I have always thought that a sound athletic program was good for a university," he later wrote. "It is good for the athletes, if they are full-time, bona fide students who must maintain satisfactory standards of scholarship and performance. Athletics unify a university probably more than any other feature of the institution. They merge the enthusiasm of students, alumni, faculty, friends and supporters of the university, and all to the university's good."

In 1998, the *State News* celebrated the university's first half century in the Big Ten. In addition to rerunning several 1948 articles, the paper solicited the perspective of the current administration. "Joining the Big Ten changed the way we saw ourselves and what we became thereafter," Michigan State president Peter McPherson said, citing the school's metamorphosis "from a regional university to a true statewide university and much more." Former MSU president Walter Adams, who had been a member of the economics faculty in 1948, echoed Hannah's belief that Big Ten membership was just as important to academics as it was to athletics: "Joining the Big Ten was a tremendous boost for our academic programs. It opened up new opportunities for both faculty and students. It helped us recruit talented teachers. It brought prestige we might not otherwise have received. I attended a conference in 1949 or 1950 and professors from other colleges and universities came up to me and extended congratulations. Hell, some were more interested in my thoughts on Big Ten membership than in my views on economics."

And despite Hannah's protestations, Adams also thought not only that the MSC president had played a huge role in pressing for MSC's admission to the conference but also that his efforts had constituted a significant milestone for college athletics. "It was one of the first times that a college president, not the athletic director, was calling the shots for a university's athletic program. Ralph Young was very helpful. Biggie Munn was very helpful. But admission to the Big Ten was because of John Hannah." Sportswriter Francis J. Powers had

said much the same thing in a 26 May 1949 *San Francisco Chronicle* article: "Strangely, admission of Michigan State was rather coldly received in some conference schools. The Spartans' campaign for membership . . . was supported by the presidents of several conference schools. With this presidential support there wasn't much for the Faculty Representatives and Athletic Directors to do but accept Michigan State into the fraternity."

The MSU football brass soak up the sun before a 75-0 win over Arizona in 1949. (*Left to right*) are *unidentified*, Lyman Frimodig, Jack Heppinstall, John Hannah, Biggie Munn, and Duffy Daugherty. Courtesy of Michigan State University Archives and Historical Collections.

THE FIRST YEARS IN THE BIG TEN

MSC became an official member of the Big Ten on 20 May 1949 and began competing in all sports except football during the 1950–51 school year. Because football schedules are made up several years

Charles Schmitter became Michigan State's fencing coach in 1939 and produced such All-Americans as Francis Thalken, Ed Popper, Chandler Washburn, William Lacey, Richard Berry, Fred Freiheit, and Mark Haskell. Courtesy of Michigan State University Archives and Historical Collections.

Robert "Bob" Devaney came to MSC as an assistant football coach in 1953. He would eventually go on to become an outstanding coach at the University of Nebraska, compiling a 101-20-2 record in eleven seasons. Courtesy of Michigan State University Archives and Historical Collections.

in advance, Michigan State did not begin competing in that sport until the fall of 1953. MSC quickly established itself as a conference sports power, winning the tennis crown in 1951 on the strength of the play of Leonard Brose and John Sahratian. Other Spartan teams also did well during their first year of conference competition. Karl Schlademan's cross-country squad finished second in the Big Ten as well as at the National Collegiate Athletic Association championships. The gymnastics team finished second in the conference, with Mel Stout taking five individual titles. The swimming team also finished second, with Bert McLachian and Clark Scholes each taking two individual titles. The wrestling team took third, led by George Bender and Eugene Gibbons. And the track team, with stars Jesse Thomas, Dan Makielski, and Robert Carey, finished second indoors and third outdoors. During 1951–52, MSC proved that its first-year athletic performances had been no fluke as the school's cross-country team took first in the conference; the fencing, gymnastics, swimming, and tennis teams finished second; and the wrestling team turned in a third-place showing. Individual stars included basketball player William Bower, fencer Dick Berry, wrestler Orris Bender, and baseball player Robert Ciolek.

MSC FOOTBALL IN THE EARLY 1950s

Despite not beginning conference competition until 1953, Munn still found himself at the head of—potentially, at least—one of the nation's top football programs. Munn and his coaches frequently used the Big Ten acceptance in their recruiting pitches, and it likely played a large role in the arrival of many outstanding athletes on the East Lansing campus over the next several years. Part of Munn's overall success resulted from his ability to hire talented assistant coaches. All three members of his initial staff—Taylor, Evashevski, and Daugherty—went on to become head coaches (at Oregon State, Washington State, and Michigan State, respectively). Later Munn assistants also secured prestigious head jobs, including Red Dawson at the University of Pittsburgh, Steve Sebo at the University of Pennsylvania, Dan Devine with the NFL's Green Bay Packers and at Notre Dame, and Bob Devaney at the University of Nebraska.

Munn's 1950 team showed strong indications that MSC's football program was going to become a Big Ten power. After beating Oregon State 38-13 in the opener, the Spartans traveled to Ann Arbor looking for Munn's first win over the Wolverines. "Michigan State 14, Michigan 7," Alderton wrote the next day. "There is no news in Lansing or East Lansing this night to take precedence over that score. The Spartans, hungry for victory after a 13-year fast, gobbled up the Wolverines. State last won from Michigan in 1937, 19-14." The win was fueled by some of the greatest football names in Spartan history. Sonny Grandelius scored two touchdowns, Don Coleman starred on both offense and defense, quarterback Al Dorow was masterful, and Dorne Dibble made a key defensive play. The hero, however, may have been assistant coach Red Dawson, who told the players the night before the game that he would touch the player who would be the hero the next day and then rubbed Jesse Thomas's head. As Alderton related, "Michigan's hopes died completely when Jesse Thomas, a star all day, intercepted a desperation pass on the Wolverines' 24-yard line as the clock lit up the big 'o' on the scoreboard."

The next week, the University of Maryland handed the Spartans a surprising loss, mainly as a result of a new Terrapin option offense that caught Munn by surprise. MSC then racked up six straight wins, including victories over Indiana, Notre Dame, and Minnesota. The squad's 8-1 record was the best Michigan State had posted since 1934, when Bachman's team posted the same mark. Grandelius, Dibble, and end Bob Carey received All-American honors. And for the first time in its history, an MSC team finished the year ranked in the top ten in national polls, coming in eighth in the Associated Press rankings and ninth in the United Press International poll.

MSC began 1951 with a 6-0 squeaker over Oregon State but followed up by trouncing Michigan. Alderton enthused, "Michigan's gold-caped band played the 'Victors' this afternoon at the end of the football game with Michigan State—but it wasn't for Michigan. It was for a sharp, powerful Michigan State team that buried the Wolverines, 25-0. A second quarter touchdown by quarterback Al Dorow started the Spartans toward victory. They scored two more in the third quarter by halfbacks Don McAuliffe and LeRoy Bolden, and a final TD in the fourth period by halfback Vince Pisano. . . . It was the widest margin of superiority over Michigan that State has ever

Bob Carey was an All-American end for Biggie Munn in both 1950 and 1951. Courtesy of Michigan State University Archives and Historical Collections.

Halfback Don McAuliffe won All-American honors for Michigan State in 1952. Courtesy of Michigan State University Archives and Historical Collections.

enjoyed. . . . It was Michigan's widest margin of defeat [at Michigan Stadium] since Minnesota whipped the Wolverines 34-7, in 1935." The Spartans went on to beat Ohio State, Penn State, and Notre Dame, and ended the season at 9-0, their first unbeaten campaign since 1913. Both national polls ranked the Spartans second at the end of the season. Michigan State had a fifteen-game winning streak.

With winning teams and participation in the Big Ten rapidly approaching, MSC's difficulty in scheduling top teams vanished. On 22 October 1951, University of Detroit president Celestin J. Steiner wrote to Hannah to suggest that the two schools renew their annual football rivalry: "Whether we played at East Lansing or at Briggs Stadium in Detroit, you would be assured of capacity crowds," Steiner suggested. "Not only Michigan State alumni here but civic officials and actual and potential benefactors of both institutions would be interested." When Hannah asked Emmons for advice on handling Steiner's request, the dean quickly responded, "I think the only answer one can give Dr. Steiner is that our commitments in the Big Ten, with Notre Dame, with an eastern school and a western one, which we feel we must arrange to have a schedule attractive to future athletes who sometimes are influenced by the opportunities for profitable and pleasant trips, are such that it is extremely unlikely that we will at any time in the near future be able to schedule additional games in the State of Michigan. I see no reason why we should not make it perfectly clear at the present time that the probability of future scheduling of football contests with the University of Detroit is extremely remote." Hannah quickly rejected Steiner's request.

In the spring of 1952, Dick Cullum of the *Minneapolis Tribune* acknowledged the Spartans' bright future: "This is the last year in which the Big Ten will be able to settle its football championship without listening to what Michigan State has to say. In 1953 what the Spartans do will count. . . . The Spartans are absolutely loaded with young talent that will be around at that time. Last year's greatest of all Michigan State teams, the one which overwhelmed Notre Dame 35-0, has been pretty well scattered by graduation. . . . However, their upcoming stuff is of high grade, particularly in the backfield. Tom Yewcic, Billy Wells and Jim Ellis have two more years of service and LeRoy Bolden has three. These are among the best backs in sight. . . . When [MSC] comes into the Big Ten race it will come a-roaring."

THE 1952 AND 1953 FOOTBALL SEASONS

The Spartans' 1952 schedule was probably the toughest in their history, with six opponents—Michigan, Texas A&M, Syracuse, Penn State, Notre Dame, and Purdue—listed among the nation's top teams in preseason polls. Michigan State turned in impressive wins over Michigan (27-13), Texas A&M (48-6), Syracuse (48-7), Penn State (34-7), and Notre Dame (21-3) on the way to another 9-0 season, and both polls named the Spartans national champions.

The game with Notre Dame was especially significant. The Spartans had won the two previous years by scores of 36-33 and 35-0. The Irish had been embarrassed by the previous year's shutout, the worst defeat ever suffered by a Frank Leahy–coached team, and Leahy, a former Spartan assistant coach under both James Crowley and Bachman, found the loss to his old employer particularly galling. But MSC also had plenty of motivation: the sold-out crowd at Macklin Field; the lure of three straight victories over the Irish; and the chance to extend the school's winning streak to twenty-one games. The Fighting Irish never gave themselves a chance, fumbling the ball away seven times. Richard Tamburo recovered three of the fumbles, McAuliffe scored twice, and Bolden ran twenty-four yards for another score.

The 1952 team produced eight All-Americans—Dorow, Robert Carey, Coleman, Ellis Duckett, Yewcic, Tamburo, McAuliffe, and Frank Kush—many of whom would go on to succeed in professional football. Moreover, Munn was named Coach of the Year at season's end. The program received additional prestige when defensive back John Delane Wilson, a Lapeer native, received a Rhodes Scholarship, the first football player since future U.S. Supreme Court justice Byron "Whizzer" White to do so.

Nearly thirty members of the 1952 team returned to East Lansing for the 1962 Homecoming game against Minnesota to celebrate the tenth anniversary of the national championship. When Alderton asked Munn why this team had been so good, the coach answered,

First it was their closeness and their feeling for one another. Second it was their ability to deliver their best when a big play was needed. Thirdly, it was their tremendous offensive power and their ability to score from any place on the field. During the year they scored

Halfback Billy Wells was the MVP of the 1954 Rose Bowl. He, along with Tom Yewcic, LeRoy Bolden, and Evan Slonac, formed one of the smallest but most talented backfields in college football during the early 1950s. Courtesy of Michigan State University Sports Information.

John "Thunder" Lewis was a star end in the early 1950s for the football teams coached by Biggie Munn and Duffy Daugherty. Courtesy of Michigan State University Sports Information.

312 points to their opponents' 84. The 84 proved that the defensive team was as strong as the offensive group. . . . There was a background of buildup for the 1952 team. The year before, when we had an undefeated season, the boys felt they had been the victims of a bad decision. Tennessee was moved into the No. 1 position in the polls late in the season. Many of us felt that our team deserved the championship, having played a much better schedule than Tennessee, and so in 1952 we had the opportunity to prove the decision had been wrong. . . . This 1952 team always had an unusual flair for paying attention to small details because small details will win in a game where teams are equal. This team had it. No detail was too small for it to master. I am most proud of every one of the players, especially for what they have done in the last 10 years. They have been able to fit into whatever endeavor they have chosen.

In the fall of 2002, many members of the 1952 team returned to campus to celebrate the fiftieth anniversary of the championship season. *Spartan* magazine sent two writers, Jim Comparoni and Jack Nowlin, to spend time with the returning players. "It was no secret that Biggie Munn wanted his Michigan State teams to be faster and in better physical condition than their opponents," the magazine reported. "That meant most practices involved lots of running." According to linebacker Hank Bullough, "The defense would hold dummies, we always held dummies, and the offense had to practice take-offs. That's all [Daugherty] talked about . . . take-off, take-off, team take-off, running. The offense would work their asses off and the defensive guys, we wouldn't do a hell of a lot. We would set up in our defense and go through a few drills, but [practice] was set up for the offense. The returning players remembered that Munn would never say anything bad about his players to the media but that didn't mean he was not a tough coach." "We used to go into what we called 'The Pits' down in Jenison on Monday nights to look at the films," offensive lineman Larry Foster said. "You would think on Saturday, particularly if you had won, that you had played a decent game; until you got down there Monday night. All the little blemishes would show up and Biggie would sit there and run them back and forth. That was a teaching technique for him so you didn't make the same mistake again. He would humiliate you, but it would never go outside the building."

The 1952 season marked the twentieth anniversary of football broadcasting by MSC. The first broadcast had taken place in 1932, and after a one-year lapse, the college station carried each week's game. The broadcasts were picked up by a network of twenty-seven stations; the flagship station also produced a fifteen-minute weekly show, *Spartan Sports Special*, hosted by WKAR sports director Bob Shackelton. The first show of the 1952 season featured Munn, team captain McAuliffe, and Michigan head coach Bennie Oosterbaan.

In 1953, with Duckett and Yewcic returning and emerging stars Bullough, Wells, Bolden, and James Neal, MSC was among the teams favored to win the Big Ten, despite the players' relatively small size. The biggest player was sophomore end Carl Diener, who weighed 220 pounds; the smallest was Bolden, at 163 pounds; the average Spartan weighed 188. Munn's teams had always been known for speed and quickness instead of height and weight. Munn nevertheless seemed concerned about his '53 squad, writing to State Board of Agriculture member Forest Akers on 21 May, "To tell you the truth, the Michigan State champions of 1952 graduated and it worried me plenty when the second team scored 26 points on the first team [during spring practice]. The first can't be too good. Actually we had planned this to be a rebuilding year as our squad will be predominantly sophomores and juniors. There will be only 11 seniors on our squad of 55. I hope that the people around Michigan State will not allow our program to drop too fast. I look at the Detroit Tigers and find what a difficult time they are having getting back on their feet—it may take another five years. If the people here allow us to drop too fast, it will take them ten years to get back on their feet." In a 3 June letter to his team, Munn reiterated the fact that many of the 1952 national champions had graduated and added that the first two games would be on the road and that most opponents would be gunning for the 1953 squad. He also reminded his team that substitution rules had been tightened, forcing players to play on both offense and defense and thus requiring them to be in top physical condition. He then concluded with his usual philosophy: "You must realize that winning is usually accomplished by doing the things the other fellow won't do. It may not be a big thing because all men who play the game must have it or they wouldn't pay the price it takes. . . . Let us not forget the objective of playing is to win. Sure I insist on fair, clean play but what the score board reads as we leave the field, well that's it. Do not do anything to lessen your effectiveness as a player this summer."

Munn was at the top of his coaching career as he entered the 1953 season. He was liked by the media, who appreciated his help; he was a player's coach, sitting with the substitutes on media day so that they would not feel left out as the star players received all the attention; he excelled at public relations tasks, sending personal responses to fans who wrote to him or suggested plays; and he found the time to be with his family, often spending hours on a boat with his son, Mike, as they fished Canadian trout streams. But most important from the school's point of view, he was winning football games. "There is a secret to Munn's amazing success at Michigan State," wrote *Grand Rapids Herald* sports editor Charles L. Clapp. "It's a simple secret. Somewhere along the road from Minneapolis to East Lansing Munn learned the actual, physical act of coaching is only a part, a division of big-time college football leadership. So Biggie became a coordinator, a chief of staff. That ability has made him a tremendous success."

MSC took a twenty-four-game winning streak into its first Big Ten season. The campaign opened on the road against Iowa on 26 September 1953, with the Spartans beating the Hawkeyes 21-7 on the strength of Yewcic's passing and Wells's running and receiving. Because the Big Ten required visiting teams to wear white jerseys, the Spartans left their traditional uniforms at home and wore new road uniforms that consisted of white jerseys with green numerals and green stripes on each sleeve, with solid green pants with thin white stripes running down each side. The home uniform consisted of a green shirt with white numerals and white stripes on each sleeve, with white pants with a thin green stripe running down each side.

Victories over Minnesota, Texas Christian, and Indiana followed before Purdue upset the Spartans 6-0 at West Lafayette. The streak had ended. George Alderton described the loss: "In ancient history, the Spartans ruled their part of the world, but they fell from fame and fortune in a battle still remembered at Thermopylae. In the season of 1953, Michigan State had won 28 games over almost three years of football. The game was at Purdue and the morning of that game at West Lafayette, Indiana, the whole city was tense. . . . The Purdue student newspaper came out that morning with a one-word front page in big type—THERMOPYLAE. And it happened. . . . Campus bells were ringing, whistles were blowing, downtown streets were crowded with people, and there were lights in houses all over town that night, people talking in the streets. The Spartans had encountered their Thermopylae."

The Spartans rebounded quickly. The next week against Oregon State in East Lansing, Ellis returned a punt seventy-six yards for a touchdown, and MSC won 34-6. Then Bolden rushed for 126 yards and three touchdowns in a 28-13 win over Ohio State. Against Michigan, the Spartans posted a 14-6 win as Bert Zagers intercepted two Wolverine passes and the defense held the Wolverines to eighty-one yards rushing. The Spartans finished the season with a 21-15 win over Marquette. Michigan State's 5-1 conference record was good enough to make the Spartans the Big Ten cochampions with Illinois, but it was not clear whether the conference members would select MSC to participate in the Rose Bowl. Illinois had turned in an impressive 39-14 win over Northwestern in its final regular-season game, a sharp contrast to the Spartans' uninspiring victory over Marquette. Moreover, Michigan State supporters worried that University of Michigan officials would resent having MSC go to the Rose Bowl after the school's first season in the conference and consequently would vote to send Illinois. Some members of MSC's camp tried to convince Michigan athletic director Fritz Crisler that sending the Spartans to Pasadena would benefit the entire state of Michigan. "[We] in Michigan are very proud of the State of Michigan, and feel that representation by the University of Michigan or Michigan State at the Rose Bowl would bring great credit to the State of Michigan," Senator Haskell L. Nichols of Jackson wrote. "The Legislature appropriated more than thirty million dollars the present fiscal year for the two schools. The State of Michigan appropriated nearly three hundred thousand dollars for the Tourist Council for the present fiscal year to advertise Michigan. . . . I realize there is much rivalry between the two schools, and believe it is wonderful as long as it remains friendly. . . . [I]t seems as if the University of Michigan should be the first to support Michigan State at the Rose Bowl on January 1st."

Whether these efforts had any effect has never been publicly discussed. The schools' conference representatives first voted on the matter via telegraph, but the result was a 5-5 tie, forcing a meeting in Chicago the next day. After five ballots had been taken, one school changed its vote, and MSC was on its way to the Rose Bowl. Stabley remembered that the Spartans received the news in a phone call from Big Ten commissioner Tug Wilson:

> The call . . . was intended for MSC faculty representative Ed Harden. But Harden had wearied of the long vigil and gone home, leaving [Stabley's] smoke-filled, camera, tape recorder, and typewriter-littered house to the 40 or so newspaper, radio and TV people who had been awaiting the news since mid-afternoon. "Well," Wilson began. "The athletic directors have voted to send Michigan State. . . ." [Stabley] clapped his hand over the mouthpiece, turned to his rapt audience, and said, "We're in!" It was like flipping a lighted match into a bucket of gasoline. The media people exploded from the house to make quick phone calls to their offices and track down Biggie across town. Wilson's further words were lost in the confusion but no more were necessary.

News of the bowl invitation quickly spread through campus, and students, faculty, and townspeople began to celebrate. The *State News* reported the next day that "more than 9,000 students went on a mass 'toot' last night, but the only ill effects they're feeling this morning are a severe lack of completed homework and a slight ringing of the ears." A string of cars had wound its way along Grand River Avenue, honking their horns. Remembered longtime East Lansing resident Verna Hodge, "The night they announced that the football team was going to the Rose Bowl a big crowd of students marched past our house singing and yelling. When the end of the group came by, the last few students picked up the empty pop cans that had been dropped in the street and on our yards."

Many observers expressed surprise that MSC had beaten out Illinois for the bowl invitation. "Illinois, as an old-line Big Ten power and one of the dominant members of the conference, was felt to possess too much inner-council political influence to lose the bowl vote," wrote Tommy Devine of the *Detroit Free Press*. Devine and others cited the Illini's two previous Rose Bowl wins, a better record against the teams' three common opponents, and a stronger finish in the conference as pluses for Illinois. MSC skeptics also suggested that Hannah's earlier outspoken opposition to postseason play would work against the Spartans.

Crisler was unable to get a flight from Detroit to Chicago and thus did not attend the selection meeting. But he stayed in contact by phone, and some observers credited him with playing a major role in the conference's decision despite his earlier lack of enthusiasm for having the Spartans join the Big Ten. Vera Munn always maintained that despite her husband's on-field rivalry with Crisler, the two men remained close friends and had enormous respect for each other. MSC's athletic director, Young, and his Illinois counterpart, Doug Mills, had agreed not to take part in the meeting, but Young believed that Michigan supported the Spartans. "I don't know how any of the other schools voted," Young told the *Detroit Free Press* a day after the meeting. "All that I'm certain of is Michigan State received the majority it needed. But I have a positive feeling that Michigan voted for us. Like I say, I can't prove it, but I feel certain Ann Arbor was with us." MSC was gracious in victory, and Illinois reciprocated, with the two athletic directors issuing public statements praising each other. Biggie Munn's seventy-nine-year-old mother, Jessie, told *Minneapolis Star* reporter Dick Gordon that although she was delighted by her son's success, she felt "so sorry for those other boys. They must have been very disappointed."

THE 1954 ROSE BOWL

Michigan State College was on its way to Pasadena to play Pacific Coast Intercollegiate Conference representative UCLA on New Year's Day 1954, venturing into territory that had been somewhat hostile to Big Ten teams in recent years. According to Stabley, when Denison, Hannah's assistant, and the rest of the Michigan State representatives arrived in Los Angeles to meet with Tournament of Roses Committee members and make arrangements for the game, the Californians at first were "stiff and formal. . . . But no one could stay reserved long with the hearty back-slapping extroversion of MSC business manager Lyman Frimodig or the gusty geniality of Ralph Young. The bowl officials quickly broke down and enjoyed 'the new kind of Big Ten people,' as they themselves put it."

Munn boosted MSC's popularity in California by breaking with the earlier Big Ten practice of prohibiting West Coast reporters from attending practices while welcoming journalists from the Midwest. The Spartan players also proved to be public-relations whizzes. Billy Wells took actress Debbie Reynolds to the Big Ten Club dinner as his date, and their photo appeared in newspapers throughout the country. The team hobnobbed with other movie stars, looking nothing like country bumpkins from the Midwest. And when their hotel caught fire, players Joe Badaczewski, Evan Slonac, Bill Quinlan, and Hank Bullough helped evacuate guests and pour water on the flames, while Tom Yewcic carted away hundreds of rolls of film that reporters had stored at the hotel.

When 1 January arrived, Munn and his team took the field against the Bruins. As had happened fourteen times in its string of thirty-two wins in thirty-three games, the Spartans fell behind, trailing 14-0 in the second quarter. Before halftime, the Spartans closed the gap to seven points when Duckett blocked a UCLA punt and returned the ball six yards for a touchdown. In the locker room before the second half, according to Alderton, Munn "fished a bit of paper out of his pocket, handed it to Captain Don Dohoney and said for all to hear, 'I was up at dawn this morning. I sat in my room watching the sunrise, thinking about the game. Something came to me and I wrote it on this piece of paper. Captain Dohoney, will you read this to your team?' Dohoney, face sweat-streaked and soiled, took the paper and read: 'Get off the floor in '54.' A snicker ran through the room, then a laugh. Then faces straightened and Munn grinned."

In the second half, Billy Wells took over the game. Wells, who had had just a single carry and had gained no yards before the break, scored twice in the second half, including a sixty-two-yard punt return for a touchdown. Bolden also scored, and the Spartans won 28-20.

The Spartans' participation in the Rose Bowl prompted congratulatory cards and letters to flood Jenison Field House. Congressman Gerald R. Ford Jr., a former University of Michigan football player and future U.S. president, wrote, "Although I will be in Washington on January 1st, I will certainly be a partisan spectator when State and UCLA get together. The Big Ten could not have selected a better team to represent the conference. As a matter of fact I am looking forward to a wager or two with some of my always too enthusiastic California colleagues." Former quarterback Al Dorow wrote to Munn, "I'd like to offer my congratulations on your great Rose Bowl victory. I only wish I could have been there. . . . The Spartan team never looked better and that last half was a great exhibition. . . . You must have really inspired the boys at half-time much like the many times you had to do the same for us in 1951. It made me feel real proud to see the Spartans come thru once again." And Professor William M. Seaman of MSC's foreign language department told Munn, "As a teacher of Latin, Greek and ancient history, I do not get many of your football men in my classes. But those I have had impressed me by their cooperation, their fine attention and their splendid attitude. None of them have been stupid and some have made very fine grades. Some cynics may wonder what football has to do with a teacher of the classics. But let me tell you that a winning football team makes the college known nationally and when I go to meetings or have contact with classicists in other schools, they know me as being on the faculty of a school which has that great team. And they don't confuse Michigan State with another university anymore."

10

A Tradition Continues

For several months in late 1953 the media reported rumors that Biggie Munn would resign as football coach after the season and replace the retiring Ralph Young as Michigan State's athletic director, seemingly the next logical step in Munn's move up the career ladder. It also seemed logical that Duffy Daugherty would become MSC's new football coach. Just four days after the Spartans' Rose Bowl victory, the *Detroit Free Press* reported that Michigan State officials had tapped Daugherty as the school's new football coach. Daugherty denied the report, pointing out, "Biggie hasn't resigned and I haven't been asked to accept his position." At the 16 January meeting of the State Board of Agriculture, however, Fritz Mueller, acting on Michigan State President John Hannah's recommendation, moved that Munn be appointed athletic director and Daugherty be appointed head football coach. After praising Munn, Mueller said, "Duffy is a good football coach, trained under the best man in the country, and there is no need to look further." Later that day, in front of a phalanx of cameras, Munn tossed a symbolic football to Daugherty, signifying a new era in MSC sports. According to the *Detroit Free Press*, Daugherty, the first MSC football assistant to move into the head job, "made an easy, certain catch."

Daugherty's hometown of Barnesboro, Pennsylvania, was ecstatic. On 17 February, five hundred people filled the Legion Home to honor the new Spartan coach. When Daugherty and his family arrived, the crowd offered a standing ovation. Daugherty then took a seat on the stage, where he was treated to a Barnesboro rendition of the popular television program *This Is Your Life*. The main speaker for the evening was Edgar Harden, MSC's dean of education. "Duff always accentuates the positive," the *Barnesboro Star* quoted Harden as saying. "He is a person who is what he is because he has been what

Earl Morrall was an All-American quarterback at MSU in 1955 and went on to star in the National Football League. Courtesy of MSU Sports Information.

he has been. He is not content to fail. He will be great because he believes in greatness." Daugherty responded by paraphrasing Winston Churchill's comments in regard to the Battle of Britain: "Never has one person owed so much to so many."

Daugherty was a logical choice for head coach because he was close to both Munn and Hannah. He had served as line coach during the entire Munn era, starting out, according to longtime *Lansing State Journal* sports editor George Alderton, as a "third string assistant" with the paltry salary of eighteen hundred dollars a year but rising to become Munn's "first lieutenant" during the last years of his tenure. Recalled Alderton, "I don't believe [Daugherty] ever dreamed that he could eventually become one of the leading coaches in college football."

The new coach faced an enormous challenge. Not only was he succeeding a legend and taking over a team that had just won a Rose Bowl, but graduation had taken a heavy toll on the squad, which lost Billy Wells, Tom Yewcic, Evan Slonac, Jim Neal, Don Dohoney, Bill Quinlan, and Larry Fowler, among others. Still, many observers believed that returning veterans LeRoy Bolden, Hank Bullough, and Ferris Hallmark as well as such talented but inexperienced players as Earl Morrall, John "Thunder" Lewis, and Clarence Peaks would play well enough to give the Spartans a winning season. Daugherty, responding to questions about the upcoming campaign, said, "Well, I feel like a pilot on a long flight who has passed the point of no return. There's no looking back. Everything, success or failure of the mission, lies ahead."

Daugherty, like Munn, selected talented assistant coaches. He retained Bob Devaney, Don Mason, and John Kobs from Munn's staff and hired Sonny Grandelius, Burt Smith, and Bill Yeoman. Daugherty was even more willing than Munn to delegate authority to his assistants. Recalled Muddy Waters, "Biggie was more of a hands-on coach, while Duffy was more of a coordinator. I can even remember him coming to practice with a golf club and practicing his swing while his assistant coaches did the actual coaching." Playwright and MSU graduate Jim Cash, an avid Spartan football fan who worked as a *State News* reporter during the 1960s, noted, "Duffy always had time for me when I needed to finish an article. He'd take me to a quiet place, even in the middle of practice, and give me the information I needed. There I was, a reporter for the student newspaper, huddled with this famous football coach, while the assistant coaches helped the players prepare for the next game. When I told him how much I appreciated his time, he told me that helping the media was a big part of his job."

Not surprisingly, given this attitude, Daugherty was a media favorite, particularly given his penchant for what became known as "Duffy humor." He liked to tell a story about going fishing with University of Alabama football coach Bear Bryant at an Alabama lake. After talking about some of his football accomplishments, Bryant said, "You know Duffy, there are some folks out here in Alabama who actually think I can walk on water." Then, according to Daugherty, Bryant decided to try it. Standing at the end of the boat, he took a step into the water and immediately went under. Daugherty jumped in and pulled Bryant to safety. "Duffy," Bryant sputtered, "you've gotta give me your solemn promise that you'll never tell any of these good folks down here in Alabama that I actually tried to walk on water." Daugherty agreed not to "breathe a word of it, provided he never told folks up north I helped pull him out."

Duffy's Shaky Start

MSC managed just a 3-6 record in 1954; even more disappointing was the fact that the season saw the beginning of the Daugherty-Munn rift that continued for the next fifteen years. The two men had previously been close, and Munn's recommendation had been the key factor in Daugherty's appointment as head coach. Munn had expressed the strength of their friendship in a letter to the new football coach's mother, Elizabeth Daugherty, written shortly after he took over the team:

> In every way Duff has earned this job through his untiring efforts and loyalty to Michigan State and me and I have often considered Duff to be just like my son. We do have tremendous admiration for one another that has somehow brought success. This success has not been brought about by any extreme brilliance on our part but through effort and great faith in the players we have coached. Now

I see no reason why this relationship should be any different than it ever was. In fact, my door will always be open if he would care to have me help him in any way. . . . You have been a mother of a wonderful young man. All things start from their bringing up and you certainly have every reason to be proud. With great love to the mother of my best friend—Biggie.

Midway through the dismal 1954 season, however, Munn entered a coaching-staff meeting in Spartan Stadium and began criticizing Daugherty's assistants. "Then came what must have been the shock of Biggie's life," Michigan State sports information director Fred Stabley later wrote. "Duffy told him to shut up and get out, that he was the head coach and not Biggie. Biggie left angrily. That confrontation had two consequences. It established Duffy as head coach standing squarely on his own two feet and sowed the first seeds of ill feeling that would burst into the open several years later. The days of the father-son relationship were over."

Back to Pasadena

While the 1954 season cast doubt on Daugherty's chances of proving himself a worthy successor to Munn, 1955 vaulted him into the fraternity of big-time college football coaches. Preseason expectations for the Spartans were low, but future stars Morrall, Peaks, Lewis, Norm Masters, Buck Nystrom, and Jim Hinsley turned in breakout years. With the assistance of a talented group of sophomores, including Walt Kowalczyk, Jim Ninowski, Dave Kaiser, Pat Burke, and Dan Currie, the squad posted a 9-1 record marred only by a 14-7 loss to Michigan in Ann Arbor. Key wins included a 21-7 victory over Notre Dame and a 42-0 pasting of Minnesota, Munn's old school. Morrall, Masters, Nystrom, and Gerald Planutis were named All-Americans, the team finished the year ranked second in the national polls, and Daugherty's fellow coaches named him Coach of the Year.

The icing on the cake came when MSU was picked to represent the Big Ten in the Rose Bowl, where the Spartans would again face UCLA. "Plans were quickly made for six special trains to carry some 2,700 State students and faculty advisors to Los Angeles," Stabley later wrote in *The Spartans*. "Another 1,800 students planned to travel by plane and automobile." Bob Voges of the Associated Press reported that the migration represented "the largest peace-time, non-military point-to-point mass movement by train in history." According to Voges,

> When the team boarded its plane at Capitol City Airport, some 500 Spartan boosters, among them Gov. G. Mennen Williams, cheered, danced and sang the "Spartan Fight Song" with the MSU band. The pace picked up quickly once the team arrived in California and the press began its spate of extravagant stories. Most writers said the 1955 Spartans were the best team ever to come out of the Big Ten. Duffy followed Biggie's lead in his cordiality of two years before by announcing practice sessions would be open to all the press. The preceding December Woody Hayes had reverted to the standard Big Ten policy of banning West Coast writers but Duffy declared, "If I didn't think I could trust the newspapermen, it would be a pretty poor reflection on both of our professions. The job of a sportswriter is to write, so I figure my job's to help him." However, Duffy went Biggie one better, much to the consternation of his assistant coaches. At the open house affair, meant mainly for the press to take pictures and talk to coaches and players, Duffy ran the team through dummy plays and explained them to some 3,500 spectators in the stands via a public address system. "We showed them just about everything we used this year," he said afterwards. "I figure [UCLA coach] Red Sanders had us pretty well scouted, so what's the harm in showing the folks our stuff."

As in 1954, the Spartans fell behind 7-0 in the first quarter of the Rose Bowl. But thanks to an outstanding performance by Kowalczyk, a touchdown by Peaks, and a Peaks-to-Lewis touchdown pass, the Spartans led 14-7 early in the fourth quarter. With nine minutes left in the game, UCLA tied the game, setting up one of the biggest plays in MSU football history. With only seven seconds left and the ball on UCLA's twenty-four-yard line, Dave Kaiser came in to try his first collegiate field goal. Although the ball was snapped early, Kaiser booted the ball straight through the uprights, giving MSU the 17-14 win.

In honor of both the Rose Bowl win and MSU's Centennial, horticulture department chair Harold Tukey contacted Eugene Boerner

Duffy Daugherty was highly respected as a winning football coach and renowned as a humorous after-dinner speaker. Courtesy of the MSU Museum Collections.

at Jackson and Perkins, one of the nation's leading rose growers, and suggested that a new rose be named after the university. The result was the Spartan rose, a floribunda type hailed as the "rose of the decade." Said Boerner, "Like your teams, it is a real winner."

An Era of Highs and Lows

Duffy Daugherty enjoyed telling a story about a letter he received from an alumnus: "In 1958, we failed to win a single conference game, but the thing that hurt most was a critical letter I got from an old grad. It wasn't his choice of words, but I objected most to the fact that the letter arrived promptly on my desk and the only address on the envelope was 'Duffy the Dope.'" After the 1965 regular season, during which MSU went undefeated, Daugherty received another letter from an anonymous author that read, "Duffy: If the East Lansing Post Office delivers this to you—I guess you can assume that they follow your career very closely." The envelope was addressed only to "Duffy the 'Genius,' East Lansing, Michigan."

The contrasting dope-genius salutations in a sense symbolized Daugherty's coaching career. His teams often had spectacular success; at other times, they were mediocre—or worse. During the fall of 1956, Duffy was considered a genius. He was coming off a Rose Bowl win, his current squad had beaten both the University of Michigan and Notre Dame, and the coach appeared on the cover of the 8 October issue of *Time*. Inside the magazine, readers found nine pages of text, photos of Daugherty and his players, and even diagrams of plays devised by the "master craftsman of the most intricate offense in modern football": "With so much dogged making of muscle and butting of heads, fans are often fooled into thinking football is a game for muscleheads. The men who play for Duffy Daugherty know differently. On autumn Saturdays, when the chips are down, the Spartans play a game as intricate as any yet devised. Where other teams are satisfied to practice and perfect a single style of attack—the single wing, which piles blockers into a bludgeoning phalanx ahead of the ball carrier; the T-formation, with its quick opening plays and tricky handoffs; the split-T, which spreads the defense for exasperating option plays—Michigan State uses all three." MSU fisheries and wildlife professor George Petrides, working in Africa, wrote home that "Michigan State's football prowess is well known over here. Duffy Daugherty's picture on *Time* was well-distributed. We saw it at Cairo, Khartoum and even in the back country here in Uganda."

Just over a month later, on 17 November, the *Saturday Evening Post* featured Daugherty in a story titled "The Merry Maestro of Michigan State." Author Red Gleason referred to Daugherty as an "outsize leprechaun" and wrote, "Winning or losing . . . Daugherty injects into big-time football the almost-forgotten ingredient of fun. It is this that sets him apart in the ulcer-prone coaching profession. This is also the quality that links him most closely, in the minds of some, to the little people of the Irish moonlight. . . . He is forty-one years old, five feet nine and a half, and weighs 190 pounds. His face is a map

Halfback Clarence Peaks won All-American honors in 1956 and went on to star in the National Football League. Courtesy of MSU Sports Information.

of Ireland divided by rivers of laugh lines. His nose is an impudent, flaring thing. His chin is strong. His eyes are blue. His once red hair is graying but curly. In the interests of accuracy, it must be reported that his ears do not come to a point nor do his toes curl up, as they do in the classic leprechaun, but perhaps these characteristics of the breed are dying out." Gleason concluded by writing about Daugherty's laid-back approach during the Rose Bowl game. "The Spartans had a good time. They usually have a good time. Duffy Daugherty has convinced them that victory can be a laughing matter."

The laughter continued during 1956 and 1957. The 1956 season may have represented his best coaching job, when the squad overcame injuries to tackles Joel Jones, Palmer Pyle, and Pat Burke; halfbacks Clarence Peaks and Walt Kowalczyk; and ends Dave Kaiser and Bob Jewett on its way to a 7-2 finish. The 47-14 win over the Fighting Irish was especially impressive as MSU rolled up 494 yards of total offense. The polls ranked the Spartans first in the country following that victory, but they lost the top slot the next week when they lost to the University of Illinois. Daugherty nevertheless retained his sense of humor. "You know, I've got a real problem this year," he said. "I'm expected to win football games with halfbacks named Blanche [Martin], Clarence [Peaks] and Dennis [Mendyk]. Now I ask you, how can fellows with names like that play this rough game of football?"

In 1957, Daugherty's squad turned in another fine year, rising as high as the No. 1 spot in the polls before losing their only game of the season to Purdue. MSU's 8-1 record included a 35-6 thrashing of Michigan in which Kowalczyk gained 113 yards on offense and recovered a fumble on defense. "Michigan State's Spartans called the turn on the toss of the coin in this spacious stadium this afternoon, and kept right on setting the pattern of play for the annual gridiron clash between this state's two great universities," wrote Alderton. Both halfback Kowalczyk and linebacker Dan Currie received All-American honors, while Kowalczyk, Currie, Sam Williams, Jim Ninowski, and Pat Burke were named to the All–Big Ten team. The Spartans finished the year ranked third in the country, trailing only Auburn and Ohio State. "I have never seen a finer all-round team," Stabley commented. "There were more top-quality boys in this year's club than have been at M.S.U. for many years. I am proud to be affiliated with a school that fields such an outstanding team."

With a 24-4 record from 1955 to 1957, the Spartans had high expectations for the 1958 season despite the loss of twenty-two seniors from the 1957 team. But the squad managed only a disappointing 3-5-1 record, with some of the few highlights a 12-12 tie with Michigan and the play of end Sammy Williams, who made several All-American teams. Hannah began receiving letters from Spartan fans complaining about Daugherty's coaching performance, and just before the season's end, the president sent a personal reply to one disgruntled writer:

> Not being a football expert, I hesitate to attempt to explain why the football team failed to live up to newspaper predictions this year. I say "newspaper predictions" because our own publications and publicity made no extravagant prophecies, pointing out that an unusually large number of men of exceptional ability were lost to the squad through graduation, and that this was to be a year for rebuilding. I do know that the team has had an extraordinary number of injuries to key players. [Against Minnesota] Coach Daugherty was forced to use every man on his traveling squad because of injuries. . . . He was not nearly as rich in personnel resources as he was reported to be, and I am sure that this had its effect on the team's play. It is interesting to note that although the team has lost five games, and has won but two and tied one, it has been outscored by only 25 points, and that in the all important statistical categories. . . . [T]he team has a clear margin over combined totals for opponents. . . . Considering these facts, it is hard to understand why the team has not won more games; one is almost tempted to concede that there has been an extraordinary run of bad luck. But these things seem to balance out in the long run, and I think we all look forward with confidence to an improvement in the Spartans' football fortunes in the immediate future.

DISSENT IN ATHLETICS

The team's fortunes in 1958 bothered fans less than did rumors of rifts in the athletic department—specifically, suggestions that Munn and Daugherty simply could not get along. Hannah received a letter from Kenneth D. Lawson, an alumnus and president of the CTL Company in Wausau, Wisconsin, expressing support for Daugherty and suggesting that Munn undoubtedly constituted the source of any problems at MSU: "Duffy Daugherty has been an incomparable asset to Michigan State," Lawson wrote. "He has stood head and shoulders above the rest of the nation's 'character builders,' a clan whose ranks include many men of questionable moral standards and, most especially, bad judgment." Students also entered the fray. "I think Duffy is a good winner, but more than this, a superb sport in losing," wrote Robert Beystrum. "I can respect Duffy more for his behavior during the year's losses than I ever can Munn for his victories. I hope most sincerely that the administration will do anything possible to insure that MSU will continue to have both Duffy's services, and Duffy's brand of football."

As media reports regarding the Daugherty-Munn rift became increasingly frequent, Hannah met with both men on 18 November. Apparently satisfied that no significant problem existed, the president issued a press release the next day: "Last night, I had a long and profitable discussion with Director Munn and Coach Daugherty and was gratified to have them confirm my belief that reports of differences between them have been greatly exaggerated. . . . We expect and enjoy the cooperation of the faculty and staff in advancing the best interests of Michigan State, and on the basis of my conversation with Mr. Munn and Mr. Daugherty, I am happy to reassure faculty, students, alumni and friends of the University that in athletics as in all other activities, all of our people are going down the same road together in harmony, accord and understanding. As far as I am concerned, and as far as Mr. Munn and Mr. Daugherty are concerned, this is a closed incident, and there will be no additional comment." But matters were not closed. In a 17 February 1959 memo to both Munn and Daugherty, Hannah again referred to the relationship between the two men: "I am afraid that I was a little harsh in my comments this morning, and if so I regret it. . . . What I tried to say, but probably didn't succeed in saying, was that I think in spite of well intentioned efforts on the part of both of you that quite unconsciously at times strained situations develop that could have been prevented if the two of you would only sit down together with no outsiders and with all the doors closed for at least one hour each week. . . . I am sure if you would just do this, concentrate your thinking and your conversation on the best interests of this university, the best interests of the athletic program, and the best interests of our football program, you both could be very happy; and if you are both happy I will be happy and the University will be happy."

One point of contention may have been Daugherty's and Hannah's tendency to eliminate Munn from the chain of command. According to Daugherty, soon after he became head coach, Hannah encouraged him to feel free to contact the president—in effect, bypassing Munn. At least in some cases, Hannah also dealt directly with Daugherty. For example, in one instance, Hannah rebuked Daugherty for providing the media with information about a recruit's academic status: "I am sure that [you have no] idea how much harm you do the cause of athletics by publicity items of this kind. This irritates our academic faculty, causes them to take the attitude that some of them do toward athletics in general." On another occasion Hannah wrote to Daugherty, "Sometime before you take off for your coaching responsibilities in connection with the East-West game and other post season games, I would like an opportunity to visit with you for a few minutes alone. . . . The purpose of this session that I have in mind is a little well intentioned fatherly advice."

In his autobiography, Daugherty wrote about his relationship with Munn:

> When Biggie became athletic director and I became head coach, it was a difficult transition for both of us. He had been accustomed to the spotlight and now it was my turn. Perhaps Biggie thought I wasn't appreciative enough, I don't know. But we both had pretty good-sized egos, and we had our clashes. Certain people magnified them, and there were factions that supported Biggie, and factions that supported me. I always thought that was ridiculous. Why did anyone have to be a Biggie person or a Duffy person? Everyone should have been content just to be a Michigan State person, because the school will be around a long time after the two of us and all the All-American athletes have vanished. . . . [W]hen I took the job it was agreed that when Biggie and I disagreed—and it was inevitable that we would—I would have the right to go directly to the president. Down through the years I never felt I was going over

Gideon Smith, one the first black collegiate footballers, played for Michigan Agricultural College between 1913 and 1915. Courtesy of MSU Archives and Historical Collections.

Biggie's head or behind his back because I took the job with that understanding.

Munn and Hannah had a close personal relationship, and they fished together on northern lakes during the summer. Munn opened his letters to Hannah with "Dear John," a sharp contrast from most of the president's other official correspondents, who opened their letters with "Dr. Hannah" or "President Hannah." Still, Hannah did not let friendship prevent him from criticizing Munn when he felt that doing so was warranted, as in 1960, when he wrote,

> You will recall that I asked you in one of our recent conferences about the morale of the people in your department. I have some reason to suspect that the morale is not nearly as good as you think it is, and I am not referring to the football staff. . . . I think it might be well for you to get together all of your key people and give them an opportunity to express any of their unhappiness and go on from there. I suspect that part of the problem is the feeling that football is given first consideration always, and that other activities receive less attention. . . . I learned long ago that it is much better to let people speak their pieces. It does not cost very much to ask for their advice. You don't have to follow it, but they always have the satisfaction of knowing that their views were at least given consideration, or might have been given consideration before the final judgments were arrived at.

Both Munn and Daugherty had huge numbers of supporters, and the negative publicity about their relationship never seemed to go away.

INTEGRATION AND THE FOOTBALL PROGRAM

Despite their rocky relationship, Munn and Daugherty agreed on the value of black football players to their program. Since the early part of the twentieth century, a scattering of black athletes had participated on Spartan athletic squads. Gideon Smith, one of the first black intercollegiate football players, starred on the 1913–15 teams. Walter Arrington, Jesse Thomas, Fred Johnson, and Horace Smith participated on MSC's track teams from 1939 through the late 1940s.

But Munn's and Daugherty's football teams truly integrated sports at Michigan State. Munn's black recruits included LeRoy Bolden, Don Coleman, Ellis Duckett, and John "Thunder" Lewis. One Munn recruit, Willie Thrower, went on to become the NFL's first black quarterback when he replaced Chicago Bear George Blanda on 18 October 1953, completing three of eight passes for twenty-seven yards in what would be Thrower's only NFL appearance. "I felt like the Jackie Robinson of football," Thrower recalled. Thrower, a Pennsylvania native, had won All-State honors in high school, but many college coaches had lost their initial interest in him after realizing that he was a black player. Not Munn. The highlight of Thrower's Michigan State career, during which he was part of the squad that won twenty-eight games in a row and a national title, occurred during his senior season in 1952. According to Robert B. Van Atta, Thrower "came off the bench in a close and crucial game against Notre Dame with the Spartans holding a narrow 7-3 lead. Thrower threw for one touchdown and directed the team to another to spark a 21-3 win for his team."

Daugherty expanded Munn's efforts, recruiting black players not only from the Midwest but also from other areas. By the late 1940s and 1950s, black players from the South began migrating to northern universities because southern schools refused to recruit black athletes no matter how skilled they were. Daugherty's southern black recruits included Sherman Lewis, George Webster, Charlie Thornhill, and Gene Washington, and by 1962 the coach's efforts generated notice, as the Associated Press reported that the Spartans had seventeen black players, the "largest delegation of Negro players in the history of major college football." Those players included such current and future stars as Lewis, Ernie Clark, Matt Snorton, Lonnie Sanders, and Dick Gordon. Games broadcast on television also showed the nation that Michigan State was a good place for black students. Lewis, athletic director Clarence Underwood, and urban affairs dean Robert Green said that watching Michigan State's black football players on television during the 1950s made the university seem an attractive place to attend college.

In *Spartan Seasons*, Lynn Henning assessed the campus atmosphere black athletes encountered during the Daugherty years:

> Off the field Daugherty . . . managed to keep peace and a racially mixed team from splitting or collecting in black or white cliques. Most Southern black players came to East Lansing half-terrified that the white society they had come to know would be at least as hostile in the North. Most discovered, to their surprise, it was far different. People treated them courteously, especially assistants like Vince Carrillot. Arriving players found Daugherty gracious and friendly, and only rarely was he a screamer on the field. The culture shock came in huge classrooms where competitive athletes were now expected to be competitive students. Segregated Southern schools had not always provided the strongest elementary or secondary education, which for many athletes meant intense work with tutors during their freshman years, and even later as they tried to catch up. And whether one was dealing with it in a dormitory or at a drug store, racism could be found. Older black players told new recruits to avoid dating white women if they expected to play. Thornhill was studying in the lobby at Jenison Field House one day when a white coed sat down a few feet from him. He jumped from the sofa and left the lobby, hoping his playing chances hadn't been damaged by a two-second indiscretion. Daugherty one night came into the post-practice dining room to see whites sitting with whites and blacks sitting by themselves at dinner. He exploded. "You play together, dammit, you eat together." It was the last time tables were segregated.

By March 1965 black athletes had become so accepted on the Michigan State campus that football star Clinton Jones was selected as Mr. MSU. The *State News* ran a front-page photo featuring Jones posed in front of Beaumont Tower with Miss MSU, Anne Lawrenz, a white woman.

Many of Michigan State's black players during the 1950s and 1960s went on to have successful professional football careers. "Squirmin" Sherman Lewis, a 1963 All-American whom Daugherty called the best small back he had ever coached, eventually became a top NFL assistant coach, as did quarterback Jimmy Raye. Black

Michigan State alumni from this era who played in the NFL include Herb Adderley, Clinton Jones, Bubba Smith, George Webster, Gene Washington, Eric Allen, Jerry Rush, Dick Gordon, and Ron Hatcher, who became the first black player for the Washington Redskins. Many more of Michigan State's early black athletes found success in other fields: Blanche Martin became an East Lansing dentist and the first black member of the university's Board of Trustees; basketball player Lee Lafayette went on to work with delinquent and neglected kids in the Lansing area; Bolden became an educational psychologist in California; and basketball great Julius McCoy found a job as equal-opportunity director for the Pennsylvania Highway Department.

THE 1959–1962 SEASONS

Both white and black players contributed to the Spartans' improved performance in 1959, as they posted a 5-4 record and a second-place finish in the Big Ten behind Wisconsin. Wins included a 34-8 trouncing of Michigan and a 15-0 shutout of Purdue. *Look* magazine named quarterback Dean Look an All-American. Other outstanding players included Martin, halfback Herb Adderley, receiver Fred Arbanas, future assistant coach Larry Bielat, and future Detroit Lions coach Wayne Fontes. MSU put together an even better record in 1960, going 6-2-1 and finishing the season ranked thirteenth in the nation. The campaign's highlights included a 24-17 win over Michigan and a 21-0 win over Notre Dame. Perhaps the most talked-about game of 1960 was the Iowa contest, which pitted two of Munn's protégés against each other. Both Iowa head coach Forest Evashevski and Daugherty had played for Munn—Evashevski at Michigan and Daugherty at Syracuse—and they had served as Munn's assistant coaches at Syracuse and at Michigan State. The two had faced each other twice before, with Evashevski winning both meetings, 14-10 in 1954 and 37-8 in 1959. Evashevski was stepping down as Iowa's coach to take over as the school's athletic director, so 1960 would be the last time they would face each other. According to Alderton,

> You could argue all night about who was the better coach. . . .
> Both have had Rose Bowl champions, both developed several

MSU's All-American halfback Sherman Lewis went on to a distinguished college and professional football coaching career. Courtesy of MSU Sports Information.

all-Americans. Evy has had two Big Ten Champions. . . . Duffy has never fashioned one for himself, missing twice by the margin of half a game. But Duffy won a coach-of-the-year award, an honor that has escaped the big, square-jawed Hawkeye boss. . . . Of course Evashevski wants to finish off with a winner. Any coach would have such an ambition—to quit at the top of a wave. So far it looks as though he would. Evashevski hasn't admitted it in so many words, but there are observers who are saying the current team may be the best of all he has developed at Iowa City. . . . All the previous meetings of State and Iowa have been at Iowa City. This is the first on the Spartan home grounds. Winning here would give Evashevski more than the usual amount of satisfaction, and you can be sure his old staff mate Duffy Daugherty has just as big a yen.

But the home-field advantage was not enough, and Iowa topped MSU, 27-15.

Over the next four years, Daugherty's squads alternated winning and mediocre years, going 7-2, 5-4, 6-2-1, and 4-5. He twice shut out Michigan and beat Notre Dame three out of four years. Prior to the 1962 Michigan game, Daugherty shared his football coaching philosophy with *Detroit Free Press* writer Bob Pille: "The game is really simplicity," he said. "Maybe we out-coach ourselves with all our talk. Teaching and execution . . . that's all there is to football. There is no magic formula except blocking and tackling. They will be ready and we will be ready. The team that is tougher physically will gain and stop the other team." On the afternoon of 13 October 1962, Michigan State was the tougher team. The seventy-seven thousand fans who filled Spartan Stadium saw Sherman Lewis score three touchdowns, Dewey Lincoln run for 139 yards, and George Saimes run for 99 while the Spartan defense held Michigan to just 112 yards total offense in the 28-0 win.

After Saimes gained 158 yards against Notre Dame, including touchdown runs of 54, 59, and 15 yards, Pille began touting him as a Heisman Trophy candidate:

Invoking days of glory past, Notre Dame last weekend adorned its football program with five portraits. . . . They were Angelo Bertelli, John Lujack, Leon Hart, John Lattner, and Paul Hornung—all

winners of the Heisman Trophy. On the field, hammering the Irish with the facts of the football present, was the player who should win the trophy this year. He was—and is—George Saimes of once-beaten Michigan State. The Heisman award goes to the player judged to be the season's best. If there is anybody around better than Saimes, he hasn't been heard from. The game he threw at the Irish was the finest by a Spartan back ever seen by old MSU hands. Better than LeRoy Bolden in the 1953 conquest of Ohio State, better than Walt Kowalczyk's 172 yards against Wisconsin in 1952, better than the best day ever enjoyed by Clarence Peaks or Earl Morrall or Lynn Chandnois. . . . He looks at football with a coach's analysis. Asked if the Notre Dame game was his best, he said: "Maybe it was . . . offensively and defensively . . . I'd have to see the movies first."

Spartans George Saimes, Duffy Daugherty, and Dave Behrman are not really trying to predict the outcome of the team's 1962 season. Saimes received the glass ball to symbolize his selection to the Crystal Ball All-America team. Behrman had been selected an All-American during the previous season. *Courtesy of MSU Archives and Historical Collections.*

Saimes finished seventh in the Heisman Trophy balloting but was named an All-American at season's end. He went on to become an All-Pro NFL safety and was named to the Buffalo Bills Silver Anniversary Team in 1984.

In the second game of the 1962 season, a 38-6 win over North Carolina, Ronald R. Rubick, a 170-pound junior halfback, broke the Michigan State single-game rushing record, gaining 207 yards and three touchdowns on just fourteen carries. The Spartans set another team record with 472 yards rushing.

FAN SUPPORT

MSU's football squad continued to receive enthusiastic support from its fans. One of the highlights of each season was Homecoming. In 1960, *Cleveland Press* sportswriter Jack Clowser marveled over a typical MSU Homecoming.

It's Homecoming at Michigan State, the night before the big one with Ohio. Out on the band practice field, lights illuminate a platform built for the occasion. Everyone's coming to the rally. Streaming from each dormitory, the boys and girls rendezvous. Hand-in-hand they walk gaily to their destination. Already, the band is there, filling the air with the old songs, the loved songs of campus. Overhead, the moon burns through the light mist. Its rays dance along the bosom of the Red Cedar, placidly gurgling between rows of giant elms. A soft breeze stirs. Burnished leaves shimmer downward to join the emblems of the season. For this is autumn, the loveliest time of the year.

The old grads have motored in the day before the big one. Drawn by the nostalgic lures of Homecoming, some of them stream across campus to watch—to live again the priceless days of their youth. There is nothing quite like Homecoming, and they stand about on the fringes of the crowd, trying to appear nonchalant. Sometimes they don't succeed. Who doesn't swallow hard if he's an old Spartan and the band's playing the marching song? I know, Homecoming is much the same at every campus. The old friends to be met, and conviviality, raising a glass to victory, and hoping your own youngsters realize college days are the most enjoyable of their lives. For me, Homecoming at Michigan State is a particular joy. Nowhere in the broad expanse of Big Ten territory is there more genuine hospitality for the visitor. From Athletic Director Biggie Munn down, everyone in the sports family goes out of his way to make us feel at home. You sense it at the press dinners, the eve of the game. Duffy Daugherty, the most genial of football coaches, stands at the entrance to the dining room, making certain he gets in a little personal greeting to all. Though I've been watching athletic contests at Michigan State only since the university gained entrance to the Western conference in 1949, there is a definite conviction. Here is a school to which hospitality and courtesy are basic ingredients, a steadfast policy.

I'm an Ohioan, and want the Buckeyes to win. But the next afternoon, after the overtense Spartans had fumbled, dropped passes in the end zone and made other grievous mistakes, I still couldn't help feeling sorry for Daugherty. There he sat in the locker room, disappointment showing in his eyes, but still managing to be agreeable as we clustered around him. In my mind, there should be no such thing as a "good loser." A gracious loser, yes. But there is a difference, and Daugherty exemplified it. He's a credit to the school and the great game of football. I hope everyone at Michigan State knows that. May you have many happy Homecomings, Duffy.

And even without the events of Homecoming weekend, football games generated enormous enthusiasm among students. On Friday nights before home games, bands of students often paraded around campus, singing the Spartan fight song and chanting cheers as they circled Sparty. In 1961, with the Spartans holding onto a No. 1 national ranking, pregame activities started earlier and became more boisterous before the 21 October game against Notre Dame. On Wednesday night, an estimated thirty-five hundred students formed an impromptu pep rally, marching around campus shouting "Go State" and "Rose Bowl, Rose Bowl." Some marchers blocked traffic on Grand River Avenue, rocking automobiles and pounding on car tops. Seven were arrested and immediately brought before the municipal judge, who fined them $13.50 each and gave them a harsh lecture about mob psychology. The next night, one thousand students marched through campus and downtown East Lansing; another seventeen students were arrested, fined, and lectured. Two days later, Michigan State beat Notre Dame, 17-7.

MSU police also had problems with University of Michigan students, who would sneak onto the East Lansing campus and paint Wolverine symbols on campus buildings. Prior to the 12 October 1963 Michigan–Michigan State game in Ann Arbor, nine MSU buildings, including the library, museum, Beaumont Tower, and Jenison Field House, as well as Sparty were splattered with blue and gold paint. Police caught four of the offenders and forced them to clean off the paint. "I expect they may be at it for quite a while," MSU director of public safety Richard O. Bernitt said. "It's elbow grease work now." Of course, Michigan State students at times returned the favor, splattering green paint on Wolverine landmarks in Ann Arbor.

Other fan-related problems surfaced when the *Ingham County News* published a 6 November 1963 editorial expressing concern over drinking in Spartan Stadium. "Speaking of football and the Red Cedar institute, universities and law authorities had better start taking action to curb the bottle addicts. State, relatively free of hip flasks, is beginning to take on the aura of Michigan stadium with open guzzling, in many cases right in front of the law." Hannah responded immediately, writing to Munn, Bernitt, and John Fuzak, MSU's dean of students: "I have had comments made after each of our previous home games that we have much more drinking in the stands than is usually the case," he observed. "If the Notre Dame game follows the usual pattern, it will be the wettest of them all. The purpose of this letter is to call this matter to your attention with the request that we take every step that we can to discourage drinking in the stadium."

THE 1963 SEASON

As with many successful coaches and athletic directors, consistent rumors had both Daugherty and Munn leaving MSU for other positions. In 1962, both men continually denied imminent departures—Daugherty to either Stanford or Notre Dame and Munn to his alma mater, the University of Minnesota. Daugherty insisted that he was already preparing for the 1963 season, and Munn announced that he was too involved in building an upper deck in the stadium and increasing stadium seating to consider other offers. To quell the rumors, Hannah recommended in late 1963 that the Board of Trustees give Daugherty a five-year contract extension. The board unanimously approved the extension but left his $20,500 annual salary unchanged. Some fans disagreed with the extension of the coach's contract: as one Lansing resident wrote to the president, "You sure pulled a good one when you gave Duffy Daugherty a five year contract. . . . I wouldn't go to any more of your games if you paid me. I hear those same remarks all over Lansing and out of town also. Daugherty never has had a good team at MSU. . . . He just can't mold a team together, and he gets the best material in America. He uses the same plays game after game, and the result is that teams know how to play a defense against them, they know where the ball is going and who is going to carry the ball. Watch your attendance really go down. Also, football players are going to quit coming to MSU as long as you keep Daugherty. He might develop into an after-dinner speaker."

Daugherty also retained his supporters, both within Michigan and across the country. On 20 November, Florida's *Miami Herald* enthused, "When Dr. John A. Hannah, president of Michigan State University, announced that Duffy Daugherty will continue to coach the Spartan football team through 1968, he set a fine example for college presidents everywhere." The article continued,

> If more [college presidents] would take such firm action to protect coaches who are doing a good job from uninformed critics who think they should do better, football would be healthier. . . . Daugherty each year faces a challenge unlike that confronting any other coach in the Big Ten and, perhaps, the country. The challenge is three-headed. Duffy is expected to win the Big Ten, beat Michigan and beat Notre Dame. Because he has failed to do all three, some people (mostly losing bettors) have cried out for his removal. . . . Heckling Daugherty must have reached its apex of silliness in 1961. The Spartans had a 7-2 record, yet Duffy was hung in effigy. His question, "What's wrong with a 7-2 record?" was appropriate. . . . Fortunately for Daugherty, Michigan State and college football, Dr. Hannah is a man with a deep sense of fairness. He sees the football picture in accurate perspective. He understands that while

the Spartans usually field fine material, so do their opponents. He appreciates not only Duffy's ability to coach well, but his plusses beyond the field: the regard for real values which he instills in his players by precept and example, and the extraordinary popular image which he projects of Michigan State everywhere he goes.

The Michigan High School Coaches Association also supported the extension, with executive secretary Paul Smarks writing to Hannah, "On behalf of the [association] and its 3,000 members, I want to commend you and the Board of Trustees for the confidence you have in Coach Duffy Daugherty and in keeping him at M.S.U. . . . The athletic future of a great school like M.S.U. largely depends on getting boys from its own state who are fine athletes and good students to come there. . . . Boys go to M.S.U. because the high school coaches and their players love and respect Duffy Daugherty. . . . There isn't a college coach in the nation who does more for a high school coach than Duffy does for all of us. . . . President Hannah, the world knows that you practically single handed made M.S.U. what it is today and in keeping Duffy Daugherty as your head coach you added just that much more to your wonderful record."

On the field, the 1963 season started out with a 31-0 drubbing of North Carolina. A brief slump followed, with the Spartans losing to Southern California and tying Michigan before winning four straight Big Ten games and squeaking past Notre Dame 12-7. On 2 November, Michigan State defeated Wisconsin 30-13, delighting future MSU trustee Patricia Carrigan, who wrote to Daugherty to express her pleasure:

Congratulations to you and the Spartans on what sounded like one of the finest games of the season in yesterday's victory over Wisconsin. Like all other loyal supporters, I would be delighted to see this spirited team finish on top of the conference. Unlike some, I believe that other factors should weigh more heavily in judging the success of a collegiate football team, and it is this which prompts my letter. None can deny that winning teams bring prominence to a university, nor that such prominence encourages the support of alumni necessary to continued growth of its educational role and facilities. Winning teams assuredly bring peace of mind to the coaching staff, often loudly criticized under less fortuitous circumstances. Nonetheless, I think it is important to remember that participation in intercollegiate [sports] has a critical educational role; only if this is true can support be justified for such programs in institutions of higher education. In my years as a student at MSU, and in the 13 years since I graduated, I have seen many brilliant performances by Spartan teams, and some not so brilliant. I have cheered at spectacular victories and been dismayed by hard-fought losses. I have heard praise for the coaching staff, and criticism of it—the latter more often, of course, for it is human nature to search out reasons for failure, where success often goes unanalyzed. In this time, I have not once been disappointed with the broader evidence of success in the training of these fine young athletes.

I have never seen a Spartan team come onto the field without apparent enthusiasm and determination, nor leave the field with poor grace in defeat. Remarkable individual efforts have impressed me less than the team support for these efforts. . . . The exuberance with which a football toted over the goal line is tossed into the air, the evident joy and enthusiastic congratulations by teammates for the young man who has momentarily gained the limelight, the unfailing determination by the team as a whole to do its best, no matter what the score—these things, to me, are the best evidence one can ask for the success of an athletic training program, and I know of no team which can surpass the Spartans here. Whatever these young men choose to do with their lives, the qualities of loyalty, determination, and team spirit encouraged by their athletic participation will serve us well. One can hope that these important lessons will be accompanied by rewarding victories on the gridiron, but one cannot insist on it. Credit must be given to the character of the Spartan players individually, and hence to many who have guided their previous development. At the same time, it cannot be supposed that our boys have been unique in this potential, and credit for their outstanding displays of these qualities must, therefore, go to the coaching staff as well.

In the season's final conference contest, the Spartans were to face off against an Illinois squad in East Lansing on 23 November with the Big Ten championship and a Rose Bowl berth on the line.

Even without upper decks, Michigan State's football stadium was an impressive sight. The top decks were added in 1957. Courtesy of MSU Archives and Historical Collections.

A day before the game was to take place, however, President John F. Kennedy was assassinated in Dallas. Although many college teams postponed their games scheduled for that weekend, MSU and Illinois did not. "In making our decision we have taken into account that it would be difficult to reschedule the game for another time in view of the approaching Thanksgiving Day holiday and the approaching final exams at Michigan State," Hannah stated. "The alternative of canceling the game could not be reasonably considered in view of its singular importance in deciding the championship of the conference. . . . A memorial service is being arranged to precede the game in which all of those attending will be asked to join. The usual pregame and half-time program of entertainment by the band has been cancelled. This decision is final subject only to a request by President

Johnson that all public events be cancelled in this period of national mourning."

Many members of the Michigan State community reacted negatively, including education professor and Athletic Council member Milosh Muntyan, who immediately wrote to Hannah to resign from the council. As more and more Saturday events were canceled, school officials decided that the MSU-Illinois game should be postponed until the following Thursday, Thanksgiving Day. Hannah returned Muntyan's letter, and Muntyan remained on the council.

The postponement, however, proved disastrous for MSU. By the time the game was postponed, the Illinois players had already arrived in East Lansing, and according to Stabley, the "Illinois coaches were joyful as they took their club back home. . . . They had felt their team was not emotionally keyed for the game, and this delay looked to them like a reprieve from disaster. Spartan coaches, conversely, felt their club had never been more eager and ready. To let off steam, the team ran through a dummy scrimmage that Saturday afternoon in the indoor baseball arena of the Men's IM building and simply exploded with spirit and ferocity. But State was flat in practice the following week and never regained the fine competitive edge it had on Saturday." Illinois won the game, 13-0.

When MSU and Illinois initially decided not to postpone their game despite the assassination of President John F. Kennedy in 1963, education professor and Athletic Council member Milosh Muntyan objected and resigned from the council, although he retracted his resignation after the decision was changed. Courtesy of MSU Archives and Historical Collections.

THE 1964 SEASON

Facing a tough schedule and heavy graduation losses, MSU was not highly rated going into the 1964 season. "Last season the Spartans came within one game of playing for the Big Ten Championship, but this year it looks like the title is more than a mile away," *State News* sportswriter Jerry Morton wrote. "Senior members of the 1963 MSU club accounted for 2,049 yards rushing and passing as the Green and White proved to be one of the most surprising teams in college football. That means more than a mile of yardage must be replaced if the Spartans are to come close to duplicating last year's accomplishments." Morton named Harry Ammon, Dick Gordon, and Eddie Cotton as the most likely candidates to handle the ball-carrying duties, while sophomore halfback Clinton Jones was listed as one of the "other contenders."

The Spartans had a rough season, losing to North Carolina, Michigan, Indiana, Notre Dame, and Illinois. The Wolverines' victory was their first over Michigan State since 1955. Still, a few bright spots could be found. After MSU beat Southern California 17-7 in the season's second game, United Press International named Daugherty Coach of the Week. Gordon starred at running back and receiver, Jones showed flashes of outstanding running ability, Gene Washington set a single-season receiving record with thirty-five catches, and Bubba Smith and George Webster showed some defensive potential. Despite its 4-5 overall record, MSU finished the season ranked twentieth by UPI, the first losing team to place in the top twenty polls.

RECRUITING AND SCHOLARSHIPS

With no computerized recruiting services, no Internet, and much less media involvement, recruiting in the early 1960s differed greatly from the process today. Alumni and other university supporters provided coaches with leads regarding promising high schoolers. In 1964, for example, Michigan State assistant coach Vince Carrillot, who headed the school's recruiting in southwestern Michigan, received more than two hundred recommendations and investigated all of them plus about two hundred more. Athletes signed letters of intent that meant that they could not attend any other Big Ten school, but they could still sign with schools outside the conference. Consequently, MSU coaches could never be sure an athlete would play for the Spartans until he officially enrolled in college.

In September 1965, the *MSU Alumni Association Magazine* described Michigan State's recruiting of Mitch Pruiett, a 1964 All-State back from Benton Harbor. "State's coaches became aware of this young man's abilities during his junior year. . . . Films and newspaper clippings were collected during that season and the next. [Pruiett] exhibited superior athletic ability and—of great importance—he had a 'B' scholastic average. A talk with his high school coach, plus another look at some films revealed that Mitch had three basic things necessary to make Duffy Daugherty's varsity: desire, speed and size." As rules permitted, the Pruiett family visited campus, and Carrillot made one visit to the recruit's home. Pruiett liked Michigan State, and

Michigan State liked him. He joined the team in the fall of 1964 and went on to earn three letters as a Spartan.

Another major contrast between the athletic programs of the early 1960s and those of the early twenty-first century lay in the way in which scholarships were funded, although changes occurred during that time. Previously, money for scholarships had come from ticket sales, but around this time the university created the Ralph H. Young Scholarship Fund, which accepted donations from alumni and supporters of the athletic programs, thereby increasing the amount of money the university had available for such scholarships.

The 1965 Season

Despite his team's mediocre performance in 1964, Daugherty was optimistic heading into the following season: "We had good talent returning, and our players were eager to wipe out the bad memories of the previous season," he wrote. Outside observers did not share his optimism, however: most preseason football magazines had MSU finishing somewhere between third and fifth in the Big Ten. The *Detroit Free Press* had them third, behind Michigan and Purdue and just ahead of Ohio State. *Free Press* sportswriter Bob Pille thought the Wolverines would be outstanding, especially if they avoided stumbling against the Spartans on 9 October. Daugherty spent the early fall going over every aspect of kicking and kick coverage, and he later recalled, "On the Thursday night before our opening game, I naturally wanted to find out if the lecturing had sunk in and if all the work on the kicking game had any impact. So I pointed to a young sophomore lineman and asked, 'Norm, where are most football games lost?' 'Right here at Michigan State, coach,' he shot back."

Over the next two seasons, however, the Spartans lost only one game. MSU beat a highly regarded UCLA team in the 1965 opener, 13-3, as Bob Apisa turned in the best performance ever for a running back playing in his first MSU game—ninety-nine yards on thirteen carries, including a twenty-one-yard touchdown run. But Apisa was not the only MSU player to emerge as a star. Wins over Penn State, Illinois, Ohio State, Purdue, Northwestern, Iowa, Indiana, and Notre Dame made the names Steve Juday, Harold Lucas, Clint Jones, George

Halfback Clinton Jones starred on Michigan State's 1965 and 1966 championship football teams and later played for the NFL's Minnesota Vikings. Courtesy of MSU Archives and Historical Collections.

Webster, Bubba Smith, Ron Goovert, and Don Japinga famous in national football circles. And Michigan indeed fell before Michigan State, 24-7, with the Spartan defense holding the Wolverine runners to an extraordinary fifty-one yards rushing. Other outstanding individual performances in 1965 included barefoot kicker Dick Kenney's 47-yard field goal against Illinois, Jones's four touchdowns against Iowa to clinch the Spartans' trip to the Rose Bowl, and Washington's three touchdowns and Dwight Lee's 103 yards rushing against Indiana. And in the final contest of the year, a 12-3 win over Notre Dame, the Spartans held the Irish to twelve total yards.

As the victories continued, Daugherty and the Spartans received more and more national media attention. Wrote Roy Damer of the *Chicago Tribune*, "Of course, nobody could accurately predict the incredible success achieved by Michigan State this year. It was thought no team could go through the seven-game Big Ten schedule undefeated, let along post a 10-win mark as the Spartans did." The *Tribune* also printed an Associated Press story about the team's return home after the Notre Dame win: "Nearly 4,000 excited Michigan State rooters engulfed a Lansing railway station to greet their team tonight after its 12-3 victory over Notre Dame. The yelling, sign-waving fans—mostly students—climbed atop buses and baggage carts and lined up perilously close to the railroad tracks in cheering their top ranked team. 'It's a wonderful reception and very fitting for a wonderful team,' said Coach Duffy Daugherty from the train. 'We can't tell you how much we appreciate this. . . . Our defensive team played the most magnificent game any college team ever played.'"

The 28 December issue of *Look* magazine included a piece describing the Spartans' connection to Hawaii, which had sent three players—Dick Kenney, Bob Apisa, and Charlie Wedemeyer—to East Lansing. The story explained that the "migration of island players began in 1947–48 with games between MSU and the University of Hawaii. Later, Hawaii coach Tom Kaulukukui did graduate work at Michigan State and returned home as a volunteer scout for the Spartans. Bob Apisa and Dick Kenney heard not only from Kaulukukui but from other Hawaiian émigrés that natives of MSU were friendly. Apisa wanted Michigan State because 'They're known for running a fullback.' Other schools saw him as a blocking halfback. More important, 'Duffy was the first coach who took an interest in me as a person.'"

The 35-0 win over Iowa had both guaranteed the Rose Bowl trip and clinched a tie for the Big Ten title. The 27-13 win over Indiana a week later gave MSU its first undisputed Big Ten championship. And after the Notre Dame win, UPI declared the Spartans national champions. Then, on 28 November, the National Football Foundation and Hall of Fame announced that MSU had been selected to receive the MacArthur Bowl, signifying excellence in college football. Several organizations named Daugherty Coach of the Year, while Apisa, Goovert, Jones, Juday, Lucas, Smith, Washington, and Webster were named All-Americans.

The Rose Bowl would pit the Spartans against the UCLA Bruins, a team MSU had already defeated 13-3 earlier in the season. Assistant coach Hank Bullough, who had played on State's 1954 Rose Bowl team, was now getting the defensive line ready for the 1966 game. "The Rose Bowl isn't fun like many people think," Bullough told the *State News.* "Players have to go out there with the idea of winning. And since Big Ten rules permit only a certain amount of days for the game, teams have to practice twice a day when they get to California." Bullough also noted the changes in coaching methods since he had attended college. "One of the big changes is to platoon football which is used now. . . . With the responsibility of coaching only a few players, and teaching them only offense and defense, the coach can devote more time to each player, and can develop more personal pride in the work of each boy. . . . The biggest change in coaching has come through the use of films. The films of our games and of our opponents' games makes work harder for the coaches since we must spend so much time watching films to spot our own mistakes and our next opponent's weaknesses." The other differences Bullough noted between the football of the 1950s and that of the 1960s included bigger players, more passing, and larger high school staffs that could turn out talented young men in greater numbers.

While Bullough and the other assistant coaches were getting the team ready for the Rose Bowl, Spartan fans and friends were busy honoring the Big Ten champs. University of Michigan President Harlan Hatcher telegraphed Hannah, extending "WARMEST CONGRATU-LATIONS TO YOU ON MICHIGAN STATE'S FINE FOOTBALL TEAM AND COACHES AND ON THEIR BIG TEN CHAMPIONSHIP AND ROSE BOWL INVITATION. WE ARE DELIGHTED TO HAVE YOU KEEP THESE HONORS WITHIN MICHIGAN AND WE

WILL BE CHEERING FOR YOU ON JANUARY 1." Hatcher included a resolution passed by the UM Board of Regents, wishing MSU victory in the Rose Bowl and congratulating the school for exemplifying the "finest in sportsmanship." Future U.S. president and UM alumnus Gerald R. Ford Jr. sent his congratulations, as did U.S. Vice President Hubert Humphrey and Alabama football coach Bear Bryant. *Cleveland Press* sportswriter Jack Clowser, who had written several positive articles about MSU football, typed a Christmas Day letter to Daugherty:

> I would very much like, through this letter, to extend my very sincere thanks to the members of the football squad for autographing that ball you brought to Cleveland and gave me. In more than 40 years of sports writing, I have accumulated several autographed footballs, but believe me, this one from the 1965 national champions is the finest gift of all. Now I would like to extend to the team, before the big game, a few final words. I know how hard they've worked to climb the heights. I know a perfect season calls for marked dedication and superb attitude. But now, having come this far, wouldn't it be a crushing blow not to end it up in Glory? For each and every Spartan out there with you, let him fully realize what the effect would be to win the Big Ten championship, go unbeaten and untied, and then to meet defeat in the oldest and most glamorous bowl game of them all. Relatively few football players ever get to play in the Rose Bowl. It's something to boast about for the rest of your lives. In the years to come, let everybody remember you as the team that not only won the national championship, but finished up the job by being one of the greatest since the first Rose Bowl was played in 1901. At the final gun, let them rank you with the super teams. The glory and satisfaction will illuminate your entire lives.

Clowser's ominous warning turned out to be prophetic. The Spartans quickly fell behind UCLA, 14-0, and, as Stabley put it, were "already beaten, although nearly three quarters remained to be played." MSU launched a comeback, scoring on a forty-two-yard run by Apisa late in the third quarter and again in the fourth on a quarterback sneak by Juday, but the Spartans failed on two-point conversion attempts after both scores and lost, 14-12. "That team could have gone down in history as one of the all-time great aggregations in the history of the College game," Daugherty later wrote. "Then we came to the Rose Bowl a three-touchdown favorite in a rematch against UCLA. Obviously all our players believed that. We really thought we were the 'jolly green giants,' but we played like mice for three quarters. We had five turnovers. Believing all that junk said and written about us was fatal. We weren't emotionally ready for the game and I knew it, but there wasn't a thing I could do about it. It was an absolutely helpless feeling."

MSU Alumni Association director Jack Kenney wrote an epitaph for the season that appeared in the January–February issue of the association's magazine:

> As the sun sank in the west on New Year's Day, several thousand Spartan hearts sank with it, as the final score stood UCLA 14–MSU 12. The heavily favored unbeaten Big Ten Champions had been outplayed and out-fought by the Bruins in one of the biggest upsets in Rose Bowl history. It was a completely frustrating day for the Spartan football team and for the Spartan fans. Ranked as the number one team in the country, State could do nothing right, and by comparison, UCLA was crisp, poised and ready! UCLA deserved to win and it was to the credit of State that they fought back and nearly salvaged a tie in the waning moments. . . . Despite the loss of the game, there were some positive factors for your University. It was a real honor for Michigan State to be designated the representative of the Western Conference in the Rose Bowl, and a richly deserved one based upon an outstanding season. Thousands of alumni and fans had an opportunity to watch the team either in person or on television New Year's Day. There will be more football seasons and more Rose Bowl games, and undoubtedly Michigan State will win its fair share.

THE 1966 SEASON

Because of the Big Ten's rule that no team could play in consecutive Rose Bowl games, the Spartans went into the 1966 season knowing that they would not see bowl action. Nevertheless, they were still playing for the Big Ten title and the national championship. Juday,

Goovert, Lucas, Japinga, and Robert Viney had graduated, but the team retained Jones, Smith, Washington, Apisa, Kenney, Jerry West, Dwight Lee, and Jesse Phillips, among others. Jimmy Raye, a mobile quarterback who could create excitement, would replace Juday. The biggest concern seemed to be that highly talented Spartans would, as in the Rose Bowl, take their opponents too lightly. But MSU rolled to easy wins over North Carolina State, Penn State, and Illinois, outscoring their victims by a combined 96-28.

Michigan was next. When asked the significance of the game, Daugherty told the *State News*, "I think it's a game that means more to us because of the great interstate feeling. . . . It's a big aid to your recruiting of Michigan athletes and it's something we always look forward to. . . . I am sure that in the hearts and minds of all true Spartans, the Michigan game will always be the most important." In 1966, as in most years of that era, the Spartans defeated the Wolverines, this time by a score of 20-7. "Michigan State added just enough finesse to a slam-bam football effort to trip upset-minded University of Michigan this afternoon," *State Journal* sportswriter Bob Hoerner reported. "The almost 79,000 fans might have been a bit uncomfortable packed in the 76,000-seat stadium, but you can bet not one of them would have traded for a place on the field. The playing surface at Spartan Stadium was no place for a timid soul. State's No.1–ranked Spartans and Coach Bump Elliot's Wolverines played without thought of life or limb from start to finish. It was a rip-snorter all the way. Maybe not all the tackles were heard on Grand River Avenue, but a couple of times when Spartan and Wolverine met head-on the windows in Ag Hall must have rattled."

The next week, in heavy rain and wind at Ohio State, the Spartans struggled into the fourth period with an unusual 3-2 lead. Ohio State then scored on a fifty-yard pass play but missed the extra point to surge ahead 8-3. MSU stormed back on an eighty-four-yard drive, with Raye completing four of seven pass attempts and handing off to Apisa for the last yard and a touchdown. With a 9-8 lead, State tried a trick play, and kicker Kenney passed the ball to holder Charlie Wedemeyer for the two-point conversion and an eventual 11-8 win. "It meant a field goal would not win for Ohio State," Daugherty would say later. "It changed their strategy because they were not playing for a tie."

Wins over Purdue, Northwestern, Iowa, and Indiana gave MSU its second straight outright Big Ten title. A foot of snow had buried East Lansing two days before the MSU-Iowa game, but by kickoff, reported the *Chicago Tribune*, "seats in Spartan Stadium were clear, but wet." According to the paper, seven hundred people had shoveled out the stadium "at a cost of approximately $35,000. Calls for volunteers had gone unanswered until authorities broadcast an offer of $2 per hour. In the next 30 minutes there were seven 'volunteers' for each of the 700 shovels available. 'Michigan State does not turn out any dumb students,' observed a spokesman, summing up the project."

Next up would be the 19 November season finale against undefeated Notre Dame at Spartan Stadium. "Like the freight train rumble of an approaching tornado which gradually amplifies into an engulfing roar—that is the way the 1966 Notre Dame–Michigan State football game grew in the national consciousness," Stabley wrote in his history of MSU football, calling the contest the "Game of the Galaxy." ABC-TV promoted the game as "the greatest battle since Hector fought Achilles." On the day before kickoff, *State Journal* reporter Marcia Van Ness wrote, "The eyes of the nation . . . were on East Lansing today. Hotels and motels were sold out, highways and airlines were clogged and Lansing residents were braced for visits from relatives and friends they haven't seen in years. . . . Excitement spread through student living units Thursday night, sending an estimated 500 to 600 youthful marchers marching across the campus, singing and shouting. MSU Police said they had no reports of property damage or malicious destruction as the paraders left one group of dormitories and headed for another just as other groups reversed the process. . . . MSU's stadium press box will be jammed with an estimated 700 newsmen—outpulling this year's Michigan game which drew more than 500 sportswriters and broadcasters." Because Michigan State still had the three Hawaiian players, the game would be transmitted on live television via satellite to the islands. The odds appeared to be strongly in the Spartans' favor: since taking over the reins in 1954, Daugherty had compiled a spectacular 9-2 record against the Fighting Irish.

After all the buildup, the game itself was something of an anti-climax. A touchdown pass from Raye to Regis Cavender followed by a Kenney field goal gave the Spartans a 10-0 lead. The Irish tied it

One of the most remarkable Spartans from the Daugherty era was Charlie Wedemeyer. His catch of a two-point conversion against Ohio State was a key play in the victory over the Buckeyes and an undefeated 1966 season. He later was diagnosed with Lou Gehrig's disease and confined to a wheelchair, but he nevertheless coached his high school football team to a sectional championship, a story featured in a PBS documentary and a CBS movie. Courtesy of MSU Sports Information.

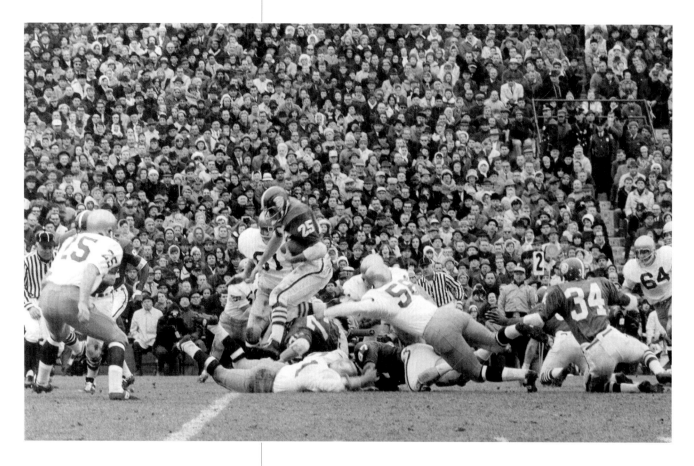

MSU's Regis Cavender (#25) runs for eleven yards against Notre Dame in the famous 10-10 tie with the Irish in 1966. Three plays later Cavender scored from the four-yard line to give the Spartans a 6-0 lead. Courtesy of Michigan State University Archives and Historical Collections.

at 10-10 and then ran out the clock. Many observers criticized Notre Dame's decision to play for the tie, but when the next week's polls were released, AP rated Notre Dame No. 1.; the UPI poll had MSU on top. State's season had ended, but Notre Dame had a final game against Southern California. After crushing the Trojans 51-0, the Irish took the national championship.

The game had tremendous significance, both on and off the football field, as Allen Barra summarized in the *New York Times* thirty-five years later:

> The most talked about game in college football history [ended] not with a bang but with a whimper. . . . No football game, college or pro, had ever been so anticipated. . . . All over the country people worked their schedules around the game; one Michigan newspaper calculated that the lives of thousands of deer in Michigan and Indiana would be saved by taking potential hunters out of the woods and putting them in front of their television sets. . . .

The controversy stirred by the final vote in the polls . . . prompted the A.P. and U.P.I. to move back the voting until after the bowl games. . . . The Irish had shunned bowl games on the premise that they interfered with final exams. But the wire services' decision made it clear that Notre Dame would never again be able to vie for a national championship while staying home on New Year's Day. Within three years, Notre Dame entered the bowl scene. . . . The Big Ten soon dropped the archaic rule that did not allow its members to play in the Rose Bowl two years in a row or in any other bowl game at all. . . . More important than the money and politics were the social implications. Coach Duffy Daugherty's 1965 and 1966 Michigan State Spartans were one of the first major-college powers to field a team with a nucleus of black stars (Notre Dame had only one black player, the All-American defensive end Alan Page). . . . Jimmy Raye was one of the first black players to play quarterback on a major-college team.

. . . No college game can again be so controversial because none can be so important. With the advent of overtime, coaches no longer have the option of playing for the tie, and controversies about whether or not to "go for it" are muted. Big games are now merely preliminaries to a dizzying series of conference championship and bowl matchups. In 1998 the Bowl Championship Series, an approved system for determining an official champion, did away with the "mythical" that usually accompanied the phrase "national championship." Thus, one of college football's most cherished rituals—the year-round debates over who should be, who was, and who would be ranked No. 1—was history. For better or for worse, what was unique about the game was gone, and college football settled down to accept its role as the N.F.L.'s junior partner.

Daugherty's teams never again approached such lofty heights, and he retired after the 1972 season. In 1984, three years prior to his death, he was inducted into the College Football Hall of Fame, and in 1985 Michigan State named its new football facility in Daugherty's honor. The *Pigskin Post* named Daugherty one of the fifty best college coaches of all time, but he is perhaps best known for his colorful quips, which include, "A tie is like kissing your sister"; "Football is not a contact sport. Football is a collision sport. Dancing is a contact sport"; and "When you're playing for the national championship, it's not a matter of life and death. It's more important than that." A few months after Daugherty's death, his beloved Spartans returned to the Rose Bowl for the first time in twenty-two years. The program for that game included Stabley's fitting tribute to the man who had taken Michigan State to the pinnacle of the college football world:

> [Seeing] the Spartans in the Rose Bowl for the first time since his own team played in the 1966 game would have sent him into ecstasy. He would have come down from his retirement home in Santa Barbara early on and spent joyful hours with Spartan loyalists, many of them his own former players, delighting everyone with his fabulous wit and humor, dropping in at practice and surely—at Coach [George] Perles' invitation—saying a few rousing words. A massive spectacle like the Rose Bowl experience with all its facets—luncheons, banquets, side trips, New Year's Eve balls, parade, and finally the big game—would have been for the chubby, ebullient extrovert as the Broadway stage is for a master actor. . . . Rarely has a sports personality made such a lasting impression on his university as well as the general sports public. . . . The splendid new football building near Spartan Stadium named in his honor is the visible evidence of the esteem in which he is held. The rest is in the hearts and minds of thousands of Michigan State–related people—past and present students, staff, faculty and alumni, as well as sports fans everywhere.

11

The House That Ralph Built

T HE YEAR WAS 1957, AND IT WAS A BLISTERING HOT DAY ON THE MSU campus. John Hannah was sitting in the bleachers of the ice arena in Demonstration Hall. "A newspaper reporter recently accused me of only liking football," the university president said, gazing out at the skaters practicing their routines. "That's not true. I like all sports." The ice arena was the coolest spot on campus, but Hannah was probably there because of the athletic talent. "Some 150 of the best amateur figure skaters from the United States and Canada, including six of America's top seven national stars and a Canadian national titlist, are working out daily on the M.S.U. ice," the *Lansing State Journal* reported that summer. The skater receiving the most attention was seventeen-year-old world champion Carol Heiss, soon to win an Olympic gold medal. The person most responsible for assembling such a wide range of skating talent was the arena's manager since 1948, Norris Wold, who had been a professional skater and who knew most of the world's top skaters and skating instructors. His friendship with Pierre Branet, instructor for the Heiss family, was instrumental in attracting top skaters.

ORIGINS OF THE MODERN ATHLETIC PROGRAM

By the 1940s, when John Hannah became Michigan State's president, the college already had a long history of athletic success. During the late 1880s and early 1890s, the school's representatives consistently won the annual Michigan Intercollegiate Athletic Association Field Day, largely as a result of the efforts of the State Agricultural College's first sports superstar, Leander Burnett, a Native American. Sprinter Harry Moon achieved a national reputation during the early 1900s;

Fran Dittrich became head cross-country and track coach in 1959. Courtesy of MSU Archives and Historical Collections.

Ralph Young served as Michigan State's athletic director from 1923 to 1954 and was known for his ability to hire talented coaches. Courtesy of MSU Archives and Historical Collections.

Fred Tillotson starred as a long-distance runner in 1910 and 1911; Clark Chamberlain became the NCAA two-mile champ in 1931; and in 1936 Walter Jacobs captured the college's first National Collegiate Athletic Association (NCAA) wrestling championship. Michigan State's teams also tasted success during the 1930s: the tennis team went 32-3 in dual meets between 1932 and 1934, and the Spartan basketball team compiled a 16-1 record during the 1930–31 season. From 1938, when the event was inaugurated, until 1964, Michigan State hosted the NCAA cross-country championship meet. The Spartan harriers took their first national title in 1939, following up with eight more before the championship left the East Lansing campus.

Long-distance runner Tom Ottey was a member of the 1932 U.S. Olympic team and won numerous regional and national titles in both cross-country and track during the early 1930s. When he and his MSC teammates won their second straight cross-country national championship in the fall of 1934, the front page of the *State News* trumpeted, "Ottey Outruns Fast Field for Second Win in Successive Years." Tom Warner's accompanying story reported, "Capt. Tom Ottey, blonde Olympic distance runner from M.S.C., placed first for the second consecutive year and became the first man in the history of this annual classic to do this feat." The archetypical "Big Man on Campus," Ottey also served as president of the senior class. The team's coach, Lauren Brown, had been an All-American runner and team captain at MSC in 1928, setting school records in the steeplechase and two-mile run.

RALPH YOUNG

By 1934, when Hannah became MSC's board secretary, Ralph Young had been building the school's athletic programs for more than a decade, serving as football coach for five years (1923–27), as cross-country coach for one year, and as track coach for sixteen years. Young was especially busy during 1923, when he not only headed all three programs but also served as athletic director, which was also his sole position from 1941 to 1954. Under Young's stewardship, Michigan State's athletic department found remarkable success, and Young's successor, Clarence "Biggie" Munn, continued that tradition.

One of Young's strengths was his ability to recruit and retain coaches. During his twenty-nine years at MSC, basketball coach Ben Van Alstyne compiled a 232-163 record and produced the school's first All-American in the sport, Chester Aubuchon. Karl Schlademan headed an outstanding cross-country program during the late 1940s and 1950s, winning NCAA titles in 1948, 1949, 1952, 1955, and 1956. Gymnastics coach George Szypula produced such NCAA individual champions as Steve Johnson, Dale Cooper, Jim Curzi, Dave Thor, and Toby Towson and led the team to a tie for the NCAA championship in 1958. Baseball coach John Kobs racked up a 576-377-16 record while turning out future major leaguers Robin Roberts, Dick Radatz, Tom Yewcic, Ron Perranoski, and Dean Look. Swimming coach Charles McCaffree compiled a 190-57-2 record, and his teams featured NCAA champions George Hoogerhyde, Clark Scholes, Billy Steuart, Frank

Before football gained prominence on college campuses, games often coincided with other athletic contests. In this 1934 photo, Michigan State's cross-country runners compete while the school's football players face off against Marquette. Courtesy of MSU Archives and Historical Collections.

The 1945 baseball team compiled a 12-4 record. The team included Coach John Kobs (*second row, center*), trainer Jack Heppinstall (*second row, far right*), and future MSU administrator Jack Breslin (*first row, center*). Courtesy of the MSU Museum Collections.

Modine, Don Patterson, Gary Dilley, and Ken Walsh. Wrestling coach Fendley Collins, whose squads consistently placed high in national championships, produced NCAA titlists Gale Mickles, Jim Sinadinos, and Ken Maidlow. Coaches specialized less during the Young era than in later years. Van Alstyne, for example, also compiled a 140-117 record at the helm of Michigan State's golf team. In addition to his baseball duties, Kobs served as head coach of the hockey teams and as a football assistant. And James Crowley and Harry Kipke served as both football and golf coaches.

Athletes, too, sometimes excelled in more than one sport. Roberts starred at Michigan State in both baseball and basketball during the mid-1940s before going on to a Hall of Fame baseball career. Yewcic was a catcher on the baseball team and a quarterback in football and went on to play both sports professionally. Steve Garvey played both football and baseball in the 1960s and later became an all-star first baseman with the Los Angeles Dodgers. And Look, a standout football and baseball player in the 1950s, played baseball for the Chicago White Sox, played football for the New York Titans, and subsequently became a National Football League official.

Coach Charles McCaffree gives pointers to five of his swimmers—(*top to bottom*) Howard Patterson, Bob Trout, Rod Quigley, Jim Quigley, and Don Reynolds—in 1949. Courtesy of MSU Archives and Historical Collections.

Other key members of the athletic department included support personnel, such as trainer Jack Heppinstall, who served on the school's staff from around 1914 until 1959. According to *Lansing State Journal* sportswriter George Alderton, Heppinstall "was like the spreading maples on the campus. He was always there. He is probably the person that the returning athletes from other days always wanted to greet and thank for the attention he had given them for their years at Michigan State." Before Hannah began expanding the college's athletic staff, the English-born Heppinstall served as the trainer for all sports but also was in charge of the athletic equipment for all sports, served as the instructor for the soccer classes, and substituted as a public speaker when a coach had a scheduling conflict.

MSC's 1931 golf team, coached by James Crowley, compiled a 5-4 record. Courtesy of MSU Archives and Historical Collections.

Another East Lansing fixture was Heppinstall's brother-in-law, Albert Amiss, who oversaw Michigan State's athletic fields. Wrote Alderton, "I feel sure that he could have grown sod on pavement with a wave of his hand. . . . I thought Albert counted the blades on the football field, and if one was missing he would replace it. Grounds keepers from other Big Ten schools often came to talk with him and learned some of his secrets of turning the earth green. . . . The baseball field was his pride and joy. Anyone who ever saw Albert in his dress-up clothes at the baseball games will never forget him. He was always attired in freshly laundered white overalls and he would have the whole stage to himself before the game began when he marked off the batter's box with lime. The diamond was always in Sunday dress on game day."

Another member of the Spartan sports staff, photographer Everett Huby, pioneered the making of play-by-play movies of football games. In 1923, he suggested to Young that the college film its football games. Young liked the idea, and Huby, a newsreel photographer for Lansing's Reo Motor Car Company, began filming

Burl Jennings, Bill Maxwell, and Merle Jennings
won NCAA wrestling championships in 1942.
Courtesy of the MSU Museum Collections.

the most important games. State could only afford to hire him part-
time, and he also began working for the University of Michigan, the
Detroit Lions, the Chicago Bears, and the Green Bay Packers. In 1938,
Michigan State made him a full-time employee, and he began filming
all home football games. Basketball, wrestling, gymnastics, hockey,
and boxing eventually were added to his schedule.

At first, Huby could not develop the film locally. Immediately
after each football game, he would drive to the Kodak laboratories
in Chicago, returning with the developed film so the coaches could
review it on Sunday. "I always thought that the entry of the motion
picture camera into sports was really a hardship for the players,"
Alderton wrote. "The coaches took the pictures apart play-by-play
in slow action and they could watch the move of every player, both
offensively and defensively. The poor player could not even pause for
a brief rest. He had to go all out all of the time or the camera would
tell on him when he took a rest."

Lyman Frimodig served as a key member of Michigan State's athletic department and also as mayor of East Lansing. Courtesy of Michigan State University Archives and Historical Collections.

Perhaps the most valuable member of the MSC athletic department was Lyman L. Frimodig. A ten-time letterman in football, basketball, baseball, and track while a student from 1914 to 1917, he went on to become an assistant coach in basketball, baseball, and football and an assistant athletic director in charge of athletic records and financial data. In addition, he served as East Lansing's mayor from 1933 to 1937. "He was always there," Alderton wrote. "He remembered everybody. He knew their first and middle names, too. His accounting was letter perfect. He never had a bad word about any of the coaches or his associates. He worked early and late, and asked no extra pay. One summer he joined the paint crew that had to re-paint all the seats in Spartan Stadium."

HANNAH AND ATHLETICS

Michigan State's longtime president enjoyed athletics, even achieving some notoriety for the number of consecutive football games he attended. He ended the streak "after Ripley in his *Believe It or Not* cartoon in the daily newspapers made reference to the fact that John Hannah, President of Michigan State, had attended 120 or more consecutive football games," he wrote in his biography. "With that I decided neither I nor M.S.U. needed that kind of publicity." As interested in competing as in winning, Hannah often sent notes to coaches before athletic events, telling them that win or lose, the college was proud of them. He also saw the nonathletic benefits of sports. "My interest in athletics gave me an opportunity to know a cross section of students, to know them personally, to know what their problems and concerns were," he said. "And out of that I learned much that was useful to me over the years in dealing with student affairs. . . . One of the greatest satisfactions of my life is the fact that some of the closest friends I have were students on the Michigan State athletic teams, many of whom have gone on to do interesting and worthwhile things in a great many fields." Hannah sometimes journeyed to great lengths to support MSC athletes. Heppinstall remembered Hannah traveling to London to encourage Spartan athletes participating in the 1948 Olympic Games. "After greetings I asked Dr. Hannah what I could get or do for him. He said, first, 'I need a pitcher of good cold drinking water, then get all our Michigan State boys together so that I can congratulate them for making the trip and tell them what is expected of them as competitors.'" Boxer Chuck Spieser, swimmers Howard Patterson and George Hoogerhyde, wrestlers Robert Maldegan and Leland Merrill, and walkers Adolph Weinacker and Ernest Crosbie gathered around the MSC president: as Heppinstall recalled, Hannah gave "one of the nicest talks I have ever heard given to a bunch of athletes." Frimodig echoed Heppinstall's recollections, noting that Hannah "seemed to take great interest in the athletes. Their scholastic trouble, their personal problems and their aches and pains. He enjoyed their successes both on and off the field."

Frimodig also credited Hannah with being influential in the hiring of baseball coach Danny Litwhiler; cross-country coaches Karl Schlademan, Fran Dittrich, and Jim Gibbard; golf coach Bruce Fossum; gymnastics coach George Syzpula; hockey coach Amo Bessone; wrestling coach Grady Peninger; sports information director Fred Stabley; and ticket manager Bill Beardsley. Frimodig also gave Hannah much of the credit for increasing stadium seating in 1936, 1948, and 1957; for building the track in 1936 and Jenison Field House in 1940; for enlarging and renovating the old men's gymnasium in 1958 for use by women; and for opening the Forest Akers Golf Course, the swimming pool, the tennis courts, and the intramural building in 1958.

However, Hannah often argued that although athletic competition had a place on the college campus, that place was secondary to academics. At a 9 April 1949 luncheon in honor of the NCAA boxing championships, which MSC was hosting, Hannah encouraged the NCAA visitors to inspect the whole campus, not just the athletic facilities. "It would be unfortunate if you went away thinking of Michigan State College only as an institution fortunate in possessing unusually good facilities for intramural and intercollegiate athletics," he told his audience. "That would not be accurate because it would give the impression we give undue emphasis here at Michigan State. We recognize the importance of athletics but we do not over-emphasize athletics." Sports, Hannah explained, were an important part of American culture, or "folkways." He frequently referred to the popularity of wrestling matches, foot races, canoe competitions, and shooting matches long before the first football game on a college campus. "I think that it would not take much research to prove that

Danny Litwhiler had a ten-year major league career before becoming Michigan State's baseball coach in 1964.

Americans have been vitally, actively interested in sports since this country began, and it does not take much foresight to predict that sports will continue to be prominent on the American scene for many decades to come," he said. Hannah asserted that colleges and universities would not be doing their job if they did not make a place for organized athletics in the educational program.

Despite his commitment to and love for collegiate athletics, Hannah did not hesitate to criticize the system in its current form. During the late 1940s and early 1950s, educators and the media launched a series of attacks on college sports, bemoaning their overemphasis, the lack of faculty control, differing policies regarding grants-in-aid, and the extent of alumni groups' power. Hannah had strong views on the subject, and Big Ten commissioner Tug Wilson gave Michigan State's president a national platform from which to present his ideas, inviting him to address the 1946 NCAA convention in St. Louis. Hannah told the delegates that colleges and universities too often ceded control of athletic programs to alumni groups and other special interests, producing a "circus side-show to which the college has loaned its name for publicity purposes." He argued that the rules controlling collegiate athletics were fine but almost impossible to police because of the many loopholes. And he urged association members to "adhere publicly and privately to some reasonable code of sportsmanship and ethics rather than drawing up a lot of rules and regulations that clever alumni and employees of the athletic department can find means of circumventing without violating the written word."

Hannah provided two simple solutions for restoring integrity to college athletics. First, he proposed that all athletic scholarships and remuneration for employment be administered by the same faculty organization or committee or procedure as for nonathletes. "I would not require that athletes be eligible only for the same grants as are non-athletes, but I would require that all grants and scholarships and payments either of a gratuitous nature or for services be handled by the same officer or committee of the faculty that administer the same program for the non-athletes, and all such records be available upon request to any recognized accrediting association or to the officers of this association." Second, he proposed limiting team membership to full-time students who had completed at least one full year on campus and one year's work toward a college degree. "I want to be assured that the persons competing against my teams are bona fide students, proceeding at a rate that would graduate them in the regular four years or five years required for graduation of all other students," the president said.

Hannah also argued that playing athletic events off of college campuses promoted commercialism and encouraged control by for-profit entities: "My judgment may be wrong, but I see in the bowl games a powerful force for tearing down the efforts of this association for maintaining athletics as part of the educational program of our colleges and universities. Why? Because to play in a bowl a team must win most or all its games. To do that there must be high-powered coaching and superlative material and non-representative schedules. . . . If football coaches regard their work as a profession, if our colleges regard intercollegiate athletics as an educational activity, then both the coaches and the colleges better de-emphasize the bowl business. . . . If intercollegiate athletics are part of the educational program, let's keep these games and contests on our college campuses. There is more at stake than our athletic reputations."

Hannah closed his speech with a couplet by Edwin Markham:

> We are blind until we see
> That in the human plan
> Nothing is worth the making
> If it does not make the man.
>
> Why build those states glorious,
> If man unbuilded goes?
> In vain we build the nation unless
> The builder also grows.

Hannah's commitment to integrity in sports continued for the rest of his time at the Michigan State helm, with his recommendations for reform built on the same two solid pillars: coincidental administration of athletic and nonathletic scholarships, and full-time enrollment required for participation. "If those two conditions prevail," he argued on many occasions, "I'm not going to worry too much about rules and regulations that bind the colleges, but have no effect on alumni groups, downtown coaches organizations and booster clubs."

Hannah's efforts received more national publicity in a June 1949 *Sports Illustrated* article written by *Detroit Free Press* sportswriter Tommy Devine. "The powerful Western Conference is to become the proving grounds for one of the greatest experiments of modern intercollegiate athletics," Devine wrote. "Into the sprawling, 53-year-old conference there is being introduced a new member—Michigan State—and a new leader—Dr. John Hannah. Hannah is president of Michigan State. It may be a bit startling to spotlight a college president in an athletic program, but that is the situation that prevails at East Lansing. Hannah brings to the influential and affluent Big Ten a different outlook on the ills and evils of collegiate sports—and strong convictions on how to eradicate them. He gives the conference an Ivory Tower touch in the locker room." The article quoted Hannah as saying, "If an athletic department, or a separate athletic association which is set up for that specific purpose, is allowed to handle all sports funds and builds reserves, there inevitably is too much emphasis placed on money grabbing." Moreover, he continued, "The most satisfactory plan, I think, is to handle the athletic department expenditures and revenue along with the general fund, just as you do any other department."

Hannah continued his crusade in a 10 January 1950 speech at the Maxwell Club dinner in New York City held to honor Notre Dame end Leon Hart as the year's best collegiate football player. Hannah told his audience that athletics should be returned to faculty control and that alumni groups should not be allowed to dictate athletic policy. "No college will get into trouble with its athletic program if it remembers that its football players are students first and athletes second," he said. "Universities must be true to their traditions as centers for the preservation and discovery of knowledge. It is only when they desert those traditional roles for the pursuit of athletic glory that they damage themselves and the games they prostitute." The speech won the endorsement of the dean of American sportswriters, Grantland Rice, who wrote, "I would like to see Dr. Hannah put in charge of the handling of all college football. There will, of course, be no seconds. College football hasn't gotten that sane."

In late 1951, Hannah became head of an American Council on Education committee to study intercollegiate athletics. The committee members—ten college and university presidents—would "examine at close range the total college sports picture and recommend changes which will maintain these sports as a valuable and respected part of American life." Hannah's influence on the committee's final recommendations is unmistakable:

- The department of athletics to be under university control on the same basis as any other department, with faculty status, tenure, salary and other rights of staff personnel to be comparable to the rest of the institution;
- Admission standards to be the same for all students, athletes or non-athletes;
- Eligibility of athletes to be based on normal progress toward a degree;
- Scholarships to be granted on the basis of academic excellence and need; to be administered by the university agency and not to exceed the cost of board, room, tuition and books at the given institution;
- Seasons for practice and play of the major team sports (football, basketball and baseball) to be limited to specified periods of time with out-of-season practice and play prohibited.

The full membership of the American Council on Education later approved the committee's recommendations, and they ultimately became the blueprint for the administration of intercollegiate athletics. However, the reforms had little effect in East Lansing: "Few changes in departmental organization, athletic policies or practice will have to be made at Michigan State," Stabley wrote in the *MSC Record*. "Alumni with a knowledge of the athletic situation at their Alma Mater will find most of the president's program quite familiar."

Despite Hannah's position at the forefront of the movement to reform collegiate athletic programs, the university found itself in some trouble with the Big Ten. In the early 1950s, Wilson began hearing rumors that a Lansing-based organization, the Spartan Foundation, was providing inappropriate financial aid to Michigan State athletes. Young and Munn admitted having heard of the organization but denied any MSC involvement. After the Big Ten and MSC failed to resolve the matter, Wilson contacted Hannah directly, stating that if more progress was not made, the Big Ten would have no choice but to bring formal charges against the school. Hannah quickly replied to Wilson with the information that the "Spartan Foundation had agreed to turn over $2,000 to the Michigan State scholarship fund and that after May 1, 1952, all scholarships funds would be processed through college channels."

Two major points of disagreement remained, however: whether a college could be responsible for controlling an outside organization and whether the conference commissioner had the authority to impose penalties. Wilson ultimately decided to put Michigan State on probation for one year; Hannah immediately requested a formal hearing. When the hearing produced no solution, Wilson took steps to put the probation into effect. MSC appealed, and on 2 February 1953, Dean Lloyd Emmons presented the college's case to the Big Ten faculty representatives, arguing that no conference rules had been violated, that the Spartan Foundation had no connection with MSC, that the conference handbook did not provide for any sort of probation penalty, and that the commissioner lacked the authority to impose penalties not spelled out in the handbook. The appeal was denied. In the wake of the incident, Wilson declared, "To Michigan State's great credit it cleared up the situation in a hurry, and our subsequent investigation showed that all Spartan Foundation funds had been turned over to the scholarship committee. [Alumni are allowed to] raise all the money they [like,] but it must be turned over to the university and be administered by the regulating agency in conformity to the rules."

One of Hannah's favorite sayings illuminates the basis for his commitment to integrity in athletics. As he wrote to Young regarding a possible NCAA rules violation, "I would like to again call your attention to a quotation from my predecessor, Mr. Shaw, which I think is as applicable today as it was then: 'Remember always that no player, no team, no coach, no sport is ever more important than the good name of Michigan State College.'"

Nevertheless, Hannah's attitude toward sports had its detractors. Writing in 1969, Harold B. Tukey, a prominent horticulturist and a member of the MSU Athletic Council during the 1950s, offered a less-than-positive assessment. Although Tukey "had the impression that [Hannah] would be just as well pleased if athletics were a little better controlled by the University," the professor also believed that they represented Hannah's "blind spot." "He enjoyed athletics and really saw nothing too evil about what was going on. He felt that they contributed heavily to the University drama, which they undoubtedly did." By "what was going on," Tukey meant academic dishonesty and even under-the-table payments to players, all of which, he believed, simply constituted part of competing in the Big Ten. Wrote Tukey, "How well I remember the man from western New York who used to stand up and wave his hat at me when one of 'his players' made a touchdown. He was definitely . . . paying them on the side, and no question about it, in full violation. But the athletic people never took a stand that would put anyone before a Grand Jury." No evidence has been found to support Tukey's allegations of unauthorized payments to athletes, and another member of the Athletic Council during the 1950s, communications professor Gordon Thomas, had no memory of any such instances, although he did know of cases where coaches and parents pressured faculty members to be lenient with athletes encountering difficulty in the classroom.

Horticulture professor Harold B. Tukey was a member of Michigan State's Athletic Council in the 1950s. While dedicated to that role, he criticized the operation of college sports. Courtesy of MSU Archives and Historical Collections.

THE FIGHTING PROFESSOR

During Hannah's tenure, Michigan State produced many athletes who excelled in their sports. None, however, matched the honors of boxer Chuck Davey, who went undefeated in every college bout he fought, was three times voted the NCAA's outstanding boxer, and fought at the 1948 Olympics (although he had gone shopping and missed Hannah's London speech to the athletes). When Davey died in 2002, *Detroit News* columnist Pete Waldmeir wrote,

> Boxing was barely out of the bare-knuckle, barroom brawling stage when Davey came along in the early 1940s. It's never been a Big Ten varsity sport, but several colleges—including Michigan State, Army, Navy, even Penn State—pulled together teams and convinced the NCAA to sanction their competition in the early '40s. This was the heyday of the Golden Gloves and the AAU, which ran the amateur competition nationwide. Unlike football and basketball, the colleges weren't pro boxing's minor leagues. It was the rare collegian who made it into the rough and tumble game for pay. Davey was the first and most marketable of those collegians. A four-time NCAA

MSC's 1948 boxing team placed second in NCAA competition. Ernie Charboneau (*first row, left*) won an individual title at 125 pounds, while Chuck Davey (*first row, third from right*) won an individual championship at 136 pounds. Courtesy of the MSU Museum Collections.

champion, bearer of both bachelor's and master's degrees from Michigan State College, he was exactly the kind of clean-cut, well-educated gladiator that the promotion-conscious International Boxing Association (IBA) was looking for in post–World War II America. Besides that, he was left-handed. And while he wasn't a banger, he could box a little and move a lot.

Labeled the "Fighting Professor," Davey became a star on the *Cavalcade of Sports* television shows that attracted large audiences on Wednesday and Friday nights. He compiled a 39-0 record and defeated such well-known fighters as Rocky Graziano, Chico Vejar, and Ike Williams. In 1953, however, Dave finally lost to an up-and-coming Cuban, Kid Gavilan. Despite the defeat, the bout netted Davey the biggest paycheck of his career—forty-six thousand dollars.

Michigan State produced other championship boxers as well. Bill Zurakowski, Ernie Charboneau, Gerald Black, Charles Spieser, Tom Hickey, Herb Odom, Choken Maekawa, and John Horne won

NCAA titles in the 1940s and 1950s. Under coach George Makris, the Spartans won the NCAA team championship in both 1951 and 1955. Beginning in 1958, Horne won three straight NCAA titles at 178 pounds. The feat was more remarkable because Michigan State disbanded its boxing team after the 1958 season, so Horne won his last two titles with no boxing schedule to sharpen him, no regular coach, and no regular sparring partners, often working out alone in Jenison gymnasium.

BASKETBALL, POLO, AND ROTC

MSC basketball did not achieve the consistent success of the cross-country squads, but magical moments nevertheless occurred. Beginning in 1930, games were played in Demonstration Hall, which could hold around 5,500 fans. "Its shortcomings included restricted availability for basketball and large vertical 'I' beams which would impede vision of the floor," Frimodig and Stabley wrote in *Spartan Saga*. "Demonstration Hall was the last major athletic structure at State to be erected with public funds appropriated through the legislature, and was intended for joint use of the athletic department and ROTC. The arrangement which was worked out required all home basketball games to be played during the first six weeks of winter term. The portable floor then had to be removed so that ROTC could use the area. Indoor polo was another complicating factor." Still, Van Alstyne managed some success. While the 1930–31 squad suffered only a single loss—to Michigan—the team probably gained more fame as the first U.S. collegiate sports team to fly to a game, when Van Alstyne and players Dee Pinneo, Art Haga, Randall Boeskool, Edward Scott, and Roger Grove flew to Milwaukee to take on Marquette, winning 24-21 on 28 February 1931. Between 1927 and 1935 Van Alstyne put together eight straight winning seasons that included seven victories over Michigan.

Basketball shifted to the newly built Jenison Field House in 1940, giving the Spartans better facilities and larger crowds. According to Lansing businessman Duane Vernon, a student of Spartan basketball history, "The first game ever played at Jenison Field House was on January 6, 1940, when we played the University of Tennessee and

Benjamin Van Alstyne compiled a 232-163 record as Spartan basketball coach between 1927 and 1949. Courtesy of MSU Archives and Historical Collections.

Wendell Patchett captained the 1934 basketball team. Courtesy of MSU Archives and Historical Collections.

won the game 29-20." The contest also showcased Michigan State's first All-American, Chet Aubuchon.

In 1942, when Michigan State faced off on 12 February at home against the University of Michigan, the game pushed war news off the front pages of the local newspapers. Dudley Jones scored twenty-five points to lead the Spartans to their biggest margin of victory against the Wolverines, 57-34. *State News* columnist Marshall Dann was so impressed that he chased down Jones and his parents after the game. "My mother and dad were up for this one," Jones explained. "It's the first college game they ever saw me play. I had to do something different for them." Dann also reported that the "impressive sight of the men's glee club singing the Star Spangled Banner before the game is one memory that will never be erased, and that the crowd of 8,300 is the largest which has or will see a basketball game in Michigan this year." At the end of that season, during which MSC compiled a 15-6 record, Dann asked Van Alstyne to choose his all-time Spartan basketball team:

> "Sure I'll pick a team," the MSC coach responded. "I've got two All-Americans on this year's team, Chet Aubuchon and Joe Gerard to start with and I'll find three more to fit in with them." Van Alstyne then consulted his small, black notebook that contained the records of every player he had coached in his seventeen years at State and said, "Aubie (Aubuchon) is a sure player at one guard position and Bob Herrick (class of 1935) goes at the other. They're the same type of ball player—cool, good ball handlers and real quarterbacks when it comes to running a team. Max Hindman can't be left off the team at center. . . . The forwards are the toughest to pick—can't we have three forwards on this team? Gerard surely has earned one place, and I can't choose between Marty Hutt and Ron Garlock for the other spot." You just couldn't beat that outfit. Every one of those boys was a star in his own right, yet they were the ideal team players.

Van Alstyne also insisted on naming a second team, whose members included Roger Grove, Don Grove, Jim Van Zylen, Jerry McCaslin, George Falkowski, and Bob Phillips as forwards; Arnie Van Faasen and Maurice Buysse at center; and Art Haga, Mike Rouse, Al Kircher, Lee Callahan, and Mel Peterson as guards.

Van Alstyne retired in 1949 and was replaced by Alton Kircher for one season before the highly respected Pete Newell took over for the next four. Newell subsequently had great success at the University of California in his native state, where he won the 1959 NCAA championship, and as coach of the 1960 U.S. Olympic team, which included Oscar Robertson and Jerry West and brought home the gold medal. Newell had only moderate success in East Lansing, compiling a 45-42 record, but nevertheless became a Spartan legend. His Michigan State players held an annual reunion with their former coach. A writer for *Spartan* magazine, Tom Shanahan, attended the 2003 gathering in San Diego and reported that the "70ish Spartans—their hair receding, graying or matching the white of their old coach—rose from their table one by one to speak of what Newell meant to them both a half-century ago and today. They called him a mentor who made them better players and successful men. They spoke with such fondness they sounded as if they had just finished playing for him two or three years ago." One star player, Al Ferrari, declared that Newell had a profound influence on his charges: "What he taught us as a coach lasted us a lifetime. The fellows here have succeeded because of the discipline he instilled in us."

When Forddy Anderson took over for the 1954–55 season, however, MSC started to gain the national respect it would enjoy in later decades. Anderson inherited a player who would eventually deflect some of the attention from the stars who played for the championship football teams of Biggie Munn and Duffy Daugherty—Julius McCoy. A native of Farrell, Pennsylvania, McCoy starred in football and track as well as basketball. Although the team managed only a 35-31 record during his three years at MSC, McCoy averaged 20.9 points for his career and an outstanding 27.2 points and 10 rebounds per game in his senior season. Fans who had never been excited about Spartan basketball attended home games just to see the scoring phenomenon, and local kids emulated McCoy in their playground contests. On 28 January 1956, MSC played Ohio State, pitting McCoy against OSU's scoring whiz, Robin Freeman, in what became one of the most famous shootouts in college basketball history. When the dust settled, Freeman had scored forty-six points and McCoy forty, but the Spartans won 94-91 with McCoy stealing the ball and scoring the winning basket. In an 84-78 win over Notre Dame during the same season,

Julius McCoy, one of the best shooters in Spartan basketball history, was selected to the All–Big Ten team in 1956. Courtesy of MSU Sports Information.

McCoy tallied forty-five points, prompting the *Lansing State Journal's* Lad Slingerland to write, "Seven Notre Dame firefighters tried in vain to put out the blaze but were forced back by the flames."

While many fans thought that McCoy's departure after that season would take the excitement out of Spartan basketball, Anderson's 1956–57 squad turned out to be one of MSU's best. After a sluggish 4-7 start, players Johnny Green, Jack Quiggle, Larry Hedden, George Ferguson, Bob Anderegg, Chuck Bencie, and Pat Wilson came together and tied Indiana for the Big Ten title. Because Indiana had gone to the NCAA Tournament in 1954 and MSU had never represented the conference, the Spartans went on to compete for the national title. They opened with an 85-83 win over Notre Dame, paced by Green's 20 points and 27 rebounds. In the next game, against Kentucky, Green fouled out midway through the second half, but MSU nevertheless upset the Wildcats 80-68 to reach the Final Four. In the national semifinals, MSU was matched against the No. 1–ranked North Carolina Tarheels, who needed three overtimes to edge out the Spartans, 74-70. The game was televised, and thousands of Spartan faithful saw game officials rule Quiggle's apparent game-winning shot from half-court a fraction of a second late. At season's end, Quiggle received All-American honors, while Quiggle, Green, and Ferguson were named to the All–Big Ten first team.

Anderson's team turned in a 16-6 record in 1957–58, once again winning the conference crown and representing the Big Ten in the NCAA Tournament. Green, Hedden, Quiggle, and Anderegg continued their key roles and were joined by a new star, rebounding ace Horace Walker. Green was named an All-American in 1959. Over the next six years, however, Anderson's teams posted only one winning season, and he was fired in 1965. While many fans, students, and alumni accepted Anderson's dismissal as the logical result of losing seasons, some did not. Opined a *State News* editorial,

> In light of Thursday's discharge of basketball coach Forddy Anderson, Michigan State has seen fit to employ the hire-fire brand of athletic management that has contaminated the high school, college and professional sports scenes. . . . [E]ven if Spartan fans weren't impatient, Athletic Director Clarence Biggie Munn was. . . . Anderson was not without his flaws, the least of which was the

Fans carry basketball player John Green off the floor after a 1957 win. Courtesy of MSU Archives and Historical Collections.

impulsive, highly volatile way he responded to criticism. And Munn was not without his criticism—especially when it deals with a favorite subject of his, Big Ten championships (or the lack of them). Hence, force-meet-force. . . . Thus, exit Anderson. That an injustice has been done to Anderson is, to our way of thinking, an undeniable and irremediable fact. Whether Munn had the final word or President John Hannah (who conveniently scheduled a trip to Nigeria the day of the firing) matters little. Either way, the net result leaves Anderson holding the bag.

Some *State News* readers agreed. Graduate student George Colburn, later a member of the East Lansing City Council, suggested that Munn's loss of power at the university had contributed to Anderson's dismissal:

Biggie was a very real MSU hero. This gave him power—very real power. He had taken MSU out of the deep dark woods of inferiority and obscurity. Power was Biggie's reward. But then something strange happened at MSU. Biggie's athletes through the 1950's had given MSU a name known to just about everybody in the United States. This is what certain people at MSU desired. The time had arrived to make MSU a real institution of higher learning. The University had a name. . . . The "egg heads" could recruit scholars now that they had a "name" to use. Biggie and his well-paid amateurs had done their job well. They gave MSU the quick way to national fame. Now libraries could be built instead of additions to football stadiums. [Munn], sinking deeper and deeper each year into oblivion at MSU, was finally given his opportunity at the end of this basketball season to show everyone he was not yet a paper tiger. He knew that Anderson lost only two players from last year's team and there was height and real promise on the freshman team. With Anderson's well-known talents, [Munn] knew he'd never get another chance to lower the ax. . . . The new powers in the University must realize that this must not happen again. They must realize that no one is the loser in this case except the University, its students, alumni and faculty.

Freshman James Spaniola, who subsequently chaired MSU's journalism department, also wrote to the *State News*:

An 11-year era of MSU basketball history came to a sad and shocking end for the man who led the Spartans to national prominence and maintained an aura of respect even in defeat. But such is the fate of basketball coaches at colleges and universities throughout the country, the pundits tell us. When completing a winning record, a coach can do little wrong. But let that same coach start losing no matter if he's forced to play five midgets, the once tumultuous cheers quickly turn to jeers and quickly become scarce. . . . In his 11 years at MSU, Anderson coached more than his share of outstanding ball players. He developed such stars as Johnny Green, the human jumping jack who never played basketball until his service days and then at MSU. Forddy Anderson worked tirelessly with him on fundamentals and the fine points of the game, so that he could eventually lead State to two Big Ten Championships. Then there was Pete Gent, the small-town boy from Bangor, who led his team to a state championship in his Class C prep days. But how did he make the jump to college ball and then become one of the highest scorers in MSU history? Again, Forddy Anderson played an important part to bring this all about. It's all over now. He's gone from the scene. But it will be "many a year" before MSU finds a man of the stature, ability and character of Forddy Anderson. When the decision was made, MSU chose to rid itself of a fine coach—and a true gentleman.

Despite such dire predictions and hand-wringing, MSU's next men's basketball coach, John Bennington, was also a man of stature, ability, and character. "During his four years as Spartan coach, Bennington would probably draw as much affection from campus and community as any prominent head coach had managed at Michigan State," Lynn Henning wrote in *Spartan Seasons*. "The kicker was he never had to try very hard. Father of nine children, he was regarded as a nice man, but no goody-goody. In contrast to the yarn-spinners who worked an audience almost manipulatively, Bennington's was a Will Rogers–style humor that branched off into practical jokes, particularly if he could get an appropriate person to swallow a put-on telephone call." His team notched a 17-7 record in 1965–66 and followed up with a 16-7 finish and a tie for first in the Big Ten in 1966–67. Two mediocre seasons followed before Bennington died of a heart attack on 10 September 1969.

Spartan Hockey

Michigan State's hockey program did not have an auspicious start. Between 1922, when the college fielded its first official team, and 1930, the squad never turned in a winning season. Things then got even worse: from 1931 to 1949, no intercollegiate hockey competition took place.

In 1949 Michigan State officials restarted the school's hockey program by installing an ice rink in Demonstration Hall, enabling games to be played indoors. Harold Paulsen became the team's coach, putting together a 6-25 record over the 1950 and 1951 seasons. Paulsen's successor, Amo Bessone, who had previously coached at

The 1954 Spartan hockey team in action in Demonstration Hall. Courtesy of MSU Archives and Historical Collections.

Michigan Tech, fared little better during his first fourteen years in East Lansing, going 134-196-9. In 1958–59, however, Bessone's Spartans finished 17-6-1 and took second place in the NCAA. Despite minimal recruiting efforts during these years, Michigan State had a number of outstanding players, including goalies Joe Selinger and John Chandik, forwards Bill MacKenzie and Tom Mustonen, and defenseman Ed Pollesel. Games at Demonstration Hall rarely sold out, a fact that is not surprising in light of the building's atmosphere. According to Henning, "Fans were seated on three sides of the building, most of them in a dark balcony that offered bloodthirsty front-row customers a position from which they could hang over a railing and verbally abuse enemy players." Moreover, on-ice "fights only heightened madness in the student section."

Bob Ritter broadcasts an MSC baseball game in 1938. Courtesy of WKAR Radio.

In 1965–66, Bessone's program reached the top of the hockey world. After finishing the regular season with a 9-11 record, good for sixth place in the Western Collegiate Hockey Association, Spartan goalie Gaye Cooley; defensemen Don Heaphy, Bob Brawley, and Tom Mikkola; and forwards Mike Coppo and Brian McAndrew played their best hockey during tournament time. The team beat Michigan and Michigan Tech in the WCHA championships, slipped by Boston University in the NCAA semifinal game, and whipped Clarkson 6-1 to take the national title, becoming "college hockey's greatest Cinderella team ever." The following season, the hockey Spartans reached the national semifinals, where they lost 4-2 to Boston University.

SUCCESS ON THE DIAMOND

The high point for Michigan State's baseball team during the Hannah years was the 1954 season, when, led by coach John Kobs, the Spartans posted a 25-10-1 overall record and an 11-2 conference mark to take their first Big Ten title, clinching the championship with a 6-5 victory over Ohio State when outfielder Bob Powell's bloop single brought home Dan Brown. Catcher (and football quarterback) Tom Yewcic was named a first-team All-American, and outfielder Jack Risch was

In the years before Michigan State fielded interscholastic athletic teams for women, they competed in a variety of intramural sports, as this photo of members of a 1933 women's tumbling squad demonstrates. Courtesy of MSU Archives and Historical Collections.

chosen to the second team. Yewcic, Risch, and first baseman Charles Matthews were named All-Conference; shortstop John Matsock and pitcher Ernest Erickson made the second team; and Powell, second baseman George Smith, and pitcher Ed Hobaugh were picked for the third team. The Spartans reached the NCAA finals, where they lost to Missouri, 4-3.

Intramural Athletics

In keeping with his vision of sports as an integral part of the collegiate experience, Hannah strongly supported intramural contests, some of which the *State News* extensively covered. On 23 August 1962, for example, the paper ran a front-page story trumpeting the Butcher Boys' 5-1 victory over the Biology Institute to take the intramural softball championship.

In 1958, Michigan State constructed the state-of-the-art intramural building, which featured both indoor and outdoor swimming pools as well as facilities for a variety of other sports. Students could

also go ice skating in Demonstration Hall, use the outdoor track for leisurely jogging or dedicated training, visit the Women's IM, and bowl in the basement of the Student Union. In addition to serving as the site for numerous intercollegiate athletic contests, Jenison Field House provided facilities for student classes in swimming, handball, and track and field and hosted Friday-evening open basketball competitions that included high school students, college students, and MSU faculty as well as more accomplished local sports personalities.

Michigan State, like many other schools of the time, did not field women's intercollegiate athletic teams during Hannah's presidency. Nevertheless, women competed as individuals and on intramural squads. Gymnast Ernestine Russell, a Canadian who graduated from MSU in 1960, won five gold medals at the 1959 Pan American Games and represented Canada in the 1956 and 1960 Olympics.

Field hockey was a popular sports activity for women in the 1930s. This team posed for its official photo in 1932. Courtesy of MSU Archives and Historical Collections.

Calm and Chaos in the 1960s

O N 12 JUNE 1960, THE *LANSING STATE JOURNAL* PUBLISHED SEVERAL articles about the "typical" MSU male graduate. Reporters Bill Burke, Doris Jarrell, and Harry Stapler created a "composite man" whom they described as serious and hardworking, with no strong political convictions, but tending to be conservative, preoccupied with his career, looking forward to raising children, and seeing religion as important. "He is not ready to lead a crusade for peace nor for war," they wrote. "He has a vague hope that nuclear bombs will be outlawed and looks upon a war as an unpleasant interruption of his home-community-career role. . . . He has no wild oats to sow and no world exploring to do."

Some faculty members found the news disturbing. "These kids need a challenge," economics professor Walter Adams told the reporters. "They've got to believe something and know why they believe as they do. . . . There is something unwholesome about their preoccupation with fringe benefits and a ranch type home. . . . In the 1960 frame of mind, our ancestors and their descendents would not have crossed the continent, would not have preserved the American way of life through the Depression and would not have mobilized the nation to win World War II." Others, such as English professor Russel Nye, were slightly kinder. "He [the 1960 graduate] is hard-working and almost grim," Nye said. "He has done a lot of thinking, on his own, about what is important in life, and in a flexible, fluid and complex world, he is searching for basic values. . . . He is not the kind of man who will lead a crusade and is not going to jump off the deep end. . . . This graduate knows exactly where he is going. . . . [H]e seems to know almost too exactly where he is going."

The *State Journal* writers were likely correct in their 1960 assessment. After all, the big news on campus when students returned

Senator John F. Kennedy of Massachusetts
appeared on the MSU campus in the fall of 1960
in his successful bid for the U.S. presidency.
Courtesy of Michigan State University Archives and Historical
Collections.

for the fall term of 1960 was the upcoming Farmers' Week in early
February. The event had been a tradition for forty-six years. The
State News had given it special front-page coverage on numerous
occasions, and the *State Journal* devoted a 29 January special section
to the opening. "Modern highways and speedy automobiles make it
possible for farm families to drive into East Lansing for the day and
return in time to do the evening chores—perhaps a bit late," a *State
Journal* writer explained. "In early days, visitors would come to Farmers' Week and stay out the entire week or several days at least. Some
still do, but a vast majority make the trek home for chores. . . . It is
not a repeat showing of a well-worn epic, but an ever-changing show
that is updated annually by science learned by researchers, new wants
expressed by consumers and the combined squeeze on the farmer by
higher prices for what he buys and lower, or constant, income for
what he has to sell." An estimated fifty thousand visitors attended
the event, which featured $1 million worth of new farm machinery,
ranging from self-propelled combines to automatic egg conveyers.
Some of the guests weren't farmers. "City people, too, flock in to see
these machines," said Arthur Farrall, head of agricultural engineering.

"Start up a tractor and you'll always draw a crowd." Special programs included a beekeepers' school, a youth tour of the museum, a muck farmers' luncheon, a session on plant disease control, and a livestock auction.

THE ADVENT OF "THE SIXTIES"

By 1962 philosophies seemed to be changing, and more students seemed willing to "lead a crusade." The *State News* noted in a 31 January story that enrollment in courses on communist theory and practice had doubled since the year before. Political science professor Alfred G. Meyer attributed the increase partially to a changing student body that was more interested in liberal arts and was turning away from the bread-and-butter courses of a narrow professional education. David Gottlieb, an assistant professor of sociology and anthropology, suggested that students were beginning to realize that business was being conducted on a worldwide basis and that employers could send their employees anywhere. Whatever the reasons, the issue of communism was at the center of one of the major battles the university faced in the 1960s. In one of the most publicized incidents, the Board of Trustees voted to bar communist speaker Robert G. Thompson from speaking on campus in the spring of 1962 and directed President John Hannah to prevent the use of the Union or any other campus facility for the speech. The Delta Sigma Phi fraternity loaned its backyard for the talk, and more than two thousand people attended. Although the speech broke no new ground, it seemed to start a surge of student activism that dominated campus throughout the rest of Hannah's tenure.

While many students questioned the right of the university to control what speakers appeared on campus in 1962, a conservative columnist was asking questions about the quality of education those students were receiving. "Michigan State today—once a good agricultural college with some commendable associated schools—is a prime example of the damage done to higher learning in America by the empire-building university president, bent upon quantity and positively hostile to quality," wrote Russell Kirk in the 28 August issue of the *National Review*. Kirk, who was formerly both a student and a faculty member at the university, went on to charge that MSU had only one "Negro" on its faculty, stifled freedom of expression, allowed administrators to control the student newspaper, and permitted doctoral candidates to write dissertations about such subjects as the impact football helmets had on preventing serious injuries. Most of the blame for the university's "low" academic standards was placed directly on its president. "The energumen at MSU is a gentleman who was once desk-clerk in the student union, married the president's daughter, was appointed secretary to the college's board of trustees, and in due course was invested with the hereditary majesty of the MSU presidency: Mr. John Hannah."

The column was not the first time Kirk had attacked MSU, and for much of his career he also criticized other universities and American education in general. In a 1983 article appearing in *Horizons*, a publication of Grand Valley State University, for example, he objected to the dependence on technology by American educators, questioning the value of using such "gadgets" as film projectors, sound systems, and even computers. Knowledge, he argued, was becoming secondary to the age of electronics. Many dismissed Kirk, believing his conservative views to be outside the mainstream of modern education. But he had a following and was called the "prophet of modern conservatism" by President Ronald Reagan. Saralee Howard, a former associate editor of *Michigan History*, also considered Kirk a legitimate scholar.

> As an historian and teacher of Michigan history, I have read many of Kirk's works. . . . He was an incomparable Michiganian of letters as well as a national and international thinker of lasting repute. . . . I knew him personally and visited his home and knew his family. He was no fan of modern consumerism and his life in his ancestral home, "Piety Hill," in Mecosta, Michigan, reflected that—no TV, no word processing for his extensive and constant stream of writings and letters, no internet but rather a far-reaching, beautiful library. I found him to be extraordinarily generous and open-minded. Visits to Piety Hill were always an experience. I never knew whom I might share dinner with at the large Kirk table—refugees from other lands, students from St. Andrews in Scotland, thinkers of every political stripe, journalists and simply folks who found solace in a loving and animated household.

Many—especially MSU administrators—disagreed with Reagan and Howard. After Kirk criticized MSU in a March 1962 *National Review* column, Hannah wrote a 27 March memo to university attorney Leland Carr and aide James Denison:

Attached is a copy of a note to Rocky Gust who is a respectable member of the Constitutional Convention. You will notice he has now filed as a candidate for Lieutenant Governor on the Republican ticket. . . . Yesterday he handed me [a copy] of the issue of the *National Review* with Kirk's latest diatribe, and asked me for the other side of the evident controversy. This disturbs me only in that it indicates that people who do not know what the facts are give credence to these articles. At yesterday's breakfast meeting Lee Carr indicated he thought there would be some gain in suing Mr. Kirk just for the purpose of shutting him up. I will appreciate it if the two of you will document whatever case we have so we can discuss the possibility of discussing this with our Trustees when they meet. If the Trustees feel there would be some gain in legal action, perhaps we should give consideration to that possibility. While I do not like these attacks, I am more concerned with the damage they do this University in the eyes of people who do not know what the facts are.

MSU did not sue. Five years after Kirk's two 1962 *National Review* columns, in a letter to a University of North Carolina colleague dated 5 September 1967, Hannah assistant James Denison summarized MSU's experience with Kirk, likely reflecting the view of many in the Hannah administration:

Kirk was a brilliant student here who had so much promise that the University waived some of its regulations, after he was appointed to the faculty, to enable him to complete his work for the doctorate. What happened subsequently to make him such a bitter and unreasonable critic of Michigan State, no one seems to know. The best information I can get is he had a fight with his department head, and that soured him forever. He has long carried on a one-sided vendetta against President Hannah, again for unknown reasons. At times his attacks—mostly in the *National Review*—have been intensely personal and potentially libelous. We have a thick file of them, and may have to take action some day. . . . He considers himself the intellectual mentor of conservatism, as you may know. He wrote and published *The Conservative Mind,* which got fine reviews in some right-wing papers in the U.S., but was roundly criticized in England. . . . As you have already detected, there are flaws in his vision. What I may have been able to explain is why his vision is flawed, or distorted by his unfounded enmity for the university where he was educated. It is a curious case; we have learned to live with this perpetual thorn-in-the-side, but it isn't easy for one of my temperament.

MSU lived with the Kirk attacks by generally ignoring them, but after the 28 August 1962 column appeared, the University of Michigan student newspaper, the *Michigan Daily,* asked Hannah for a rebuttal. Hannah complied, and his response was printed in both the UM paper and the *State News.* "Mr. Kirk has been using the columns of *The National Review* for the past several years to castigate me and to criticize Michigan State University. I would not be honest if I did not say I have not been pleased by this acrimony. Up until now, I have not dignified it by any notice or response. A president of a public university learns early that he had better develop a thick hide and calm spirit, or life could become rather unpleasant at times." Hannah pointed out that there were several minorities on the faculty, that the university had made dramatic advances since Kirk first enrolled as a freshman in 1936, that he was appointed president by the Board of Trustees and not his father-in-law, and that MSU "is a respectable and respected university." He concluded by saying, "I suspect Michigan State University will continue to survive the buzzings of Mr. Kirk."

Not everyone who made jabs at MSU created controversy. Phil Frank became well-known for cartoons that he contributed to the *State News* while he was a student in the early 1960s. His biting art often made fun of student life, sacred university institutions, and even John Hannah. MSU's president didn't seem to mind, however, and once even wrote the introduction to a Frank book, saying in part, "If he has a message, it must be that we should not take ourselves and the work we do too seriously." Frank eventually moved to San

Francisco, where he became known for his *Farley* cartoon, depicting a reporter on a metropolitan newspaper. His San Francisco popularity was confirmed when a citizen's committee chose him as one of 160 great writers (Frank was sometimes called "a journalist who draws his stories") who would have their names engraved on a sculpture at the main city library. Others included Robert Frost, Amy Tan, William Faulkner, James Joyce, Gertrude Stein, and Samuel Beckett.

The university was positively depicted in the media, as well. Paul Engle, a Rhodes scholar and member of the English faculty at the University of Iowa, praised MSU in a 1960 *Saturday Evening Post* article titled "In the Defense of the State University." He wrote, "America's first state agricultural college is now turning itself into one of the country's first universities in total service to the world and in pursuit of total knowledge. It offers courses in Arabic, Hindu, Chinese and Japanese by day, and by night provides a rich sequence of visiting ballet companies, orchestras and its own theater. It is inconceivable that any alert human being could not find his interest at this university, where one can study anything from artificial insemination of cattle to astrophysics."

THE RISE OF STUDENT ACTIVISM

While Hannah and Kirk disagreed on the "state of the university" in 1962, the year was an important one in its history—a time when students began the move from complacency to activism. At the beginning of the fall term more than five thousand students, the largest freshman class in MSU history, assembled for Hannah's welcoming address. "No better beginning could be made than to repeat what you have been told so often—that Michigan State University has high academic standards, and will expect performance at a high level from you," Hannah said. "That is not sales talk or advertising, but the cold truth." Hannah reminded students that they were no longer in high school but were now in the "big league," that MSU was a friendly place, and that their education should not be used for purely selfish purposes but should help contribute to the welfare of fellow human beings. He suggested that students go to high school to be taught but to a college or university to learn.

He also stressed the diversity of the student body. "Another point of pride at Michigan State University is the quality and diversity of our students. This entering class is the best prepared of any freshman class in our history. You will have students here from every county of Michigan, and from all states in the Union. You will rub elbows with students from small towns and large cities and rural areas, and the suburbs in between. You will find that they come from families both well-to-do and families which must make real sacrifices to send their children here." Hannah warned the students about proper behavior. "I strongly urge upon you the desirability of striking a sensible balance in your activities. We expect good classroom performance, but we know that non-academic activities, too, contribute to getting an education. The trick is to achieve a balance between them. In this sense, balance includes the employment of good judgment in the number of outside activities you undertake, and good judgment in behavior. I have seen many generations of students come and go, and it is my experience either automobiles or liquor are contributors to many of the difficulties in which students may find themselves. Freshmen are not permitted to have automobiles on the campus for the simple reason that they offer too much potential for distraction."

Hannah concluded his address by saying:

All of us can take comfort in the thought that great social gains have followed in the wake of technological improvements in this free country. We live today on a scale of comfort that would have been undreamed of a few short decades ago. Despite our social ills, still they are far less than when your parents were young. The world that awaits you beyond this campus is a world hungry for the leadership it looks to educated men and women to provide. It cries for those who can think and can do. It will reward both materially and emotionally those who prepare themselves well for the tasks awaiting them, and work hard at those tasks when they come to hand. The advances to be made in the decades ahead will be pioneered by young people like you who are now in college. In such a fast-paced age, opportunity does not knock, but pounds on the door of those who are ready to answer.

Changes in Campus Life

MSU had a tremendously diverse and opinionated student body and faculty in the 1960s. New issues and events seemed to emerge daily. Compulsory Reserve Officer's Training ended during the 1962 spring term, and thereafter students could choose not to enroll. MSU was not, nevertheless, out of step with the U.S. military agenda. Many universities, with the Defense Department's approval, had eliminated their ROTC programs. A 29 May parade, attended by Commanding General Herbert Powell of the U.S. Continental Army Command, marked the official end. "In view of the university's splendid accomplishments in the past, I have no doubt that the transition to the elective ROTC will be smooth and will not weaken the present efficient program," Powell said. "We will still rely on enlightened and patriotic supporters among faculty and students to point out to each and every man at State the absolutely essential nature of the ROTC program."

Probably just as dramatic to some was the university's decision to no longer require men to wear coats and ties when eating dinner in residence halls. The formal dress rules had been in effect since the end of World War II, but a student survey indicated the restrictions were not popular. The new rules stipulated that males should wear neat and clean dress slacks (jeans and shorts were not allowed), conventional dress shirts (no T-shirts, knit shirts, plaids, or bold stripes), and conventional dress shoes (no slippers, tennis shoes, clogs, or thongs).

Students wanting to live off campus were given some encouragement in 1962. Previously, only male undergraduate students who were twenty-one years and older, were at least in the junior class, and had maintained a C average were allowed to live off campus in unsupervised housing. Exceptions were made for veterans and local students. Similar rules applied for women, except they had to be twenty-five years old. Trustees changed the rules in May, allowing men and women students over twenty-one to live where they pleased, provided they had their parents' approval. East Lansing city officials immediately expressed concern—suggesting that in the past, students living in unsupervised housing had caused problems with noise and partying—and instructed the city attorney to study the issue. MSU trustees didn't base their decision solely on a desire to give students more independence; they also believed it might relieve a housing crunch on campus. "However," Dean of Students John Fuzak told the *State Journal,* "we feel sure the students are mature enough to accept the responsibility."

Students saw a rise in the cost of tuition in 1962, when in-state tuition increased from $309 to $324 a year, and out-of-state from $830 to $870. Parking violation fees also increased, staying the same $2 for a first ticket but rising dramatically for multiple tickets. That year fall enrollment on the East Lansing campus totaled 25,014 students—an increase of 2,290 over the previous year. Seventy-six percent of the entering class was ranked in the top quarter of their high school graduating classes, and more than two hundred were either valedictorians or salutatorians. Twenty-four were National Merit Scholarship winners. However, MSU administrators were even more proud of the student success rate after enrollment: 93 percent of the 4,917 freshmen who enrolled in 1961 were academically qualified to continue into their second year of studies. Also significant were the increasing numbers of students who were coming from educationally and economically disadvantaged homes. "Most of their parents have not had the opportunity for higher education; most of them do not work in occupations that provide the level of income that made it possible to build up large savings accounts for college expenses or that today can stand the additional expense of paying for all of the college investment," the MSU admissions office reported. "Many of these students while still in high school must work afternoons and nights and weekends to supplement the family income. Literally hundreds of their families have incomes so low they have not paid one dollar of federal income tax the past two years."

INDIVIDUALS WHO MADE A DIFFERENCE

A student walking around the MSU campus in the early 1960s would have run into numerous fascinating classmates who eventually reached outstanding success in their chosen fields of study. One was Robert Little, the half-brother of civil rights leader Malcolm X. Little became director of Michigan's Office of Youth Services and the top child welfare administrator in New York City before returning to MSU's social work department to conduct research in kinship care for children—care by grandparents or other relatives. Little, who was raised in foster care, never considered a civil rights career like his older brother. "I think my brother did a lot of good for people," he said. "I hope I'm also contributing in what I chose to do." Another later-to-be famous student was James P. Hoffa, son of legendary union leader James R. Hoffa. The younger Hoffa briefly played football at MSU and was a member of the Alpha Tau Omega fraternity. Elected president of the International Brotherhood of Teamsters in 1998, he credited MSU economics professor Walter Adams and history professor Fred Williams as having positive influences on his success. Those watching the Spartan marching band might have noticed John Kornblum, who became a U.S. ambassador to Germany. Ambassador Kornblum played both the tuba and the trombone and was a member of the Honors College. A student who made a name for himself in Hollywood was Walter Hill, who became a respected movie director, producer, and screenwriter. His films include *48 Hours, Alien, The Getaway,* and *Last Man Standing.* Another student to go on to Hollywood success was Joe Vecchio, a soon-to-be professional baseball player who eventually produced *Oscar,* starring Sylvester Stallone. Budding politicians such as future Michigan governor James Blanchard and future Lansing mayor David Hollister were preparing for their careers in the public sector. Future MSU president Peter McPherson was a student in 1962, as were eventual trustees Joel Ferguson and Donald Nugent.

East Lansing screenwriter Jim Cash argued, however, that the most talented students of the 1960s were his fellow writers. "There were just some extraordinary writing talents going to school at MSU then," he said, specifically mentioning Jim Harrison, Tom McGuane, and Dan Gerber. Harrison wrote novels such as *Dalva, The Road Home,* and *Legends of the Fall,* and the *New York Review of Books* once called his writing "among the most lucid and sensitive English being published today." McGuane authored *The Sporting Club, Ninety-Two in the Shade,* and *Keep the Change,* and is considered an outstanding chronicler of fly-fishing. Gerber is an award-winning poet, and from 1968 through 1972 he coedited the literary magazine *Sumac.* Other outstanding writers educated at MSU include Pulitzer Prize–winning novelist Richard Ford, poet Gary Gildner, and novelist Ted Weesner. Cash, who practiced his writing skills in the mid 1960s by covering the football team for the *State News,* was also a talented writer, teaming with MSU graduate Jim Epps to author such screenplays as *Top Gun, Legal Eagles, The Secret of My Success,* and *Dick Tracy.* "I really like this university and this community," he said when asked why he never moved to Hollywood. Cash showed his love for the area by donating his time to teach a film history course at MSU; throwing receptions at his home for visiting dignitaries, such as former MSU student and film actor James Caan; and hosting special events for new MSU personnel, such as the assistant coaches Nick Saban hired when he first took over the Spartan football team. Cash was passionate about MSU football and was one of the university's most knowledgeable persons about its history. "What number did Walt Kowalczyk wear?" he would ask a friend over a drink at the Harrison Roadhouse in East Lansing. When the friend responded with the right answer, Cash would exclaim, "That was way too easy. What number did Dorne Dibble wear?" When he received only a blank stare, he would supply the correct answer.

Author Glendon Swarthout featured Michigan State in one of his books. Born in Pinckney, Michigan, in 1918, Swarthout earned his bachelor's and master's degrees from the University of Michigan before receiving his doctorate in Victorian literature in 1955 from MSU. He taught English at Michigan State from 1951 to 1963, and in 1960 he wrote *Where the Boys Are,* the first comic novel about college students on spring break. The featured students were, of course, from MSU, and the novel was soon made into a hit movie. Swarthout wrote a total of sixteen novels, including The *Shootist,* which became a movie starring John Wayne, and *They Came to Cordura,* which became a movie featuring Gary Cooper and Rita Hayworth. Michigan State University Press would later publish a volume of his short stories. Before he died in 1992, Swarthout won many awards for his westerns, and he was twice nominated for the Pulitzer Prize by his publishers.

Carl Rollyson Jr. wrote biographies about such celebrities as Lillian Hellman, Norman Mailer, Marilyn Monroe, and Rebecca West. In 1997 he wrote an article for the spring edition of the *MSU Alumni Magazine* describing his MSU education.

I suppose my career as a biographer began when I was an under-graduate, during what I called my "eighteenth-century quarter" at MSU. I was an English major taking nearly as many credits as my main subject. It occurred to me in my sophomore year (1966–67) that I could simultaneously take surveys of eighteenth-century British history and the novel, as well as seminars on eighteenth-century British poetry and on continental history. This was my most exciting quarter, as I compared and integrated the courses and got to know my professors, who were then quite a study: a gruff, brilliant dietician whose Brooklynese reminded me of Ralph Cramden, an elegant (Agnew would have said effete) British lecturer, a dour Alexander Pope adept, and a cheerful, flaxen-haired Midwesterner who relished Lovelace's devious entrapment of Clarissa in Samuel Richardson's great novel.

The Campus Dialogue

Students, famous and not-so-famous, had the opportunity to discuss key university issues with MSU administrators at the Spartan Round Table, held periodically in the Student Union. Begun by Hannah in 1947, the Round Table provided student leaders of various organizations with an opportunity to interact with the administration and report back to their organizations. "After dinner—held alternatively at the Union and Cowles House—there followed an hour or more of questions and answers, with the students posing the questions, administrators attempting to answer them to the students' satisfaction," Denison recalled. "These sessions often provided an opportunity for the president to announce forthcoming proposals for changes in matters affecting student life, to explain budget difficulties which stood in the way of academic improvement, and to enlist the understanding, if not the support, of student leaders. This practice was continued with a high degree of success until President Hannah ended his tenure and, in the opinion of many administrators, helped keep student discontent at a minimum." The first Round Table meeting of the 1962 fall term was held on 16 October and provided a lively discussion of many topics important to the student representatives. According to the minutes from the meeting, subjects ranged from how tickets would be distributed for the upcoming MSU–University of Michigan football game to the possibility that compulsory ROTC would be reinstated. When a question was raised about the university's position on spontaneous pep rallies, Dean of Students John Fuzak pointed out that they were not encouraged, because of the extra manpower required and the chance a rally might turn into a riot. When asked why so many graduate students were teaching undergraduate classes, Provost Clifford Erickson stated that MSU had fewer graduate students teaching than any other major university in the country. When students proposed limiting the amount of time a visiting band could play during halftime of a football game, the suggestion was referred to band director Leonard Falcone.

Scholarship at MSU in the Sixties

The MSU student in the 1960s had opportunities to study with a large number of distinguished professors. Six were honored in 1962 with Distinguished Faculty Awards, based on nominations by students, faculty, and alumni, and were rewarded with $1,000 stipends from the Development Fund. Education professor Carl H. Gross was one of the winners. A staff member since 1947, he was a member of the board of directors of the History of Education Society and the coauthor of *School and Society,* as well as the author of many journal articles. "He always has time for the student and spends long hours in individual work with his students," wrote one of his nominators. "He conducts his classes in such a way that even the most reluctant feel compelled to contribute," said another.

Metallurgical engineering professor Howard L. Womochel had arrived at Michigan State in 1938 as a research assistant at the engineering experiment station, and earned a doctorate at MSU in 1954. Nominating comments included, "Many students have discovered unknown capabilities when challenged and encouraged by Professor Womochel's teaching" and "Professor Womochel's research activities are as distinguished as his classroom activities. He is an authority on the metallurgy of gray cast iron and has contributed greatly to the knowledge of this extremely complex material."

Dairy professor Earl Weaver was honored for his ability to communicate with his students. Weaver had been head of the dairy department at Oklahoma State University before accepting the same position at MSU in 1929, later spending time as a dairy consultant and as head of MSU's mission in Colombia. Nominating statements included, "No class of his was ever a sea of faces. Each student was an individual, was treated as such and was stimulated to develop to the maximum of his individual capacities. Even in class the student felt he was being spoken to personally. . . . He inspired people to wish to accomplish."

Physics professor Donald J. Montgomery was honored for his combination of teaching skills, innovative research, and loyalty to the university. A faculty member since 1953, he spent parts of 1959 and 1960 on leave to do research and lecture at the University of Grenoble on a Fulbright grant. His nominators described him as "going out of his way to help students" and praised him "for his great capacity as a teacher, for his originality and enthusiasm as a scientist, and for his bounteous concern as a teacher. . . . He thinks in terms of service

John Hannah began the Spartan Round Table in 1947, providing students an opportunity to discuss key issues with MSC administrators. Dinner was served at Cowles House or the Union and was followed by a question-and-answer session, such as this one in 1949. Courtesy of Michigan State University Archives and Historical Collections.

Sociology and anthropology professor John Useem received a Distinguished Faculty Award in 1962. One of his nominees wrote, "I was most inspired by his ideas and manner of presentation—more so than any other teacher at MSU." Courtesy of Michigan State University Archives and Historical Collections.

to the department and the university as a whole. So far as research is concerned, one need only look into many of the world-famous research journals and scholarly books to see his articles and work mentioned."

Music professor H. Owen Reed was honored for his published musical compositions and his talents as a teacher. A faculty member since 1939, he also authored three music textbooks and spent 1948–49 in Mexico studying music composition on a Guggenheim fellowship. His nominators said he had brought "distinction to the University as a whole and the Music Department in particular through his efforts in musical composition. His works have been widely performed by prominent organizations throughout the country and his numerous publications have commanded the highest respect. . . . Dr. Reed is also a most effective and dedicated teacher. . . . He has given much more of his time and energy to the University than is expected."

Sociology and anthropology professor John Useem had one of the most interesting backgrounds of the award winners. Before coming to MSU in 1949, he was governor of Palau, an American trust colony, and taught at the University of South Dakota, Columbia University, and the University of Wisconsin. He also conducted research projects in India and served as a consultant to the U.S. Department of the Interior and the Department of State. "I was most inspired by his ideas and manner of presentation—more so than by any other teacher at MSU," one of his former students wrote in nominating him. "As a result of his influence I earned an advanced degree in sociology and have become a practitioner in the field." Another wrote, "Dr. Useem does not even remember me—I was not that kind of student—yet I will always remember him." And a third stated, "He was one of my most challenging teachers."

The awards continued each year, and in the later 1960s they recognized such professors as entomology professor Gordon Guyer, whom students described as "accessible, sympathetic, informed and enthusiastic"; chemistry professor Harold Hart, whom a colleague described as "ranking among the outstanding physical-organic chemists in the world"; horticulture professor Sylvan Wittwer, who was especially known for turning out advanced degree students who went on to distinguished careers in the sciences; agricultural economics professor Glenn Johnson, who was honored for his "enthusiasm and intellectual drive as a teacher"; and history professor Norman Rich, for his "positive commitment to quality, sincerity and dedication in the pursuit of wisdom and understanding."

Sometimes recognition came in the form of an appointment to a prestigious government commission. For example, Jack Stieber, professor of economics and director of the School of Labor and Industrial Relations, was appointed executive secretary of the President's Advisory Committee on Labor Management Policy. Stieber, who earned his doctorate from Harvard University, had extensive experience as an arbitrator in labor-management disputes. Other times, it was the Board of Trustees who honored faculty excellence. In February, English professor Russel Nye was named Distinguished Professor of English. He was a nationally recognized scholar and teacher, probably best known for his Pulitzer Prize–winning biography *George Bancroft, Brahmin Rebel.*

Another faculty member who received national attention in the early 1960s was MSU ornithologist George Wallace, who played a key role in Rachel Carson's 1962 classic environmental book *Silent Spring.* Carson identified the spraying for Dutch elm disease as a major environmental problem, frequently citing the work of Wallace and one of his graduate students, John Mehner, in the process. Carson wrote:

> Spraying for Dutch elm disease began in a small way on the university campus in 1954. The following year the city of East Lansing (where the university is located), joined in, spraying on the campus was expanded and, with local programs for gypsy moth and mosquito control also under way, the rain of chemicals increased to a downpour. During 1954, the year of the first light spraying, all seemed well. The following spring the migrating robins began to return to the campus as usual. Like the bluebells in Tomlinson's hunting essay *The Lost Wood,* they were "expecting no evil" as they reoccupied their family territories. But soon it became evident that something was wrong. Dead and dying robins began to appear on the campus. Few birds were seen in their normal foraging activities or assembling in their usual roosts. Few nests were built; few young appeared. The pattern was repeated with monotonous regularity in succeeding springs. The sprayed area had become a lethal trap in which each wave of migrating robins would be eliminated in

MSU ornithologist George Wallace became internationally known for his research involving the negative impact of pesticides on wildlife. He was even featured in Rachel Carson's classic work, *Silent Spring.* Courtesy of Michigan State University Archives and Historical Collections.

about a week. Then new arrivals would come in, only to add to the numbers of doomed birds seen on the campus in the agonized tremors that precede death.

At first Wallace believed the birds were dying of a disease that attacked their nervous systems. But, even though the insecticide companies seemed confident that their sprays were safe, he began to suspect insecticidal poisoning. Eventually, after extensive study, Wallace and other scientists were able to prove their poisoning theory, paving the way for drastic changes in the way tree diseases and other environmental problems were addressed. Wallace's writings, such as his 1960 *Audubon* magazine article "Another Year of Robin Losses on a University Campus," helped educate both scientists and the general public about the dangers of insecticides.

Nineteen sixty-two was also the year dairy professor Clinton Meadows developed a calculating wheel that predicted how much milk a cow would produce in a year. The wheel helped dairy farmers improve their herds by weeding out poor-producing cows. Meadows, who came to MSU in 1957, was considered an expert in translating the knowledge presented in the classroom to the everyday needs of the dairy farmer. His awards included membership in the National Dairy Shrine's Hall of Fame and distinguished service awards from the Michigan Farm Bureau, the Michigan Animal Dairy Breeder Association, and the Michigan Milk Producer Association. The Michigan legislature once honored him with Clint Meadows Day, and a Clinton Meadows Endowment Chair was established in his honor.

Chemistry professor Barnett Rosenberg arrived on campus from New York University in 1962. He brought with him an interest in studying the effects of electrical current on bacteria growing in a liquid medium. Rosenberg eventually teamed with microbiologist Loretta Van Camp and chemistry graduate student Thomas Krigas to discover Cisplatin, one of the world's leading cancer drugs.

Another newcomer to the campus in 1962 was visiting professor Alvin Hansen. When economist Paul Samuelson accepted his Nobel Prize in 1970, he explained how to win the award. "The first thing you must have is great teachers. For the sake of the economists present here, let me do some name dropping concerning my own good fortune in this regard. If you have had Jacob Viner and Frank

Knight and Paul Douglas as teachers, and then went on to be blessed by having Joseph Schumpeter, Wassily Leontif, Gottfried Haberler and Alvin Hansen—then you have met one necessary condition for the problem." Hansen was seventy-five years old and considered one of the world's all-time great economists when he arrived at MSU. He taught regularly at Harvard University and had spent the previous year as a visiting professor at Yale University.

MINORITIES AT MSU IN THE 1960s

Nevertheless, students had few opportunities to learn from black faculty members. In 1957, Hannah's position on faculty hiring was spelled out in the *New York Times* for the world to read: "It's not the policy or practice of the university to examine the color of a man's skin for the purpose of either qualifying or disqualifying him for employment." Unfortunately, from an affirmative action perspective, there were many more white males with advanced degrees looking for jobs in the 1940s than minorities. But David Augustus Daly Dickson, who was hired in 1948 as MSC's first full-time black faculty member, was superbly qualified. He arrived with impressive credentials—a bachelor's degree from Bowdoin College, and a master's and doctorate from Harvard University. He had served in the armed forces from 1943 to 1946 and was a teaching fellow at Harvard prior to his arrival in East Lansing.

Dickson wrote about his upbringing in New England:

My father and mother were both natives of Jamaica, British West Indies, who emigrated to this country and were married in Portland, Maine in 1912. . . . Then they raised five children, four boys and a girl, educated them all to a high degree by dint of their own foresight and industry and with the great help of American philanthropy. Two boys became physicians, one an optometrist, one a college professor, and the daughter an Associate Director of Scholarships for the College Entrance Examination Board. Mother was named Mother of the Year for the State of Maine in 1960. . . . Though Negroes, we were never permitted by our parents to be embittered or enervated by infrequent but difficult rebuffs; we were taught to turn shoves into forward pushes, to lament America's

John Hannah continued as chairman of the U.S. Civil Rights Commission until he resigned upon his retirement from MSU. He poses with members of the 1960 commission, including his good friend Theodore Hesburgh (*left*, president of Notre Dame University) and George Johnson (*right*) who would later fill several key positions in the Hannah administration. Courtesy of Michigan State University Archives and Historical Collections.

limitation in the interracial area but to appreciate the many people who were especially kind to us of the minority.

Dickson rose from instructor to associate professor of English between 1948 and 1963. His classes were popular, and he earned a Distinguished Faculty Award. He left MSU in 1963 to become chair of the English Department at Northern Michigan University.

The second full-time black faculty member at MSU was Professor William Pipes, who was hired in 1957 and taught American thought and language. Pipes also brought outstanding credentials. He earned a bachelor's degree from Tuskegee Institute, a master's from Atlanta University, and a doctorate from the University of Michigan, and he had served as president of Alcorn College in Mississippi. Like Dickson, Pipes was considered a talented teacher. In 1967, while still at MSU, he published a book titled *Death of an "Uncle Tom."* While largely philosophical, the book included two references to his treatment at the university:

With a Ph.D. Degree from the University of Michigan (1943), after some twenty years as a College Professor, Academic Dean and

President, and having published two books and more than a score of articles, I was surprised when Michigan State University offered me an academic rank of less than full professor. Department Head [Paul] Bagwell reminded me I was being honored (at any rank) as only the second Negro teacher hired by the school in its 103-year history....

Negroes resent being called "George." All Negro bellhops, shoe-shine boys and the like are called "George" by many whites. Negroes resent the term because it suggests inferiority.... a professor in my department at MSU addresses me as "George," despite the fact I've told him I resent it. But here is my chance to practice what I am preaching. When this man calls me "George," I should ask myself, "How would Christ react? What would Jesus do?" Thus, a basis of mental non-violence in the Negro revolt.... I did talk to Dr. ———; he no longer calls me "George."

While Dickson and Pipes went on to jobs at other universities, another black professor spent almost his entire career at MSU. Dozier Thornton came to East Lansing in 1965 from the University of Pitts-burgh, where he had earned his bachelor's, master's, and doctorate in psychology. During his almost forty years at Michigan State, he taught psychology, served as both assistant and associate dean of the graduate school, and became acting dean of Urban Affairs Programs. He was also one of the key founders of Listening Ear, a 24-hour all-volunteer crisis center in East Lansing. Thornton said he first came to MSU because of the research facilities and good salaries, and because the university really seemed to want him to come.

He first lived in Spartan Village, and then moved into Cherry Hill Apartments. "I didn't know when I first moved here it would be so hard to buy a house in East Lansing," he remembered. "In the late 1960s a faculty member in the Flower Gardens [the subdivision directly southeast of Breslin Center] sold me his home. I didn't go through a realtor." Nevertheless, Thornton did not recall much discrimination on campus. "I felt respected and highly regarded by my white colleagues," he said. "I feel welcome and comfortable as a black professor at MSU."

Thornton was not involved in leading civil-rights marches, even though he believed the movement "helped both black and white students

David Dickson became Michigan State's first black faculty member in 1948. He came with a bachelor's degree from Bowdoin College and a master's degree and doctorate from Harvard University. He rose from an instructor to associate professor of English between 1948 and 1963, leaving in 1963 to become chairman of the English department at Northern Michigan University. Courtesy of Michigan State University Archives and Historical Collections.

American Thought and Language Professor William Pipes was MSU's second black faculty member. Hired in 1957, he had previously served as president of Alcorn College in Alabama. Pipes published a book in 1967, *Death of an "Uncle Tom,"* while he was still on the MSU faculty. Courtesy of Michigan State University Archives and Historical Collections.

to become involved in a variety of causes." Instead, he encouraged black students to become excited about academics, meeting frequently with those who had strong intellectual interests. While many of his black students moved on to successful careers, he specifically recalled Larry Davis and James Jackson. Davis became dean of the social work school at the University of Pittsburgh after a distinguished career as a social work professor at Washington University in St. Louis. Jackson became a psychology professor at the University of Michigan and director of its Program for Research on Black Americans.

Davis and Jackson were just two of many black MSU graduates during the Hannah years who experienced success. Robert Clark graduated in 1959, returned to his Mississippi home, and eventually became the first black elected to the Mississippi legislature since Reconstruction. Jack Jones, a 1960 graduate, earned a law degree at the Detroit College of Law and served in a variety of positions for the U.S. Department of State. Marcellette Williams earned her bachelor's degree in 1968, and later her master's and doctorate, eventually becoming a top administrator at the University of Massachusetts. Richard Butler also earned his bachelor's degree in 1968, and later two master's degrees, eventually becoming dean of the Division of Business and Management at Alverno College in Milwaukee.

One the most fascinating black students to attend MSU during the Hannah years was Ernest "Ernie" Green, a 1962 graduate. Green was famous before he even arrived in East Lansing. He and eight other black students risked their lives by walking through a hostile crowd to integrate Little Rock Central High School in 1957. He was the first black student to graduate from Central High School in 1958, and he was later awarded the Congressional Gold Medal by President Bill Clinton in a White House ceremony in 1999. His experiences were documented in a movie titled *The Ernie Green Story*. He became an investment banker and managing director of Lehman Brothers in Washington, D.C. Why did he choose to attend MSU? "During the school year at Central, I got a notice I received a scholarship to MSU," he told the *State News*. "I was unaware of who the donor was." Green continued to be unaware until he returned to MSU in 1994 and was given the name of his benefactor. It was John Hannah.

One Lansing black who decided to stay home and earn his degree at Michigan State was Wilbur D. Howard. A graduate of Lansing

Sexton High School, he received a bachelor's degree in social work in 1955. Howard went on to eventually become deputy director of the Michigan Department of Civil Rights, helping guide the agency through some of its most challenging years in the 1970s and 1980s. In 1992 he retired, devoting much of his life to black family genealogy. He was largely responsible for forming the Lansing Area African American Genealogy Society in 2001, only the second of its kind in the state. "I think black family history has been largely ignored," he said in a 2003 interview. "But everyone should know where they came from." Howard helped dozens of mid-Michigan families search for their ancestors. Personally, he spent more than fifteen years tracing his own ancestors, traveling throughout the South looking for long-forgotten records. "It's really a thrill to learn more about yourself," he said. Still, despite these examples of success, it was not until the end of the 1960s that MSU began aggressively recruiting black students and faculty to its campus.

The Campus Confronts Anti-Semitism

Jewish students and faculty members sometimes felt discriminated against because of their religion, but they never mobilized to the extent the campus blacks would. The most visible signs of anti-Jewish sentiment were the swastikas that were sometimes smeared on the walls of classrooms or residence halls. Nothing seemed to rile Hannah more than painted swastikas on public property. When a series of swastikas were discovered on classroom walls in early 1960, he issued a stern warning to the perpetrators and to anyone else contemplating similar actions. "Defacing public property is a serious offense," he said, "but the daubing of swastikas has far more serious implications. This is not the work of light-hearted pranksters and it isn't funny. . . . We went to war not too many years ago because the principles of what the swastikas represented menaced all we hold sacred. The cost of the war in blood and suffering was too great for anyone [to view] the reappearance of the swastika . . . with indifference. There is no place within the university community for anyone found guilty of flaunting the swastika in the faces of decent people."

Despite the prohibition of discrimination clauses in fraternity and sorority charters, the issue of whether Jewish students were welcome in the Greek system surfaced from time to time. In 1965, for example, two freshmen accused fraternities of discriminating against Jews. In a letter to the *State News,* they wrote, "We are participating in fraternity rush this week, and consider the friendship and brotherhood which fraternities represent to be a step toward our social goals. To our surprise, however, this step seems to be misleading. Several of our fraternities carry in their charters a 'White Christian' clause which limits their membership to White Christians only. How terribly disappointing this clause is! Does it not seem strange that these same fraternities present their rush programs as being open to all interested students?"

Rabbi Philip Frankel, who taught religious classes at MSU for many years, did not think that discrimination against Jewish students or faculty was a major problem. "I would guess it happened from time to time," he said, "but it was not as prominent here as at many other colleges and universities." Chemistry professor Harold Hart, however, believed the university's hiring practices did discriminate against Jews:

> I was hired on the spot by the department chairman [in the late 1940s] without meeting with or being interviewed by the organic faculty. . . . I have always suspected that I was hired by mistake; Larry Quill [department chairman] had Irish ancestry, and I suspect that Hart sounded like a good Catholic name. Little did he suspect, until too late, that he had hired the department's first Jew [the next was not to be hired for over two decades]. Before World War II, neither the chemical industry nor academia hired Jews, with a few rare exceptions. I strongly suspect that this issue was a major factor in not making an offer to H. C. Brown at the time he wanted to leave Wayne State and was interested in Michigan State. The future Nobelist went to Purdue—our loss and their gain. The same issue raised its ugly head in the early 1960's when we had a chance to bring in J. J. Katz, then at Argonne, as department chairman.

GENDER IMBALANCE

Women also held minority status at Michigan State in the early Hannah years. Traditionally, they had filled the roles of secretaries or employees in nonacademic fields. Hazel Shuttleworth Meyer, who was a student at MSC in the mid-1940s, took a position as a food service administrator in 1950 and wrote about her experiences in a memoir for the MSU Museum in 2000:

> Policies toward women employees were quite different than today. The college hired only single women, and only if no other relative worked for the college. I had an uncle by marriage who was an electrician in the Physical Education Department, but that was considered acceptable since he was not a blood relative. If a woman employee married, she was permitted to continue working until she became pregnant, at which time, she was allowed to work from three to six months on some jobs, but then she had to quit. I married in 1952 and continued working until mid-1953 when I was expecting my first baby. I asked to return to work, but I was not allowed to until after my third child was born. Following the same pattern with my fourth child, I again had to quit my job and then received a phone call asking me to rehire six to eight weeks after his birth. Quitting and rehiring meant losing all seniority and benefits and starting from scratch as a new employee. I am happy to say I had a role in changing this unjust policy in 1962 when I was pregnant with my fifth and last child. As my time to deliver drew near, I requested a medical leave of absence as my doctor advised. The male administrator to whom I made the request had 10 children and had never been required to lose time or benefits. When he said my request was contrary to policy, I pointed out that two male employees had received medical leaves of absence and returned to their jobs. With a small smile and a twinkle in his eye, he said he would check further into my request. The next day, he gave me written permission for a leave of absence. I believe that I may have been the first woman employee at the college to receive a medical leave of absence for pregnancy. In any case, I received 10 phone calls from other female employees asking how I had gotten my leave.

In 1941, Agnes McCann, secretary to engineering dean H. B. Dirks, was featured in the *State News:* "She plays an important role in the men's world of the Engineering division," the paper reported, adding that she was completing her twenty-fourth year in the division.

Gwendolyn Norrell arrived on campus in 1945 and quickly became one of the most prominent members of Michigan State. In the next several decades she became the first woman to serve as a faculty representative to the Big Ten Conference, significantly influenced such areas as athletics, the counseling center, the Honors College and won a Distinguished Faculty Award. Courtesy of Michigan State University Archives and Historical Collections.

In tribute to her excellent help to students she was initiated into Tau Beta Phi, Engineering honorary, last year as an honorary sister member which she says was the nicest thing ever to happen to her. Her boss, Dean Dirks, said, "She is indispensable to the Engineering division. We couldn't get along without her. She always works from the student's standpoint." . . . Other duties of Miss McCann include being on the college schedule committee, having a hand in the defense work being done by the division and regular secretarial work. Besides this, Miss McCann is the official "Gripe tender" for all Engineers. They bring their problems to her including those of registration, dean calls, course trouble, and even financial and other muddles. . . . Her favorite job is helping with the Engineers' ball.

One woman who flourished on the male-dominated campus was Gwendolyn Norrell. The Arkansas native arrived in East Lansing in 1945 after earning a doctoral degree in counseling from the University of Colorado at Boulder. Over the next three decades, she worked as assistant director of the counseling center, became the first woman to serve as a faculty athletic representative in the Big Ten Conference, served as vice president of the NCAA, and received MSU's Distinguished Faculty Award and Honorary Alumnus Award.

The few women who held faculty-level positions were often concentrated in departments such as nursing and home economics. In 1964, the university released a listing of faculty with the rank of full professor. Of 553, there were only 23 women. There was a scattering of professors with Oriental and Hispanic names, but the vast majority appeared to be white males. Eleven of the twenty-three women were members of the College of Home Economics. Other departments, such as agricultural economics, horticulture, history, music, marketing and transportation, electrical engineering, and chemistry, did not include a single female member with the rank of full professor. Females with that rank, not including those in home economics, included Miriam Kelly and Gertrude Nygren of the Extension Service, Alma Goetsch in art, Elizabeth Rusk in English, Helen Green in business law, Elizabeth Drews and Loraine Shepard in education, Florence Kempf and Helen Penhale in nursing, Lucille Barber in social work, Nora Landmark in American thought and language, and Beatrice Moore in the counseling center.

GEORGE ALDERTON'S RETIREMENT

One man who had the reputation for treating everyone equally was George Alderton who, along with sportswriter Dale Stafford, had given the sports teams the nickname "Spartans." Alderton retired in 1962 after many years as sports editor of the *State Journal,* and Hannah gave the main speech at Alderton's 6 November retirement dinner.

> We are grateful that he promoted the use of the name "Spartans" for our athletic teams. The change came at a time when Michigan State was changing from a good agricultural, engineering and technical college into a university with a great deal of promise. . . . I have a good personal reason to think of him often. I will carry a physical reminder of his prowess as an athlete with me for the rest of my days. Many years ago, when he and I were much younger and more carefree, we used to join Fred Jenison, Dr. Heckert, and two or three others in getting a little exercise by throwing a football around while the football squad was at practice. He threw the ball at me one memorable evening—hard and true—so hard, and so true, that it broke my finger. Here is the finger to prove it. I'll always remember George Alderton, the demon passer. . . . I have another good reason to remember him, too. Over the years I have made no secret of my interest in and enjoyment of football. Up until recent years, I had not missed a single game in which our team had played since I was here as a student. But my record was always a little dimmed by one fact—George Alderton had seen even more games. Now that he is leaving these parts, maybe I'll have a chance to exceed the record of the only man who has seen more Michigan State football games than I. . . . Many years ago, this university conferred on George Alderton the status of honorary alumnus. We thought then that he deserved the honor—we have hundreds of additional reasons to believe it now. He has always been a good friend of Michigan State University.

BUILDINGS AND SCHOLARSHIP IN THE SIXTIES

Some faculty members complained in the 1960s that too much money was being spent on "bricks and mortar," and not enough

Few women achieved the rank of full professor before the mid-1960s. Two who did, however, were Alice Thorpe (*above,* home economics) and Elizabeth Drews (*below,* education). Courtesy of Michigan State University Archives and Historical Collections.

on hiring new faculty and retaining veteran faculty members. Walter Adams, who would succeed Hannah as president, was one of the most vocal. Adams, who had found no fault with the campus building boom immediately after World War II, now charged that when funds became available, the money was spent on buildings and administrators, not teachers. This was becoming a frequent complaint by students, faculty, and alumni. Hannah's responses were almost identical. "No buildings are being constructed on this campus with money that could be used for any other purpose," he wrote in a 26 May 1962 letter to a concerned former student. "They are being built with funds appropriated by the legislature for new buildings or with loans that are paid back by student tuition." Still, almost everyone agreed that faculty salaries were too low. At a 25 May 1962 board meeting, Provost Clifford Erickson ran down a long list of professors who were leaving MSU because of better offers from other schools. The *State News* reported that "some were small universities in Alabama and Tennessee which had outbid M.S.U. for teaching talent." Erickson gave an example of an economics professor earning $10,900 at MSU who had received a $14,000 salary offer from the University of Illinois; of a sociology and anthropology professor earning $11,500 who was leaving for a $17,500 position at the University of Texas; and of a philosophy professor who went from $10,000 annually to a $15,000 job at a Washington university. While trustees expressed concern and a desire to increase salaries, the problem of low-pay for faculty continued to plague the university throughout its history.

MSU administrators were planning major additions to their scientific facilities in 1962. Ground was broken for both a $2.8 million cyclotron building and a $400,000 planetarium. "The new cyclotron will make MSU a leading center in nuclear physics," physics professor Henry Blosser said. He was right. The cyclotron, which would be called the premier university-based nuclear science research facility in the United States, became a frequent stop for research scientists from all parts of the world. Blosser quickly established himself as a leading American scientist. MSU also announced the purchase of a $1,387,000 computer in 1962 that, according to the *State News,* put MSU "in a league by itself." The Control Data computer was supposedly twice as fast as the IBM model and had more overall potential than the Burroughs machine. It was available to a wide range of campus academic departments and individual researchers.

Other innovations were occurring in the dormitories. Case Hall, which opened in 1962, was a combination of academic classrooms with adjacent quarters for men and women. The *State News* dubbed the coeducational dormitory "Fishbowl Hall" because everyone seemed to be watching what happened to one of the nation's newest educational experiments. Forty classes—in such disciplines as American thought and language, natural science, social science, and mathematics—were offered in Case, where men and women also ate and socialized together. Professors were provided office space in the dormitory. The new concept was intended to reduce travel between classes, facilitate communication between professors and students, build "esprit de corps," and create an atmosphere that encouraged academic excellence. "Things are 1,000 times more normal here," said Donald Adams, head adviser for men at Case. "It's more like life," said head women's adviser Beverly Belson. "The atmosphere in the dining room is very relaxed and they [the students] enjoy themselves. We haven't had any trouble in the co-educational areas." Hall manager Robert Underwood did notice one significant difference compared to the single-sex dining rooms of the past. "There's less noise in the dining room," he said. "And the men dress better and the women don't come to eat in hair curlers." At the end of winter term the project was declared a success, and a similar dormitory, Wilson Hall, was scheduled to open in 1963.

Renewing a practice the university began in the 1940s, forty-four signs describing how campus buildings were financed were put up during Christmas vacation in late 1961. The signs indicated that the buildings were paid for in one of four ways—with gifts from foundations or individuals, legislative appropriations, student fees, or self-liquidating sources. University secretary Jack Breslin told the *State News* that from 1945 to 1961 more than $107 million was spent for construction of buildings. The signs cost $70 apiece and, as Breslin was careful to point out, had been approved by both Hannah and the Board of Trustees.

Marcia Van Ness was a *State News* editor in the 1960s. Despite claims by some that the student newspaper was a propaganda arm of the Hannah Administration, Van Ness would later say that she felt no pressure from anyone to print only stories that placed Hannah or his policies in a positive light. Courtesy of Marcia Van Ness.

Reorganizing the Curriculum

The big academic news of 1962 was the splitting of the College of Science and Arts into the College of Natural Science, the College of Arts and Letters, and the College of Social Science. The new concept, according to Provost Paul Miller, would move departments such as political science and economics from the business college to a more appropriate position in social science. It would also allow MSU to put more emphasis on liberal arts at the undergraduate level, facilitating (as the *State News* put it) "the development of the total man and his relationship to modern society." The first dean of the College of Social Science was psychology department chair Louis McQuitty. A faculty member since 1956, McQuitty was popular with both the teaching staff and students. When he died in 1986, a full-page obituary, written by MSU colleagues Clarence Winder and Charles Wrigley, appeared in *American Psychologist.* "Lou was fair, tough-minded, and congenial. As occasion demanded, he demonstrated his deep commitment to basic academic values, such as the primacy of the faculty in academic decisions. He understood that colleges and universities can be great transforming agencies for individuals and for the society that supports higher education, and he labored to preserve and enhance the impact and quality of the academic enterprise for the benefit of people. McQuitty was a model academic administrator."

The new dean of the College of Arts and Letters was history professor Paul Varg. When the appointment was announced, the *State News* admitted "mixed feelings." While it praised Varg's potential as a dean, it called the appointment a blow to students. "Those who have taken his three-term course in American foreign relations and listened to his stimulating, sophisticated and thought-provoking lectures are already asking the question, Who will replace Dr. Varg? It will not be easy to fill his shoes. . . . We feel Dr. Varg will make an excellent administrator, but are sorry to lose so fine an instructor." Richard Byerrum, assistant provost and acting head of the Institute of Biology and Medicine, was appointed the first dean of the College of Natural Science. Byerrum had been honored for his research on the chemical mechanism by which tobacco plants make nicotine and, at the time of his appointment, was serving as an MSU health consultant in Okinawa.

Two other colleges were "tooting their horns" in 1962. College of education dean William B. Hawley presented his annual report to the MSU trustees on video tape over closed circuit television—perhaps a first at the university. His college, he said, had doubled in size during the past ten years, and the number of degrees granted had increased nearly 500 percent. Sixty-two percent of students admitted to teacher education in 1960 were in the upper quarter of their class, and 74 percent of the education faculty held doctorates in 1961. Also at this time, the College of Communication Arts changed its name to the College of Communication. In stressing the importance of communication studies, Dean Fred Siebert told the *State Journal* that history is filled with stories of wars fought because someone or some nation was misunderstood, and that wives have konked their husbands with pans because one spouse was not able to communicate clearly. He also emphasized the importance of the media for learning in the twentieth century. "We are in business here to insure a broad, liberal education for all students," he said. "We want these people to have a clear understanding of the role of communications media in society."

Enhancing MSU's research facilities in 1962, especially for historians, was a gift of more than eight thousand recorded voices, donated by freelance recording engineer G. Robert Vincent. Records, tapes, and cylinders—containing the voices of such historical figures as Theodore Roosevelt, Sarah Bernhardt, William Jennings Bryan, and Buffalo Bill—estimated to be worth $100,000–$150,000, were deposited in the library. "The Vincent collection is a very significant acquisition because the voices are important library materials and will be useful to students and faculty just as books are," library director Richard Chapin said when the gift was announced. Vincent was eventually hired to direct the voice library. Across Circle Drive, the MSU Museum received one of its more unusual donations in 1962—a six-ton African elephant from Kenya. The animal was shot and donated by wildlife hunter Jens Touberg, and it arrived on campus in five large packing boxes weighing four-thousand pounds. Touberg had earlier donated a South American jaguar and two Indian tigers.

Though MSU was moving toward a greater emphasis on the liberal arts, teacher training, and communications, it did not ignore Michigan farmers. Many were grateful for the university's continuing

History Professor Paul Varg became dean of the College of Arts ad Letters in 1962. *The State News* had mixed emotions. "We feel Dr. Varg will make an excellent administrator, but are sorry to lose so fine an instructor." Courtesy of Michigan State University Archives and Historical Collections.

Richard Byerrum, acting head of the Institute of Biology and Medicine, was appointed the first dean of the College of Natural Science in 1962. Courtesy of Michigan State University Archives and Historical Collections.

support of agricultural issues, and Hannah was honored for that dedication at a special Kellogg Center tribute on 26 May. More than five hundred dirt farmers, dairy producers, fruit growers, and livestock breeders showed up. Speakers, according to the *State News*, called Hannah "the architect who sculptured Michigan State University in its modern form. . . . a poultryman's poultryman. . . . one who understands the importance of agriculture in the state. . . . a tireless servant to mankind. . . . an enthusiastic supporter of the land-grant system of education. . . . [and a] servant and leader in education, agriculture, business, industry, government and international affairs."

The subject of sports was not mentioned in the Hannah tribute, but the MSU president, as he had in previous years, voiced strong opinions about the role of athletics in the nation's colleges and universities. In his address at the Big Ten dinner in March, he expressed concern to conference representatives that schools were placing too much emphasis on intercollegiate teams and ignoring the non-varsity athlete. "The increasing emphasis on identification before enrollment in the university of almost all students who are ever to participate in intercollegiate athletics, the concentration of all coaching on a very few—producing a small corps of gladiators to perform in the arenas . . . tend to move all of the components of the university into a spectator status," he said. Hannah then went on to suggest that more attention be placed on providing athletics for all students, featuring programs that address strength, fitness, vigor, courage, sportsmanship, and the ability to win or lose with equal grace. "These are real values that you can contribute to our universities, and in so doing hold your heads as high and be as deserving of respect as one with a knowledge of Dr. Einstein's formula or its after effects."

Hannah was probably pleased by the way the *State News* covered not only varsity sports but also intramural contests. When the Butcher Boys beat Biology Institute 5-1 for the intramural softball championship on 23 August, the newspaper ran the story on the front page. For a day at least, many students knew the name Ron Marshall. The Butcher Boys' star pitcher, Marshall gave up just one run and four hits in the seven-inning game, striking out nine and walking three.

There were a wide range of facilities for the intramural athlete, including the intramural building west of Spartan Stadium, Demonstration Hall, the outdoor track, the Women's IM, and the basement of the Union, as well as Jenison Field House, which was used by intramural as well as intercollegiate athletes. Students could ice skate, jog, swim, play handball, and play basketball at these facilities.

For varsity sports, 1962 was one of the most important years in MSU football history. The Spartans 5-4 record was a bit disappointing, even though two of those wins were over Michigan, 28-0, and Notre Dame, 31-7. The biggest wins of that year, however, would not be known for several years. Players such as Steve Juday, Don Japinga, Harold Lucas, Boris Dimitroff, and Don Weatherspoon entered MSU that fall, and Duffy Daugherty was in the process of recruiting such high school stars as Clint Jones, George Webster, Gene Washington, and Bubba Smith for 1963. This group would form the nucleus of the great championship teams of 1965 and 1966.

CAMPUS ENTERTAINMENT

Those looking for entertainment other than intramural competitions or intercollegiate sports in 1962 could participate in a full range of activities ranging from farcical plays poking fun at college life to serious discussions of international events. Faculty and students watched closely as President John F. Kennedy confronted the Russians over bringing missiles to Cuba in late October, and many November activities in East Lansing centered around Russia and Cuba. On 12 November, for example, Anthony Hall hosted a debate between students from MSU and students from England's Oxford University on the subject of Fidel Castro's regime in Cuba. Two weeks later, a panel discussion by ATL professors T. B. Strandness and John Cary, political science professor Alfred Meyer, and foreign language professor Nikola Poltoratzky addressed the Soviet Union's attitudes toward American history.

There were many other forms of entertainment on campus in 1962, as well. In January, for example, the Lecture-Concert Series brought to East Lansing a production of *The Miracle Worker,* starring Eileen Brennan. In June, the university's Summer Circle Theatre staged *The Front Page,* which Ute Auld reviewed favorably in the *State News:* "Director James Brandon, associate professor of speech, has not toned down the coarse characterizations and

WKAR music program director Ken Beachler (*left*), joking with graduate student Garnet Schafer, was beginning to make a name for himself in the 1960s. He would go on to become the first director of MSU's Wharton Center. Courtesy of WKAR Radio.

brutally humorous lines in his interpretation of the play, but nevertheless it does not come across as vulgar, but merely as a 'fun' play to see and also to act, which is apparent in the enthusiasm of the actors." Other activities that received good attendance in 1962 were the showing of the award-winning movie *Rickshaw Man,* an appearance by the Boston Pops, a lecture by diplomat Ralph Bunche, a concert by violinist Isaac Stern, and a performance of *Romeo and Juliet* by the Old Vic Company. While Russian communists were looked at with suspicion, the Leningrad Philharmonic drew a positive response when it performed at the MSU Auditorium in November. The 107-man ensemble was touring the United States as part of an exchange program sponsored by the U.S. State Department and the Soviet Ministry of Culture, while the Robert Shaw Chorale was conducting a concurrent tour in Russia. Begun in the mid-nineteenth century, the Leningrad orchestra was known for its skill in combining contemporary with more traditional works and the MSU audience was treated to the music of Prokofiev, Samuel Barber, and Tchaikovsky.

Canoes made their reappearance on the Red Cedar River in the spring of 1962. During the construction of Bessey Hall, the canoe shelter had been torn down and the canoes stored. When Bessey was completed, a new shelter was opened and the canoes were brought out of storage. The rental rate was forty-five cents an hour. "Coeds and dates will be able to paddle down the river to the strumming of a guitar or a ukulele once again," the *State News* reported. "When the canoes glide down the Red Cedar you can be certain that spring is here."

THE CENTENARY OF THE MORRILL ACT

Almost lost in the barrage of activities in 1962 was the celebration of the one hundredth anniversary of the signing of the Morrill Land Grant College Act, which marked the advent of land-grant colleges. While the attention of the college community was mainly focused on other issues, the MSU Alumni Association, mostly through the *Michigan State University Magazine,* attempted to present the land-grant philosophy in a modern-day context. In its 2 February 1962 issue, the magazine stated that

> In the century that has passed since U.S. Congressman Justin Morrill presented his radically new concept to Congress, the University on the banks of the Red Cedar has experienced phenomenal growth in national prestige, educational stature and physical facilities. . . . Three small buildings on $10,155 worth of land (677 acres) constituted the University's beginning physical plant. Today, it has a total at-cost value of more than $154,000,000. Land holdings in Michigan total 17,450 acres. . . . Yet despite its vast size and huge personnel (more than 1,200 faculty members are in the instructional program alone) MSU never has lost sight of its fundamental objective. This objective is to prepare students for full participation in the society in which they live and, in addition, to be of greatest possible service to all of the people. What has been accomplished toward reaching this objective appears on the record of the past 100 years. What the future holds for MSU we cannot tell, but we do know the plant and the personnel are awaiting greater things and, come what may, will be ready for them. Students of the second century will probe the unknown, explore as the pioneer explored and build as their predecessors built in the first."

The Year of Bigness

The 1963–64 school year could perhaps be called the "year of big-ness." For the first time in its history MSU could boast of more students than the University of Michigan—just over thirty thousand, including those at Oakland University. But the largeness also caused problems. Some new dormitories were not completed, and students had to stare at unpainted walls in Wonders Hall and to wait several days before taking a shower in McDonel Hall. Increasing numbers of people both on the campus and in East Lansing were also playing havoc with one of the area's aesthetic landmarks—the rows of elm trees that lined Grand River Avenue. In August 1963, state highway department workers removed many of the trees, leaving open spaces where the green leaves of the elms had once given homeowners, faculty, and students the feeling of a city in a forest. Interestingly, the trees were removed not because of the dreaded Dutch elm disease but because of human overcrowding. Problems such as sidewalks covering much of the area and preventing adequate rainwater from reaching the tree roots, heavier pedestrian traffic, and increased salt-ing of the roads in the winter all were cited as reasons contributing to the ill health of the trees and the need to remove them.

In addition to the difficulties caused by a growing population, there were also social problems. In the 1960s, parents who lived away from campus towns frequently read newspaper reports or saw television news about rape, drugs, drinking, and premarital sex at the schools their children were attending. When Olin Health Center director James Feurig announced in 1965 that illegitimate pregnancies were on the increase at MSU, he received statewide media attention. "With the present attitudes toward free love, and the changing of moral attitudes, the incidence of illegitimate pregnancies has been on the ascendancy here and elsewhere," he told the *State News*. Feurig was especially concerned about the number of female students who had to drop out of school to take care of their newborns. When parents saw these kinds of stories, they often wrote university presidents expressing fear that their children were not receiving proper supervision. Hannah got his share of those letters. The MSU president almost always took time to compose a personal response to a distressed parent. In early 1967 he wrote to an Essexville mother who had expressed concern over the well-being of her daughter.

> Surely your daughter must have told you that this University has not abdicated responsibility for the welfare of its students. . . . For example, all freshmen, both men and women, are required to live in residence halls or with relatives, and are not allowed to move off-campus until they have developed considerable maturity. Freshmen are not allowed to operate automobiles, this on the theory that automobiles are so often involved when students get into trouble in the community. Again, we provide trained personnel as counselors in the residence halls, and certain standards of conduct are enforced by both residence-hall personnel and by the students themselves. It may be unfair to require women students to be in their residence halls by certain hours and leave the young men to their own devices, but years of experience have taught us that if the women have returned to their halls, the young men tend to turn in soon afterwards. There is nothing to keep them from "roaming the town" all night, except they would find very little to do in East Lansing or Lansing, either, and the demands of the academic program tend to keep all but the irresponsible and frivolous under reasonable control. As for drugs, we find little or no evidence of their use by our students, and we keep a pretty close watch. Certainly drugs are not available on the campus as such, and community officials are just as diligent in their observation and control.

One person who did not seem affected by the increasing population or the social problems was the unofficial campus hermit, Del Bennett. Bennett lived in a ramshackle house on two acres of land near the intersection of Hagadorn and Bennett roads, which had once been part of a farm his father had donated to MSU. He often walked to the Union Building, where he always drew the attention of curious students. Friendly, as well as an engaging storyteller, Bennett frequently agreed to interviews with local reporters. In 1966 *State News* writer Bobby Soden visited Bennett at his home. "In the midst of the frantically, busy multiversity, a grizzled little man about 65, wearing a pair of denim overalls, sat on top of the huge woodpile on his front porch and watched us hike through the jungle that had once been a front yard," she wrote. Bennett apologized for the holes in his overalls, explaining that, "The price of overalls went up 30 cents, ya know. That's just too much to pay." Two signs, reading "Occupant" and "Occupied," stood in his yard. "I put up those signs a few years back so's people would know somebody lives out here. Some lovers from State used to come out here and didn't think nobody lived here. Not that I mind lovers, ya know." And when Soden began to leave, he said, "Come back and see my rock collection some day. I'm a full-fledged member of the MSU Rockhound Club, ya know." Reporters were not the only people who sought Bennett. John Hannah was known to cross the lounge at the Union to say hello to Del Bennett. Bennett was considered by many to be a contemporary landmark.

East Lansing almost lost another one of its landmarks in the winter of 1965, when a late-afternoon fire at Peoples Church on 8 February caused an estimated $150,000 worth of damage, in a blaze that city fire chief Arthur Patriarche deemed the worst fire in the city's history. "The organist, Corliss Arnold, was giving a lesson when the organ suddenly stopped," the *State News* reported. "Arnold noticed smoke coming from beneath the console area, and immediately alerted Rev. Wallace Robertson, pastor, who phoned the Fire Department." The interdenominational church, created in the same year as the city of East Lansing, had been a longtime social and religious headquarters for generations of MSU students and city residents. It was quickly rebuilt and has functioned in a similar capacity into the twenty-first century.

A View of the Campus in 1965

While East Lansing and MSU celebrated the survival of Peoples Church in 1965, they also celebrated the tenth anniversary of Michigan State's status as an official university. "We'd been a university for many years," Denison told the *State News.* "But only in 1955 were we given official recognition." Denison said that the quality of students had increased during the first year of the name change, that recruiting faculty and securing appropriations from the legislature became easier, and that foreign countries were more receptive to aid from Michigan State when it became a "university" instead of a "college." He said that other major areas of progress since 1955 included the creation of the Honors College; the completion of the Kresge Art Center, the men's intramural building, and the Cyclotron; and the establishment of the College of Human Medicine.

By 1965, one man who had established himself as a major force in university decision making at MSU was Jacweir (Jack) Breslin. The former star athlete graduated from Michigan State in 1946 and spent the next four years as a district manager of the Dodge Division of Chrysler Corporation. He returned to MSC in 1950 as assistant director of alumni relations, served as director of the placement bureau, and in 1959 became a special assistant to President Hannah. In 1961 he became secretary to the Board of Trustees. Breslin was known for his skill in working with the Michigan legislature. "When I'm in the legislature, I have to work with both sides," he once told the *Lansing State Journal.* "I don't believe the legislators look at me as either a Democratic or a Republican but as a representative of Michigan State University." By 1965 Breslin was the only MSU employee authorized to communicate with the legislature. "As we move into the 1965 legislative session, I want to call to the attention of all the deans and other administrators that it is essential that ALL CONTACTS WITH THE LEGISLATURE BE HANDLED THROUGH MR. BRESLIN," Hannah wrote on 9 February. "Secretary Breslin has been designated by the Board of Trustees and by the University as the only official contact between the University and the legislature. In some of the recent legislative sessions, the University has been subjected to possible embarrassment through the activities of friends of the University who have sometimes involved members of our staff in representations before members of the legislature. I will appreciate it if you will call this University policy to the attention of any of your department chairmen or staff members who might be possibly involved in presentations before the legislature."

While Breslin was trying to make MSU look good to members of the legislature, others were criticizing MSU over conflict-of-interest issues. In 1966, Michigan passed a new law that prohibited any state official "from having a direct or indirect interest, financial or otherwise, in a contract with the state or any of its political subdivisions." Hannah, who served on the boards of two institutions that did business with MSU, immediately asked Attorney General Frank Kelley for a ruling. Kelley indicated that Hannah was in conflict and should resign from both boards. Hannah immediately complied. Hannah was later accused of buying up property near the university—land which some suggested he would someday sell back to MSU for a profit—and with channeling university business to his brother-in-law, who was a construction executive. Hannah was eventually cleared of any wrongdoing, and the land in question eventually housed a shopping center and other private developments. For Philip May, however, the outcome was different.

Kelley had ruled that May, MSU's chief financial officer, was in conflict of interest because of business connections with companies doing business with the university. On 12 November 1968 the attorney general cleared May, based on his assessment that May had sold all his business interests that had been in conflict. "The matter is closed as far as this office is concerned," Kelley announced. But certain Board of Trustees members were not willing to let it go at that. A battle between Democratic members (who generally favored firing May) and Republicans (who generally opposed any firing) continued for more than a year. At the Board's September 1968 meeting, members deadlocked 4-4 on a motion to fire May. At the October meeting, May requested retirement, and it was unanimously accepted. May said that unfair publicity and continued attacks by several trustees made it "unpleasantly difficult" for him to continue in his position.

Hannah was a strong May supporter, and would later write:

From the day of his arrival to the date of his departure Mr. May gave the university service of the highest quality. We had, under his management, the best university business office that could be found anywhere in America; he handled our fiscal affairs efficiently, effectively and well. The president or the trustees could call for and get from him all the information they needed about any facet of university business affairs or procedures—often in a few minutes. Under his guidance, M.S.U. funds were always carefully and prudently collected, handled and expended in accordance with the budget and the policies of the university as agreed by the trustees. An effective administrator of financial affairs does not often win popularity awards. Too often, he has to say no for requests for funds or for relaxation of rules. Unfortunately two or three trustees became disenchanted with Phil May. In later years, they persistently and often maliciously were publicly critical of him, so that in the end he was hounded out of the university and eventually requested an early retirement. I should like to take this opportunity to repeat what I said years ago to one of the trustees who was a leading critic of Mr. May—that by their tactics, they deprived the university of one of its most able and faithful servants, much to its disservice.

The College of Human Medicine

Despite the charges of inappropriate behavior by university administrators, the 1960s produced major innovations at Michigan State that benefited the university for years to come. In 1967, for example, the university received permission from the state Board of Education to develop a four-year, degree-granting medical school. While most MSU supporters considered the decision to be a major victory, some were also stung by the almost decade-long battle for approval. The decision to establish a medical school in East Lansing was not hasty. As early as 1948, State sociologist Charles Hoffer had published articles on the availability of and access to medical care in Michigan. His findings indicated that there was a clearly uneven distribution of medical care in the state, especially in the rural areas. Michigan State professor John Thaden supported Hoffer's findings in the early 1950s, and also found that between 1940 and 1944, only 44 percent of Michigan's medical school graduates stayed in the state to practice medicine. In 1961 the Board of Trustees decided to begin a two-year program, the Institute of Biology and Medicine. The program was intended to provide two years of medical education to students, to prepare them to transfer to a four-year school.

Alumni Relations director Jack Kinney sought to put things in perspective in a story in the November 1964 issue of the *Michigan State University Magazine:*

When classes begin in the fall of 1965 your university will mark one of the most significant milestones in its colorful history. Included among the more than 30,000 enrolling students, will

Philip May, MSU's chief financial officer, was criticized for being in conflict of interest due to his personal business dealings. He was cleared by the state attorney general, but was strongly criticized by several board of trustee members. John Hannah, however, called May one of the university's "most able and faithful servants."
Courtesy of Michigan State University Archives and Historical Collections.

be a handful of keen young people who will be the first students of human medicine at MSU. The human medicine program at MSU will be a two-year preclinical course for students seeking to become physicians. Upon successful completion of this two-year course students will be qualified to transfer to a four-year medical school for the final two years of work needed to receive the M.D. degree. . . . President Hannah has stated that only a two-year school is planned. A major reason for MSU's involvement in medical education is the shortage of M.D.s in this country. More medical schools are needed to even maintain the present doctor-patient ratio. . . . [The foundation] was laid two years ago with the establishment of the Institute of Biology and Medicine. This program, directed by Dr. William H. Knisely, coordinated and integrated many of the studies that were being conducted on the campus. With the recent founding of the College of Human Medicine these studies will be jointly administered by their present college and the new college. For MSU to add human medicine to its academic structure it was necessary to create but one new department— Medicine—to be composed of physicians to introduce students to the problems of patients and their illnesses. . . . One of the most important steps was the appointment of Andrew D. Hunt Jr., M.D., as Dean of the College of Human Medicine. He was an associate professor of pediatrics and director of the ambulatory service at Stanford University. He is now organizing the curriculum and hiring the new staff members. In early September the Kellogg Foundation granted the University $1,250,000 to help initiate the program. With the support of foundations such as Kellogg and the blessings of the Michigan Medical Association, the human medicine program at MSU is assured. Thus our University stands at the threshold of one of its most notable accomplishments.

A four-year medical school was approved by the State Board of Education in 1967 and two years later the state legislature gave its approval.

The move to establish a medical school was as popular in Ann Arbor as the admittance to the Big Ten and the name change from college to university had been. Hannah would later write in his memoirs:

It was certain from the beginning that any interest expressed by Michigan State in human medicine would meet immediate resistance from the medical school and the administration at the University of Michigan. And it did, vehemently, loudly and politically. Wayne State was encouraged by some of M.S.U.'s critics to believe that somehow or other it would be better for Wayne if there were only two medical schools in Michigan, at Michigan and at Wayne State. As a result, certain people at Wayne State joined with the University of Michigan in opposition. The opposition enlisted some of the most powerful members of the legislature to resist every suggestion that M.S.U. develop any kind of program in human medicine. On the other hand, the medical profession in Michigan, by and large, joined in supporting us.

MSU's first dean of the new medical school, Andrew Hunt, arrived on campus in 1964 and quickly discovered firsthand the political realities of UM's opposition. "[My] first night in East Lansing was bitter cold," he told writer Brooke V. Heagerty in 1985. "I fell on the ice outside the motel room and on the 11:00 news was treated to a diatribe by the Michigan President, Harlan Hatcher, addressing a Michigan alumni group, and blasting Hannah and MSU for having the temerity of wasting the public's money on an expensive and obviously futile adventure; namely a medical school. This obbligato of ridicule, patronization, subtle innuendo or outright virulent antipathy from the much of the legislature, the Detroit newspapers, most UM alumni, and much of the national medical education establishment was almost constantly in evidence during the first five years of my tenure at MSU."

In an 8 February 1970 article in the *State Journal* Hunt talked about the past and the future. "During the 1960s, we went through gestation and early development," he said. "During the 1970s, we expect to pass through adolescence and into maturity. Moreover, we think we will be able to avoid inflexibility and other pitfalls of middle age through a constant process of self-examination and experimentation." Seven months later, at the fourth annual convocation of medical students and faculty at the Erickson Kiva, Hunt and other members of the medical school provided a look at what future MSU doctors would be like. Pictured as a composite of the old-fashioned family doctors and the modern medical scientists, they would start learning skills of dealing with patients within three weeks of entering the college; would learn to understand the sociological as well as the psychological aspects of patients' problems; would work with patients in hospitals in Lansing, Grand Rapids, Flint, Howell, and Alma; and would learn to understand the role of the medical profession in society, the relationship of the medical world to the outside world, and the value of contributing to the community.

COLLEGES IN A UNIVERSITY SETTING

At the same time the new medical school was being created, MSU administrators were also looking into the feasibility of creating small and semi-autonomous colleges within the framework of a large university setting. The first was Justin Morrill College, which opened its doors in 1965. According to its first dean, Gordon Rohman, it was created "mainly because students were being turned off by the impersonal environments of the emerging multiversity of MSU. As one solution to all that bigness, JMC brought some smallness in the form of a residential college." Rohman had been an associate professor of English, had earned a bachelor's degree at Syracuse University in 1948, and then spent the next seven years in the print media in Utica, New York, before returning to Syracuse and earning a master's and doctorate. He was a prolific writer, authoring two books and numerous journal articles. His new college's orientation was liberal arts, and it was housed in the Snyder-Phillips dormitory and classroom complex, providing the student with a living-learning way of life. The college had an international studies emphasis and would initially require two years of university-level foreign language study. "We were to make a fresh start on an old problem: how to best use the four years of an undergraduate's time to best serve the ends of a liberal education," Rohman wrote in a pamphlet titled *JMC: The Liberating Journey*. "Our guidelines established that we should weave study in the humanities with social sciences, and natural sciences around the integrating theme of international understanding and service. We were to take advantage of the living-learning setting to do this on the premise that environment and program are inseparable in liberal education. Our size was fixed at 1,200. We were to stress independent study for students, and innovation in administration, teaching and curriculum."

JMC students quickly became known as intelligent, free-thinking, and independent, and were sometimes described as "wandering minstrels." JMC faculty member Glenn Wright added a few other descriptions of the JMC graduate: he/she should be a "Renaissance Man," exemplifying the best ideals of earlier liberal arts education; a "generalist," capable of approaching and engaging a variety of issues; an "ecologist of the imagination," whose perspective was not limited to specific ideas per se, but rather to how ideas coexisted and interacted generally; a sort of "commando," in the sense that the JMC graduate should be capable of "parachuting" into the middle of an issue or problem and by virtue of his/her education be equipped to assess the relevant factors and take effective action; and have an intellectual commitment to anti-intellectualism.

MSU continued its "small college within a big university" approach with the opening of James Madison and Lyman Briggs colleges in 1967. Briggs was a residential learning community located in Holmes Hall, and was devoted to studying the natural sciences and their impact on society. Its first dean was Frederic Dutton. Madison, housed in Case Hall and sometimes called Justin Morrill's "little brother," was designed for the student interested in major social, economic, and political issues. Its first dean was Herbert Garfinkel. "When John Hannah retired as president of MSU in 1969, the three residential colleges, Morrill, Madison, and Briggs were flourishing, although Justin Morrill College was already suffering from some of the problems that ultimately led to its demise," Paul Dressel would write in his history of the Hannah years. "James Madison, with its emphasis on public policy, had started with a clearer mission than Morrill, by focusing on a concern common to many social scientists of that period, and was thus able to draw a broader segment of faculty from the various social sciences and give rein to their interests in the policy problem. Lyman Briggs, in the beginning, had defined its role as providing programs for the variety of students who were interested in the broad field of sciences. Lyman Briggs also opened the possibility for students interested in the philosophy of science, the history of science, or the impact of science on modern culture. James Madison and Lyman Briggs continued into the twenty-first century. Justin Morrill did not."

Student Unrest, Segregation, and Vietnam

But to many, the 1960s at MSU were not about excellent professors, new buildings, small colleges, or great football teams. They were about student demonstrations. It did not take much to prompt a protest. MSU students, geographically at least, seemed to be in an environment conducive to demonstrations against the university establishment. In 1960, the radical Students for a Democratic Society held its first national meeting in Ann Arbor. Two years later, SDS held its first convention in Port Huron, Michigan, adopting a political manifesto that criticized the country's political system for failing to achieve international peace and to confront society's social problems. In addition, the university was attracting a number of younger faculty members who were aggressive in criticizing administrative decisions and who urged students to do the same. An easy target, of course, was John Hannah, who had completed twenty-five years as a top Michigan State administrator in 1961. To students looking for someone to blame for what they saw as a university unresponsive to critical issues, he symbolized everything that was wrong about what was happening on campus.

Students, sometimes led by activist faculty members, marched on city hall in East Lansing and the Administration Building on campus, protesting a lack of progress in meeting their demands for racial integration. Sometimes they loudly defended non-tenured faculty who were not rehired. Other times they took to the sidewalks and streets chanting antiwar slogans in opposition to the Vietnam War. Once they organized a sit-in supporting students who had been arrested on charges of selling marijuana. They protested against tuition increases, verbally attacked the university for buying California grapes, and sought to disrupt speeches given by Hannah. MSU students sometimes took their antiwar protests to Washington, D.C. In April 1965, SDS and other groups sponsored two busloads of students traveling to the nation's capital to join the 17 April March on Washington. The

itinerary included a stop at the White House and visits to the Capitol, the Washington Mall, and other government buildings. That same month, a teach-in protesting the war was attended by about 1,500 students in the Auditorium. The featured speaker was interrupted by John Donoghue, chair of the Faculty Committee for Peace in Vietnam. "I'm sorry to have to announce this, but our freedom of speech has been threatened," he said. "There has been a bomb threat." The building was evacuated and searched, but no bomb was found. The teach-in continued.

The Vietnam protests could become especially confrontational. Sometimes campus antiwar demonstrators took their grievances to the state capitol. In early May 1965, approximately fifty members of the Committee for Peace in Vietnam marched to downtown Lansing carrying signs reading "War Is Hell" and "Get Out of Vietnam." Police officers lined the route, making sure the demonstrators and the largely unsympathetic crowd did not clash. "We have the right to picket," a demonstrator claimed. "And we have the right to take a club and bust in your head," a member of the crowd responded. One legislator suggested taking the protesters to the barber shop for

Civil Rights marches on campus and in the city of East Lansing were common in the 1960s. Students and faculty marched for open housing in the city, and for the hiring of more minority faculty and administrators on campus. Courtesy of Michigan State University Archives and Historical Collections.

haircuts. The march ended peacefully, without anyone being clubbed or forced to get a haircut. Antiwar protests on campus were often more innovative than simply marching, carrying signs, and shouting slogans. At the university's career carnival in the fall of 1965, dozens of local and national employers set up booths in the Union to discuss future job possibilities with MSU students. One of the participants was the United States Marine Corps. Quickly, however, the Marine representatives found their booth flanked by unapproved booths set up by the MSU Committee to End the War in Vietnam. The group distributed antiwar literature, and five members (four students and one nonstudent) were arrested when they refused to leave. Some of the marines were pleased by the appearance of the antiwar group, saying it attracted even more attention to the Marine Corps display. Another was not quite so sure. "If our sergeant was here, we'd beat the hell out of them," he told the *State News.* Carnival chair John McQuitty later said his committee would have considered approving a booth for the antiwar group if it had made a request through official channels.

The campus antiwar protest movement continued into 1966 when, for example, two MSU students were asked to leave a local Kiwanis Club meeting after causing a disturbance during a speech by Michigan Selective Service director Arthur A. Holmes. Sometimes the protests impacted studying students. "I remember one night there was a big riot," library director Richard Chapin said. "It was about the Vietnam war. I came back to campus and got a phone call—'Shut the library down. Close the library.' I picked up the phone and called Dick Bernitt, head of public safety. . . . 'Hey Dick. I've got 2,000 kids in here and I'm not going to dump them out on the street.' So, he said, 'Ok, keep them.'"

Sometimes student demonstrations were quiet and somber. On 17 April 1966, approximately 250 students carried handmade white crosses through campus, eventually placing them in a symmetrical arrangement, similar to a military cemetery, on the lawn near Beaumont Tower as a memorial to Vietnam War casualties. Many stayed all night at the mock graveyard. Earlier that day, the demonstrations had been noisier, as students gathered outside Bessey Hall to listen to assistant biochemistry professor Burke Zimmerman complain that he had been pressured by his department to avoid discussing issues related to biological and chemical warfare. "Should the content of science courses be limited to technical aspects or should it include the social and political consequences of the research of that field?" he asked. The ultimate protest, however, may have happened during finals week in the spring of 1966. On several nights students gathered outside the dormitories. Rocks were thrown, obscenities were chanted at the police, and students shouted, "Kill the cops"; fortunately no one was killed or even badly hurt. The reasons protesters later gave for their involvement were surprising. Some just shrugged their shoulders and said, "No reason in particular." Others said they were disgusted with dorm food. Some talked about hostility displayed toward them by East Lansing businessmen. Some said they were angry about losing recreation space at Brody Hall. And one even said he was protesting the bad seats he had been assigned for football games.

Reading through the state newspapers of the 1960s, it is easy to get the impression that everyone was against the war. The campus antiwar effort was well organized, it effectively recruited activists from off campus, and it often drew journalists looking for a controversial story. "Young journalists found stories about murder, sex, and Vietnam-war activists very exciting in the 60's," *East Lansing Towne Courier* publisher Harry Stapler would later say. But many students supported the war or were too busy with academic pursuits to get involved in either side of the controversy. During the anti-Vietnam teach-in that produced the bomb scare, more than one hundred members of the student-organized Ad Hoc Committee to Support President Johnson attended, and at one point, some members of the audience interrupted a speech by standing and singing "The Star Spangled Banner."

While newspapers generally gave front-page coverage to the antiwar effort, their editorial pages did not always support the protesters' actions. The arrests at the 1965 career carnival, for example, received the support of a *State News* editorial. Under the headline "Arrests of Protestors Defended Majority Rights," the paper argued:

> The four students and one non-student arrested . . . seem to be clearly out in left-field in regards to the methods they used to call attention to their thoughts on the Vietnam War and University regulations. They seem to have disregarded other individuals' rights to carry on other activities at this University. Their individual rights obviously seem more important to them. They seem to care little for

A student demonstration in 1969 showed the anti–Vietnam War sentiment on campus in 1969.

Courtesy of Michigan State University Archives and Historical Collections.

the rights of others. A professor on this campus has a right to conduct a class without interruption from without. The football team has a right to play ball in Spartan Stadium without other persons running around on the playing field. The MSU band has a right to practice on a University field without interference. . . . An insurance salesman does not have the right to start hawking during a history lecture. A group of lacrosse players do not have the right to use Spartan Stadium during a regularly scheduled football game. An ROTC Drill Team does not have the right to use a field designated for a band practice. . . . In a free society, any individual should be allowed to do anything he chooses as long as he doesn't interfere with the rights of others to do what they choose.

Student protests definitely caught the attention of almost everyone in the mid-Michigan community. Media organizations, church groups, social work practitioners and a variety of civic groups frequently addressed the motives behind student activism. On 16 May 1966, for example, a discussion titled "Unrest on Campus" was held at the Kellogg Center as part of the Twelfth Annual National Institute on Police and Community Relations. MSU psychology professor Milton Rokeach explained that much of the student unrest was partly due to alienation, and that students felt powerless in a world seen as big and hostile. He also suggested that there were strategic motives by some of the protest leaders as they confronted law enforcement agencies. "Student-police battles generate lots of publicity and that publicity helps recruit new members for the protest groups." Two years later, faculty members Irvin Lehman and Walker Hill, of the Office of Evaluation Services, made a further contribution to understanding students of the late 1960s when they released their study that compared student attitudes in 1958 to those in 1967. They found that the freshmen of the latter class were brighter, better readers, and had more ambitious educational plans than their counterparts of 1958. The 1960s students tended to question concepts regarded as absolute by their elders, and to believe that anything was fair game for a challenge. More than half of the contemporary students felt they were mature enough to determine when a rule was inappropriate, and almost a third stated they would break a rule just "for the hell of it." The study also noted a decrease in out-of-state students from 21 to 14 percent, but an increase in the number of Roman Catholic students on campus.

By 1968, protesters were complaining about the overly aggressive efforts of local law enforcement to control them. In early June 1968, several hundred students marched on both the city hall in East Lansing and the Administration Building on campus, demanding an end to police harassment and asking that campus police be put under the control of a student-faculty committee. On Wednesday, 5 June, eighteen demonstrators refused to leave the Administration Building and were arrested. Concerned about campus disruption, the MSU Varsity Club entered the controversy. At Hannah's 11 February 1969 farewell address at the Auditorium, the athletes had their first confrontation with demonstrators, when they sided with MSU administrators and local police in attempts to keep order. The club explained its actions in a prepared statement:

As varsity athletes we know that we can live in unity, brotherhood and mutual understanding with all people. Let it be known that the MSU Varsity Club stands in full support of the right and privilege of each ENROLLED student of MSU to voice his personal opinion through organized channels of legal dissent. We feel legal dissent DOES NOT include those activities that are detrimental to the normal functioning of our University. However, in the face of the current controversies and incidences in which OUTSIDE AGITATORS have proven to be involved, we feel an obligation to MSU, our fellow students and ourselves to publicly voice our disapproval of those forces solely intent upon causing student unrest, rather than creating genuine, constructive administrative reform. Therefore, we urge the students of MSU to reexamine their beliefs on the current campus disturbances and to formulate a consensus as to the basic problems at hand. We recognize that a dissatisfied group of individuals cannot express the total voice of each and every student. It is the majority voice and ONLY the majority voice which can legitimately express the opinion of the entire student body.

In 1969, the MSU Alumni Association decided to dedicate almost two pages of its April magazine to the students' perspective of campus unrest. Peter Ellsworth, then chair of Associated Students of MSU, presented his views of the university and protesting students:

Michigan State has been lucky—lucky that it has not joined the list of American universities torn in recent years by violent student unrest. While the President's office was being burned at Stanford and students were striking at San Francisco State things were functioning smoothly at Michigan State University. Although there have been student protests and demonstrations, not a single class has been canceled, almost no damage has been done, and only a small percentage of the student body have been even mildly interested in mounting any sort of attack on the institutions of the University. Recent student activity at Michigan State has probably been less rambunctious and more meaningful than the rallies and panty raids of an earlier era. Michigan State has been spared the embarrassment and inconvenience of student disruptions not because her students are less intelligent, less aware, less concerned or even more responsible than students on other campuses. Indeed MSU would seem to possess all the ingredients necessary for a turbulent situation. We have a large school with large classes. It's an impersonal place where it's easy to feel lost. MSU has an active campus where students are exposed to an enormous number of different ideas. And we have our hard core of disaffected students who firmly believe that confrontation is the only way to cure the ills that plague our University. But the most important ingredient for violent student unrest is missing at Michigan State. That one important ingredient is an all-pervasive frustration.

Ellsworth suggested that frustration at MSU had been decreased because of opportunities for students to participate in the decision-making processes—representation on faculty committees, input in updating student regulations, and a say in determining Hannah's successor:

> But it would be a mistake to assume that Michigan State students are contented. There is unrest on campus—the kind of unrest which should stimulate the University to progress both in terms of responsibility to its students and in terms of responsibility to society. Michigan State students share with students elsewhere a dissatisfaction with many of our nation's modes and institutions. We are told that we as a group are better informed and more aware than any other generation of students. With our education has come a knowledge of many of the evils which plague our country and our world; we have seen discrepancies in what is and what ought to be and we demand more be done about them. . . . We have questions about the proper role of Michigan State University. . . . MSU students are also not satisfied that we are getting the best education the University can provide. . . . MSU students feel the University should remove itself from decision-making areas which affect the non-academic aspects of our lives. Social regulations should be left to student organizations to determine.

Despite all the analysis related to the relationships between students and their university, campus unrest and confrontational marches continued. There was one student march, however, that everyone seemed to support. On 20 January 1965, the MSU marching band performed at the inaugural parade for President Lyndon B. Johnson in Washington, D.C. It was the only band invited from Michigan, and it led the entire Michigan parade delegation. Band members were sponsored by the Oldsmobile Division of General Motors and traveled by train, where they were allowed to eat and sleep during their stay. The trip, however, was only one high point of the band's remarkable history. It had played at both the 1954 and 1956 Rose Bowl games and been featured at the 1964 World's Fair in New York. Band members would soon be on their way to the 1966 Rose Bowl parade and game. Band leader Leonard Falcone was no stranger to dramatic events. His earlier "military band" had once played for President Herbert Hoover, and had accompanied the football team to numerous football games throughout the country. In good times and in trying times, the Spartan marching band always seemed to bring pride to the university. More than twenty years after the band performed for President Johnson, a local magazine ran a contest to determine the best band in the Lansing area. The MSU band won easily over the many rock-and-roll and country-western bands that were also nominated. "I first became a fan in the 1960s," one nominator explained. "I still am. No matter what happens on campus or in East Lansing, good or bad, the Spartan marching band, as it comes out of the tunnel in Spartan Stadium, makes you feel great."

13

Academic Freedom

ON A RAINY 11 APRIL 1935, A GROUP OF MICHIGAN STATE students threw the Reverend Harold P. Marley and five other demonstrators into the Red Cedar River. The tossing did not result from an overzealous celebration of a football victory nor from youthful exuberance at the coming of spring. Rather, Marley and his companions had been exercising their right to free speech, demonstrating in concert with thousands of others on college campuses throughout the United States to express support for world peace and to oppose U.S. involvement in any future war. MSC administrators backed—and maybe even instigated—the dunking: "This peace meeting is a blind for a radical gathering," college secretary John Hannah had announced before the gathering. "The administration of the college will have no objection if other students toss these radicals in the river."

The demonstration was sponsored by the Social Problems Club, a group that apparently included nine students, had no faculty adviser, and was not officially recognized by the college. Its leader was Louis Weisner, one of the six people who ended up in the Red Cedar. Club members claimed that President Robert Shaw had originally given them permission to meet in a room in the Union but had later rescinded that permission and that the *State News* had refused to give their group any publicity. The club eventually met across from the campus in the former Farm Club fraternity house on Grand River Avenue, and organizers distributed a pamphlet. "We are bewildered," it read. "When we studied history and civics, we found in the constitution of the United States and the Declaration of Independence that we as citizens had certain rights, such as freedom of speech and assembly and freedom of the press. . . . But apparently these things are not true."

Word had spread that trouble might arise, and the *Detroit Free Press* sent a reporter to cover the story:

> When the pathetic and rainsoaked group opened the meeting, more than 500 students, many of them in R.O.T.C. uniform, abandoned their drill in the armory and closed in. Showers of eggs and fruit rinds greeted the first speaker, Louis Weisner of Alpena, a sophomore student. A ripe orange struck him in the face, but he removed his glasses and continued. He introduced Maurice Wilsie of Ann Arbor, a graduate student at the University of Michigan. . . . Wilsie denied he was a Communist or a Socialist, when someone shouted "Back to Moscow." "I am against war. . . . I know it is unpopular to fight against it now. I know also that that it is your prerogative to throw me into the river if you want to." He was interrupted as the crowd surged forward. The group on the platform was seized, half carried, half pushed across the street to the campus and to the river bank, a half-mile away. At the students' favorite dunking spot, where generations of students have been hazed by their fellows, [the demonstrators] were pushed into the river. They were permitted to crawl out of the cold water on the opposite bank and were not otherwise molested. One of the group received a black eye as he was pushed toward the river. Mr. Marley took refuge in the parsonage of Peoples Church, where the pastor, the Rev. N. A. McCune, provided the dunking victim with a bucket of hot water for his feet and a change of socks.

Two years later, on 7 June 1937, demonstrating members of the United Auto Workers of America stormed downtown Lansing to protest the arrest of union pickets, virtually shutting down Michigan's capital city. Then, with Lansing under their control, union members headed east down Michigan Avenue to East Lansing, where they encountered a group of MSC students. According to James Sheridan of the *Detroit Times*,

> Trouble broke out when the union men, it is alleged, gave James Brakeman, proprietor of a small shoe shop, "5 minutes to close the place up." Brakeman is a former Michigan State football star and popular with the student body. He refused to close. The students

then dragged the three union leaders over the road, across the campus, and threw them into the river. A few minutes later, students said, five car loads of union men, armed with clubs, entered the campus from the east entrance and indicated they proposed to avenge the incident. "Get off the campus you Communists," yelled the students. "Don't think you're running this place." The irate students then pulled nine of the occupants from the cars and likewise dumped them into the river. One of the UAW members fainted as he was dragged to the muddy creek. He quickly revived when he hit the cold water.

The confrontation quickly became part of campus lore, and the story of the event was told and retold for many years. In addition, anti-union editorialists lauded the actions of the MSC students. Parents saw the East Lansing campus as a healthy environment for children who soon would be of college age. And forty-six members of the state legislature sent a letter to President Shaw declaring, "[We] heartily congratulate you on your success in turning out the type of young men and women who had instilled in their characters the high standards and ideals of our great nation, together with the force and courage to carry them out."

While admitting to being a communist or a socialist might get someone thrown in the river in the 1930s, the atmosphere had changed, at least somewhat, by 1940. On 30 October, the Socialist Party candidate for president, Norman Thomas, appeared at the MSC Auditorium to speak on "Our Dying Democracy." Classes were dismissed from two to three P.M., just as they had been for the appearance of candidates from the Democratic and Republican Parties, and the talk was broadcast over WKAR Radio. Shaw and Hannah appeared delighted. "It is of educational value for students to hear discussions of political, economic and social problems by outstanding individuals in the country," Shaw told the *State News*. Hannah added, "I would recommend Thomas' lectures to any thinking individual. This will be the last time in the present campaign that classes will be dismissed for political speeches. In giving the three major parties an opportunity to address the entire student body, we feel that every student who is of voting age should cast a more intelligent ballot in this presidential election."

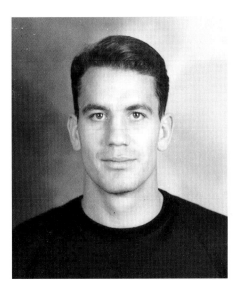

Football players such as Arthur Brandstatter lent their muscles to turn back labor union members when they attempted to shut down East Lansing in 1937. Brandstatter, an early friend of John Hannah, went on to become a leading Michigan State faculty member, achieving an international reputation for his expertise in criminal justice.
Courtesy of Michigan State University Archives and Historical Collections.

Communism on Campus

The World War II years on the Michigan State campus were patriotic times. Led by Hannah, most faculty and students supported the U.S. troops' role in the war. Soldiers trained on campus, and members of the MSC family died on foreign soil. Still, Hannah did not discourage faculty members from speaking their minds when they had something important to say.

After the defeat of the Axis powers in 1945, returning veterans received warm receptions on campus, but a widespread fear of communism created an atmosphere that was not always receptive to freedom of thought and expression. Newspapers, newsmagazines, radio news broadcasts, and newsreels suggested that innumerable "communist plots" endangered America. Opportunists took up the issue: Joseph McCarthy used it to win reelection as a senator from Wisconsin. Others, including Richard Nixon, founded political careers on anticommunist rhetoric, attacking their opponents as "un-American." It was not a popular time to question American values. "It was inevitable . . . that Michigan, home of the Big Three Auto Companies, the United Auto Workers, and several large universities and colleges, would be a major battlefield in the campaign to purge the Red Menace," MSU graduate student David Edmund Murley wrote in his 1992 master's thesis, "Un-American Activities at Michigan State College: John Hannah and the Red Scare, 1946–1954."

Flint native James Zarichney provided MSC with one of its first Red Scare challenges. Zarichney's parents struggled to make a living, eventually working in the state's Thumb area harvesting beets with migrant workers. The Communist Party tried to organize the laborers, convincing Zarichney that its philosophy might be the right approach for the struggling workers of the sugar-beet fields. His attraction to the party was a result of the "sheer horror of being an agricultural worker and not an intellectual decision." He became a student at Michigan State in the later 1940s, still retaining his belief in the soundness of the communist philosophy. In 1946, a group called American Youth for Democracy (AYD) applied to the student council for recognition as an official campus organization and received permission to hold meetings during the summer on a probationary status; in the fall, however, officials denied AYD's request to become an official student organization. The group apparently continued to function at MSC, even distributing handbills on the campus. After the student council recommended in early 1947 that "offending members" of AYD be disciplined, the Faculty Committee on Student Organizations placed organization members on probation, which prevented them from participating in extracurricular activities.

Zarichney and five other students were notified they had been placed on disciplinary probation on 6 February, and over the next few months, all except Zarichney were removed from probation. He, however, faced additional charges, including his roommate's accusation that he had been using their room as a headquarters for the distribution of communist literature. The dean of students suggested to Zarichney that he transfer to some other institution; however, Hannah told Zarichney that he "would be permitted to re-enroll at Michigan State College on strict disciplinary probation to continue his academic career . . . and forego active participation in organized extra-curricular activities and he agreed orally to those conditions."

In December 1948, Zarichney arranged for a meeting that featured Carl Winter, a member of the Michigan Communist Party, at College House, a building directly across the street from campus and owned by the Peoples Church. "From his investigation of the affair, the Dean of Students determined that Mr. Zarichney had violated the terms of his probation, which required him to refrain entirely from active participation in organized extra-curricular activities. The Dean notified Mr. Zarichney on December 18 by registered letter addressed to his home that he would not be permitted to register at the opening of winter term. . . . Attorneys for Mr. Zarichney asked the Michigan Supreme Court on January 12, 1949, for a writ of mandamus requiring the College to readmit him as a student on the grounds that his constitutional rights as a citizen had been violated. On January 13, the Supreme Court denied the petition. On February 28, the Supreme Court denied a petition for reconsideration of its action of January 13."

James Zarichney, now in his eighties, is retired and lives in Florence, Massachusetts. After leaving Michigan State, he earned a degree in math from Columbia University and eventually went to work as a computer programmer at Florida State University. He is still active in left-wing politics and describes himself as a "communist with a small c." He says he is not bitter about his Michigan State experience but, when asked about Hannah, says, "He was probably pretty good as a chicken farmer." Zarichney does not dispute much of the "official report" contained in the Hannah files, but does say he did not realize his organizing the session with the Communist speaker at the Peoples Church facility violated his probation, because it was held off campus. He also suggests he had strong student support for his positions, and that several members of the student council in the 1940s were communists. But, he does admit, "When I was at Michigan State I was very political and totally ignoring my studies."

On 22 June 1950, the *Michigan State News* published an editorial written by Russell McKee, who eventually became the editor of *Michigan Natural Resources* magazine, contending that the American Legion's Boys State Convention, held annually on the MSC campus, was not a democratic exercise but an opportunity for legion members to pass out "their American bill of goods which consistently reads as follows: Preserve Americanism. Preserve militarism. Stamp out communism, because it threatens Americanism, and stamp it out by any means available, fast, slow, fair, foul, but stamp it out." The editorial continued, "Communism itself may be good or bad; but that isn't the point. The point is that there is little room left in this country for the other point of view."

The American Legion complained that the statement "Communism may be good or bad" was inappropriate, that the editorial was probably communist-influenced, and that communism was a "poison to the people." Legion members demanded a retraction and an apology, insisted that those involved be disciplined, and suggested that an investigation of the incident might be in order. MSC suspended publication of the paper for the remainder of the summer, and Hannah apologized to the American Legion. However, 238 faculty members signed a petition supporting the *State News*.

As American anticommunism heated up during the 1950s, Michigan State professors soon found it advantageous to avoid even the appearance of any sort of association with left-wingers. According to Murley,

> During the 1950–51 academic year, the wife of a prominent physician in the area took a micro-economics course from Anthony Koo, a young faculty member who was born in China. The woman had

received a poor grade on her exam and went to Koo about getting her grade changed. Apparently she could not fathom the concept of diminishing marginal returns, the process whereby adding inputs of labor with fixed amounts of capital will ultimately result in diminishing additions of output. She contended that under America's capitalist system, hard work will always lead to higher yields. When Koo refused to change her grade, explaining that she did not understand the concept, she complained to her husband about her supposedly Communist professor and the "Red" textbook he used to support his theories (future Nobel Prize winner Paul Samuelson's *Economics*). Her husband, a prominent Republican, began contacting legislators about the "Chinese Communist" on the MSC staff. (That Koo was a Communist was strongly implied but never explicitly stated.) Those legislators contacted Hannah, wanting to know who this man was and why he was being kept around. Hannah began an inquiry into the nature of the charges, asking his staff what other universities used Samuelson's textbook. Members of Hannah's staff contacted the publisher, McGraw-Hill, which sent a list of other schools using the text. The list was several pages long, and included the United States Military Academy, Catholic University, and the General Motors Institute. That was good enough for Hannah. Professor Koo's background was also explored. Koo, it turned out, was hardly a Chinese Communist subverting our nation's youth. He was the nephew of Wellington Koo, the Taiwanese Ambassador to the United States and an ardent supporter of Chiang Kai Shek and our anti-Communist efforts in Korea.

In the fall of 1953, however, an actual—albeit former—communist was found on Michigan State's campus. The English department's Arnold Williams admitted to reporters that he had been a member of the Communist Party while serving as an instructor at the University of North Carolina. Even though Williams had left the party fifteen years earlier, the media still thought that the story was important. Williams told reporters that he had joined the party in 1936 because he believed that the Communists opposed fascism and racial discrimination. He said that during the two years he had been a party member, no discussions ever took place about overthrowing the U.S. government. When asked if he had ever attempted to bring

During the 1950–51 school year, a student asked Anthony Koo (*above*), who taught economics at the college, to change her grade. He refused. She then implied he was a communist who was using a "Red" textbook. Hannah would eventually support Koo. Courtesy of Michigan State University Archives and Historical Collections.

In 1953, English Professor Arnold Williams admitted he had once been a member of the Communist Party before he came to Michigan State, joining the party in 1936 but leaving it in 1938. His dean, Milton Muelder, supported Williams, suggesting he was a valuable member of the faculty. Courtesy of Michigan State University Archives and Historical Collections.

Communist doctrine into the classroom, he said, "Teaching English, you would have to drag Communist propaganda in by the heels if you were to try to teach it. I never did that. I am primarily interested in scholarship and truth in my profession." He also stated, "Having been a member of the party I discovered rather abruptly the superiority of the American system for preserving and maintaining the values of a free society. I hope that my experience has helped me to interpret these values to my students and to others with whom I have come in contact." Milton Muelder, dean of the School of Science and Arts, issued a statement of support for Williams. "I am convinced that Dr. Williams is telling the truth and has complied with the college's policy on Communism and loyalty. I believe he was a member who has renounced all party affiliation." Russel Nye, chair of the English department, agreed. "I have known Dr. Williams for 13 years and have been his department head for seven years. I have always regarded him as a loyal citizen and an excellent scholar and teacher. After hearing his statement and talking with him I still so regard him. I am glad to give him my support. I have no doubt of his loyalty and his continual value to Michigan State College."

Nevertheless, college officials would not so easily have forgiven current membership in the Communist Party. As Hannah aide James Denison wrote, "There is a strong feeling here that public funds should not be used to employ any individual who is committed to the destruction of our social and political system, and it is my judgment that any Communist discovered to be a member of the faculty would not be with us very long." An art professor was accused of being a Communist, a graduate student destroyed an undergraduate paper about communism for fear of being accused of having leftist leanings, and a politician wondered if MSC invited to campus too many communist-leaning speakers as part of the Lecture-Concert Series. However, the president appears to have handled the situation well. In Murley's words,

> Hannah's actions in response to charges during the Red Scare
> follow a certain pattern—to collect all relevant information, to gain
> as much knowledge of an accused faculty member as possible. Im-
> passioned, foolish decisions were not part of his modus operandi.
> Having then reached a conclusion as to whether charges might

be valid, only then might he call a faculty member in and discuss the matter. . . . No faculty review boards, special committees, or meetings before the Board of Agriculture—Hannah was willing to shoulder the responsibility of deciding how an accused Communist should be dealt with.

Even after McCarthy was discredited and the Red Scare fervor of the 1950s had died down, the issue of communists on campus remained. In an impromptu 17 May 1962 meeting, for example, the MSU Board of Trustees voted to bar a campus speech by Robert G. Thompson, an ex-convict and member of the U.S. Communist Party who had been invited by the university's Young Socialist Club. "Students need to be taught and to learn about communism," the board stated, "but they should get their facts from faculty members who are competent in the field, and who respect the obligation to tell the truth. The University never has and never will knowingly invite a communist to preach his treason on our campus, for we see no point in providing a platform for an exponent of 'communism' who is not bound by any obligation to tell the truth." The trustees denied that politics had influenced their decision, but resolutions protesting Thompson's appearance had been introduced in both the Michigan Senate and the House of Representatives.

The *State News* quickly criticized the board's decision, calling it "an insult to the intelligence of every student on this campus. To assume that students will be duped by the irrational arguments of one implies a lack of confidence in the young men and women who soon will become the leaders in their communities. Fearing the unpopular ideas of one man because he dissents too much and arbitrarily designating agents to teach the 'truth' stands incongruous with the cherished principles underlying our society." Hannah supported the ban, using the podium at the annual award ceremonies for student publications to state his reasons. "It was not an easy decision and was not taken lightly," he said. The trustees "do not distrust our students or their judgment or lack confidence in them."

Members of the Delta Sigma Phi fraternity were not intimidated and offered the backyard of their fraternity house: Thompson spoke there on 23 May. Delta Sigma Phi president James Eggert told the *State News* that the students had enough intelligence and insight to evaluate the opinions of the speaker critically and open-mindedly. Ac-cording to *Lansing State Journal* reporter Jerry Chiappetta, more than 2,300 students and faculty members attended the talk: "No one could be sure if anyone in the audience carried a new ideology from the backyard of the Delta Sigma Phi fraternity house, but they did come away with all-American, giant mosquito bites. Students who were interviewed later said they were disappointed by the New York com-munist's speech which was interrupted repeatedly by boos, cheers, wisecracks and barbed questions like 'What About Hungary?'"

Three days later, a *State Journal* editorial approved the decision to ban Thompson from campus, stating that "Actually this country is at war, be it called hot or cold, psychological or shooting. . . . Somehow, an invitation to a Commie speaker to appear anywhere does not seem to us to be an issue of preserving the great privilege of free speech. . . . It's just that the idea of giving aid and comfort to the enemy is repulsive. . . . This newspaper commends Dr. Hannah and the board of trustees for their forthright action. The Commie speaker should not only have been denied the facilities of the university, he should have been swept under the rug." Many faculty and students disagreed and reacted negatively to the board's decision. "It seems to me that by forbidding Thompson's appear-ance MSU is taking a step in the direction of ostracizing those who disagree with popular or majority doctrines," economics department graduate assistant Harvey Ackerman wrote to the *State News*. "Let the Communists speak. Let us decide for ourselves whether their dogma is sound or not. Let us not use totalitarian methods to protect democracy." Joining the individual protesters were the All Uni-versity Student Government (AUSG), the Campus United Nations organization, and the Michigan chapter of the American Association of University Professors (AAUP). English professor and Michigan AAUP president Herbert Weisinger issued a statement represent-ing his organization's position: "We cannot be persuaded that the institutions of the home, the church and the school have failed so miserably in teaching our young people the values of democracy that a single talk by a Communist will undermine their beliefs," he wrote. "On the contrary, we believe that exposure to opposing ideologies of the left and right alike [will] strengthen our students' faith in their values, for they will have met and passed the test of public scrutiny." The *State News* agreed. "The simple fact remains that if students are old enough to be sent to Laos and fight for American ideals they are discriminating enough not to be swayed by the ravings of an extremist, be it a right-winger or a leftist," the paper editorialized.

There were repercussions. The Delta Sigma Phi alumni board fined the ten-member fraternity board fifty dollars each for allowing Thompson to speak on fraternity grounds. It also requested and accepted Eggert's resignation. The president of the alumni board, Harold Balbach, told the *State News* that he believed that the fraternity could get a bad name from associating with a Communist. The student newspaper disagreed, publishing a 1 June editorial that criticized the alumni board's action. "Eggert, the members of the fraternity executive board and the chapter deserve a vote of thanks from the students of this university. They realized that punitive action would be taken because of their decisions, but went ahead anyway. It took real conviction and courage to allow the Communist speaker to use the fraternity's facilities."

The matter resulted in the formation of a student-faculty speakers committee responsible for approving campus speakers, who in turn had to be sponsored by official campus organizations. While the committee's rules permitted communists to speak as long as they did not advocate change by violent means, the fact that any restrictions at all existed did not sit well with some observers. On 8 October 1962, the heads of nine student organizations, calling themselves the Campus Club Conference, met at the Union and heard three representatives of the Student Non-Violence Coordinating Committee talk about their experiences registering voters in the South. The speakers had not been cleared by the speakers committee, and three weeks later, the Faculty Committee on Student Conduct removed six of the organizing students—AUSG president Bob Howard, Young Socialist Club president Jan Garrent, Humanist Club president Peter Werbe, Young Democrat president Bob Hencken, National Student Association coordinator Dick McClellan, and Forensics Union president Tom Steinfatt—from office and placed them on "strict disciplinary" probation. Probation included barring the students from holding any campus office or driving a car on campus. "Apparently this is what you get for biting the hand that's trying to hit you," Howard told the

State News. "The most repulsive thing to me about Soviet Communism is the limitation it places on individual freedom. In some degree
this is the path we're following at this University."

Economics professor Walter Adams voiced his disapproval of the
Faculty Committee's action. Students picketed, and future Michigan
governor James Blanchard helped start a petition drive. Edwin
Wilson, president of the American Humanist Association, strongly
objected to Werbe's ouster and to the university's practice of requiring speakers to be cleared in advance. "This prior censorship appears
to us as a violation of the spirit and letter of the First Amendment to
the United States Constitution providing for civil religious liberty,"
he wrote to Hannah on 8 November. The student leaders ultimately
were taken off probation, and the Board of Trustees voted to allow
any speakers, including Communists, on campus as long as they did
not advocate violence or sabotage; nevertheless, the requirement that
speakers be registered remained in place.

A few months later, in early January 1963, the Young Socialist
Club received permission to have Herbert Aptheker, editor of the
Communist magazine *Public Affairs*, speak at the Union. Aptheker's
17 January talk attracted only about one hundred listeners, a far
smaller number than had gathered to hear Thompson. Argued a 22
January *State News* editorial, "The two incidents clearly show how
crackpots can make an issue where there should be none and then
proceed to blow it out of proportion. Fortunately, the crackpots didn't
stand a chance this time thanks to the new policy. Academic freedom
reigned supreme last week on our campus. It didn't rate headlines.
There were none. That's the way great universities operate."

FACULTY MEMBERS AND ACADEMIC FREEDOM

Academic freedom at MSU also made national headlines in 1962
when Samuel Shapiro, an assistant history professor at the Oakland
campus who held a doctorate from Columbia University, was denied
tenure. *American Heritage*, the *Nation*, and the *Atlantic Monthly* had
published articles by Shapiro that criticized U.S. policies toward
Cuba at a time when many Americans saw the Caribbean island as a
menace to their safety.

The denial of tenure came under fire from a variety of angles. The *Detroit Free Press*, the Detroit branch of the American Civil Liberties Union, and Delta College's AAUP chapter questioned the decision. An MSU chemistry professor on sabbatical in Cambridge, England, entered the fray. "The foul smell of infamy travels far and swiftly," wrote Harold Hart in a letter to the *State News*. "Whether one agrees with Professor Shapiro's views regarding U.S. policy toward Cuba or not is beside the point; his attempts to evaluate the situation first hand are laudable in an academic or social science sense, and his academic freedom to present the results of his investigations as he sees them must be defended. MSU will never be a first-rate University unless it requires an administration which will resist rather than succumb to public pressure, which will defend its faculty's right to inquire into all areas of human activity and publish its findings, no matter how unpopular they may be."

In a 14 December editorial, Harvard University's student newspaper suggested that state government officials had pressured MSU to get rid of Shapiro. On 10 January 1963, the *National Guardian* described Shapiro as a "brilliant young man" and noted that he had written many articles in scholarly journals as well as a book, *Richard Henry Dana, Jr.*, published by the MSU Press. According to the *Guardian*, "Since publication seems to be the criterion for faculty standing these days, it would seem that Shapiro had met the requirement admirably." Like the *Harvard Crimson*, the *Guardian* charged that academic freedom was the issue, encouraging readers to express their concerns in writing to the AAUP and to Hannah, with copies to Shapiro.

Hannah received numerous letters on the subject. To a high school student from Uniondale, New York, who suggested that MSU was stifling Shapiro's academic freedom, Hannah responded,

> I regret to see a high school student as obviously interested in education as you tilting at windmills as you are in this case. It would surprise me to learn you have anything better than second-hand knowledge of this case, and are not depending on the interpretation placed upon it by someone else in making your judgment. You have somehow overlooked the point that the decision not to reappoint Dr. Shapiro was made by his professional colleagues, who must be

Chemistry Professor Harold Hart was not afraid to speak out on issues he thought negatively affected Michigan State. When he was on sabbatical in England in 1963 he read about Samuel Shapiro's difficulty in getting tenure and wrote to the *State News* saying Shapiro's academic freedom must be defended. Courtesy of Michigan State University Archives and Historical Collections.

John Moore, an associate professor of natural science, was an outspoken conservative, who accused the *State News* of being a puppet of the anti-conservative university administration and who believed there was a preponderance of left-wing reading material in campus lounges. Courtesy of Michigan State University Archives and Historical Collections.

presumed to have as much concern for the protection of academic freedom as you. The decision was not, as you seem to assume, whether he should be free to speak his mind, which of course he is. The decision was whether they wanted to accept him as a permanent member of the faculty, and they made their judgment on considerations other than you cite.

A 7 January 1963 *State News* editorial suggested that the Shapiro case seemed to have had two results: first, "MSUO rid itself of a controversial professor—a fact which makes some people happy and others unhappy"; second, a "self-conscious Michigan State, concerned with presenting a favorable image of itself, was given once again a black eye—however careful it was in trying to duck the punch." One Lansing television station took the opposite stand, suggesting that state-supported institutions should not be a "refuge for communists" and that perhaps Shapiro should consider teaching in Cuba.

The case was resolved when Shapiro agreed to accept the findings of an AAUP investigation into the matter. On 14 February, Edward Huebel, president of the Oakland chapter of AAUP, announced that the university had followed accepted procedure in deciding not to retain Shapiro. "Both the national office and the local chapter, after examining the circumstances, find no evidence that Shapiro was released for reasons inconsistent with academic freedom." The *State News* then declared the controversy ended. "The AAUP is a highly respected organization and would be the first to stand behind and defend one of its people if he had been wronged," the paper editorialized. "If Dr. Shapiro is willing to accept the decision of the AAUP, so are we." Several months later Shapiro landed a job as a history professor at Notre Dame University, where he taught Latin American history until his retirement in 1991. In a 2003 interview, he sounded more amazed than bitter over his treatment by MSU–Oakland. "They fired me on Christmas Day," he remembered. "For a while I couldn't get a job because everyone seemed to think I was a communist. My writings were not pro-Castro, they just questioned U.S. policy in Cuba," said Shapiro, who stated he was jailed in Cuba twice for what Castro supporters believed were anti-communist statements. He had predicted a U.S. invasion of Cuba would fail and that Castro would remain in power for a long time. He, of course, was right.

While Shapiro's supporters had contended that the university had punished him for his liberal views, Michigan State's treatment of John Moore, an associate professor of natural science, raised charges that conservative viewpoints were not tolerated. Since arriving on the East Lansing campus in the mid-1940s, Moore had frequently accused the university of favoring liberals and discriminating against persons with more rightist points of view. Administrators had largely ignored his charges until he spoke to the Van Buren County Farm Bureau in Paw Paw, Michigan, on 20 September 1960 and claimed that some professors were anti-Christian and anti-parental, that campus lounges and libraries contained a preponderance of left-wing reading material, and that the faculty had voted 400-1 against requiring students to sign a loyalty oath before receiving government scholarships. Word of Moore's address did not begin to circulate immediately, but when it did, his accusations eventually provoked another controversy. In December 1961, *Detroit Free Press* columnist Judd Arnett examined Moore's charges and questioned the university's commitment to academic freedom; a 9 December 1961 *Muskegon Chronicle* article took the opposite stand, suggesting overreaction by those on the far right, who tended to see a "Communist behind every bush."

Hannah received numerous letters supporting Moore's charges. One Detroit woman wrote,

I spent one year at MSU. My sister is a graduate. We have known for some time that Socialism is being taught, outright and slyly under cover of fancy terms and phrases. I sent my son to Bowling Green University for this reason. I know many others who did the same for the same reason. A prominent member of G. Mennen Williams' official family took his son out of MSU and sent him to U. of D. in Detroit because the text books at MSU were too socialist. May I remind you that this is a public institution financed by public money. . . . The Communists plan to take over this country. Not by force, but by infiltration into schools, churches and all methods of thought control and shaping. . . . The people of this country are constantly being hounded for more money for education. For what? To train young people to work for our own destruction? Are we supposed to furnish the money and then sit in the classrooms to hear what is being taught? Are we supposed to collect and study your textbooks to see what is going on? That Dr. Hannah is what we are paying you for and a great many of us are very unhappy with the job you are not doing.

Hannah wrote a lengthy reply to one such vitriolic correspondent:

It being quite evident that you based your letter . . . on hearsay and incorrect information, perhaps my best response would be to correct your misapprehensions as to the situation at Michigan State University. [No] professor at Michigan State University is known to have questioned the value of the marriage ceremony. The remark to which you allude was made by a visiting lecturer, and he was promptly repudiated by the University. . . . I am not aware of any decline in morals among our students. I have the advantage of more than 20 years of intimate observation of our students, and I think no finer, more wholesome group of young people ever were students here. . . . As for discouraging students from thinking, the very opposite is true, and it is not the university, but its critics who would impose conformity upon students, and deny them the right to decide for themselves what is right and best.

The charge that seemed to generate the most concern to many was Moore's contention that MSU's Academic Senate had voted almost unanimously to ask Congress to strip the loyalty-oath requirement from the National Defense Education Act. On 15 December 1961, Hannah issued an official statement explaining that the senate had not favored eliminating the loyalty oath, in which students agreed to "bear true faith and allegiance to the United States of America and [to] support and defend the Constitution and laws of the United States of America against all its enemies, foreign and domestic," but rather its sister document, an affidavit in which a student was required to "solemnly swear (or affirm) that I do not believe in, and am not a member of and do not support any organization that believes in or teaches, the overthrow of the United States Government by force or violence or by any illegal or unconstitutional methods." Hannah pointed out that a majority of leading colleges and universities had taken the same action, as had the American Association of Land-Grant Colleges, and that President Dwight D. Eisenhower had urged Congress to repeal the disclaimer requirement.

An ad hoc committee of the MSU Academic Council was established to investigate Moore's charges, but he failed to appear at a 6 February 1962 meeting that would have allowed him to present evidence or other materials on his behalf. The entire Academic Council then unanimously approved a report that concluded, "Professor Moore has no charges against the University or its faculty which he is willing to bring to a faculty committee. The Committee is naturally concerned over the kinds of charges reported and allegations made. It concludes that material damage has been done, needlessly, to the reputation of Michigan State University." The controversy died down, and Moore remained at Michigan State, teaching and advocating his conservative point of view. Perhaps partly in response to the Shapiro and Moore incidents, on 5 February 1963 the MSU Academic Council formally adopted the academic freedom principles endorsed by the American Association of American Colleges and the AAUP, including:

- The teacher is entitled to full freedom in research and in the publication of the results, subject to the adequate performance of his other academic duties; but research for pecuniary return should be based upon an understanding with the authorities of the institution.

- The teacher is entitled to freedom in the classroom in discussing his subject, but he should be careful not to introduce into his teaching controversial matter which has no relation to his subject. Limitations of academic freedom because of religious or other aims of the institution should be clearly stated in writing at the time of appointment.

- The college or university teacher is a citizen, a member of a learned profession, and an officer of an educational institution. When he speaks or writes as a citizen, he should be free from institutional censorship and discipline, but his special position in the community imposes special obligations. As a man of learning and an educational officer, he should remember that the public may judge his profession and his institution by his utterances. Hence he should at all times be accurate, should exercise appropriate restraint, should show respect for the opinions of others, and should make every effort to indicate he is not an institutional spokesman.

In 1966, the issue of academic freedom again made news when a faculty committee of the American thought and language (ATL) department recommended that nontenured professors William Gary Groat, John Kenneth Lawless, and Robert S. Fogarty not be rehired. The three men claimed that they had been given no reason for their dismissals, while the department chair, T. Ben Strandness, contended that reasons had been given and that the three men, or possibly some of their supporters, were turning a professional matter into a political football. A 2 November *State News* editorial suggested that the decision might have been based in part on the perception that the three instructors were "dissenters, trouble-makers, persons who rock the boat of the otherwise tranquil ATL department" and that Groat and Lawless had contributed articles to *Zeitgeist*, a non-mainstream local magazine. The paper ran numerous news stories about the controversy, printing many letters to the editor from students who believed MSU was getting rid of some of its most talented teachers. On 27 November, the *State News* ran a letter in which Lawless questioned his dismissal:

> Is the Ivory Tower a cloister? Yes. Should it be? No. I have been released from the ATL Dept. for breaches of academic decorum. I admit to these, but I deny their validity as grounds for my release. I broke academic decorum two ways: I spoke in a manner considered rude at faculty meetings and I wrote a story with deeper roots in Tropic of Capricorn than Catcher in the Rye. I have been chided, and released for the tone of voice used in my dissent at faculty meetings. It was my intention to speak effectively, not rudely, but I will admit that an element of rudeness did enter my speech. I was fighting what I considered ignorance in high places on important issues. The phrase "community of scholars" has been used here as a synonym for conformity here. . . . I hadn't known the community of scholars was a nunnery.

ATL associate professor Jerry West, a member of the faculty committee that had chosen not to rehire the three instructors, wrote to the *State News* to express a different point of view: "We're so damn democratic in ATL that we have a lot of familiarity which sometimes breeds contempt and children. We're trying to get rid of some of the children, partly because they keep stealing all our toilet paper to throw at cops and old ladies, but mainly because a lot of us don't want students taught by people who are immature, snobbish, narrow and intolerant. . . . I do want you to know that I think I was right in voting with the majority on the committee."

Despite a student vigil at Bessey Hall in support of the instructors, pickets protesting the ATL department decision at the football "game of the century" against Notre Dame, discussion sessions in individual dormitories, and national wire-service coverage, Lawless, Groat, and Fogarty were not rehired. All evidence indicates that this and other decisions regarding the denial of tenure were handled at the university's lower administrative levels and that Hannah played no role. When asked his opinion about the ATL controversy, the president replied that he knew only what he "had read in the *State News.*" In a 1966 statement, Adams, who later succeeded Hannah as MSU's president, shared his belief that "MSU's record on academic freedom in the 19 years I have been here has been outstanding."

One of the last battles over academic freedom during President Hannah's tenure occurred in early 1969, when the university decided not to rehire Bertram Garskof, an assistant professor of psychology. Garskof apparently gave A grades to all his students and let them decide what should be taught. His loyalists claimed that he stood for a free and unrestricted exchange of ideas between student and teacher: "Why would the university want to get rid of such a wonderful teacher?" asked one female student. Critics were concerned that students signed up for Garskof's classes to receive the automatic As, not to learn. As in earlier such instances, participants took their battle beyond the department's tenure committee and fought in the media. In a remarkably balanced 31 January editorial, the *State News* lauded Garskof for his forward thinking but expressed some reservations. "Sadly, his lofty ideals have been debased by the large numbers of students who flock to his class solely for a guaranteed A. These students are neither interested in his innovative methods nor in contributing to what is certainly a rich and rewarding learning experience. There are therefore large numbers of students who are learning nothing

When the university decided not to rehire Bertram Garskof, an assistant professor of psychology, both supporters and detractors debated his future. "Why would the university want to get rid of such a wonderful teacher?" one of his students asked. Courtesy of Michigan State University Archives and Historical Collections.

from Garskof's class. That they enrolled only for a good time is probably true; that they provide grist for those who disparage his teaching
concepts is, unfortunately, also true."

STUDENTS AND ACADEMIC FREEDOM

Paul M. Schiff, a New York native, arrived in East Lansing in 1963
with an economics degree from Rutgers University. Schiff did graduate work in economics for two years before withdrawing from the
university in the spring of 1965 to work on his thesis. He then decided
to change his field of study to history and applied for readmission.
He received a letter of acceptance from the history department on
3 June, but on 21 June received another letter, this time from the
registrar's office, denying readmission. Schiff charged that the denial
was based on his political beliefs—he had served as president of the
Young Socialist Club, was a member of the steering committee of
the Committee to End the War in Vietnam, and was on the advisory
council of the East Lansing Civil Rights Movement. The university
countered that he disrupted the university by illegally distributing
literature door-to-door in the dormitories, exhibiting an "open, defiant
and deliberate course of discrediting conduct," refusing to abide by a
university regulation requiring official recognition of student organizations before they could operate on campus, and exhibiting negative
conduct toward a public official who was speaking on the MSU
campus. Schiff denied the charges, then sued the university. Perhaps
in an effort to avoid an unsatisfactory legal decision, the university
allowed Schiff to enroll for the winter term of 1966, disappointing
many observers. The *State News* editorialized on 19 July,

> The question is still unanswered: Must a university be democratic
> in its relations with students? . . . When the University rejected Paul
> Schiff's application last fall, because he had opposed University
> policies, it was not showing democracy at work. It was showing how
> people get squelched when they react too strongly against strong
> forces in a mass society. When Schiff took his case to court there
> was hope the court would answer the question: must a university be
> democratic? A decision in Schiff's favor would have set a precedent

forcing schools across the country to use democratic methods in making admissions selections. But the leaders of MSU had a change of heart and re-admitted Schiff, making the suit a moot issue—no precedent. . . . The arbitrary decision of the leaders of the school to re-admit Schiff is little consolation to students upset by its earlier arbitrary decision not to re-admit him. . . . At a university whose atmosphere more closely resembles a big business corporation than a traditional ivy-covered academic institution, students want and need legal guarantees.

The End of an Era

THE 1960S HAD NOT BEEN AN EASY DECADE FOR JOHN A. HANNAH. Protests against the Vietnam War and for increased civil rights, conflict-of-interest charges, and a faculty that seemed to be more rebellious than in the late 1940s and 1950s made many observers wonder how much longer the MSU president would stay at his job, especially since he was an attractive candidate for a political or administrative position at the state, national, and international levels.

In late 1966, Paul Varg, dean of the College of Arts and Letters, broached the subject of retirement with Hannah. "In the meeting of the Administrative Board this morning, I believe you used the term 'retire' three times," Varg wrote on 1 November. "To be sure, you did not leave an inference that you were about to do so. However, I fear that this may be on your mind and, therefore, I would like to have you know my feeling on the matter. Goodness knows, you've earned freedom from the heavy responsibilities that have been on your mind for so long a time. I would not begrudge you this freedom. On the other hand, the very difficulties in this period of transition that would promote such a decision constitute the reasons why this University so desperately needs your leadership. The ferment among students, among the faculty, and among the Board of Trustees, is disturbing. This is why we so desperately need understanding leadership. Only you can provide this leadership at this time." Hannah's response was short. "I have no intention to abandon the ship regardless of how rough the weather may get. Your kind words were appreciated."

Other people connected to MSU thought it was time for the president to leave. At a fall 1968 meeting of the Board of Trustees, board member Clair White, a frequent Hannah critic, attempted to force his retirement by sponsoring a resolution calling for the MSU president

An attempt by two members of the Board of Trustees to force Hannah's retirement in 1968 failed by a 6-2 vote. Trustee Don Stevens (*left*) supported Hannah. Courtesy of Michigan State University Archives and Historical Collections.

to reveal his retirement plans before the 5 November general election. The resolution attracted support only from White and one other Democrat, Allen Harlan, and failed by a 6-2 vote, with Democrats Don Stevens, Frank Hartman, and Connor Smith joining Republicans Frank Merriman, Stephen Nisbet, and Kenneth Thompson in support of Hannah.

Hannah biographer Richard Niehoff suggests that Hannah may have grown tired of serving as Michigan State's president. In 1971, for example, Hannah's administrative assistant, James Denison, wrote that around 1965–66, the president "began to lose interest to a degree in the University itself and its on-campus operations, and transferred that interest to international projects. This loss of interest, if substantiated, could be attributed to many things: he had accomplished so much, and comparatively little of consequence needed to be done, or

John Hannah spent much of his presidency chairing the U.S. Civil Rights Commission. MSU Press Director Lyle Blair (*right*) and Hannah discuss Foster Rhea Dulles's history of the Civil Rights Commission that was published by MSU Press in 1968. Courtesy of Michigan State University Information Services.

was well in hand, in the areas of planning and building . . . and he had attained most of the honors available to men in his profession."

Hannah had always balanced his love for Michigan State with his feelings of obligation to participate in other areas of public service—working for the Defense Department, the U.S. Civil Rights Commission, and even as a delegate to Michigan's Constitutional Convention in the early 1960s.

In early 1969, rumors began to circulate that Hannah was in line for an appointment as director of the U.S. Agency for International Development (USAID), and on 5 February he met with trustees for an informal discussion of the university's direction if he received the nomination. "Hannah said that if he should accept an appointment, it would be in the best interests of the University for him to remain president in name at least, until the end of the current academic year," *Michigan State News* staff writer Ron Ingram reported. Ingram also quoted Hannah as saying, "My obligations are to MSU. I intend to keep that commitment."

The rumors also prompted *State News* editors to assess Hannah's presidency and speculate about his successor:

The 28 years of Hannah's administration have seen the explosive growth of small and obscure Michigan State College to our sprawling

John Hannah's ideas were solicited by many world leaders, including U.S. Presidents Franklin D. Roosevelt, Harry Truman, Dwight Eisenhower, Richard Nixon (*above*), John F. Kennedy, and Lyndon Johnson. Courtesy of Michigan State University Archives and Historical Collections.

multiversity. . . . Within his generation of college presidents Hannah has earned a reputation as a brilliant, sometimes controversial innovator. . . . To students Hannah has been a mythological character—on official occasions the subject of ritual praise, and during periods of revolt the object of ritual blasphemy. . . . Whatever final assessment of Hannah's contribution to MSU may be it will be difficult to find a man to take his place. . . . The choice of a new president for MSU will have to be made with violently conflicting goals and concepts of the University's future in mind. The legislature is worried about student unrest, immorality on campus, and leftist agitation, and would like to see a "good, solid, respectable man" appointed who would understand and sympathize with their worries. The faculty is tired of "cramped and creaky" facilities and "paltry" budgets for academic activities and research. And it would be nice to have a "liberal, scholarly president" who would respond to their needs. Students have a long list of complaints, most centering about their powerlessness within the University community and the meaningless and competitiveness of their classes. The revolt has been growing for years and is approaching crisis proportions. . . .

The choice of a new president, if it can be made without provoking major shake-ups in the University, will in any event mean major changes in its directions. We can go on to become the world's first megaversity, or stop growing physically and become great academically. We may be known in the future for our literary and artistic greatness, or for our advances in crop research. The possibilities, like MSU itself, are enormous.

On 11 February, Hannah delivered his annual State of the University address. Four or five hundred students attempted to disrupt the speech by banging on the doors of Fairchild Theater and building a bonfire outside. In the theater lobby stood police from MSU, Lansing, and East Lansing, armed with billy clubs and gas masks. Outside the building, a group of varsity athletes tried to help police maintain order. Activist professor Bertram Garskof stood among the crowd, using a bullhorn and shouting for "student action against the establishment." Hannah told the audience he would accept the position of USAID director. He urged the Board of Trustees quickly to select his successor but first to consult with faculty, students, and alumni.

The alumni association was always important to John Hannah. Above he talks with Pontiac Press publisher Harold Fitzgerald (*left*), General Motors vice president Jack Wolfram (*second from right*), and aviation pioneer Talbert "Ted" Abrams (*right*) at an alumni reception. Courtesy of Michigan State University Archives and Historical Collections.

He also took the opportunity to criticize intentionally disruptive agitators and suggested that the use of police officers was appropriate to guarantee that "those who teach, those who learn, those who do research, those who do public service will not be interfered with by those who want to destroy the establishment, and who would substitute chaos for order, repression for opportunity, allegiance to their point of view for freedom. . . . The very impracticability of many of the demands explains their true purpose—not the improvement of our society, but confusion, disruption and chaos." An after-speech reception was canceled, and Hannah, the trustees, and an audience estimated at around five hundred were led out the back door to prevent a confrontation with the demonstrators. The episode contrasted sharply with Hannah's 1952 departure for a temporary job in the Defense Department, when he was escorted to a farewell ceremony and greeted by cheering students.

On 27 March, the U.S. Senate confirmed Hannah's appointment as head of USAID, prompting encomiums from Michigan's politicians. Democratic senator Philip Hart said, "There are few men in the civil rights field whom I grew to admire more," continuing, "Dr. Hannah always told it the way it was—north or south. . . . One way to judge a man is by weighing the strength of the institutions that he heads. And certainly MSU stands as fine testimony to Hannah's ability." Republican senator Robert Griffin concurred: "Hannah is one of the most able leaders that the state has produced. I have no doubt he will do an excellent job."

• • •

His impending departure prompted Hannah to reflect publicly on what he had accomplished at Michigan State and to share his hopes for the institution he had played such an important role in shaping. In an early March 1969 interview with the *Kalamazoo Gazette*, Hannah suggested that MSU, then boasting an enrollment of around thirty-nine thousand students, should never grow bigger than forty-five thousand. He foresaw a law school in the university's future, and he argued that education should not be left up to professional educators but should be the responsibility of all society. And when asked about campus unrest, he said that the demonstrators received the lion's share of the media's attention while the good news went unreported, and that in his day, the rest of the students would have thrown protesters in the river "when they became too much of a nuisance." Finally, Hannah offered some advice for his successor: "If a university president hopes to be successful, he should have some understanding of the role of education in society, and . . . try to look at the university as an agency of society working to forward the aspirations of its people. I think he also should have a thick hide and a calm spirit."

The *State News* published a lengthy front-page story in which editor in chief Edward Brill interviewed the retiring president. When asked if he could have conceived of MSU's growth into a forty-thousand-student multiversity, Hannah replied, "The answer is of course no. One, when starting a career, does not look forward to its end, so I'm sure I didn't have any preconceived notion of what the University would be like 28 years later. . . . One of the interesting things about this university is that it has re-appraised itself every few years and it has developed logically, not only in its program but in its campus. Of course it still has a long way to go. There's nothing ever so good that it couldn't be better." Brill then asked Hannah what he envisioned for MSU. "I hope that Michigan State University is going to go that last mile," Hannah answered. "There isn't any reason why this can't be one of the truly great universities of the world." Brill also asked about the qualities Hannah's successor would need:

> First of all, we must recognize that a modern university is a big, complex organization. There was a time when a university president needed to be a scholar, and he was usually a preacher with long hair and a calm spirit that behaved well in a social setting. But it's not that kind of a world anymore. He still has to have some understanding, however, of the academic area of the university which is its real objective. So I think right off the bat that an adequate president must come from the academic arena. I'm always irritated when a presidency falls open and the newspapers suggest that some political figure or maybe several of them or someone who has been an army general or a business tycoon is the man they ought to look to. . . . The second part of it is the president can't succeed unless he has the support of his faculty. . . . I think I should stop there because many times I have watched what universities go through

when they change presidents and watched what happens when the outgoing president dabbles in the selection of his successor. I have said and I mean to keep it that I'm not going to participate in the selection of my successor. And I'm going to keep out of his way after he's once selected. Mr. Shaw, my predecessor, happened to be my father-in-law. I was always grateful to him for the fact that he never stepped his foot on this campus for the first two years after I became president.

. . .

ONE OF HANNAH'S STRONGEST CHARACTERISTICS HAD ALWAYS BEEN HIS consistency. But in his final few years as Michigan State's president, that consistency became a liability: the student body was changing, but the president was operating in much the same way as he had during the 1940s, the 1950s, and the early 1960s. Nevertheless, his departure prompted numerous positive assessments of the impact of his presidency. For example, under the headline "Exit Methuselah," the 21 March 1969 issue of *Time* described Hannah as

> an evangelist for land-grant colleges, which engineered the farm revolution and now boast "the world is our campus." His approach makes purists shudder. As they see it, M.S.U. is a big "service station" that fills up students with trade-school courses like Sewage Treatment or the Dynamics of Packaging. To Hannah, the criticism is almost a compliment: The object of the land-grant tradition was not to de-emphasize scholarship but to emphasize its application. Under Hannah, M.S.U. has grown from a sleepy agricultural college of 6,390 students to a 5,000 acre "megaversity" with an enrollment of 42,541 and an annual budget of more than $100 million. Critics point out that Hannah began building the reputation of M.S.U. by building a championship football team, and the school's free-wheeling recruiting tactics earned N.C.A.A. censure in 1964. They sometimes overlook the fact that Hannah has also succeeded in recruiting many bright young professors. . . . A charismatic speaker, he also made a point of frequently outtalking the rival University of Michigan for state funds. . . . This year M.S.U. boasts more Merit Scholars than any other campus in the country—684 compared with second-place Harvard's 503.

John Hannah was always a willing speaker, continually promoting Michigan State or any other project that benefited the people of Michigan. Many times he was the featured speaker at economic club meetings, a local Farm Bureau, or a horticultural society. Sometimes his appearances took on a less serious note as when he appeared with movie director Otto Preminger (*left*) and actress Lee Remick (*center*) in honor of a film shot in Michigan, *Anatomy of a Murder*. Courtesy of Michigan State University Archives and Historical Society.

Provost Howard Neville, who had filled various positions at MSU since 1955, offered *State Journal* reporter Helen Clegg his assessment of Michigan State's progress under Hannah: "I think that if you were to select the top 50 universities in the world, by almost any standard, MSU would be among them—where would depend on what measure you were using. . . . I am sure that when the history of post-war higher education is written, John Hannah . . . will be among the great educators who developed the multi-university and the large, complex institutions as we know them today."

Agricultural engineering department chair Arthur W. Farrall described Hannah as "at heart an aristocratic individual [who nevertheless] always kept his interest in the common man and the underprivileged at a high pitch. . . . He was willing to accept suggestions from anyone—I do not know whether this directly affected him, but I noted shortly after I made the suggestion that we should have a bus system on the campus, to help students get around, it was provided. . . . His motto was 'get the job done' and he did his part to push projects along. He did not stand on ceremony, but got to the nub of a problem and acted."

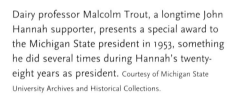

Dairy professor Malcolm Trout, a longtime John Hannah supporter, presents a special award to the Michigan State president in 1953, something he did several times during Hannah's twenty-eight years as president. Courtesy of Michigan State University Archives and Historical Collections.

Ira Baccus, a professor of electrical engineering who had previously offered outspoken criticism of some of Hannah's actions, found kind words for the president's overall tenure: "I believe most, if not all, of those who really knew Dr. Hannah considered him a just and honorable person in all his associations with others. He was generous (sometimes to a fault) and had great faith in people until those involved proved his faith was not well founded. Even then he was far more tolerant of any shortcomings of the person than most Administrators would have been. These characteristics helped to retain many outstanding faculty members on the MSU staff even though they were offered excellent positions with other institutions." Longtime secretary Marie Mercier wrote, "I feel sure that President Hannah will go down in history as the outstanding President of Michigan State University. He had a way of inspiring confidence in people and I believe that is why he was able to accomplish so much during his tenure at MSU. As long as he had confidence in his own ideas and he knew what he was doing was right, criticism never bothered him."

Twelve years after Hannah's death, MSU officials announced that a statue dedicated to Hannah would be placed outside the Administration Building. Vice President Emeritus Milton Muelder sent a letter to the *MSU Alumni Magazine* expressing his approval of the memorial: "To thus honor and commemorate John A. Hannah for his remarkable achievements provides succeeding generations an occasion to know and draw inspiration from the underlying values and goals which defined his long and fruitful incumbency. What a visionary and in so many respects one for succeeding generations to emulate. A list alone of firsts of the University under his administration, now copied by others, would fill a page by itself. And the root of his successes at MSU he ascribed to involving so many faculty and administrators. I loved the man!"

In 2003, the president of Northern Kentucky University, James Votruba, who had graduated from MSU during the 1960s and later worked as an administrator in the provost's office, uttered a succinct and eloquent tribute to Michigan State's longtime president: "John Hannah had the capability to dream big dreams and then make them happen. He inspired me. He sent me on the way to my eventual career. Hannah had dreams and dreams inspire people. Because of John Hannah, a small agricultural college became a great university."

Milton Muelder, a longtime Hannah loyalist and university administrator, wrote the *MSU Alumni Magazine* when a statue was erected in Hannah's honor in 2004. "What a visionary and in so many respects one for succeeding generations to emulate. A list alone of firsts of the university under his administration, now copied by others, would fill a page by itself. And the root of his successes at MSU he ascribed to involving so many faculty and administrators. I loved that man!" Courtesy of Michigan State University Archives and Historical Collections.

Bibliography

Materials drawn from the *Lansing State Journal* and the *Michigan State News* were used throughout the text.

CHAPTER 1. MR. SHAW AND MR. HANNAH

Interviews by the Author
Patriarche, Jack. Series of interviews, 1999.

Correspondence
Geib, H. V., to Robert Shaw. 5 September 1935. Michigan State University Archives.

Michigan State College faculty to Robert S. Shaw. 28 January 1933. Michigan State University Archives.

Shaw, Robert, to H. V. Geib. 31 October 1935. Michigan State University Archives.

Other Unpublished Sources
Alderton, George. "Down Memory Lane." 1991.

Bachman, Charles. Manuscript regarding John Hannah. Ca. 1970. Hannah Archives Project, Michigan State University Archives.

Baldwin, Joseph A. Press release. 25 November 1932. Michigan State University Archives.

Brandstatter, Arthur. Manuscript regarding John Hannah. Ca. 1970. Hannah Archives Project, Michigan State University Archives.

Coleman, Robert. "A History of Radio Station WKAR." N.d. Michigan State University Archives.

Farrall, Arthur. Manuscript regarding John Hannah. Ca. 1970. Hannah Archives Project, Michigan State University Archives.

Frimodig, Lyman. Manuscript regarding John Hannah. Ca. 1970. Hannah Archives Project, Michigan State University Archives.

Gardner, V. R. "Peddling Campus Rumor and Criticizing Administrative Officers." Ca. 1932. Michigan State University Archives.

Heppinstall, Jack. Manuscript regarding John Hannah. Ca. 1970. Hannah Archives Project, Michigan State University Archives.

Herbert, Paul. Manuscript regarding John Hannah. Ca. 1970. Hannah Archives Project, Michigan State University Archives.

Hudson, Jean M. "Ralph S. Hudson: A Brief Sketch of the Life of Ralph Stowell Hudson." 1972. Michigan State University Museum.

Kuhn, Madison. Manuscript regarding John Hannah. Ca. 1970. Hannah Archives Project, Michigan State University Archives.

Mallman, Walter L. Manuscript regarding John Hannah. Ca. 1970. Hannah Archives Project, Michigan State University Archives.

Mercier, Marie. "32 Years of Association with John Hannah," ca. 1970. Hannah Archives Project, Michigan State University Archives.

Michigan Great Lakes International Horse Show Committee. "The Men and Horses of Michigan State." N.d. Michigan State University Museum.

Shaffer, Terry. "Farming at Michigan State University." February 1999. Michigan State University Museum.

Stack, J. W. Undated notes, transcribed by Val R. Berryman. 4 March 2003. Michigan State University Museum.

Statistics sheet containing information about football star John Pingel. N.d. Michigan State University Archives and Historical Collections

Thompson, William Fawcett. Biographical information and filmography. Available online at *brokenwheelranch.com/pete.htm*.

Towar, James. "History of the City of East Lansing." 1933. Library of Michigan.

Published Works

"And Now It's Macklin Field." *MSC Record,* November 1935.

"Bachman of Florida Named New Coach." *MSC Record,* February 1933.

Baker, Ray Stannard. Letter to the editor. *MSC Record,* July 1939.

"Don't Get Excited." *Ingham County News,* 22 September 1932.

"Eleventh President of M.S.C." *MSC Record,* July 1941.

"Enough of Muckraking." *Lowell Ledger,* 2 February 1933.

Eustace, H. J. "Thomas L. Gunson Completes Forty Years of Service at Michigan State." *MSC Record,* May 1931.

"Extension Service Solving Rural Problems." *MSC Record,* January 1933.

"Federal Money Aids Building Program at State." *MSC Record,* July 1938.

"Foresters Honor Life Work of Dr. Beal by Dedicating Memorial at Pinetum." *MSC Record,* June–July 1932.

Gianettino, Robert L. "The Remarkable Dean Emmons." *The Lamplighter,* April 1997.

"Gifts to Michigan State." *MSC Record,* July 1939.

Graff, George. "Chace Newman: A Pioneering Spirit." *The Lamplighter,* April 1997.

Greenough, Sarah. *Harry Callahan.* Washington, D.C.: National Gallery of Art, 1996.

Hannah, John A. "Keeping Informed." *MSC Record,* October 1940.

———. *A Memoir.* East Lansing: Michigan State University Press, 1980.

———. "Some Facts about State." *MSC Record,* April 1940.

"Hannah Directs Poultry Code." *MSC Record,* January 1934.

"He Finds Work for Students: That's Glen O. Stewart's Job in Administering the N.Y.A. Program, in Addition to His Alumni Duties." *MSC Record,* November 1935.

"How Music Expanded at State." *MSC Record,* January 1940.

"Judge Denies All Charges: One-Man Grand Jury Investigator Finds No Substantiation." *Grand Rapids Press,* 3 November 1932.

Kenyon, Norman. "President Shaw Completes Ten Years as College Head." *MSC Record,* July 1938.

Kestenbaum, Justin. *At the Campus Gate: A History of East Lansing.* East Lansing: East Lansing Bicentennial Committee, 1976.

Kuhn, Madison. *Michigan State: The First Hundred Years.* East Lansing: Michigan State University Press, 1955.

Ludders, Arthur R., ed. *Michigan State University Lecture Concert Series: The First Seventy-five Years.* East Lansing: Michigan State University, 1987.

"Meet the State Board." *MSC Record,* December 1938.

"Name Hannah College Secretary." *MSC Record,* December 1934.

Niehoff, Richard O. *John A. Hannah: Versatile Administrator and Distinguished Public Servant.* Lanham, Md.: University Press of America, 1989.

Noble, William T. "Dr. Hannah: The College He Built Just Grew and Grew." *Detroit News Magazine,* 6 November 1966.

Norman, Ralph. "WKAR Steps Up." *MSC Record,* January 1940.

"President Shaw Retires July 1; Hannah Succeeds." *MSC Record,* January 1941.

"Scholastic Ratings Improved." *MSC Record,* September 1930.

"Spartans Look Back on Successful Year: Jimmy Crowley and Assistants Overcome Many Obstacles." *MSC Record,* December 1930.

Stewart, Glen O. "College Mourns Passing of 'Uncle' Frank Kedzie." *MSC Record,* January 1935.

———. "Thomas Gunson: 1858–1940." *MSC Record,* January 1941.

"39 Years of Progress: Dr. Shaw, President for 15 Years, Gives 10,084 Degrees." *MSC Record,* April 1941.

Trout, Peggy. "He Lives Informally with Students [Robert Shaw]." *MSC Record,* April 1941.

Chapter 2. The College Goes to War

Unpublished Sources

Baccus, Ira Bishop. Manuscript regarding John Hannah. Ca. 1970. Hannah Archives Project, Michigan State University Archives.

"Facts and Information Concerning Michigan State College." December 1944. Typed manuscript. Michigan State University Archives.

Geil, Lloyd H. "Some Facts Concerning Alumni and Students For Year, 1941–42." Department of Journalism and Publications, n.d.

Hannah, John A. Hand-corrected, typed manuscript of remarks made to the Convocation for Men Students, 11 March 1943. Michigan State University Archives.

———. Hand-corrected, typed manuscript of remarks made to the Howell Forum, 23 February 1944. Michigan State University Archives.

———. Typed manuscript of remarks made at the Jackson Rotary Club, 11 October 1944. Michigan State University Archives.

———. Hand-corrected, typed manuscript of remarks titled "Michigan State College in a World at War," Detroit New Century Club, 2 November 1942. Michigan State University Archives.

———. Hand-corrected, typed manuscript of remarks made at President's Convocation, Freshman Week, 22 September 1942. Michigan State University Archives.

———. Hand-corrected, typed manuscript of remarks made at Women's Convocation, 17 January 1942. Michigan State University Archives.

Hutchins, Diane. "WKAR Radio, 1922–1998." 1998. Michigan State University and Broadcasting Services.

McDonel, Karl. "Post-War Building Program—Michigan State University." Ca. 1970. Hannah Archives Project, Michigan State University Archives.

MSC Publications Department. Press release describing the implementation of war efforts at MSC. 19 December 1941. Michigan State University Archives.

Published Works

Alderton, George. "Physical Fitness Highlights." *MSC Record,* July 1943.

Dressel, Paul L. *College to University: The Hannah Years at Michigan State, 1935–1969.* East Lansing: Michigan State University, University Publications, 1987.

Faulkner, James W. "Close beside the Winding Cedar: Michigan State College after World War II." *Michigan History Magazine,* May–June 1997.

Hannah, John A. "Greetings." *MSC Record,* December 1943.

———. *A Memoir.* East Lansing: Michigan State University Press, 1980.

———. "Your College in Wartime." *MSC Record,* January 1942.

"His Achievements Live [Carl F. Siglin]." *MSC Record,* February 1943.

Kuhn, Madison. *Michigan State: The First Hundred Years.* East Lansing: Michigan State University Press, 1955.

"Library Is War Information Center." *MSC Record,* October 1942.

"M.S.C. Men Cited for War Heroism." *MSC Record,* February 1943.

"M.S.C. Selected as War Training Center." *MSC Record,* February 1943.

Niehoff, Richard O. *John A. Hannah: Versatile Administrator and Distinguished Public Servant.* Lanham, Md.: University Press of America, 1989.

"Physical Fitness Demonstration on November 20." *MSC Record,*
October 1942.

"34 Bombing Missions [Captain Seymour G. Knight]." *MSC Record,*
July 1943.

Thompson, Clarice. "The War Effort." *The Lamplighter,* May 2001.

"Thousands Trained at State." *MSC Record,* December 1943.

Chapter 3. Becoming Much More Than an Agricultural School

Interviews by the Author

Adams, Walter. Series of interviews, 1997–2000.

Bagwell, Paul. Conversations, 1950s–60s.

Bates, Jack. Conversations, 2002–3.

Guerre, George. Series of telephone and in-person interviews, 1999–
2000.

Pierson, Roland. Series of interviews, 1993–99.

Varner, Durward "Woody." Conversations, 1950s–60s.

Other Unpublished Sources

Church, Howard. Unpublished history of Michigan State art department, 1950. Author's collection.

Combs, William. Manuscript regarding John Hannah. Ca. 1970. Hannah Archives Project, Michigan State University Archives.

Denison, James. History of the Hannah years. Ca. 1970. Hannah
Archives Project, Michigan State University Archives.

"Dimensions of Giving: Alma Goetsch." Pamphlet, n.d. Author's collection.

Hannah, John A. Remarks at Annual Banquet of the State Horticultural
Society, 5 December 1945. Michigan State University Archives.

———. Remarks at dedication of Sparty, 9 June 1945. Michigan State
University Archives.

———. Remarks at NCAA Boxing Championships Luncheon, 9 April
1949. Michigan State University Archives.

———. Remarks at Third Annual Meeting of the Club Presidents Assembly, 7–8 November 1947. Michigan State University Archives.

Kuhn, Madison. History of working relationship with John Hannah.

Ca. 1970. Hannah Archives Project, Michigan State University Archives.

Lockwood, Yvonne. Biographical material related to Richard Dorson. Ca. 2003. Michigan State University Museum.

Meyer, Hazel Shuttleworth. "My Food Service Career at Michigan State University." 2000. Michigan State University Museum.

Michigan State University News Bureau. Press release regarding death of Howard Church. 4 January 1993.

"135 Years Teaching Art: Whitaker, McConnell, Raynor and Gamble." N.d. Kresge Art Gallery, Michigan State University.

Reeves, Floyd. Manuscript regarding John Hannah. Ca. 1970. Hannah Archives Project, Michigan State University Archives.

Published Works

Dressel, Paul L. *College to University: The Hannah Years at Michigan State, 1935–1969.* East Lansing: Michigan State University, University Publications, 1987.

———. *Evaluation in the Basic College at Michigan State University.* New York: Harper, 1958.

Hamilton, Thomas H., and Edward Blackman, eds. *The Basic College of Michigan State.* East Lansing: Michigan State College Press, 1955.

Hannah, John A. "The Challenge to Higher Education." *Michigan Education Journal,* February 1948.

———. *A Memoir.* East Lansing: Michigan State University Press, 1980.

Hendry, Fay L. *Outdoor Sculpture in Lansing.* Okemos, Mich.: Iota, 1980.

Hungiville, Maurice. *From a Single Window: Michigan State University and Its Press, 1947–1997.* East Lansing: Michigan State University Press, 1998.

Kenyon, Norman. "Research Aids Industry Agriculture." *MSC Record,* April 1945.

Kuhn, Madison. *Michigan State: The First Hundred Years.* East Lansing: Michigan State University Press, 1955.

"MSU Shadows." *Michigan State University Magazine,* November 1962.

Narasimhan, C. V. "Remembering R. K. Narayan." *Frontline,* 26 May–8 June 2001.

Niehoff, Richard O. *Floyd W. Reeves: Innovative Educator and Distinguished Practitioner of the Art of Public Administration.* Lanham, Md.: University Press of America, 1991.

———. *John A. Hannah: Versatile Administrator and Distinguished Public Servant.* Lanham, Md.: University Press of America, 1989.

North, Bill. *The Prints of John S. DeMartelly.* East Lansing: Kresge Art Museum, Michigan State University, 1979.

"Scheele Exhibited in Union." *East Lansing Community Life,* 9 March 1934.

Thomas, Phyllis. "Edith Butler." *East Lansing Towne Courier,* 13 December 1978.

"Veterans Get Top Priority at M.S.C." *MSC Record,* January 1946.

"Veterans Return, Enrollment Tops 7,000 First Time." *MSC Record,* January 1946.

Wilcox, Richard. "Spartan Wives: Hundreds of Thousands of American Girls, Like Those at Michigan State, Are Solving the Problems of Community Life while Their Veteran Husbands Go to College." *Ladies Home Journal,* October 1947.

Chapter 4. Building a University

Correspondence

Hannah, John A., to A. F. Brandstatter. 25 February 1947. Michigan State University Archives.

——— to top MSU administrators. 5 October 1948. Michigan State University Archives.

Kuhn, Madison, to James Denison. 18 March 1960. Michigan State University Archives.

Other Unpublished Sources

Alderton, George. "Down Memory Lane." 1991.

Chapin, Richard. Remarks at retirement of librarian Jackson E. Towne, 1959. Michigan State University Archives.

Denison, James. History of the Hannah years. Ca. 1970. Hannah Archives Project, Michigan State University Archives.

Kuhn, Madison. History of working relationship with John Hannah. Ca. 1970. Hannah Archives Project, Michigan State University Archives.

McDonel, Karl. "Post-War Building Program—Michigan State University." Ca. 1970. Hannah Archives Project, Michigan State University Archives.

Mercier, Marie. "32 Years of Association with President John Hannah." Ca. 1970. Hannah Archives Project, Michigan State University Archives.

"Michigan Stained Glass Census: Alumni Memorial Chapel." September 2000. Michigan State University Museum.

"Michigan State College and the New Era in Higher Education." Ca. 1945. Hannah Papers, Michigan State University Archives.

Published Works

"The Alumni Memorial Chapel." *Michigan State University Magazine,* October 1957.

Bao, Robert. "Alumni Memorial Chapel: Celebrating Fifty Years." *MSU Alumni Association Magazine,* Fall 2002.

Berglund, Doris. "My, How Things Have Changed At Good Old MSU," *The Grand Rapids Press,* 1956.

Brookover, Edna. "Living in the Quonset Huts." Paper #2, East Lansing Historical Society, April 1993.

"Campus Landmark Razed." *MSC Record,* April 1946.

DeBruyn, Gayle, and Jill Emerson. "Brick and Mortar: An Architectural Tour of Michigan State University." Booklet published by students of the College of Human Ecology's Historic Preservation Class, n.d.

Hannah, John A. *A Memoir.* East Lansing: Michigan State University Press, 1980.

"Jenison Fieldhouse." *MSC Record,* January 1940.

"Kellogg Center at Michigan State College: 'Hotel' Plays Big Role at Michigan State." *Christian Science Monitor,* 4 October 1951.

Kestenbaum, Justin. *At the Campus Gate: A History of East Lansing.* East Lansing: East Lansing Bicentennial Committee, 1976.

"Kinney Retires as Head of B & U." *MSU Reporter,* January 1957.

"Kresge Foundation Gives M.S.U. $1.5 Million for an Art Center." *Quarterly Record of Michigan State University,* Winter 1957.

Kuhn, Madison. *Michigan State: The First Hundred Years.* East Lansing: Michigan State University Press, 1955.

Lautner, H. W. *An Oak Opening: A Record of the Development of the Campus Park of Michigan State University, 1855–1969.* East Lansing: Michigan State University, 1978.

"MSU Plans New Education Unit." *Muskegon Chronicle,* 4 May 1969.

"New M.S.C. Buildings Will Be Named for Heroes of This War." *MSC Record,* January 1946.

"New South Campus Comes to Life." *MSC Record,* October 1947.

Poole, James. "Everybody Learns at This Hotel: Kellogg Center Serves Double Purpose." *Detroit Free Press,* 11 January 1953.

"Post-War Building." *MSC Record,* December 1943.

"The Quonset Huts Are Still Hanging On . . . By Their Tinny Tin-Tins." *MSU Alumni Association Magazine,* March–April 1967.

Reed, Jan. "Kellogg Center: Now 50 Years Young." *MSU Alumni Association Magazine,* Spring 2002.

Stanford, Linda O., and C. Kurt Dewhurst. *MSU Campus—Buildings, Places, Spaces: Architecture and the Campus Park of Michigan State University.* East Lansing: Michigan State University Press, 2002.

CHAPTER 5. A DECADE OF ACADEMIC ACHIEVEMENT

Interviews by the Author

Burns, Ben. E-mail interview, 25 November 2002.

Cash, James. Series of interviews, 1995–99.

Chapin, Richard. Interview, August 5, 2003.

Howard, Saralee. E-mail interview, 27 December 2002.

Kirk, Annette. Telephone interview, 21 September 2001.

Klewicki, Edward. Series of telephone interviews, 1989–91.

McQuitty, John. E-mail interview, 15 December 2002.

Pierson, Roland. Series of interviews, 1993–99.

Ruhala, Tom and Julie, Interview, 1 August 2003.

Van Ness, Marcia. E-mail interview, 25 November 2002.

Wallington, James. E-mail interview, 24 November 2002.

Correspondence

Denison, James, addressing writings of Russell Kirk. 5 September 1967. Michigan State University Archives.

Elliott, Eugene, to John Hannah. 22 October 1962. Michigan State University Archives.

Erickson, Clifford, to Louis McQuitty. 9 March 1962. Michigan State University Archives.

Group of faculty members to John Hannah. 1 July 1958. Michigan State University Archives.

Hannah, John A., to E. L. Anthony. 23 May 1953. Michigan State University Archives.

———— to Lee Carr and Jim Denison. 27 March 1962. Michigan State University Archives.

———— to Henry T. Heald. 8 October 1958. Michigan State University Archives.

———— to Connor D. Smith. 28 February 1958. Michigan State University Archives.

Harlan, C. Allen, to John Hannah. 21 May 1959. Michigan State University Archives.

Hilberry, Clarence, to John Hannah. 1 November 1962. Michigan State University Archives.

———— to Russell Kirk. 5 April 1963. Michigan State University Archives.

Miller, Paul, to faculty. 6 June 1960. Michigan State University Archives.

Montoye, Henry J., to John Hannah. 8 October 1962. Michigan State University Archives.

Mullennix, Grady L., to Conner D. Smith. 27 February 1958.

Nixon, Richard, to John Hannah. 4 April 1958. Michigan State University Archives.

Reeves, Floyd, to Esther Knowles. January 23, 1958. Michigan State University Archives.

Smith, Conner D., to Grady Mullennix. 25 February 1958. Michigan State University Archives.

Stabley, Fred, to John Hannah. 2 December 1960. Michigan State University Archives.

Other Unpublished Sources

"About KBS." Web site, W.K. Kellogg Biological Station, Michigan State University. 27 February 2003.

Alderton Testimonial Dinner. 6 November 1962. Michigan State University Archives.

Baccus, Ira. Manuscript regarding John Hannah. Ca. 1970. Hannah Archives Project, Michigan State University Archives.

Bailey, L. H. Papers relating to genux Carex, 1884–1900, A Guide.

Gray Herbarium Library Archives, Harvard University.

Brandstatter, A. F. The Genesis and Early History of Criminal Justice Studies at Michigan State University. Typed manuscript of paper presented at the Midwestern Criminal Justice Association Meeting, Chicago, Illinois, 11–13 October 1989.

Combs, William H. Manuscript regarding John Hannah. Ca. 1970. Hannah Archives Project, Michigan State University Archives.

"Defending Our Heritage." Transcript of speech by John A. Hannah before the Economic Club of Detroit, 19 April 1954. Library of Michigan.

Delta Psi Rambler of Kappa Sigma at Michigan State College, Spring 1953.

Denison, James H. Introduction to Karl H. McDonel's "Post War Building Program—Michigan State University." Hannah Archives Project, Michigan State University Archives.

Foster, Emery G. Manuscript regarding John Hannah. Ca. 1970. Hannah Archives Project, Michigan State University Archives.

Ford, Richard (biographical information). Web site, Michigan Writers Collection. Michigan State University Libraries. 2002.

"Gordon Guyer." Biography produced by the International Adult and Continuing Education Hall of Fame, 1 March 2002.

Hannah, John A. Address to new students, 23 September 1962. Michigan State University Archives.

———. Statement prepared for presentation before the Special Senate Committee to Investigate the Labor and Industrial Relations Center at Michigan State University, 20 September 1961. Michigan State University Archives.

———. "What Religion Means to Me." Prepared at request of the *Lansing State Journal,* 29 November 1957. Michigan State University Archives.

Harden, Edgar. Biographical summary submitted by Harden to the Library of Michigan, n.d.

"Harold E. Sponberg." Web site, Gustavus Adolphus Athletic Hall of Fame: 1989 Inductees. Gustavus Athletic Hall of Fame. 2003.

"Highlights of Remarks by President John Hannah, of Michigan State University, at Big Ten Dinner." 2 March 1962. Spartan Sports.

"Highway Traffic Safety Programs." Web site, Department of Civil and Environmental Engineering. 12 March 2003.

Kirk, Annette. "Life with Russell Kirk." The Heritage Lectures (Printed Transcription), The Heritage Foundation, 17 November 1995.

"Liberty Hyde Bailey." Web site, Department of Horticulture, Michigan State University. N.d.

Mueller, Frederick. Manuscript regarding John Hannah. Ca. 1970. Hannah Archives Project, Michigan State University Archives.

Press release describing career of Dean Emeritus Lloyd C. Emmons, Department of Information Services, 1955.

Press Release outlining coaching changes, MSC Department of Information Services, 1 January 1954.

Reeves, Floyd. Manuscript regarding John Hannah. Ca. 1970. Hannah Archives Project, Michigan State University Archives.

"The Richard M. Dorson Michigan State College Folklore Collection." Web site, MSU Museum. Michigan State University. 2002.

Rykert, Wilbur Lewis, "The History of the School of Criminal Justice at Michigan State University: 1935–1963." Master's Thesis, Michigan State University, 1985.

"Questions for President Hannah at April 8, 1968, College Faculty Meeting." Michigan State University Archives.

"Robert Little: The Kinship Foster Care Program in NYC." 14 January 1998. Case Studies in Public Policy and Management, John F. Kennedy School of Government and Management, Harvard University.

Rohman, D. Gordon. "JMC: The Liberating Journey." N.d. Library of Michigan.

Sabine, Gordon A. Informational sheet describing positives of Michigan State University, 4 December 1959. Michigan State University Archives.

Samuelson, Paul. "Brief Autobiographical Sketch Delivered at the Nobel Banquet, 1970."

Smith, Alvie L. Press release describing John Hannah's first ten years as president of MSU, Department of Information Services, 29 June 1951.

Spartan Roundtable Summary. 16 October 1962. Michigan State University Archives.

Spartan Roundtable Summary. 28 November 1962. Michigan State University Archives.

"The Times to Remember." Web site, Western Illinois University Centennial.

Weesner, Ted (biographical information). Web site, Michigan Writers Collection. Michigan State University Libraries. 27 December 2002.

Published Works

Blackman, E. B. "Residence-Hall Instructional Programs." *Journal of Education,* March 1965.

Bullard, George. "No More 'Egghead U' for Oakland University." *Detroit News,* 3 March 1974.

Carson, Rachel. *Silent Spring.* Boston: Houghton Mifflin, 2002.

"Class of 1952." *New Educator,* Spring 2002.

"Committee to Select Six for Faculty Awards." *MSU Reporter,* 1 April 1960.

Croope, Jeanie. "Celebrating Five Decades of Pioneering Public TV." *MSU Alumni Magazine,* Winter 2004.

Davis, Matthew. "The Youthful Writings of Russell Kirk." *University Bookman* 34, no. 2 (1994).

"Dean Bessey: Nears Half Century of Service to MSU." *MSU Reporter,* January 1957.

"Dean Crowe Retires from MSU Post." *Grand Rapids Herald,* 8 July 1956.

Deatrick, Owen. "Board of Five to Substitute for Hannah." *Detroit Free Press,* 7 January 1957.

"Defense Official Returns to College Post Saturday." *New York Times,* 27 July 1954.

"The Department of Religion." *MSU Reporter,* November 1957.

Dobner, Jennifer. "Voice Library Lends History to Its Ear." *East Lansing Towne Courier,* 14 January 1995.

"Distinguished Faculty Awards." *Michigan State University Magazine,* May 1962.

"Dr. Bouyoucos Saves Crops and Money." *MSU Reporter,* February 1957.

Dressel, Paul L. *College to University: The Hannah Years at Michigan State, 1935–1969.* East Lansing: Michigan State University, University Publications, 1987.

Ellsworth, Peter. "No Large Waves Are Being Made at MSU, but Students Want More Determination." *MSU Alumni Association Magazine,* April 1969.

Engler, John. "Statement by Governor John Engler on the Passing of Dr. Russell Kirk." *University Bookman* 34, no. 2 (1994).

"Every Professor Had Same Choice to Make." *Michigan State University Magazine.* November 1959.

Gianettino, Bob. "The Remarkable Dean Emmons." *The Lamplighter,* April 1997.

"A Gift from Their Hearts." *Michigan State University Magazine.*

Hannah, John A. *A Memoir.* East Lansing: Michigan State University Press, 1980.

———. "Some Dilemmas of Defense." *Oklahoma A&M Magazine,* June 1954.

———. "A Willingness to Pioneer." *Michigan State University Alumni Magazine,* January 1965.

"Hannah Gets Defense Post: Will Take One-Year Leave." *Flint Journal,* 7 January 1953.

Hill, Elton B. "Historical Highlights at Michigan State University in Areas of Agricultural Economics and Farm management (1855–1965)." Agricultural Economics Department, July 1968.

Inzunza, Victor. *Years of Achievement: A Short History of the College of Education at Michigan State University.* East Lansing: Michigan State University, College of Education, 2002.

"James H. Denison is Dead." *Detroit Free Press,* 7 March 1975.

"James P. Hoffa: The Son Also Rises." *MSU Alumni Association Magazine,* Spring 1999.

"Jim Harrison: Novelist and Poet." *MSU Alumni Association Magazine,* Winter 1999.

"John Kornblum: Ambassador to Germany." *MSU Alumni Association Magazine,* Winter 1998.

Kinney, Jack. "More M.D.s." *Michigan State University Magazine,* November 1964.

Kirk, Russell. "Academic Freedom at MSU." *National Review,* 27 March 1962.

———. "Education and the Information Revolution." *Grand Valley State University Horizons,* Fall 1983.

———. "The Mind and the Head at MSU." *National Review,* 27 August 1962.

Kreifels, Susan. "UH President Led Expansion in 1960s." *Honolulu Star-Bulletin,* 8 October 1999.

Kuhn, Madison. *Michigan State: The First Hundred Years.* East Lansing: Michigan State University Press, 1955.

Kulsea, William. "MSU Center Becomes Untouchable Outpost." *Ann Arbor News,* 10 June 1961.

"Land-Grant Philosophy Today: Education Is Everybody's Business." *Michigan State University Magazine,* February 1962.

"Liberty Hyde Bailey." *MSU Reporter,* May 1958.

"Loretta Van Camp: Cisplatin Co-Discoverer." *MSU Alumni Association Magazine,* Spring 1997.

Lunde, Erik, and Gary Hoppenstand. "Spartans in Hollywood." *MSU Alumni Association Magazine,* Spring 1999.

Lutz, William W. "Famous Voices Speak: MSU Library Collection Dates Back 50 Years." *Detroit News,* 3 November 1963.

Mongeau, Martha Jane. "Sarah Hannah: The Campus Has Always Been Home to Her." *East Lansing Towne Courier,* 27 March 1963.

"MSC Museum Director Joseph W. Stack Dies." *MSC Record,* 1954.

"MSC Negro Fraternity." *MSC Record,* June 1948.

"MSU's Karl McDonel Dies at 84." *Detroit Free Press,* 3 December 1977.

"New Dean at MSC Has Wide Experience." *Detroit Free Press,* 31 May 1955.

"New Secretary for MSU Board: James W. Miller Former State Official Assumes Campus Post." *MSU Reporter,* September 1960.

Niehoff, Richard O. *John A. Hannah: Versatile Administrator and Distinguished Public Servant.* Lanham, Md.: University Press of America, 1989.

Omandam, Pat. "Library Addition Finally Gets Under Way." *Honolulu Star,* 20 October 1998.

Payne, Isabelle. *Nursing at Michigan State University.* East Lansing: MSU University Printing, 1994.

"Presenting: The State Board of Agriculture." *Michigan State University Magazine."* March 1958.

"The Printed Page: An Enduring Memorial to Liberty Hyde Bailey." *MSU Reporter,* May 1958.

"The Professor Is an Explorer, Editor and Artist." *MSU Reporter,* January 1959.

Publications of the Faculty of the University College: A Bibliography. East Lansing: University College, Michigan State University, 1966.

Richardson, Earl C. "The Colleges: Agriculture." *Michigan State University Magazine,* February 1957.

———. "What Is the Michigan Cooperative Extension Service." *Michigan Courthouse Review,* April 1952.

Rohman, D. Gordon. "JMC Today." *JMC 10th Anniversary Tabloid Paper,* April 1975.

"Questions and Answers." *Michigan State University Magazine,* November 1962.

Savage, Kay. "Chicken Is His Dish." *Detroit Free Press,* 5 October 1952.

"The Sixties at MSU." *MSU Alumni Association Magazine,* January 1974.

"Sparty Spotlights." *Michigan State University Magazine,* January 1956.

Stanford, Linda O. "MSU Alumni in the Arts." *MSU Alumni Association Magazine,* Fall 1999.

Stanford, Linda O., and C. Kurt Dewhurst. *MSU Campus—Buildings, Places, Spaces: Architecture and the Campus Park of Michigan State University.* East Lansing: Michigan State University Press, 2002.

"The State of the University: President Hannah Presents the Facts." *Michigan State University Magazine,* 1963.

"This Problem of 'Bigness' . . . And the Three Residential Colleges." *MSU Alumni Association Magazine,* January–February 1968.

Trout, Malcolm G. "John Hannah: Some Memories and Influences." *Format,* June 1969.

"Walter Hill: Last Director Standing." *MSU Alumni Association Magazine,* Fall 1998.

"We Pioneer the Honors College." *Michigan State University Magazine,* October 1957.

Winder, C. L., and Charles Wrigley. "Louis LaForce McQuitty (1910–1986)." *American Psychologist,* April 1988.

"You Are the Jury Wins Peabody Award." *MSU Reporter,* May 1958.

"Young Professor Meets J.C. Penney and an MSU Recruiter." *SLIR Newsletter,* 1 November 2000.

Chapter 6. A City-Campus Partnership

Interviews by the Author

Adams, Walter. Series of interviews, 1997–2000.

Cash, James. Series of interviews, 1995–99.

Crane, Maury. Interview, 26 January 1999.

Frame, Emily. Interview, 26 January 1999.

Green, Robert. Series of interviews, 2003–4.

Munn, Vera. In-person and telephone interviews, 2001.

Patriarche, Jack. Series of interviews, 1999.

Pierson, Roland. Series of interviews, 1993–99.

Other Unpublished Sources

Annual Reports, City of East Lansing, 1959–1970.

Associated Students of Michigan State University. City-Students Relations Banquet program. 15 November 1966.

Church, Howard. Unpublished history of Michigan State art department. 1950.

"Diamond Jubilee: East Lansing, Michigan 1907–1982." May 21–22, 1982.

Grimes, Alan P. "Remembering Lantern Hill, 1950–52." East Lansing, Michigan, November 11, 1999.

"Mass of Christian Burial for the Reverend Monsignor Jerome V. MacEachin, St. Thomas Aquinas Church, East Lansing, Michigan, 4 December 1987."

McCune, Newell Avery. "The Great Experiment: The Story of Thirty-two Years of Ministry to Peoples Church." N.d.

"Michigan Folklore Mural." Pamphlet, 1963. East Lansing Public Library.

"Mr. and Mrs. East Lansing Citizen: It's Your Move." Pamphlet, October 1968.

Newman, Chace. "East Lansing: A History and a Prophecy." N.d. Michigan State University Archives.

Peoples Church. "The Peoples Church Story." 1982.

"Remembering and Celebrating the Life of Leonard Rall, Edgewood United Church, 13 October 2002."

"Retrospective Exhibit of Creative Tapestries by Margot Evans, 1960–85." N.d. Kresge Art Museum, Michigan State University.

Thomas, David. "Creative East Lansing: Innovation in Art and Science." Program for exhibit at East Lansing Public Library, 1987.

Towar, James. "History of the City of East Lansing." 1933.

Towne Jackson E. "The History of the Friends of the MSU Library." 1963. Michigan State University Archives.

———. "Informal Brief History of the Play-Reading Group in East Lansing Covering a Period of More Than 25 Years (1934–1963): With an Attempt to Recall about 110 of the Titles of the Plays Read." N.d. Michigan State University Archives.

Towne, Mrs. Jackson. "East Lansing Garden Club, 1951–1961: The First Ten Years." N.d. Michigan State University Archives.

Published Works

"Bagwell Given Leave to Run for Governor." *Detroit News,* 22 March 1958.

Crane, Maury. "The MSU Voice Library." *MSU Alumni Association Magazine,* Spring 2000.

"Downtown: Should It Cater to Students or Residents?" *East Lansing Towne Courier,* 2 March 1965.

Gianettino, Robert L. *A History of the Marble/Bailey Communities.* East Lansing, Mich.: Gianettino, 1988.

———. "The Remarkable Dean Emmons." *The Lamplighter,* April 1997.

Graff, George. "Chace Newman: A Pioneering Spirit." *The Lamplighter,* April 1997.

Hall, Beverly. "Beer, Wine, and Liquor Sold Here: And After $2\frac{1}{2}$ Years, Some Pleasant Surprises." *MSU Alumni Association Magazine,* July 1971.

"Hayworth, Donald, 1898–1982." *Biographical Directory of the United States Congress.* Available online at bioguide.congress.gov.

Hendry, Fay L. *Outdoor Sculpture in Lansing.* Okemos, Mich.: Iota, 1980.

"How the News of Liquor Victory Came." *East Lansing Towne Courier,* 5 November 1968.

Kestenbaum, Justin. *At the Campus Gate: A History of East Lansing.* East Lansing: East Lansing Bicentennial Committee, 1976.

Ludders, Arthur R., ed. *Michigan State University Lecture Concert Series: The First Seventy-five Years.* East Lansing: Michigan State University, 1987.

Mongeau, Martha Jane. "Sarah Hannah: The Campus Has Always Been Home to Her." *East Lansing Towne Courier,* 27 March 1963.

Premer, Lee. "First by-Glass Liquor Place Opens." *East Lansing Towne Courier,* 7 October 1969.

Soria, Martin. *Zurbarán: Spain's Great Master.* London: Phaidon, 1953.

Thomas, Marc. "Dora Stockman: A Leader for Her Time . . . And Beyond." *The Lamplighter,* November 2001.

———. "Paul Bagwell: Master of Prose and Politics." *The Lamplighter,* May 2002.

Thomas, Phyllis. "Artist with Imagination and Fantasy." *East Lansing Towne Courier,* 15 March 1966.

———. "The Story behind One Piece of Sculpture." *East Lansing Towne Courier,* 6 June 1967.

Wright, Karl T., ed. *The First 50 Years: A History of the University Club of Michigan State University.* East Lansing: University Club of Michigan State University, 1982.

Chapter 7. An International University

Interviews by the Author

Riley, Harold, and Dorothy Riley. Interview, 2003.

Correspondence

Hannah, John A., to Moreau S. Maxwell. 11 October 1962. Michigan State University Archives.

——— to Paul Varg. 3 January 1964. Michigan State University Archives.

Maxwell, Moreau, to John Hannah. 8 October 1962. Michigan State University Archives.

Varg, Paul, to John Hannah, 10 January 1964. Michigan State University Archives.

Other Unpublished Sources

Cowden, T. K. "Report on Visit to Okinawa." 14–16 July 1963. Michigan State University Archives.

———. "Report on Visit to Taiwan." 16–31 July 1963. Michigan State University Archives.

Hannah, John A. "Defending Our Heritage." 19 April 1954. Library of Michigan.

International Programs Review Committee. "The International Focus at Michigan State University." 1967.

Kuhn, Madison. History of working relationship with John Hannah. Ca. 1970. Hannah Archives Project, Michigan State University Archives.

Lee, Shao Chang. "My Contribution to Michigan State's International Program, 1943–1960." N.d. Michigan State University Archives.

Office of International Programs. "Toward an International Dimension at Michigan State University." 1959. Michigan State University Archives.

"The President's Message over WKAR." 25 February 1945. Michigan State University Archives.

Smuckler, Ralph. "Report on the MSU-Vietnam Project, April 1966." Michigan State University Archives.

Published Works

Anderson, James K. "Lavish Civic Welcome Given Viet Nam Ruler." *Detroit News,* 16 May 1957.

"Columbia: Land of Sunshine." *MSU Reporter,* October 1957.

Ernst, John. *Forging a Fateful Alliance: Michigan State University and the Vietnam War.* East Lansing: Michigan State University Press, 1998.

Hannah, John A. *A Memoir.* East Lansing: Michigan State University Press, 1980.

"He Doth Protest Too Much." *Detroit Free Press,* 28 April 1966.

Hinckle, Warren. "The University on the Make." *Ramparts,* April 1966.

McKay, John. "Second Thoughts on the Vietnam Mess from an MSU Prof Who Was One of the First Doubters." *Detroit Free Press,* 11 June 1972.

Moore, Austin. *Knight Errant in Africa.* Denver: Big Mountain, 1966.

Morgan, Joseph G. *The Vietnam Lobby: The American Friends of Vietnam, 1955–1975.* Chapel Hill: University of North Carolina Press, 1997.

"Mrs. Carpenter Visits 75 Foreign MSC Grads." *The Record,* 11 August 1954.

"MSC Offers Aid Abroad." *Detroit News,* 12 October 1951.

"MSU Staffs Seminars for Communication Training." *MSU Reporter,*
    October 1958.

"MSU's Vietnam Guilt Is Shared by the U.S." *Detroit Free Press,* 15
    April 1966

Niehoff, Richard O. *John A. Hannah: Versatile Administrator and
    Distinguished Public Servant.* Lanham, Md.: University Press of
    America, 1989.

"Nigerian Adventure." *MSU Reporter,* May 1958.

Noble, William T. "Dr. Hannah: The College He Built Just Grew and
    Grew." *Detroit News Magazine,* 6 November 1966.

Norton-Taylor, Duncan. "Megaversity's Struggle with Itself: Running
    Michigan State Is Like Running a City while Trying to Teach the
    Whole Population to Grow Up." *Fortune,* May 1967.

"Okinawa." *Michigan State University Magazine,* January 1961.

"Our Scientists Probe Headhunter Country." *Michigan State Univer-
    sity Magazine,* February 1958.

"Peace Corpsmen Train on Campus." *MSU Magazine,* November 1961.

Scigliano, Robert, and Guy H. Fox. *Technical Assistance in Vietnam:
    The Michigan State University Experience.* New York: Praeger,
    1967.

Sheinbaum, Stanley K. "Vietnam—A Study in Freedom." *Michigan
    State University Magazine,* February 1956.

Smuckler, Ralph H. *A University Turns to the World.* East Lansing:
    Michigan State University Press, 2003.

"Sowing Seeds in India." *Michigan State University Magazine,* April
    1958.

Stoneman, William. "This M.S.U. Team Scores against World Pov-
    erty." *Chicago Daily News Foreign Service* (reprinted in *Michigan
    State University Magazine,* December 1957).

Taggart, Glen L. "An Investment in World Understanding." *Michigan
    State University Magazine,* March 1961.

Thomas, David. "S. C. Lee: An International Pioneer." *The Lamplighter,*
    April 1997.

"We Lend a Hand in Africa." *Michigan State University Magazine,*
    October 1960.

Whitaker, Irwin, and Emily Whitaker. *A Potter's Mexico.* Albuquer-
    que: University of New Mexico Press, 1978.

"Whitakers Write about Pottery in Mexico." *East Lansing Towne
    Courier,* 4 December 1974.

Chapter 8. That Remarkable Year, 1955

Correspondence

Hannah, John A., to Dwight D. Eisenhower. 22 July 1953. Michigan
State University Archives.

Harkins, William, to John Hannah. 20 August 1953. Michigan State
University Archives.

Hatcher, Harlan, to Wade Van Valkenburg. 27 January 1954. Library
of Michigan Vertical Files.

Other Unpublished Sources

Calendar of major MSC Centennial events, 1955. Michigan State
University Archives.

"Centennial of Farm Mechanization." 11 August 1955. Michigan State
University Archives.

Centennial Office. "What They're Saying about Our Centennial." 8
March 1955. Michigan State University Archives.

"College or University: 10 Answers to That Question." 1955. Library
of Michigan.

Denison, James. Manuscript regarding John Hannah. Ca. 1969. Hannah Archives Project, Michigan State University Archives.

Kuhn, Madison. History of Working Relationship with John Hannah.
Ca. 1971. Hannah Archives Project, Michigan State University
Archives.

Packet of Materials Opposing MSC Name Change Prepared by UM
President and Regents. N.d. Library of Michigan.

Smith, Alvie. "Progress Report of the Michigan State College Centennial." 1 November 1954. Michigan State University Archives.

"The Michigan State University Centennial: Its Planning and Execution." 1956. Michigan State University Archives.

Published Works

"Alvie Smith Appointed Centennial Director." *MSC Record,* 15 April
1953.

"And 100 Years Later . . . Beal Descendant Graduates [Ann Baker Cot-
trell]." *MSU Alumni Association Magazine,* July 1970.

Blaisdell, Thomas C., ed. *Semi-Centennial Celebration of Michigan
State Agricultural College.* East Lansing: Michigan State College,
1907.

Brody, Clark, and John Hannah. "A University—In Every Sense of the
    Word." *The Record,* 14 February 1954.

Costes, Harris. "Hatcher Warns Legislature against MSC Name
    Change." *Ann Arbor News,* 31 March 1955.

———. "MSC Name Change Bill Referred to Senate Judiciary Commit-
    tee." *Ann Arbor News,* 24 March 1955.

Daugherty, Duffy, with Dave Diles. *Duffy: An Autobiography.* Garden
    City, N.Y.: Doubleday, 1974.

Deatrick, Owen. "MSC to Become MSU on July 1." *Detroit Free Press,*
    19 April 1955.

"Famous Rose Is Named for Spartans of M.S.U." *Michigan State
    University Magazine,* February 1956.

"Founders' Day Program Opens MSC Centennial." *Ann Arbor News,*
    12 February 1955.

Hannah, John A. *A Memoir.* East Lansing: Michigan State University
    Press, 1980.

———. "Michigan State University Awaits the Future." *The Record,*
    June 1955.

"It'll Be 'Michigan State University' after July 1: U-M Makes No Com-
    ment on Name Change." *Ann Arbor News,* 14 April 1955.

Kestenbaum, Justin. *At the Campus Gate: A History of East Lansing.*
    East Lansing: East Lansing Bicentennial Committee, 1976.

Kuhn, Madison. *Michigan State: The First Hundred Years.* East Lan-
    sing: Michigan State University Press, 1955.

Kulsea, William. "Name Change Accorded 50–50 Chance in Senate."
    Ann Arbor News, 23 March 1955.

———. "Name Change Aired—But Good—as House Prepares for Vote
    Today." *Ann Arbor News,* 22 March 1955.

"Michigan State University: Legislature Approves Name Change for
    Centennial Year." *The Record,* April 1955.

"Michigan State University Enters 101st Year in '56." *Escanaba Daily
    Press,* 30 December 1955.

"MSU Makes Little Fuss over New Name." *Ann Arbor News,* 1 July
    1955.

"Name Row Stymies M, MSC Governors." *Detroit Free Press,* 19 March
    1955.

Niehoff, Richard O. *John A. Hannah: Versatile Administrator and
    Distinguished Public Servant.* Lanham, Md.: University Press of
    America, 1989.

"Regents May Act on MSC Name." *Ann Arbor News,* 2 February 1955.

"U-M Opposes 'Michigan State University' Title." *Ann Arbor News,* 26 February 1955.

"U-M to Tell Name Change View Thursday." *Ann Arbor News,* 29 March 1955.

"University Put in Middle by MSC Name Change Move." *Ann Arbor News,* 2 March 1955.

Voges, Robert E. "MSC to Start Celebration of 100th Birthday on Feb. 12." *Ann Arbor News,* 26 January 1955.

"The Vermonter's Legacy." *Newsweek,* 28 April 1955.

Chapter 9. The Man Named "Biggie"

Interviews by the Author

Adams, Walter. Series of interviews, 1997–2000.

Guerre, George. Series of telephone and in-person interviews, 1999–2000.

Klewicki, Ed. Series of telephone interviews, early 1990s.

Munn, Vera. In-person and telephone interviews, 2001.

Pierson, Roland. Series of interviews, 1993–99.

Waters, Frank "Muddy." Series of interviews, 2001.

Correspondence

Aigler, Ralph, to John Hannah. 13 April 1943. Michigan State University Archives.

Beadle, Brenda, to Biggie Munn. N.d. Michigan State University Archives.

Daugherty, Duffy, to John Hannah. 22 February 1949. Michigan State University Archives.

Dorow, Al, to Biggie Munn. 3 March 1954. Michigan State University Archives.

Emmons, Lloyd, to John Hannah. 24 October 1951. Michigan State University Archives.

Hannah, John A., to H. L. Bevis. 15 December 1942. Michigan State University Archives.

———— to Lloyd Emmons. 22 January 1953. Michigan State University Archives.

———— to Biggie Munn and Duffy Daugherty. 18 January 1954. Michigan State University Archives.

———— to Celestin J. Steiner. 26 October 1951. Michigan State University Archives.

Munn, Biggie, to Forest Akers. 21 May 1953. Michigan State University Archives.

———— to Howard Auer. 3 May 1948. Michigan State University Archives.

———— to James "Bill" Brown. 28 October 1952. Michigan State University Archives.

———— to Elizabeth Daugherty. 19 January 1954. Michigan State University Archives.

———— to Lou Little. 30 November 1948. Michigan State University Archives.

———— to members of football team. 11 December 1952. Michigan State University Archives.

———— to Tom Yewcic. 17 July 1952. Michigan State University Archives.

Reeves, Floyd, to John Hannah. 21 March 1946. Michigan State University Archives.

Ruthven, A. G., to John Hannah. 21 December 1942. Michigan State University Archives.

Seaman, William M., to Biggie Munn. 29 September 1953. Michigan State University Archives.

Steiner, Celestin J., to John Hannah. 22 October 1951. Michigan State University Archives.

Other Unpublished Sources

Alderton, George. "Down Memory Lane." 1991.

Hannah, John. Typed text of speech at football dinner, 6 December 1946. Michigan State University Archives.

Published Works

Adams, Walter. "Spartan Postscripts." *Spirit Illustrated,* September 1995.

Clapp, Charles L. "Mister Football: Biggie Munn's Secret Brings MSC Leadership." *Grand Rapids Herald,* 20 September 1953.

Cohane, Tim. "Football's Fiercest Feud: The Michigan State of

Affairs—The Spartans Licked the Opposition of Michigan to Achieve Power and Join the Big Ten, but the Fight's Not Over." *Look,* 7 December 1952.

Daugherty, Duffy, with Dave Diles. *Duffy: An Autobiography.* Garden City, N.Y.: Doubleday, 1974.

Devine, Tommy. "Junking of Grants Aided MSC Cause." *Detroit Free Press,* 14 December 1948.

———. "Michigan State Challenges the Big Ten to Clean House." *Sports Illustrated.* [Published by Dell.] June 1949.

———. "MSC's Success Is Credited to Dr. Hannah: Young President Driving Force behind Athletics." *Detroit Free Press,* 13 December 1948.

Falls, Joe. "Biggie Munn Left Mark on Michigan." *Detroit Free Press,* 19 March 1975.

Frimodig, Lyman L., and Fred W. Stabley. *Spartan Saga: A History of Michigan State Athletics.* East Lansing: Michigan State University, 1971.

Hannah, John A. *A Memoir.* East Lansing: Michigan State University Press, 1980.

Henning, Lynn. *Spartan Seasons: The Triumphs and Turmoil of Michigan State Sports.* Union Lake, Mich.: Momentum, 1987.

Hoffman, Ken, with Larry Bielat. *Spartan Football: 100 Seasons of Gridiron Glory.* Champaign, Ill.: Sagamore, 1996.

"Huskers, MAC Seek Admission into Conference." *Chicago Tribune,* 7 December 1924.

Kuhn, Madison. *Michigan State: The First Hundred Years.* East Lansing: Michigan State University Press, 1955.

Munn, Clarence "Biggie." *Michigan State Multiple Offense.* New York: Prentice Hall, 1953.

Nowlin, Jack. "Shocking Loss to Purdue Ended Historic 28-Game Win Streak." *Spartan Magazine,* 23 September 2003.

"Over 500 Persons Attend Daugherty Testimonial." *Barnesboro Star,* 18 February 1954.

Powers, Francis J. "Michigan State Will Balance Big Ten Again." *San Francisco Chronicle,* 26 May 1949.

Salsinger, H. G. "The Umpire." *Detroit News,* 13 December 1942.

Skearns, James. "Time Is Ripe for Michigan State to Seek Place in Big Ten Conference." *Chicago Sun,* 17 December 1942.

Smith, Lyall. "Column Irks MSC Alumni, but Hannah Backs It Up." *Detroit Free Press,* 4 December 1946.

————. "MSC Prepared to Pass Big Nine Entrance Test." *Detroit Free Press,* 9 November 1948.

Stabley, Fred W. *The Spartans: A Story of Michigan State Football.* Huntsville, Ala.: Strode, 1975.

Vincent, Charlie. "Biggie Munn Dead at 66." *Detroit Free Press,* 19 March 1975.

Wilson, Kenneth L., and Jerry Brondfield. *The Big Ten.* Englewood Cliffs, N.J.: Prentice Hall, 1967.

CHAPTER 10. A TRADITION CONTINUES

Interviews by the Author

Adams, Walter. Series of interviews, 1997–2000.

Cash, James. Series of interviews, 1995–99.

Guerre, George. Series of interviews, 1999–2000.

Munn, Vera. Series of interviews, 2001.

Waters, Frank "Muddy." Series of interviews, 2001.

Correspondence

Akers, Forest, to Duffy Daugherty. 20 December 1965. Michigan State University Archives.

Clowser, Jack, to Duffy Daugherty. 25 December 1965. Michigan State University Archives.

Hannah, John A., to Milosh Muntyan. 23 November 1963. Michigan State University Archives.

Hatcher, Harlan, to John Hannah [telegram]. 22 November 1965. Michigan State University Archives.

Humphrey, Hubert. Letter extending congratulations on Rose Bowl participation. 19 January 1966. Michigan State University Archives.

Minter, Ed, to John Hannah. 14 December 1963. Michigan State University Archives.

Muntyan, Milosh, to John Hannah. 22 November 1963. Michigan State University Archives.

Smarks, Paul, to Duffy Daugherty. 29 October 1963. Michigan State University Archives.

Other Unpublished Sources

Alderton, George. "Down Memory Lane." 1991.

Hannah, John A. Official statement regarding decision not to cancel football game. 22 November 1963. Michigan State University Archives.

Published Works

Adams, Walter. "Spartan Postscripts." *Spirit Illustrated,* September 1995.

Astor, Gerald. "Duffy's Hawaiian Punch." *Look,* 28 December 1965.

Barra, Allen. "Nothing Resolved, Everything Changed: The Famous Tie in '66 Altered College Football and the Way Sports Are Viewed." *New York Times,* 18 November 2001.

Berry, Jack. "He's the Old Duffy Once Again: Victory over U-M Is Nectar." *Detroit Free Press,* 14 October 1962.

Damer, Roy. "Spartans Can Clinch Title Tie Saturday." *Chicago Tribune,* 1 November 1965.

———. "Spartans Shoot for Rose Bowl Today." *Chicago Tribune,* 6 November 1965.

Daugherty, Duffy, with Dave Diles. *Duffy: An Autobiography.* Garden City, N.Y.: Doubleday, 1974.

"Daugherty Sees NCAA Grid Series." *Chicago Tribune,* 6 November 1966.

"Driving Man [Duffy Daugherty]." *Time,* 8 October 1956.

"Duffy Clears Air on Bubba." *Detroit Free Press,* 15 June 1975.

"Duffy Kept on as MSU Coach." *Detroit News,* 25 October 1963.

"Ends '56 Grid Wars With 7–2 Record." *Michigan State University Magazine,* 26 December 1956.

Falls, Joe. "Hard to Remember Last Win over MSU: U-M Has Problem." *Detroit Free Press,* 10 November 1963.

"Fast Mail Irks 'Duffy the Dope.'" *Detroit News,* 26 December 1958.

Fitzgerald, Francis J. *Backyard Brawl: The Storied Rivalry of Michigan–Michigan State Football.* N.p.: Epic Sports, 2000.

Frimodig, Lyman L., and Fred W. Stabley. *Spartan Saga: A History of Michigan State Athletics.* East Lansing: Michigan State University, 1971.

"Hannah Sets a Spartan Example: With Duffy Pact." *Miami Herald,* 20 November 1963.

Henning, Lynn. *Spartan Seasons: The Triumphs and Turmoil of Michigan State Sports.* Union Lake, Mich.: Momentum, 1987.

Hoffman, Ken, with Larry Bielat. *Spartan Football: 100 Seasons of Gridiron Glory.* Champaign, Ill.: Sagamore, 1996.

Kinney, Jack. "Rose Bowl 1966." *MSU Alumni Association Magazine,* January–February 1966.

"MSU Finishes Fourth in Big 10 Grid Race." *Michigan State University Magazine,* 28 November 1960.

Murayama, Curtis. "The Wedemeyer Name Meant Athletic Excellence." *Honolulu Advertiser,* 13 March 1990.

Pille, Bob. "Duffy Handed 5-Year Contract." *Detroit Free Press,* 26 October 1963.

———. "MSU's Sanders, Johnson Defensive Dandies." *Detroit Free Press,* 20 November 1962.

———. "Saimes Best Player in the Country." *Detroit Free Press,* 21 October 1962.

"Recruiting a Fullback: How Does MSU Get Athletes?" *MSU Alumni Association Magazine,* September 1965.

"Spartan Gridders Bounce from Last to Second." *MSU Alumni Association Magazine: Sports Special,* 10 December 1959.

"Spartan Sports Zone Magazine" (100th anniversary of MSU football edition). Michigan State University, 6 September 2003.

"Spartans Post 8–1 Season Record." *Michigan State University Magazine: Football Special,* 7 December 1957.

"Spartans Win MacArthur Bowl Award." *Chicago Tribune,* 28 November 1965.

"Spartans' Defense Eyes New Stanard." *Chicago Tribune,* 12 November 1965.

Stabley, Fred W. *The Spartans: A Story of Michigan State Football.* Huntsville, Ala.: Strode, 1975.

Stapler, Harry. "Do or Die for Duffy." *Detroit News Pictorial Magazine,* 29 September 1957.

"State Ends Season with 3-5-1 Record." *Michigan State University Magazine: Sports Special,* 5 December 1958.

Waldmeier, Pete. "Duffy-Munn Feud Still Brewing." *Detroit News,* 28 October 1962.

"Will Duffy Heed Call of West?" *Detroit Free Press,* 23 November 1956.

Wilson, Kenneth L., and Jerry Brondfield. *The Big Ten.* Englewood Cliffs, N.J.: Prentice Hall, 1967.

Chapter 11. The House That Ralph Built

Unpublished Sources

Alderton, George. "Down Memory Lane." 1991.

Frimodig, Lyman. Reminiscences. Ca. 1970. Hannah Archives Project, Michigan State University Archives.

Stabley, Fred, and Ted Emery. "The Ralph Young Story." April 1954. Michigan State University Archives.

Tukey, Harold. "Reminiscences on My Relation with John Hannah and the Athletic Program of Michigan State University." Ca. 1970. Hannah Archives Project, Michigan State University Archives.

Published Works

"Big Ten Representative" (Harold Tukey). *MSU Reporter,* 1957.

"Boxers Set Sights on Sugar Bowl Meet." *MSC Record,* December 1947.

"Campus Personalities: Ernestine Russell Carter." *MSU Alumni Association Magazine,* Fall 1968.

Devine, Tommy. "Michigan State Challenges the Big Ten to Clean House." *Sports Illustrated.* [Published by Dell.] June 1949.

Frimodig, Lyman L., and Fred W. Stabley. *Spartan Saga: A History of Michigan State Athletics.* East Lansing: Michigan State University, 1971.

Hannah, John A. *A Memoir.* East Lansing: Michigan State University Press, 1980.

Henning, Lynn. *Spartan Seasons: The Triumphs and Turmoil of Michigan State Sports.* Union Lake, Mich.: Momentum, 1987.

Kuhn, Madison. *Michigan State: The First Hundred Years.* East Lansing: Michigan State University Press, 1955.

Stabley, Fred W. "Frim: A Man and His Legend." *MSU Alumni Association Magazine,* July 1972.

Staudt, Tim. "Look Out . . . Former MSU Star Still in the NFL at Age 52." *Lansing City Magazine,* April 1990.

Trumbull, George T., Jr. "Litany of Liniment and Love [Jack Hepinstall]." *MSU Alumni Association Magazine,* May 1973.

Waldmeier, Pete. "Chuck Davey Is Gone, but Boxing Won't Soon Forget Him." *Detroit News,* 13 December 2002.

Wilson, Kenneth L., and Jerry Brondfield. *The Big Ten.* Englewood Cliffs, N.J.: Prentice Hall, 1967.

CHAPTER 12. CALM AND CHAOS IN THE 1960s

Interviews by the Author

Chapin, Richard. Interview, August 5, 2003.

Green, Robert. Series of interviews, 2003–4.

Howard, Wilbur. Telephone interview, 6 August 2003.

Klewicki, Edward. Series of telephone interviews, 1989–91.

Ruhala, Tom and Julie, Interview, 1 August 2003.

Thornton, Dozier. Interview, 26 August 2003.

Washington, Jenny. Interview, 16 October 2003.

Correspondence

Breslin, Jack, to Biggie Munn. 5 March 1969. Michigan State University Archives.

Duffy, Franklin V., [series of letters discussing living arrangements on campus] to MSC administrators. 1940. Michigan State University Archives.

Fuzak, J. A., to John Hannah. 2 November 1961. Michigan State University Archives.

Group of faculty members to John Hannah. 1 July 1958. Michigan State University Archives.

Hannah, John A., to E. L. Anthony. 23 May 1953. Michigan State University Archives.

———— to Charles C. Diggs. 6 September 1940. Michigan State University Archives.

———— to Henry T. Heald. 8 October 1958. Michigan State University Archives.

———— to Connor D. Smith. 28 February 1958. Michigan State University Archives.

Harlan, C. Allen, to John Hannah. 21 May 1959. Michigan State University Archives.

McClendon, J. J., to Robert Shaw. 16 September 1940. Michigan State University Archives.

Mullennix, Grady L., to Conner D. Smith. 27 February 1958.

Nixon, Richard, to John Hannah. 4 April 1958. Michigan State University Archives.

Reeves, Floyd, to Esther Knowles. January 23, 1958. Michigan State University Archives.

Smith, Conner D., to Grady Mullennix. 25 February 1958. Michigan State University Archives.

Stabley, Fred, to John Hannah. 2 December 1960. Michigan State University Archives.

Other Unpublished Sources

"About KBS." Web site, W.K. Kellogg Biological Station, Michigan State University. 27 February 2003.

Baccus, Ira. Manuscript regarding John Hannah. Ca. 1970. Hannah Archives Project, Michigan State University Archives.

Bailey, L. H. Papers relating to genux Carex, 1884–1900, A Guide. Gray Herbarium Library Archives, Harvard University.

Brandstatter, A. F. The Genesis and Early History of Criminal Justice Studies at Michigan State University. Typed manuscript of paper presented at the Midwestern Criminal Justice Association Meeting, Chicago, Illinois, 11–13 October 1989.

Combs, William H. Manuscript regarding John Hannah. Ca. 1970. Hannah Archives Project, Michigan State University Archives.

"Defending Our Heritage." Transcript of speech by John A. Hannah before the Economic Club of Detroit, 19 April 1954. Library of Michigan.

Delta Psi Rambler of Kappa Sigma at Michigan State College, Spring 1953.

Denison, James H. Introduction to Karl H. McDonel's "Post War Building Program—Michigan State University." Hannah Archives Project, Michigan State University Archives.

Foster, Emery G. Manuscript regarding John Hannah. Ca. 1970. Hannah Archives Project, Michigan State University Archives.

"Gordon Guyer." Biography produced by the International Adult and Continuing Education Hall of Fame, 1 March 2002.

Green, Robert L. Personal memoirs prepared by Green. 1 April 2002.

———. Typed manuscript of speech titled "Martin Luther King Jr.: His Words Ring Clear in 1995," given at Michigan State University, 16 January 1995.

Hannah, John. Typed manuscript of speech titled "Civil rights, a National Challenge," given as the Dillon Lecture at the State University of South Dakota, 12 January 1961. Michigan State University Archives.

———. Statement prepared for presentation before the Special Senate Committee to Investigate the Labor and Industrial Relations Center at Michigan State University, 20 September 1961. Michigan State University Archives.

———. "What Religion Means to Me." Prepared at request of the *Lansing State Journal,* 29 November 1957. Michigan State University Archives.

Harden, Edgar. Biographical summary submitted by Harden to the Library of Michigan, n.d.

"Harold E. Sponberg." Web site, Gustavus Adolphus Athletic Hall of Fame: 1989 Inductees. Gustavus Athletic Hall of Fame. 2003.

"Highway Traffic Safety Programs." Web site, Department of Civil and Environmental Engineering. 12 March 2003.

"Liberty Hyde Bailey." Web site, Department of Horticulture, Michigan State University. N.d.

Mueller, Frederick. Manuscript regarding John Hannah. Ca. 1970. Hannah Archives Project, Michigan State University Archives.

Norrell, Gwen. News release upon her death on 15 June 2004. MSU Media Communications.

Press release describing career of Dean Emeritus Lloyd C. Emmons, Department of Information Services, 1955.

Press Release outlining coaching changes, MSC Department of Information Services, 1 January 1954.

Reeves, Floyd. Manuscript regarding John Hannah. Ca. 1970. Hannah Archives Project, Michigan State University Archives.

"Report of the Committee of Sixteen." Typed manuscript of the committee's recommendations, 25 April 1968. Library of Michigan.

"The Richard M. Dorson Michigan State College Folklore Collection." Web site, MSU Museum. Michigan State University. 2002.

Rykert, Wilbur Lewis, "The History of the School of Criminal Justice at Michigan State University: 1935–1963." Master's Thesis, Michigan State University, 1985.

Sabine, Gordon A. Informational sheet describing positives of Michigan State University, 4 December 1959. Michigan State University Archives.

Smith, Alvie L. Press release describing John Hannah's first ten years as president of MSU, Department of Information Services, 29 June 1951.

"The Times to Remember." Web site, Western Illinois University Centennial.

Published Works

Ahern, Patricia. Letter to the editor. *MSU Alumni Association Magazine*, January–February 1968.

"And 100 Years Later . . . Beal Descendant Graduates [Ann Baker Cottrell]." *MSU Alumni Association Magazine*, July 1970.

"Board Members Condemn Anti-Race Dean at Michigan State." *Detroit World Echo*, 14 September 1940.

Bullard, George. "No More 'Egghead U' for Oakland University." *Detroit News*, 3 March 1974.

Carrigan, Patricia. Letter to the editor. *MSU Alumni Association Magazine*, March 1968.

"Class of 1952." *New Educator*, Spring 2002.

"Committee to Select Six for Faculty Awards." *MSU Reporter*, 1 April 1960.

Croope, Jeanie. "Celebrating Five Decades of Pioneering Public TV." *MSU Alumni Magazine*, Winter 2004.

"Dean Bessey: Nears Half Century of Service to MSU." *MSU Reporter*, January 1957.

"Dean Crowe Retires from MSU Post." *Grand Rapids Herald*, 8 July 1956.

Deatrick, Owen. "Board of Five to Substitute for Hannah." *Detroit Free Press*, 7 January 1957.

"Defense Official Returns to College Post Saturday." *New York Times*, 27 July 1954.

"The Department of Religion." *MSU Reporter*, November 1957.

Dickson, David. Biography prepared by Dickson for the Library of Michigan, n.d.

"Diplomat [Jack S. Jones]." *MSU Alumni Association Magazine*, January–February 1970.

"Dr. Bouyoucos Saves Crops and Money." *MSU Reporter*, February 1957.

"Dr. Norrell." *MSU Alumni Association Magazine*, January–February 1968.

Dressel, Paul L. *College to University: The Hannah Years at Michigan State, 1935–1969.* East Lansing: Michigan State University, University Publications, 1987.

"Every Professor Had Same Choice to Make." *Michigan State University Magazine.* November 1959.

Gianettino, Bob. "The Remarkable Dean Emmons." *The Lamplighter,* April 1997.

"A Gift from Their Hearts." *Michigan State University Magazine.*

Green, Robert L. "Years after King's Struggle America Still Short of His Goal." *Cincinnati Inquirer,* 16 January 1995.

Hannah, John A. *A Memoir.* East Lansing: Michigan State University Press, 1980.

———. "Some Dilemmas of Defense." *Oklahoma A&M Magazine,* June 1954.

"Hannah Gets Defense Post: Will Take One-Year Leave." *Flint Journal,* 7 January 1953.

Henning, Lynn. *Spartan Seasons: The Triumphs and Turmoil of Michigan State Sports.* Union Lake, Mich.: Momentum, 1987.

Hill, Elton B. "Historical Highlights at Michigan State University in Areas of Agricultural Economics and Farm management (1855–1965)." Agricultural Economics Department, July 1968.

Inzunza, Victor. *Years of Achievement: A Short History of the College of Education at Michigan State University.* East Lansing: Michigan State University, College of Education, 2002.

"James H. Denison is Dead." *Detroit Free Press,* 7 March 1975.

Kincaid, Barbara. "Civil Rights Movement: Is It Dead?" *East Lansing Towne Courier,* 14 February 1967.

Kreifels, Susan. "UH President Led Expansion in 1960s." *Honolulu Star-Bulletin,* 8 October 1999.

Kuhn, Madison. *Michigan State: The First Hundred Years.* East Lansing: Michigan State University Press, 1955.

"Liberty Hyde Bailey." *MSU Reporter,* May 1958.

"Mississippi's First Black Legislator in a Long Time [Robert G. Clark]." *MSU Alumni Association Magazine,* June–July 1969.

Mouat, Lucia. "Hannah Rejects University Tokenism." *Christian Science Monitor,* 13 June 1968.

"MSC Museum Director Joseph W. Stack Dies." *MSC Record,* 1954.

"MSC Negro Fraternity." *MSC Record,* June 1948.

"MSU Attacks the Traffic Problem." *Michigan State University Magazine."* February 1956.

"MSU's Karl McDonel Dies at 84." *Detroit Free Press,* 3 December 1977.

"MSU's 17 Negro Players May Top Major Colleges in Football." *Muhammad Speaks,* 31 October 1962.

"New Coaches [Don Coleman and James Bibbs]." *MSU Alumni Association Magazine,* June 1968.

"New Dean at MSC Has Wide Experience." *Detroit Free Press,* 31 May 1955.

"New Secretary for MSU Board: James W. Miller Former State Official Assumes Campus Post." *MSU Reporter,* September 1960.

Niehoff, Richard O. *John A. Hannah: Versatile Administrator and Distinguished Public Servant.* Lanham, Md.: University Press of America, 1989.

"No Time for Bias: John Alfred Hannah." *New York Times,* 24 December 1957.

Omandam, Pat. "Library Addition Finally Gets Under Way." *Honolulu Star,* 20 October 1998.

"Panelists Tell of Local Experience at School Human Relations Conference." *East Lansing Towne Courier,* 7 October 1969.

Payne, Isabelle. *Nursing at Michigan State University.* East Lansing: MSU University Printing, 1994.

Pipes, William. *Death of an "Uncle Tom."* New York: Carlton, 1967.

"Presenting: The State Board of Agriculture." *Michigan State University Magazine."* March 1958.

"The Printed Page: An Enduring Memorial to Liberty Hyde Bailey." *MSU Reporter,* May 1958.

"The Professor Is an Explorer, Editor and Artist." *MSU Reporter,* January 1959.

Richardson, Earl C. "The Colleges: Agriculture." *Michigan State University Magazine,* February 1957.

———. "What Is the Michigan Cooperative Extension Service." *Michigan Courthouse Review,* April 1952.

Sabine, Gordon. "Michigan State's Search for More Negro Students." *College Board Review,* Fall 1968.

Savage, Kay. "Chicken Is His Dish." *Detroit Free Press,* 5 October 1952.

"Sparty Spotlights." *Michigan State University Magazine,* January 1956.

"Ten Women Graduates Honored." *MSU Alumni Association Magazine,* July 1970.

Thomas, David. "Rabbi Frankel: A Valued Treasure." *Lansing City Magazine,* December 1990.

"A Time to Listen . . . A Time to Act." A Report of the United States Commission on Civil Rights, November 1967.

Trout, Malcolm G. "John Hannah: Some Memories and Influences." *Format,* June 1969.

"We Pioneer the Honors College." *Michigan State University Magazine,* October 1957.

"You Are the Jury Wins Peabody Award." *MSU Reporter,* May 1958.

"Young Professor Meets J.C. Penney and an MSU Recruiter." *SLIR Newsletter,* 1 November 2000.

Chapter 13. Academic Freedom

Interviews by the Author

Fermaglich, Kirsten. E-mail interviews, 21, 24 July 2003.

Shapiro, Samuel. Telephone interview, 21 January 2003.

Van Ness, Marcia. E-mail interview, 25 November 2002.

Zarichney, James. Telephone interview, 21 February 2003.

Correspondence

Anderson, James, to John Hannah. 18 December 1962. Michigan State University Archives.

Combs, William, to John Hannah. 13 May 1963. Michigan State University Archives.

Denison, James, to Robert Hoffman. 7 March 1963. Michigan State University Archives.

Hoffman, Robert, to John Hannah. 4 March 1963. Michigan State University Archives.

Mazey, Ernest, to John Hannah. 12 February 1963. Michigan State University Archives.

Other Unpublished Sources

Delta College Chapter of the American Association of University Professors. Statement regarding Samuel Shapiro. 11 December 1962. Michigan State University Archives.

Murley, David. "Un-American Activities at Michigan State College: John Hannah and the Red Scare, 1946–1954." Master's thesis, Michigan State University, 1992.

"Policy on Speeches by Communists or Suspected Communists." 28 December 1960. Michigan State University Archives.

Published Works

Arnett, Judd. "MSU's Angry Young Prof. [John Moore]." *Detroit Free Press,* 12 December 1961.

Cohen, Robert. "Student Movements, 1930s." In *Encyclopedia of the American Left,* edited by Mari Jo Buhle, Paul Buhle, and Dan Georgakas. New York: Oxford University Press, 1998.

"Dissent Causes 'Rough Going' on Campus and Brings the 'Other Side' into Action." *MSU Alumni Association Magazine,* March 1969.

"Freedom from Conservatives." *Richmond News Leader,* 25 June 1962.

Hungiville, Maurice. *From a Single Window: Michigan State University and Its Press, 1947–1997.* East Lansing: Michigan State University Press, 1998.

Shapiro, Samuel. *Invisible Latin America.* Boston: Beacon, 1963.

Schrecker, Ellen W. *No Ivory Tower: McCarthyism and the Universities.* New York: Oxford University Press, 1986.

"State Students Duck a Pastor." *Detroit Free Press,* 13 April 1935.

"Tenure and Truth." *National Guardian,* 10 January 1963.

"A Word to the Wise." *Harvard Crimson,* 14 December 1962.

"Yippies Leader on MSU Stump Plus Garskof and Jesse Jackson." *MSU Alumni Association Magazine,* April–May 1970.

CHAPTER 14. THE END OF AN ERA

Interviews by the Author

Chapin, Richard. Interview, 7 June 2003.

Votruba, James. Telephone interview, 4 April 2003.

Correspondence

Hannah, John A., to Paul Varg. 4 November 1966. Michigan State University Archives.

Varg, Paul, to John Hannah. 1 November 1966. Michigan State University Archives.

Other Unpublished Sources

Baccus, Ira. Manuscript regarding John Hannah. Ca. 1970. Hannah Archives Project, Michigan State University Archives.

Combs, William. Manuscript regarding John Hannah. Ca. 1970. Hannah Archives Project, Michigan State University Archives.

Denison, James. Manuscript regarding John Hannah. Ca. 1970. Hannah Archives Project, Michigan State University Archives.

DiBiaggio, John. Remarks at memorial service for John Hannah. 26 February 1991. Michigan State University Archives.

Farrall, Arthur. Manuscript regarding John Hannah. Ca. 1970. Hannah Archives Project, Michigan State University Archives.

Frimodig, Lyman. Manuscript regarding John Hannah. Ca. 1970. Hannah Archives Project, Michigan State University Archives.

Gardner, Victor. Manuscript regarding John Hannah. Ca. 1970. Hannah Archives Project, Michigan State University Archives.

Greater Lansing Chamber of Commerce and Michigan State University Alumni Club. Appreciation dinner for John A. Hannah. 20 May 1969. Author's collection.

Kinney, Edward. Manuscript regarding John Hannah. Ca. 1970. Hannah Archives Project, Michigan State University Archives.

Kuhn, Madison. Manuscript regarding John Hannah. Ca. 1970. Hannah Archives Project, Michigan State University Archives.

Mercier, Marie. Manuscript regarding John Hannah. Ca. 1970. Hannah Archives Project, Michigan State University Archives.

Michigan State University Information Services. "President John A. Hannah and Michigan State University." N.d. Michigan State University Archives.

White, Elmer. Manuscript regarding John Hannah. Ca. 1970. Hannah Archives Project, Michigan State University Archives.

Published Works

Adams, Walter. *The Test.* New York: Macmillan, 1971.

Dressel, Paul L. *College to University: The Hannah Years at Michigan State, 1935–1969.* East Lansing: Michigan State University, University Publications, 1987.

"Exit Methuselah." *Time,* 21 March 1969.

"Hannah Given OK to Take Nixon Job." *Detroit News,* 5 February 1969.

Hannah, John A. *A Memoir.* East Lansing: Michigan State University Press, 1980.

"John A. Hannah, 1902–1991." *MSU News-Bulletin,* 28 February 1991.

Niehoff, Richard O. *John A. Hannah: Versatile Administrator and Distinguished Public Servant.* Lanham, Md.: University Press of America, 1989.

Sander, Al. "Noisy Farewell to Hannah." *Detroit News,* 11 February 1969.

Trout, Malcolm. "John Hannah: Some Memories and Influences." *Format,* June 1969.

Vestal, M. S., and William Cote. "Hannah: Education Is Too Important to Be Left to the Educators." *Flint Journal,* 9 March 1969.

———. "Time to Hear from the Non-Educators: Hannah's View as He Leaves MSU Presidency." *Kalamazoo Gazette,* 9 March 1969.

Index

*Entries in **boldface** refer to illustrations and captions.*

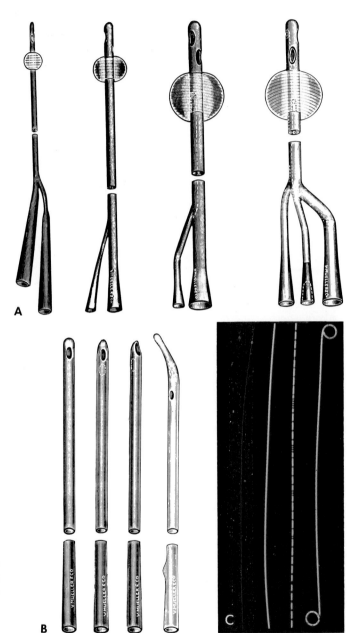

Figure 22–32. *A.* Self-retention Foley-type catheters. *Left to right*: Pediatric catheter, 5-ml retention catheter, hemostatic catheter, irrigation hemostatic catheter. *B.* Ureteral catheters. *Left to right*: Solid tip, hollow tip, whistle tip, olive tip. *C.* Assorted ureteral catheters. (*A* and *B*, Courtesy of V. Mueller Co.; *C,* Courtesy of Vance Products.)

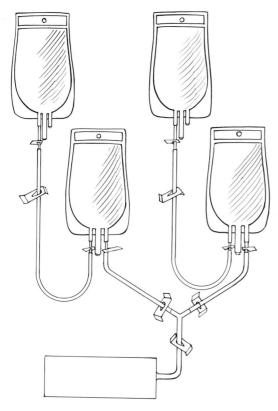

Figure 22–33. Irrigation bottles are "piggybacked" so that irrigation is continuous. One set of containers can be changed without affecting the other. (From Greene LF, Segura JW: Transurethral Surgery. Philadelphia, WB Saunders, 1979.)

in the lithotomy position, receive x-ray cassettes, and allow for drainage of irrigation fluid. The stirrups of the table are removable and differ in design according to the manufacturer. X-ray cassettes are placed in a hollow space built into the table. Irrigation fluid is directed into a drainage tray located at the foot of the table. The tray is covered with a wire mesh plate that can be sterilized for resection procedures when tissue specimens are collected piece by piece and evacuated with the irrigation solution. Proper positioning of the patient is discussed later.

Cystoscope

The cystoscope (Fig. 22–34) is a delicate and complex tool that allows the surgeon to examine, make diagnoses, and perform surgery on the urinary system. There are different types of cystoscopes; they vary according to the manufacturer. Because of these variations and because every technologist and nurse working in the cystoscopy room must become familiar with the equipment used in that particular operating room, a lengthy discussion of various cystoscopes will not be given. However, some basic guidelines are helpful in becoming familiar with the handling and care of any cystoscope.

1. Read and study the manufacturer's guidelines and instructions for the assembly of the cystoscope and its accessories *before* attempting to work with the equipment.

2. Handle the equipment gently. It cannot be overemphasized that these instruments are delicate and costly. Never use force on the various components of the instrument when assembling or dismantling it.

3. Seek help from other surgical personnel if you do not understand how to assemble or disassemble the equipment. It is better to learn from someone who is familiar with the equipment than to risk its being damaged.

4. Attend in-service lectures given by either the manufacturer or the operating room's in-service director and, if feasible, try to take written notes. Many operating rooms employ a cystoscopy technologist or nurse whose main duty is to work in the "cysto" room. Consequently, other technologists or nurses in the department may either forget or never have the opportunity to learn about the equipment. The system is efficient as long as the cystoscopy technologist is available at all times. If, however, the person is ill or otherwise unable to assist the urologist in the "cysto" room, other staff members must take over. It is often very helpful to have some written notes to serve as guidelines in these circumstances.

Regardless of the type or manufacturer, most cystoscopes have similar components and accessories.

Telescope

The telescope is the optical system of the cystoscope. It offers the urologist an unimpaired view of the bladder, urethra, and distal ureters. There are five different types of telescopes, each offering a particular angle of view, are the forward, right-angle, lateral, forward oblique, and retrospect. The telescope is a delicate instrument and must be handled gently at all times. In particular, care should be taken to avoid scratching the lens or bending the shaft of the scope.

Sheath

The sheath is a hollow tube constructed of Bakelite or fiberglass that provides a passageway for the instruments used during cystoscopy and resection. Most sheaths are designed to accept an irrigation stopcock. The tip of the sheath may be beveled or oblique. Insertion of the sheath into the urethra is aided by the use of an obturator.

Obturator

The obturator is a metal rod with a rounded tip. It is inserted into the sheath and advanced so that its blunt tip protrudes past the end of the sheath before the sheath is inserted into the urethra. This prevents the end of the sheath from abrading the mucosal lining of the urethra as it is inserted. The obturator may be straight or deflecting (able to be turned to the side).

Fiberoptic Light Cable

The fiberoptic light cable connects the cystoscope with a fiberoptic light source to provide light that is adjustable